W9-ADX-394

Advance Praise for *Life in Debt*

"*Life in Debt* will become, I predict, one of the classic ethnographies in the anthropological study of state violence, community responses, and the moral life of the global poor. Relating economic and political debt, financial and psychological depression, and caregiving by ordinary people and by social institutions, Clara Han maps our brave new world just about as illuminatingly as it has been done. A remarkable achievement."
—Arthur Kleinman, Harvard University

"In this highly sophisticated take on the ironies of neoliberal social reforms, the corporate sector, consumer culture, and chronic underemployment, nothing can be read literally. Han transforms underclass urban ethnography in Latin America by bringing readers directly into the intimate flow of relationships, experiences, and emotions in family life on the margins of Santiago, Chile."
—Kay Warren, Director, Pembroke Center, Brown University

"People-centered, movingly written, and analytically probing, *Life in Debt* deals with both the human costs and the changing structures of power driven by contemporary dynamics of neoliberalism. Combining a deep and nuanced understanding of Chile's history with a longitudinal and heart-wrenching field-based knowledge of the everyday travails of the urban poor, Clara Han has crafted an exceptional analysis of human transformations in the face of political violence and economic insecurity."
—João Biehl, author of *Vita: Life in a Zone of Social Abandonment*

"During ten years, Clara Han has gathered fragments of biographies and moments of lives to re-create the experience of Chileans after Pinochet's dictatorship. Her vivid ethnography plunges into the moral economy of a society entangled between memory and pardon, revealing the ethical work undertaken by those who accept the present without disclaiming the past."
—Didier Fassin, Institute for Advanced Study, Princeton, New Jersey, and author of *Humanitarian Reason*

Life in Debt

Life in Debt

*Times of Care and Violence
in Neoliberal Chile*

Clara Han

UNIVERSITY OF CALIFORNIA PRESS

Berkeley · Los Angeles · London

University of California Press, one of the most distin-
guished university presses in the United States, enriches
lives around the world by advancing scholarship in the
humanities, social sciences, and natural sciences. Its
activities are supported by the UC Press Foundation and
by philanthropic contributions from individuals and institutions. For more information, visit www.ucpress.edu.

University of California Press
Berkeley and Los Angeles, California

University of California Press, Ltd.
London, England

© 2012 by The Regents of the University of California

Library of Congress Cataloging-in-Publication Data

Han, Clara, 1975–

   Life in debt : times of care and violence in neoliberal
Chile / Clara Han.
     p.   cm.
   Includes bibliographical references and index.
   ISBN 978-0-520-27209-5 (cloth : alk. paper) —
   ISBN 978-0-520-27210-1 (pbk. : alk. paper)
    1. Chile—Social policy—21st century.   2. Chile—
Economic policy—21st century. 3. Political vio-
lence—Chile.   4. Neoliberalism—Social aspects—Chile.
I. Title.
   HN293.5.H36   2012
   320.60983—dc23   2012001902

Manufactured in the United States of America

12 20 19 18 17 16 15 14 13 12
10 9 8 7 6 5 4 3 2 1

In keeping with a commitment to support environmen-
tally responsible and sustainable printing practices,
UC Press has printed this book on 50-pound Enterprise,
a 30% post-consumer-waste, recycled, deinked fiber that
is processed chlorine-free. It is acid-free and meets all
ANSI/NISO (Z 39.48) requirements.

For Mom and Dad
For Mike, Alyse, Andy
For Paty
For Maarten

Contents

Acknowledgments   *ix*

Introduction   *1*

1. Symptoms of Another Life   *29*

2. Social Debt, Silent Gift   *54*

3. Torture, Love, and the Everyday   *92*

4. Neoliberal Depression   *129*

5. Community Experiments   *167*

6. Life and Death, Care and Neglect   *202*

Conclusion: Relations and Time   *231*

Notes   *239*
References   *255*
Index   *269*

Acknowledgments

Writing this book has been a process of growth. I am deeply thankful to friends and families in La Pincoya for inviting me into their lives, for their hospitality, friendship, and wisdom. Helping me understand your commitments, allowing me to accompany you in daily life, and challenging me to be a better person in the registers of my everyday life, you gave me friendship and warmth that not only led to insights for this book but also were formative for my being. I hope the writing adequately evokes the deep and meaningful commitments in this world that endure in difficult circumstances. Thank you.

I also thank the human rights activists, psychiatrists and psychologists, and public health officials who generously gave me insights into their work. I thank Dr. Fernando Lolas of the Pan American Health Organization Regional Program for Bioethics and University of Chile, who was a mentor in the early years of my fieldwork for this book. My gratitude goes also to critical interlocutors, writers, and artists in Santiago: Juan Pablo Sutherland, José Salomón, Willy Thayer, Pedro Lemebel, Héctor Nuñez, Gabriel Guajardo, Ximena Zabala Corradi, Rodrigo Cienfuegos, Davíd Maulen de los Reyes, and Raquel Olea.

This ethnography grew from my dissertation research at Harvard University. I give deep thanks to my advisor Arthur Kleinman. His commitment to worlds and to thinking sustained me as a graduate student and beyond. Kay Warren offered a richness of ideas and an energy that makes her students thrive. Byron Good has been a wonderful mentor and companion on the road of ideas that stretches to the future. Luis

Cárcamo-Huechante taught me how to be a writer and friend. I am happy to see our shared intellectual and ethical commitments grow. Allan Brandt was the calm sea during my often bewildering MD and PhD training. I thank Marilyn Goodrich for bringing art and music to WJH, and the late Joan Gillespie for the pretzels and chats. I thank the late Joan Kleinman for her wisdom.

In the first three years of my graduate training, the Friday Morning Seminar led by Byron Good and Mary Jo DelVecchio-Good at Harvard introduced me to a host of mentors, who now live in other places. My deep thanks go to João Biehl for reading so many of my papers, reading texts with me, and for reviewing this manuscript with such wise eyes. Adriana Petryna, Joseph Dumit, and Michael Fischer have been critical teachers and friends from predissertation to manuscript. Angela Garcia, Chris Dole, Duana Fullwiley, and Lisa Stevenson created sparks for thought and friendship throughout this process. Thank you for reading parts of this writing at early and very late stages. I also benefited greatly from conversations with Eduardo Kohn, Diana Allan, Jessica Mulligan, Emily Zeamer, Jeremy Greene, Erica James, Johan Lindquist, Narquis Barak, Josh Breslau, Liz Miller, Aslihan Sanal, and Chris Garces. Ian Whitmarsh generously read and reviewed the entire manuscript and provided critical comments. My warmest thanks to Vincanne Adams who believed in my future in anthropology when I was an undergraduate majoring in molecular biology.

The Johns Hopkins Department of Anthropology provided me with an intensely challenging and creative ethos. I am grateful to Veena Das, whose comments on this manuscript proved to be turning points in my formation. Jane Guyer, too, read parts of the manuscript and provided critical insights and intellectual support. I also thank Deborah Poole, Naveeda Khan, Juan Obarrio, Anand Pandian, Niloofar Haeri, Emma Cervone, and Sidney Mintz for their conversations and insights. I am especially grateful to Aaron Goodfellow, whose modesty would normally prevent me from saying that I have learned a great deal from him. Thanks to Jane Bennett, William Connolly, Randall Packard, Katrin Pahl, Jennifer Culbert, and the late Harry Marks for expanding my thinking and my world at Hopkins. Bhrigupati Singh, Prerna Singh, Isaias Rojas-Perez, and Sylvain Perdigon have become wonderful friends whose intensity of thought made me a better scholar. I am grateful to graduate students Amy Krauss, Nathan Gies, Juan Felipe Moreno, Serra Hakyemez, Patricia Madariaga-Villegas, and Grégoire Hervouet-Zeiber for their engagement. I thank my undergraduate students who engaged with parts of the manuscript for this book in classes, including Precious Fortes, Michael Rogers, Tyler Smith, Dom Burneikis, and Margaret Davidson.

I shared parts of this work over the past several years, including at Princeton's Department of Anthropology and Program in Latin American Studies, when invited by João Biehl and Miguel Centeno; at Harvard's Friday Morning Seminar; at Brown's Department of Anthropology; and at the Pembroke Center's "Markets and Bodies in Transnational Perspective" seminar, when invited by Kay Warren. I shared it virtually at UC Irvine, and I thank Bill Maurer and Tom Boellstorff for their comments. I also shared it at several meetings of the American Anthropological Association, and I thank Didier Fassin for his comments on materials presented at the AAA and workshops.

The research for this book was made possible by several generous fellowships: the National Science Foundation Predoctoral Fellowship, the Social Science Research Council International Dissertation Research Fellowship, and the National Institutes of Mental Health Ruth L. Kirschstein National Research Service Award MD/PhD Fellowship Grant No. 5 F30 MH064979–06, as well as by summer fieldwork grants from Harvard University, including grants from the David Rockefeller Center for Latin American Studies, the Department of Social Medicine's Crichton Fund, the Weatherhead Center for International Affairs, and the Film Study Center.

I thank Reed Malcolm of the University of California Press for believing in this book and for his enthusiasm, and the reviewers who provided incisive and helpful comments.

Treasuring the complexity of life comes from my family. I thank my dad, Sook-Jong Han, for his stubborn perseverance and intellectual honesty. My mom, Chung Hwa Han, passed away before she could see me graduate from college. I hope she finds that this book speaks to her life-affirming warmth. My siblings made this research and writing existentially possible. I thank my sister, Alyse, treasured soul mate, for making life fun, beautiful, and smart; my twin brother, Andy, for keeping my sense of humor alive and kicking, and my brother Mike for being a solid big brother to a kid sister. I am grateful to Paty, *alma gemela,* for her love of shared worlds. Finally, I thank my partner, Maarten Ottens—a beautiful, caring, and wise companion. Such a wonder of life and world! With great patience, he listened to every page of this book multiple times. This book is dedicated to you all.

Introduction

We waited. In La Pincoya, the lights were cut to the sector and bonfires crackled on the main street, Recoleta. On September 11, *poblaciones* (poor urban neighborhoods) commemorate the *golpe del estado* (the coup d'état) that in 1973 brought down the government of the democratically elected socialist president Salvador Allende and ushered in a seventeen-year dictatorship headed by Augusto Pinochet. It was 2005, and there was euphoria and expectation in the air, the atmosphere both celebratory and tense. Women helped children put garbage—wood, an old armchair, plastic bins—in a bonfire pile to be ignited with paraffin. Neighbors stood outside closed storefronts, greeting one another with a mixture of festivity and fear. People knew what to expect, as one woman said precisely: "At around midnight, the municipality will cut the lights to the sector. An hour later, the police will come up Recoleta [La Pincoya's main street], and then we will protest. And then the police will go up Recoleta [starting from the beginning of the *población* and moving farther into it], and then we will chase them down, and then they will come up again, and then we will chase them down again."

A choreographed dance of bullets, tear gas, Molotov cocktails, stones, and water canons was to pass through the stage of Recoleta that night. In anticipation, some young men with covered faces were preparing Molotov cocktails to throw at the police. I was in the street with my *comadre* Ruby,[1] who lived in the sector with her husband, Héctor, a former militant, and their three children. Ruby handed me a cut lemon with salt, a homemade antidote for tear gas. The police were supposed to come up Recoleta, as they usually do, in their armored vehicles with water canons and busloads of special forces. They were supposed to start firing tear gas bombs. Special forces were supposed to get out of the olive green buses and chase adolescents through the narrow passageways and lift the struggling teens into trucks. Women were supposed to throw stones at the police and then run through the passageways, laughing at and fearing the expected violent police response.

That is what happened the year before. In 2004, Ruby and I followed a march led by youths in the Grupos Acción Popular, a popular youth movement that surged during the democratic transition after Pinochet's 1990 handover of power. They held a banner reading, MENOS REPRE, + SALUD Y EDUCACIÓN (Less repression, more health and education). The leaders of the march, faces masked, stopped before the municipal police station and read a speech condemning the government in its perpetuation of the "neoliberal model." A moment later, headlights from police buses flashed on. The protestors scattered, opening their backpacks to pull out and light Molotov cocktails. Ruby and I ran down a passageway off the main street. An unknown neighbor saw us running and grabbed my arm from the door of a wooden shed.

Through the shed's wooden slats, we watched special forces carry a young man to the green truck. "Los llevan presos sólo para llevarlos no más" (They take them prisoner just to take them, nothing more), a woman whispered to me. Another whispered, "But we are used to it. It has happened for the past thirty years." Fear was mixed with a sense of the formulaic. Taking leave of the shed, Ruby and I ran farther up the main street to the point where we could observe the fighting between the police and the youths below. The police came up the street, extinguishing the bonfires. Molotov cocktails rained down on the police vehicles, and the vehicles retreated, at which point people returned to the street and threw more garbage, wood—whatever would burn—into piles for new bonfires.

But in 2005, a presidential election year that culminated in the December election of President Michelle Bachelet, the police never came. The flames from the bonfires flickered and drizzled smoke as people ran out of garbage, wood, and old broken furniture to burn. "Ya no vienen" (They're not coming), people repeated over and over again in tones of disappointment. It was as if the commemoration of the *golpe* could not be realized without the state's show of force. The back-and-forth between the forces of the state and the *población* provided a structure through which history was to be enacted and remembered.

With that structure altered by the absence of the police, a generalized sense of anxiety spread. The undertones of fear shifted from a thrilling, if predictable, confrontation with the police as commemorative practice to a sense of impending chaos when a few youths began to laugh and fire pistols in the air. Tired people nervously started to make their way to the safety of their homes, leaving the fires to burn out on their own.

As we returned to Ruby's house, an elderly man stopped me. "Madame, madame," he said. He was noticeably drunk. "Allende is present! Those assassins must die! Because they have the monopoly!" The young men around him started whistling and jeering. He continued, "Here, our *compañero* is present. Assassins, those evil Pinochet supporters! Because they are evil. And what is here? The pueblo—"

A teenage boy interrupted him, yelling, "United!" both ridiculing and predicting the man's next words. While the youth laughed, other men and women turned to walk away. The man continued, "The pueblo united will never be defeated! But, well. Excuse me, madame. Excuse me that we do not have so much education. But well, our Chile!" He turned to look angrily at the high and drunk youths encircling him, Ruby, and me. He turned back to us, saying quietly, as if addressing the nation, "Chile, they killed me . . . " A young man yelled, "Shut up, crazy idiot!" The man turned around, raising his fist. "They say that I am crazy, but you know, I, thirty-five years working! I am old, ah! And you know, you know . . . ah, you know madame, we are equal. Equal to what? For each other. Thank you, madame." He shook my hand. The young men continued to ridicule him. Ruby intervened, saying to the man, "You are the only one talking sense here. You are not the one that is crazy." The young men grumbled as the man thanked Ruby, holding both her hands.

September 11, 1973, is a critical event in the lives of the people in this book and for the Chilean population generally (Das 1995). Marking the beginning of a dictatorship that disappeared thousands and subjected hundreds of thousands to torture, fear, and insecurity in tandem with a profound reorganization of the state and market, September 11 evokes a complex mixture of pain, mourning, resentment, defiance, and rage in La Pincoya. September 11 commemorations in La Pincoya, as in other *poblaciones* of Santiago, are more than a conflictive remembering of past violence. In street scenes, grief over the loss of a political project—an alternative vision of democracy and social justice—is both ridiculed and acknowledged, crystalizing frustrations and resentments that emerge from persistent inequalities and economic precariousness that shape the lives of the poor in the present.

Since 1990, the coalition of democratic parties cast the state's project of transitional justice in terms of debts to the population. The state owed a "social debt" to the poor through the inequalities generated by the regime's economic liberalization, while society owed a "moral debt" to the victims of human rights violations. Accounting for these debts would occur partly through the expansion of poverty programs, mental health programs dedicated to low-income populations, and the official acknowledgment of human rights violations under the Pinochet regime. Through such an accounting, a reconciliation over the past would be achieved, and the unified nation could look toward a prosperous future. In casting the past as debt that could be accounted for, however, the state performatively marked a break with the past while leaving intact the actual institutional arrangements of the state and market, as well as the kind of subject imagined within social policy and interventions.

Life in Debt attends to such debts in their concrete manifestations as poverty programs, reparations for torture, and treatments for depression in the lifeworld of one *población,* La Pincoya. It explores how the moral and political subjects imagined and asserted by these interventions are refracted through relational modes and their boundaries, as well as through the aspirations, pains, and disappointments that men and women embody in their daily lives. It traces the forces of kinship, friendship, and neighborliness—and the shoring up of the boundaries between them—in the making of selves in a world in which unstable work patterns, illness, and pervasive economic indebtedness are aspects of everyday life. And it attends to how a world could be reinhabited by those who staked their existence on political commitments and aspirations for democracy, as well as by those who live today with bitter disappointment.

In this book, I attempt to bring into focus and into question this performative break with the past by considering how and when state violence is experienced as a past continuous that inhabits present life conditions. That is, rather than assume that the past of dictatorship has been sealed through a project of reconciliation, I consider the ways in which the state's "care" in the democratic transition is inhabited by that past. Therefore, this ethnography is an extended meditation on boundaries between past violence and present social arrangements of care. But it is also a meditation on care in everyday life, care that takes shape and is experienced through concrete relations inextricably woven into unequal social arrangements. This book asks: How are the claims of others experienced in the face of minimal state assistance and institutional failures, and how do obligations track along relational modes? How can anthropology attend to the ways in which individuals are both present to and failing to be present to one another? How are modes of care and living with dignity related to boundaries of speech and silence?

Although neoliberal reforms in Chile have displaced the responsibilities for care onto families and individuals, divesting the state of crucial responsibilities for the well-being of the population, an ethnographic exploration of "care" does not move smoothly across the registers of governmental discourse to lifeworlds.[2] Discourses of "self-care" and "self-responsibility" that are advanced in health and social policy presume a self that is sovereign, morally autonomous, and transparent posed against social determinations of "the poor," who must divest themselves of such determinations to be "free" (see Povinelli 2006). Simultaneously, the expansion of consumer credit and an expanded range of consumer goods impels public discourses on the disorganizing force of neoliberalism in its fragmentation of "nonmarket" regimes of value and social ties (Greenhouse 2010). How self, agency, and collectivity are conceived through these discourses, however, comes into awkward tension with relations as they are actually lived, embodied, and experimented with. Any stable or certain notion of care becomes unsettled when ethnography explores *how* individuals are always already woven into relationships and how they awaken to their relationships "thus becom[ing] aware of the way they are connected *and* disconnected" (Strathern 2005, 26).

This book is based on thirty-six months of fieldwork consisting of short two- to three-month trips between 1999 and 2003, eighteen months of continuous fieldwork between 2004 and 2005, and follow-up visits in 2007, 2008, and 2010. Throughout the chapters, I attend to life and the singularity of lives in La Pincoya, a poor urban neighborhood on the northern periphery of Santiago, while drawing on interviews with a range of institutional actors, such as psychologists, psychiatrists, social workers, and human rights activists. I explore how social and health policies manifest as group therapy sessions, circulations of psychopharmaceuticals, and point scores for poverty programs. I examine how unstable work patterns and the expansion of consumer credit has shaped experiences of poverty, experiences that are manifested and lived in intimate relations. These experiences critically recast official narratives of state violence. Throughout this book, I consider this matrix of debt and state interventions within scenes of daily life to explore how political and economic forces are realized in people's lives.

NEOLIBERAL EXPERIMENT

The aspirations, disappointments, and daily struggles that make up this book reveal how a past continuous inhabits actual life conditions, specifically through continuities in economic and social policies between the dictatorship and the democratic governments. During the dictatorship, life conditions underwent a profound reorganization through Chile's experiment in neoliberal economics. Led by Chilean economists trained at the University of Chicago's school of economics, who were known as the Chicago Boys, this experiment in free market reforms drew from a history of unequal north-south relations that took place in the cold war context.

In 1955, the University of Chicago and the Catholic University in Santiago signed an agreement for academic exchange, allowing for the training of more than a hundred Chilean graduate students at the University of Chicago (Valdés 1995). As is well known, the Chicago school proposed that economic theory was premised on "natural laws," much like physics, biology, or chemistry. These natural laws were based on the rational behavior of "man," *homo economicus,* and the autoregulation of the market. The elaboration of these natural laws was based on the empirical testing of economic theory and the coherence of economic models to "reality." Economics, from this perspective, was not a domain apart from the social. Rather, economics encompassed all of human action and sociality, and economic science was the analysis of and intervention into this reality (Burchell 1991; Lemke 2001).

As Milton Friedman states, "In discussions of economic science, 'Chicago' stands for an approach that takes seriously the use of economic theory as a tool for analyzing a startlingly wide range of concrete problems, rather than as an abstract mathematical structure of great beauty but little power; for an approach that insists on empirical testing of theoretical generalizations and rejects alike facts without theory and theory without facts" (quoted in Valdés 1995, 65). According to Friedman, more than a description of reality, economic models had explanatory power if they were predictive and could model a reality construed as what should be natural. As political scientist Juan Valdés remarks, "As a consequence, one of the central functions of theoretical analysis was in their [the Chicago school's] view the formulation of normative rules" (Valdés 1995, 65). Thus, the Chicago school's approach to neoliberalism was based not on predetermined human nature, but on the construction of the "natural" rational-economic being through normative rules that were defined through economic science.

With the *golpe del estado* in 1973, Chile became a testing ground for this normative economic approach. Scientific expertise, embodied in the Chicago Boys, combined with authoritarianism informed a new experimental and technified reality for state actors and institutions. The market, according to Minister of Economic Affairs Pablo Baraona, was the "economic manifestation of freedom and the impersonality of authority." As such, it combined freedom's normative principles with the neutral and objective practice of economic science (Valdés 1995, 31).

Viewed as the structuring principle for life itself, the market became the primary mode of governance, and the social became a terrain in which economic rational actors made choices in their own self-interest.[3] "Nature," in terms of *homo economicus,* was not an a priori given, but instead needed specific technical conditions under which it could emerge. As Baraona remarked, "The new democracy, imbued with true nationalism, will have to be authoritarian, in the sense that the rules needed for the system's stability cannot be subject to political processes, and that compliance with these measures can be guaranteed by our armed forces; impersonal, in the sense that the regulations apply equally to everyone; libertarian, in the sense that subsidiarity is an essential principle for achieving the common good; technified, in the sense that political bodies should not decide technical issues but restrict themselves to evaluating results, leaving to the technocracy the responsibility of using logical procedures for resolving problems or offering alternative solutions" (quoted in Valdés 1995, 33).

The Chicago Boys and the Pinochet regime contrasted this "new democracy" to the Allende government, which they diagnosed as causing an "immoral" and "sick" state of the economy. According to the military regime, the previous epoch of state intervention and centralization had produced a situation in which the economy, and by extension individual rational actors, had become obstructed from their "normal" or "natural" functioning. These obstructions were, in the words of Undersecretary of Economic Affairs Alvaro Bardón, "perverse" (quoted in Silva 1996, 29) and had led to a balance-of-payments crisis and soaring inflation. As the words of Minister of Economy Sergio de Castro suggest, this perversity was attributable to "the result of the years of demagogy and erroneous economic policies, the consequence of an exaggerated statism, the result of exaggerated protectionism that guaranteed monopoly profits" (quoted in Loveman 1988). The military regime therefore called for a "normalization" and "*saneamiento*" (healing) of the economy. Such normalization would be brought about through the "shock treatment" of structural adjustment.

In the Government Economic Recovery Program of 1975, Minister of Finance Jorge Cauas reiterates Friedman's emphasis on "normalization": "The purpose of the recovery program which we are discussing in general terms today is to bring about the definitive normalization of the economy by means of a drastic reduction in inflation" (Cauas 1975, 159). The military government drastically reduced fiscal spending by 25 percent, devalued the currency, and removed price controls on almost all commodities. The regime also privatized almost all state-owned enterprises, except for copper mining, and deregulated the interest rates of banks so that they could charge their clients according to their own economic measurements. Public infrastructure such as health care and education were severely curtailed and semiprivatized. And the economy was opened up to the global market by reducing trade barriers and passing new foreign investment laws that gave equal treatment to both foreign and domestic investors (Loveman 1988, 159). Between 1975 and 1979, foreign loans flooded the Chilean economy. This expansion of credit from private international banks, amounting to more than USD 6,120.9 million, allowed the regime to service Chile's public debt, which at the time was the highest in the world on a per capita basis, representing 45–50 percent of all export earnings. The costs of such measures were felt throughout the population, but especially by the urban and rural poor, who saw the minimum wage drop by 50 percent during the first two years of the military regime and the loss of disposable income sharpened by the reduction in social expenditures by the state (Petras et al. 1994, 21).

By the end of 1982, in the wake of the debt crisis that swept across Latin America, the private financial system was on the verge of collapse. The state, via the Central Bank, stepped in to bail out the private sector. This bailout—on the order of USD 6 billion, representing 30 percent of GDP each year—ushered in a new round of structural adjustment, this time promoted by the World Bank. In 1985, Chile received a three-year structural adjustment loan from the World Bank and made a three-year agreement with the International Monetary Fund. By the end of the 1980s, the payments the Pinochet regime was making to service the foreign debt amounted to USD 800 million a year, representing 3–4 percent of GDP and 18 percent of exports (Meller 1996).

With banks and their debtor companies under the control of the Central Bank, the regime initiated a new wave of privatizations of these now public properties and companies—which it sold at much reduced prices to national and international conglomerates, turning public assets into private wealth. With these privatizations also came an influx of transnational corporations that entered into partnerships with several Chilean conglomerates, since these conglomerates could not absorb the heavy debts acquired with their new companies. Transnational corporations bought heavily into public utilities, such as telephone and electricity companies, and bought significant shares of pharmaceutical and nitrite-based chemical industries, steel, and coal mines (Fazio 1997).

With such measures, the regime managed to pay off USD 9 billion of the 19 billion that it owed to external creditors. The "fiscal responsibility" of the state—itself now heavily privatized—was celebrated by the World Bank, International Monetary Fund, and Inter-American Development Bank, which together annually provided loans averaging USD 760 million between 1983 and 1987. With British Prime Minister Margaret Thatcher and President Ronald Reagan supporting the regime, the "Chilean miracle" was advanced as an argument for structural adjustment across Latin America and for neoliberal reforms in both Europe and the United States. With these economic reforms, the state itself would transform from a welfare state to a subsidiary state that addressed the inevitable generation of "extreme poverty" produced by the market. This "extreme poverty" would be addressed by focalized programs aimed at sustaining minimum requirements for biological survival.

These reforms were advanced through state violence, by disarticulating labor unions and political movements through torture and disappearances. And they produced not only a structural adjustment of the economic system but also, as literary scholar Luis Cárcamo-Huechante suggests, a profound *cultural* adjustment of the Chilean population (Cárcamo-Huechante 2007). As the 1974 Declaration of Principles makes clear, the military regime viewed itself as installing new "healthy" norms and value systems in the Chilean population: "The government of the Armed Forces and of Order aspires to initiate a new stage in national destiny, opening the way to new generations of Chileans formed in a school of healthy civic habits" (Junta Militar quoted in Vergara 1984). The exercise of competition, individualism, and ownership were some of the "healthy civic habits" that the military regime sought to potentiate through the market and by establishing a subsidiary state.

For example, with respect to private property, the military regime stated, "Chile must become a land of property owners and not a country of proletariats." Regarding morality, the regime stated, "National politics, lately characterized by low standards and mediocrity, has developed an outlook where personal success has frequently been considered as something negative, to be hidden, something for which an individual must 'apologize.' To lead the country towards national greatness, we must conceive a new outlook which will recognize the merit of public distinction and reward those who deserve it, be it for labor output, production, study, or intellectual creation" (Junta Militar 1974, 34). Women's duty was reproduction: "Finally, the present government feels the whole task it has outlined must rest solidly on the family as a school for moral upbringing, of self-sacrifice and generosity to others, and of untarnished love of country. Within the family, womanhood finds fulfillment in the greatness of her mission, and thus becomes the spiritual rock of the nation. It is from her that youth is born who, today more than ever, must contribute its generosity and idealism to Chile's task" (p. 43). In other words, these "healthy civic habits" drew from and magnified a genealogy of the liberal Chilean state that articulated sexuality with political community.

With the democratic transition, governments sought to maintain Chile's macroeconomic success in a global economy while trying to distance themselves from the Pinochet regime's use of state violence. Anthropologist Julia Paley documented the complex political processes in the early 1990s that established conditions for institutional politics as well as possibilities for grassroots mobilization today. Social mobilizations that had taken place during the dictatorship were in the process of being absorbed by the state itself in advancing a "participatory" democracy. Political mobilization in the *poblaciones* had to contend with the state's valorization of technical knowledge production in concert with its contracting out of public services to the community, in which community members were called on to "actively participate" in resolving their own local needs.

Simultaneously, in the early postdictatorship years, governments strategically advanced a discourse of "democracy" through opinion polls and community participation in order to politically legitimate the continuation and deepening of the economic model (Paley 2001). Indeed, entering into bilateral trade agreements with the United States, China, and South Korea, Chile has consolidated an international reputation of economic stability and fiscal responsibility, making it an attractive country for transnational capital and the possibility of future wealth creation. In this context, a growing private-sector credit industry, both national and transnational, has generated extreme wealth for an elite class, while economic indebtedness from consumer debts accounts for one-third of monthly expenditures in low-income households.

Chile now is registered as one of the ten most liberalized economies in the world, according to the Heritage Foundation. And according to the United Nations Development Program, it has the second-highest level of income inequality—after Brazil—in Latin America. The wealthiest 10 percent of the population earns thirty-four times more than the poorest 10 percent. The three largest private fortunes in Chile are equivalent to 10 percent of the nation's GDP (Fazio 2005, 44).

How these cultural and political adjustments manifest in everyday life, however, is not a straightforward or simple question. Yes, social policies to address poverty have posed citizens as "clients" or "consumers" of public goods, and women as mothers to be "civilized," and the consumer credit system indeed provides possibilities for advancement in perceived class status. Yet social diagnoses that proclaim the breakdown of "the family" and the generation of a consumer society seem inadequate when one is drawn into lives, when one is invited into homes and takes part in chitchat in the street, cooks, cleans, helps do chores, and runs errands. How to attend to aspirations, disappointments, and bitter compromises became my struggle in writing. The struggle lies not in grasping a world but in being receptive to it.

LA PINCOYA AND RELATEDNESS

Within the boundaries of the municipality of Huechuraba, La Pincoya is bordered on the west by new upper-middle-class condominiums. The Ciudad Empresarial, or Business City, constructed in the late 1990s, also part of the municipality of Huechuraba, forms La Pincoya's eastern border. It is populated by high-rises that contain international advertising firms, global news outlets such as CNN, and offices for international banks and software engineering companies. Green hills on its northwestern and eastern sides separate La Pincoya from these wealthier areas but also provide the backdrop for children playing in the narrow streets, as well as exceptional locations for those children to fly kites on windy spring days.

Taking a bus from Santiago center to the *población,* one goes up one main street, Recoleta, passing the highway that rings the city, Américo Vespucio. One gets off as the street ends at the base of the hills. Smaller passageways branch off the main street, and walking up those streets, one greets neighbors who sit on the front steps of their patios, gossiping and taking in the sun. Dogs of various mixes and sizes sniff the sidewalks and laze on the patios. One might be called Perla (Pearl) and another called Pelusa (Fluffy), while another might be called Monster (in English) or Bruce (after Bruce Springsteen). Wrought iron fencing separates the street from the patios, which are enclosed on the sides by walls made of bricks, wood planks, or corrugated iron. Plants line many of the patios; some are shaded by grapevines growing on trellises or by large avocado trees. Folklore music streams from the open door of one house. A few houses up, *reggaetón.* Another one, Rammstein (a German heavy metal band) blares. Shop fronts (*almacenes*) appear every few houses, interspersed every so often with Pentecostal meeting places. Shops, like Pentecostal meeting places, are part of houses, built within the patio in front of the house and closed off with a large iron gate late at night.

Shops are called by the owners' nicknames or first names, such as La Viuda (the widow), selling fruits and vegetables; Sra. Cecy, selling cheese, cold cuts, powdered milk, bread, spaghetti noodles, Coca-Cola, Fanta, and pharmaceuticals; don Rodrigo, selling scissors, crayons, different papers, toner cartridges, and pens. Shop owners have, among their neighbors, loyal customers to whom they sell goods *al fiado,* or on trust, payable at the end of the month, although neighbors also tend to occasionally buy from different shops just to support the businesses of others. Continuing up the narrow streets, one is greeted by "Hola vecino/a" (Hi, neighbor), or with a wink and "Hola muñecos" (Hi, dolls). Nicknames are constantly used with endearment or cheeky irony: *flaca* (skinny girl), *flaco* (skinny guy), *guatón* (fat guy), *negra* (black), *rusa* (russian or blonde), *huacha* ("orphan," or "illegitimate child"), *volao* (someone high on drugs). Or they relate to one's skills or profession: *zapatero* (shoe repair), *joyero* (jewelry maker), *carpintero* (carpenter), *semanero* (one who sells goods on credit and asks for weekly payments). I was called various names: *negra, flaca, chinita, huacha,* but also Clarita by friends and tía Clara (Auntie Clara) by their children.

Between 1968 and 1971, the confluence of state housing policy under President Eduardo Frei Montalva (1964–1970), and popular movements for housing (*tomas de terreno*), established La Pincoya as a *población* on the northern periphery of Santiago. The presidential election of Frei Montalva in 1964 set the conditions for La Pincoya's emergence. The Christian Democrat party advanced the slogan "Revolution in Liberty," based on combining technical expertise, liberal political doctrine, and Christian humanistic values (Smith 1982, 110). This position coincided with the Catholic clergy's growing concern for the poor, voiced in two landmark 1962 pastoral letters, and the state's desire to stem communism. Consistent with this evolving Christian doctrine, the Christian Democrats argued that instead of viewing social reality as a struggle between workers and employers, Chilean society should be understood in terms of a tension between "marginality" and "integration" (Salazar Vergara and Pinto 1999; Scully 1992; Smith 1982).

This theory of marginality was advanced by the Belgian Jesuit Roger Vekemans and the Chilean group DESAL (Centro para el Desarrollo Económica y Social de América Latina) under Vekemans's leadership between 1964 and 1970.[4] The theory drew in a selective fashion from Oscar Lewis's "culture of poverty" school, emphasizing the traits of self-perpetuating poverty to the exclusion of Lewis's insistence on fundamental structural change, such as wealth redistribution, to contend with poverty (see Lewis 1966). Thus, the urban masses were associated with a premodern, "traditional," and rural character. Upon migration to the city, these peripheral urban masses were thrown into a state of psychological anomie and political and participatory apathy. The poor, peripheral urban masses were unable to overcome their situation of marginality. They were passive subjects in need of charity and guidance to become active subjects (Castells 1983; Espinoza 1989; Tironi Barrios 1990).

As Janice Perlman explains, this idea of marginality does not signify a "group of the population that occupies the lower rungs of the social scale. They [the marginals] are actually off such a scale. Marginals have no position in the dominant social system" (Perlman 1979, 119). According to Vekemans and DESAL, those marginals, who are understood as outcasts from the social system, require "integration" into the social system and mainstream political process. Two notions of participation were crucial in understanding the nature of marginality. First, passive—or receptive—participation is that participation entailed in the receiving of material benefits from society. Second, active participation is participation in the mainstream political process. Framing poverty in terms of the duality of marginality and integration casts poverty and institutional responses to it in a specific way, as Perlman critically remarks. "The fight against marginality must, therefore, proceed through the creation of new institutions capable of administering external help to the afflicted population" (p. 121). The afflicted population—the marginals—is viewed as not having a self-organizing capacity. It is the reception of material benefits (from the state or charitable institutions) that allows them to self-organize, but within the framework of mainstream politics and sociality.

The Christian Democrats drew on this theory in their implementation of social programs that would instigate a process of internal integration of the marginals. Christian humanism and a liberal state were jointly advanced through the *estado social benefactor,* or social-benefactor state. Frei's administration began the process of agrarian reform, expropriated 51 percent of the copper mining industry as a source of national income, and expanded social policies for housing and health to address the growing pauperism in the major cities. Public spending and investment were indicators of the scale of this effort. By 1969, total public investment was 74.8 percent of all investment within the country. By 1970, public spending had reached 46.9 percent of the GDP.

To address the housing crisis and illegal land occupations on the peripheries of Santiago, the Christian Democrats advanced Operación Sitio, a new policy that sought a rapid, technical solution. Inaugurated in 1966 by President Frei, the program consisted of the provision of urbanized housing sites, cooperatives, and self-help projects with governmental support, and promoted a concept of the liberal subject who, with proper state support, would build "houses according to [his] own needs and at [his] own pace" (Castells 1983, 180). Yet, while Operación Sitio parsed land into individual properties, it did not include the installation of sewer systems, electricity, or street pavement, nor did it provide building materials for the construction of houses (see Paley 2001).

As the demands for housing went unmet by Operación Sitio, *pobladores* (the poor of the city) who were living in overcrowded conditions in neighboring sectors of the city began to organize for *tomas de terreno* on the northern and southern peripheries of Santiago. Organized into *comités sin casa* (committees of those without housing), the *pobladores* occupied the land, setting up tents and carrying wood, basic food-stuffs, and lanterns. Once established, they negotiated with the state for housing (a claim to both rights to land and assistance for building) and the basic infrastructure for urbanization, such as electricity and sewage systems. *Pobladores* as social and political actors emerged in relation to this struggle for housing during the 1960s. Through state employment, they paved the roads and installed the sewer system and organized to buy materials for houses, all of which was called *auto-construcción*. *Autoconstruction* thus implicated collective organizing to build both neighborhoods and individual houses (Márquez 2006). Outside Santiago, in all other major cities, *tomas* occurred on a massive scale. Between 1969 and 1971, 312 *tomas* occurred throughout Chile, involving 54,710 families, approximately 250,000 people. By 1970, one in six inhabitants in Santiago was a *poblador* living in precarious shan-tytown housing formed through *tomas* (Garcés 1997, 46–47).

La Pincoya was formed through this combination of Operación Sitio and *tomas*. Between 1969 and 1970, the Ministry of Housing had assigned 1,152 housing sites on the terrain of La Pincoya. The demand for housing, however, far exceeded these sites, and organized *tomas* extended the occupation of land to the hills that now establish La Pincoya's northern border. With the election of President Salvador Allende, this occupation of land resulted in the designation of 2,036 housing sites.

While organization for housing offers a rich exploration of the dynam-ics of popular social movements and political process (Castells 1983), the house as process of *auto-construcción* within a neighborhood also offers ways of approaching relatedness and the moral in everyday life. As Janet Carsten has aptly remarked, "For many people, kinship is made in and through houses and houses are the social relations of those who inhabit them" (Carsten 2003, 37). Houses as material things are con-stantly being repaired, renovated, and added onto. In the sector of La Pincoya where I worked, houses were originally built as duplexes, with two houses sharing one wall, each with its own patio. Houses originally built with wood frames, partial brick walls, and corrugated iron roofs are augmented with a second story or improved with drywall and insu-lation. *Mediaguas*, provisional wood shacks provided by government organizations and charities, expand the living space and are placed in back of the original house or in the patio. These *mediaguas* can either be free-standing or connected to the original house via a covered walkway of corrugated iron. Walls may be constructed brick by brick through patient effort when money can be spared. Adult children of the second generation live in the *mediaguas* with their partners and children while trying to save money to qualify for a state-financed home loan. When inhabited, the *mediagua* (the building material) is called a *pieza*, or "room."

The idea of the house helps us attend to the materiality and obligations of kinship. People speak of one's *casa de sangre* (house of blood) as the place of primary intimate relations. Kinship obligations are spoken of as the *compromiso con la casa* (the commitment to the house) and include helping economically to maintain the house. Women may say with relief and happiness that their children turned out to be *caseros/as* (home bodies) rather than *callejeros* (of the street), meaning that these children are not only responsive to their kin but also protected from the unpredictable forces that the world of flesh-and-blood relations constantly mitigate. The autoconstruction of the house, therefore, can also be understood as the process of constructing and achieving relatedness. That process of achieving, however, can also come with the possibility of estrangement and disconnection.

Houses, however, exist within a neighborhood life of multiple relational modes. They are interconnected through intimate kin relations that are most intensely sustained between women—between mothers and their daughters, between sisters, and between friends. Such interconnections form domestic relations that, again, mitigate the forces of economic precariousness. Separate from domestic relations of intimate kin and friends are relations with neighbors, and through neighbors there is a constant circulation of gossip (*pelambre*).

When I first arrived to La Pincoya in 1999, I met Leticia through a feminist activist in a nongovernmental organization, who picked Leticia's name out of a Rolodex. Leticia had returned to Chile four years earlier after being exiled to Argentina. She told me that to engage in the life of the *población* I would have to live in the *población*. She invited me to live with her in her house. Through her daughter, I met Ruby, and through Ruby, I met Susana. These three women introduced me to their intimate kin, friends, and immediate neighbors. I engaged in both participant-observation in daily life—that is, life as lived—and conversations and interviews with women and men who spoke about their relations, their political commitments, and actual conditions of life in the *población*. As Robert Desjarlais puts it, "The phenomenal and the discursive, life as lived and life as talked about, are like the intertwining strands of a braided rope, each complexly involved in the other, in time" (Desjarlais 2003, 6).

While engaged in everyday activities such as helping to sew, looking after children, doing the laundry, learning how to wire a doorbell or rig an electricity meter, cooking, and going to the *feria* (outdoor market), I began to appreciate how the dynamics of economic reforms, as well as state violence, were lived in intimate lives. Far from being the place of safety or take-for-granted stability, as Carsten remarks, "the house and domestic families are directly impinged upon by the forces of the state" (Carsten 2003, 50). Rather than thinking of the forces of the state as "impinging" on the house from without, however, we can think of multiple ways in which the state is layered in people's intimate lives, such that houses and domestics are not neatly overlapping. State institutions and economic precariousness are folded into people's intimate relations, commitments, and aspirations. And further, for many of the men and women I came to know, experiences of torture, exile, and disappearance were realities that took shape in their intimate lives, casting doubt on modes of intimacy themselves.

With the *golpe* on September 11, 1973, history abruptly took a different course. On that day, men and women in La Pincoya saw helicopters and jets fly over the hills surrounding the *población*. From those same hills, they saw smoke pouring out of the presidential palace, La Moneda, where Salvador Allende had given his last radio address to the nation and then died. Because of the force of social movements, as well as its association with both socialist and communist militants, the *población* was a threat to the military regime. Rumors circulated that the regime had plans to bomb La Pincoya and, as people said to me, "erase it from the map." The regime persecuted the *población,* subjecting it to military sniper fire. Men and boys were rounded up and contained on the soccer field while military officers interrogated them for suspected leftist leanings. *Allanamientos,* or household raids, were performed in order to search for contraband materials, such as pamphlets, newspapers, and books, and to take men and women into preventive detention. Men were humiliated in front of their families. Relatives and friends were disappeared, politically executed, and tortured. Those who were militants had to live clandestinely or were exiled.

Along with this state violence in the form of repression and terror, the regime advanced a policy of decentralization to fragment political organization and spatially separate the rich from the poor. According to the regime, decentralization would be the foundation of a "protected democracy." Grassroots organizations would articulate concrete, local demands to the municipality. Thus, the state, freed of political pressure, would be able to fulfill its bureaucratic technical role. Paradoxically, Pinochet decreed "local participation," instantiating "participation" through authoritarianism. In 1982, he decreed that municipalization would be institutionalized to "juridically organize the direct participation of the community in local government." He then consolidated this "local governance" into law in 1988 with the Municipal Government Law (Gideon 2001; Greaves 2005, 193). Mayors were appointed, not elected. Political demands thus became tightly circumscribed to geographic location.

In the name of "local governance" and "participation," the municipalities were now to provide for their own populations in several key areas: primary care and education, transport and public highways, sanitation, sports and recreation, and local planning and development (Gideon 2001, 224). In urban housing policy, *erradicaciones* ("eradications," the forced movement of the poor to land of low value) were undertaken to facilitate the free-market regulation of housing supply. Poor and rich were geographically separated, paving the way for social spending targeted to spatial areas (Dockendorff 1990; Espinoza 1989). Thus a decrease in social spending (from 25 percent of GNP in 1971 to 14 percent in 1981) mirrored an increase in the amount of state subsidies given to the extreme poor. In 1970, 37 percent of the income of a poor family was subsidized by the state, in 1988, this subsidy had increased to 57 percent. The subsidies, however, were barely half of what a worker would make at the monthly minimum wage.

The municipality of Huechuraba was formed through this decentralization process. In 1981, Huechuraba came into existence when the larger municipality of Conchalí, in which it had been embedded, was split into two sections. The new Conchalí was the historic lower-middle-class sector with a slightly higher income level. The new municipality of Huechuraba was, at the time of the split, comprised of *poblaciones* (the working poor) and *campamentos* (squatter camps). It now includes a burgeoning transnational business sector, called the Ciudad Empresarial. This sector is directly connected by highway to the international airport. With the influx of upper- and upper-middle-class people into Huechuraba came a pervasive rumor that has ebbed and flowed over the years: that there are plans to expropriate the entire neighborhood because of this sector's surge in property values.

In 2008, when I visited Ruby, a developer was trying to make alliances with local social leaders, such as the president of the Junta de Vecinos (Neighborhood Council), in order to gain neighborhood support for his development plan for La Pincoya that he was proposing to the state under its new "Quiero Mi Barrio" (I Love My Neighborhood) community development program. This program consists of forging public-private partnerships in the name of community development. Thus, the state contracts with private companies, selected through a competitive process, who invest in "development." I happened to be staying with Ruby when the developer visited. He plugged his pen drive into my laptop and showed us the PowerPoint. His plan involved converting La Pincoya into a *barrio bohemio* (bohemian neighborhood) of discotheques and bars for international clientele, converting the green hills to flower farms to produce blooms that could be sold to the owners of upper-class condos, and creating what he called a "head-hunting agency" (in English) to filter out the "thieves" in La Pincoya and thus find "honest women" who would be able to work as nannies in the condominiums. He explained his plan while eating a homemade *sopaipilla* and taking tea in Ruby's house with the children and Ruby's husband, Héctor. Afterward, Ruby politely thanked him for stopping by and offered more than a few niceties; but as she came back into the house, she called him a "snake." Her eldest son offered more colorful prose. Ruby talked about him to Sra. Cecy, her neighbor, who said she would chain herself to her house before anyone would expropriate it. "People in La Pincoya would not leave their houses." He did not return, and the plan has not been realized.

CHAPTERS IN TIME

For many of the men and women I came to know, memory is both an ethical practice of the self and autonomous from the self. It is tied to the self's political commitment, but it is also lived in intimate relations and in the very materiality of the house and the neighborhood. Memory also manifests through a past of state violence that is available to the present through the arrangements of the state and market today. Aspirations for democracy and disappointment with actual political and economic conditions also constitute a medium through which relations with intimate kin are lived and sometimes broken.

While I came to know men and women who had been militants in the democratic movements, I was also introduced by these men and women to neighbors whose political affiliations were completely at odds with theirs. Neighborhood life does not fall along clear fracture lines of political affiliation. There are feelings of deep betrayal among those of the same political affiliation, and differences in political commitment within families. While a neighbor might despise her neighbor's political commitments, she might also say that her neighbor is "a good neighbor," meaning that she is helpful and respectful. In La Pincoya, people inhabit different relational modes simultaneously, so that attending to others in daily life might not entail an all-or-nothing judgment. By considering how people are enmeshed in these different relations, ethnography can attend to the possibilities of solidarity, generosity, and kindness in everyday life. Thus, this ethnography does not just make the point that the self is always in relations with others, as opposed to a self-constituted "I." Rather, this ethnography considers the importance of *how* the self is enmeshed in relations. That is, the self is simultaneously enmeshed in different relations that entail different demands and desires.

Likewise, the travails of "the market" are lived through relations: in the difficulties of making ends meet, in temporary work contracts and their unstable wages, and in pervasive economic indebtedness. Indeed, keeping up with mortgage payments on the house through the help of one's intimate kin shows that the forces of the market are not disembodied market values that come from somewhere else and fragment "the family." Moreover, credit has become a resource in caring for those in one's "house of blood," a house that connects intimate kin and friends outside that house with those in the house through domestic relations. At the same time, the feelings of responsibility to multiple kin and enormous economic pressures can make this responsiveness a bitter struggle.

In each of the chapters, I attend to different emphases of the market and the state in intimate relations and neighborhood life while also exploring how the state's accounting for the social and moral debts takes shape in La Pincoya. I also write about life in time—as a movement in time, as a work of time on relations, as a past continuous inhabiting the present, or as a being in another's present. Writing in time came both with the long-term nature of this ethnography, which took shape between 1999 and 2010, and with the struggle of finding orientations to time that would open rather than foreclose an inquiry into care.

In chapter 1, I explore the domestic struggles to care for kin as these struggles become entangled with debt and violence in the home. In following the relations in one house between 2004 and 2008, I consider waiting both as a modality of care and as a force of kinship embodied by those in the house. Specifically, I attend to how domestic relations and institutional credit provide temporal and material resources for the care of mentally ill and addicted kin within the home. In this scene, care may be understood in relation to the desire to be infinitely responsive to kin and the difficulty in limiting that desire. Institutional credit becomes entangled with this desire for infinite responsibility to kin.

In chapter 2, I move from the house to the field of friends and neighbors to consider how critical moments of economic scarcity are mitigated and acknowledged through domestic relations, in popular economic forms, and among neighbors. The state sought to address the social debt by expanding poverty programs targeted to the extreme poor, and in this chapter I discuss how the technologies of verification have transformed the social debt into a debt that the poor owe the state for receiving aid; the poor are assumed to be certain kinds of subjects of aid. I then explore how economic precariousness and critical moments are acknowledged in the fabric of neighborhood life, and discuss how boundaries between neighbors and friends inform a dignity that is locally intelligible. By attending to acts of kindness in everyday life, I consider the limits of the actual justice of the social debt, a debt that is empirically accounted for through disciplinary technologies.

In chapter 3, I return to scenes of intimate life, moving between 1999 and 2006. I explore how the official acknowledgment of torture under the Pinochet regime circulated in neighborhood life, and how this official acknowledgment was animated in the everyday lives of Ruby and Héctor, who experienced torture under the regime. I attend to the existential aspects of political commitments and explore how torture is spoken of in relation to conditions of unstable work and economic indebtedness. I bring into focus how aspirations for democracy, and disappointment with actual conditions, are woven into intimate life. Seeking acknowledgment for violations becomes one of many ways in which an awakening to one's present relations might occur.

In chapter 4, I am concerned with the relations between sexuality and political community, specifically with the figure of the mother militant. I turn to the lives of Leticia and her daughter, Julieta, between 1999 and 2006 and bring into soft focus how a break with intimate kin is lived. I explore how, for Leticia, her experience of exile is amplified by a return to the conventional world of kinship relations. I consider how her children's difficulties in receiving Leticia back into the home are haunted by a liberal imagination of political community, which engenders ideas of agency, sacrifice, and the citizen and posits men and women's different attachments to the life of political community. I then consider how Julieta's experiences of the domestic also bear traces of this liberal imagination, specifically in relation to reproduction.

In chapter 5, I change register to consider the fates of community mental health treatment programs for depression in different municipalities, focusing on the creation of the state's National Depression Treatment Program for low-income women. I discuss the consequences of decentralization for this program and then examine the group psychoeducational sessions as sites of experimentation. In La Pincoya, the group sessions invited an exploration of the incorporation of conservative Catholicism into a therapeutic discourse.

In chapter 6, I return to intimate scenes in everyday life to explore care and abandonment and trace how life and death are at play in specific moments of a life. I explore how the program's antidepressants, as well as a host of other medications, are forces within concrete domestic arrangements, or affective configurations. Attending to these configurations can open further questions with respect to domestic triaging, or the domestic decision making on the care and neglect of family members. It queries the limits to an anthropological account of abandonment, particularly when access to context itself is not secure.

AN ANTHROPOLOGY OF CARE

This book's central concern is with care and limits in circumstances of poverty and economic precariousness. It is concerned with how care manifests and takes shape in intimate relations, as well as how limits are intimately discovered in the midst of institutional responses to disease, distress, and need. In Chile, and regionally in Latin America, an uneven distribution of resources for health care and public education is accompanied by an expansion of funding for the identification and treatment of specific diseases and for programs that address extreme poverty. A politics of care geared to high-profile diseases such as HIV/AIDS has constituted global health as a right to medication and has increasingly focused long-term intervention in terms of an implementation of health care delivery systems (cf. Biehl 2007; Farmer 2003), even as long-standing and emergent configurations of poverty, need, and disease go unproblematized.

In studies of urban poverty, for example, the paucity of public resources for health and education, the rise of incarceration, and drug-related violence have generated powerful representations of poor urban neighborhoods. These representations have consequences for attending to life within them. Elaborating the notion of "advanced marginality," urban sociologist Loïc Wacquant has argued that the precarization of labor, along with "state policies of social retrenchment and urban abandonment," have transformed poor urban neighborhoods from places "bathed in shared emotions and joint meanings, supported by practices of mutuality, to indifferent 'spaces' of mere survival and relentless contest" (Wacquant 2008, 241).

But such a representation may elide textures of life and the fragile efforts in self-making that are occurring in circumstances of poverty and how those efforts complexly articulate with institutions. And further, this representation does so through a specific relationship to time: it creates a break between the past and present in order to represent the past (see Strathern 1995). Thus, against the representation of "collective *oekumene*" in the past, the poor urban neighborhood of today is represented as a "social purgatory" or "territory of perdition" (Wacquant 2008, 233), in which the poor engage in "informal individual strategies of 'self-provisioning'" (p. 244). Such spaces of perdition, then, call for mechanisms of social and political incorporation to "reintegrate" these spaces back into the fold of a recognizable form of life.

Recent critiques of humanitarian reason have engaged the political and moral stakes in these representations of pervasive suffering and alienation. Didier Fassin, for example, argues that a new moral economy centered on humanitarian reason has marked a shift in the way in which "we" have come to describe and interpret the world. Representations of exclusion and suffering mobilize moral sentiments of compassion, indignation, and care, and these moral sentiments have political value, which entails specific forms of intervention (Fassin 2012). For anthropologist Miriam Ticktin, a politics of care is an antipolitics insofar as it preserves the social order rather than generates a radical political critique (Ticktin 2011). Based on the universality of suffering and pain, this politics in fact operates selectively through compassion for suffering bodies recognized as morally legitimate.

These critiques illuminate how categories of suffering and trauma migrate across domains. In the process, they begin to define new fields of intervention and redraw lines of inclusion and exclusion. Attending to the ways in which violence and harm are existentially experienced, however, shifts the anthropological exercise. Rather than focus on representations of the suffering subject to trace a general moral shift, globally speaking, an anthropological writing that acknowledges suffering engages and responds to a specific life and world. This engagement opens thought to the experience of time in relation to violence as well as the concealments and boundaries in everyday life (see Kleinman et al. 1997; Das et al. 2000). For friends, family, and neighbors in La Pincoya, acknowledgment of the effects of present-day economic precariousness falters when an anthropologist holds up a representation of collectivities and intimate relations that existed in the past in order to emphasize what was "lost." Rather, the past *presents* in specific ways and moments. These effects, or affects, are refracted through relational modes and their boundaries in the present, and invest relationships with different hopes, desires, and limits.

Through these refractions, I engage moral projects in everyday life, in which care is a problem rather than a given. I take care as being diffuse and not definable in any simple way. Attending to care is similar to attending to violence, in which, as Veena Das remarks, "contests around the question of what can be named as violence are themselves a sign of something important at stake" (Das 2008, 284). To attend to care as a problem in everyday life, rather than a category with defined borders, has implications for my relation to ethnography. Everyday life is a scene to which I am *drawn*, rather than a set of routines, practices, or interviews that I observe, evaluate, and extrapolate judgments *from*. It also has implications for how I understand and engage the moral. While there might be a great deal of moralizing in everyday life, the struggles in caring for others and the complex affects that compose a discovery of limits are existentially experienced in ways that implicate the moral fabric of self-making (Kleinman 2006, 2010). Throughout this book, I engage care as a problem within intimate life, which is itself layered with institutions. I consider the moral not in terms of moral judgments but in the very ways in which self is implicated with others.[5] This implication is where limits are experienced.

How might such limits appear in ethnographic engagements with poverty and disease? Unsettling any sentimentalized notion of the family and challenging the taken-for-granted affects that "should" manifest among intimate kin, anthropologists have elaborated such limits around the problem of abandonment. For example, Nancy Scheper-Hughes's discussion of child death in a setting of poverty and extremely high infant mortality highlights the complexity and range of what might constitute abandonment. A small error or a moment of inattention can have fatal consequences: "so much greater vigilance is required to keep an infant alive, even the smallest lapse in maternal attention and care can sometimes be fatal" (Scheper-Hughes 1992, 360; see also Das 2010b). But simultaneously, given the pervasiveness of child death and the often overwhelming circumstances of poverty, "a good part of learning how to mother on the Alto includes knowing when to let go of a child who shows he wants to die" (p. 364). In the lives of Alto women and in the face of multiple dangers to life, death is not opposed to life; rather death is a "valid part of existence, so that death, too, must be *lived*" (p. 364). A play of life and death is at work in the relationship between mother and infant; abandonment here cannot be understood solely as a discrete moment with intentionalities ascribed to it.

Focusing on the shaping of intimate relations by market forces and medical technologies, João Biehl's discussion of abandonment centers on the domestic triaging of the mentally ill and unwanted (Biehl and Eskerod 2005). The normative family is a parapolity—a "state within the state"(p. 185)—engaged in a "making live" and "letting die" of its family members (see Foucault 1978). Those deemed unproductive, economically speaking, are actively ejected from the family and relegated to zones of abandonment—a social and biological death. These works raise a further set of important questions: How is ethnographic method implicated in understandings of accountability, care, and abandonment? How do modalities and temporalities of engagement with ethnographic sites shape descriptions of the dynamics of care? How do anthropologists come to know the shifting lines of the normal and abnormal, and what are limits to an anthropological knowing?

When I first started my research as a graduate student in anthropology and a medical student, I was interested in the high prevalence of depression in Santiago, which had reached 29.5 percent in primary care. According to the World Health Organization, this prevalence of depression was the second highest in the world (WHO 2001). Psychiatrists and public health officials initiated a national depression treatment program for the diagnosis and treatment of low-income women. This program was cast as both part of a national project of moral healing and an intervention for the health of the poor. The project fit key-in-lock within a critical inquiry of the biopolitical state and the medicalization of the family, in which the woman as mother is responsible for the well-being of her children, the future of the population. But situating myself in La Pincoya, I grew uneasy with a project that focused almost exclusively on citizenship and a circumscribed medical intervention. A whole range of relations and circumstances seemed to be eclipsed through a focused critique of the normative family and "the neoliberal state."

This local density of relations suggested a different reading of Foucault's writings on medicalization, the family, and the biopolitics of the population. In "The Politics of Health in the Eighteenth Century," Foucault traces how medical politics "has as its first effect the organisation of the family, or rather the family-children complex, as the first and most important instance for the medicalisation of individuals" (Foucault 1980, 174). The "close-knit family cell" (p. 182) is the milieu of the child as future adult and is hooked in a reciprocal relation to public health and the institutionalizing and protection of the doctor-patient relation. For Foucault, this medicalization must be understood through a "history of *these* materialities," of institutional rearrangements, medical technologies, urban space, the family cell, and bodies of individuals (p. 182, emphasis mine). I do not take Foucault's point here as an explanation for the daily decision making regarding disease and illness within families today. Rather, he offers a key insight: that I might understand medicine, kinship networks, neighborhood, institutions at the margins of the state, and state violence as a *specific* history of materialities. That is, medicalization has singular histories. Through interviews and partaking in everyday life, I saw the category of depression dispersed into various bodily aches and pains that women colloquially called *depresión a ratos* (depression from time to time). Experiences of exile and torture were woven into self-making but also carefully bounded. Life was moving. Another thematic horizon took shape.

Over time, I found myself drawn into a range of relationships, from allowing myself to be claimed as a godmother—and therefore assuming responsibilities to my *hijado* (godchild) and my *comadre*, as well as to her intimate kin relations spread over three houses—to being claimed by several intimate friendships that have taken shape over a decade. As I was drawn into these relationships, it became evident to me that my concerns with care were not posed in relation to a fixed ideal of the normative family or its opposite, "nonnormative" kinship relations. Rather, because I became implicated in the lives of others in various ways, I had to engage norms in their lives: to appreciate the work of domestic relations, the stakes in concealing need, the delicate struggles over intimate relationships in which the body was staked, or the small neglects and denials that also made up everyday life.

In his essay "The Normal and the Pathological," historian and philosopher of science Georges Canguilhem asks us to treat life as "an order of properties," a precarious organization of forces rather than a system of laws against which the "individual [is] a provisional and regrettable irrationality" (p. 125). From this perspective, "living beings have a normative relation to life" (Marrati and Meyers 2008, ix). That is, they respond to their internal and external conditions. Individuality is not an obstacle to the norm but the very object of the norm itself. Paraphrasing Kurt Goldstein, Canguilhem writes, "A norm . . . must help us understand concrete individual cases. . . . An alteration in the symptomatic content does not appear to be disease until the moment when the being's existence, hitherto in equilibrium with its milieu, becomes dangerously troubled" (Canguilhem 2008, 129). Disease is therefore "an aspect of life regulated by norms that are vitally inferior or depreciated" (p. 131). We might extend this thought further to consider how living beings experience moments when the whole of their existence is called into question. Experiences of such moments are not normless. Rather, they are experiments with life. This normative relation to life, for example, is revealed in the improvisations that people engage in to mitigate and normalize pains and distress and the moments when these pains are problematized in everyday life (see Das and Das 2006; Garcia 2010; Fullwiley 2011).

Through the process of writing this ethnography, I began to further appreciate the experiments with life that were in my field notes, my interviews, and my ongoing relationships with family and friends in La Pincoya. Desires to care for kin with addiction to *pasta base* and with chronic mental illness are enmeshed in economic pressures such that the experience of care could pass a threshold and become an experience of one's limit. Everyday aches and pains from unstable work and pervasive indebtedness are treated with a local formulary of anti-inflammatories, vitamins, and sometimes antidepressants. To a large extent, these aches and pains are normalized and taken as part and parcel of the bodily experience of living. I began to appreciate the significance of boundaries: experiences of poverty in La Pincoya call for an acknowledgement of the delicate concealment of both need and assistance that occur during moments of economic scarcity. And, I learned to pay attention to experiments with genre in the efforts to make the self intelligible to others, to present the self to others and to be received by them. Reworking the conventions of the *testimonio* genre, for example, was one way of making the self present to others, but also a way to withhold the violations of life so that one's children may live normal lives.

If this book expresses a wariness of the fixity of certain critiques, it is because of this engagement with the lives of others. I am wary of a diagnosis of social fragmentation and individualism that relies on a representation of a relational past. I am also wary of a critique of this diagnosis that takes the continued presence of intimate relations as a given. Both assert fixed normative imaginaries of what an individual is and what is expected of intimate relations. To counter dominant imaginaries of the atomized individual and discourses of "self-responsibility"—whether they be of drug addiction, mental illness, or consumer desires—by asserting a fundamental human interdependency based on intimate affects of care and love may eclipse the very boundaries of specific relational modes, the uncertainty in relationships, and the problem of separateness.

Understanding the normative as experiments with life and with self-making allows for the often subtle and fragile ways in which health, or more broadly, a sense of well-being, is momentarily achieved. In the delicate task of responding to others and discovering one's finiteness amid difficult circumstances, life and death are not opposed but rather sketched into each other in different ways at specific moments in a life. I imagine the chapters of this book as leaning on each other. Each chapter takes up specific concerns; the chapters' conversation with each other may further enrich them from within. The challenge for me was to consider both the singularity of a life and the availability of social conventions and genres in which life takes shape, in which the self presents itself to another (Butler 2005). Thus, my writing offers no grand diagnosis, but instead the hope that we might be attentive to the difficulties and achievements of being in another's present.

CHAPTER 1

Symptoms of Another Life

A TIME OF PURE NERVES

"Pure nerves." Sra. Flora crumbled a soda cracker in her hands. It was the afternoon of Easter 2004 in La Pincoya. She had invited me to help her prepare an elaborate Easter lunch for her extended family. But the festive plans had abruptly dissolved with the news that her partner, Rodrigo, had lost his job in a textile factory where he had worked for the past twenty-five years. Instead, bites of homemade bread and sips of sugared tea mingled with stifled conversation.

Sra. Flora, Rodrigo, tío Ricardo, and Sra. Flora's daughters and grandchildren lived together in a two-story house that was a process of autoconstruction. First-floor brick rooms joined others of corrugated iron insulated with drywall. Above them, wood beams and iron sheets made a second floor. Outside, a gate of blue-painted iron bars and sheeting bounded the front patio. As part of the *toma* (land seizure) of 1970 that gave rise to La Pincoya, Sra. Flora and her former husband arrived on this plot of land with little more than a tent. They first built their home with materials scavenged from construction sites.

After her separation from her husband in the late 1970s, Sra. Flora and her new partner, Rodrigo, continued to build and furnish the home through bank loans and department store credit. Her daughters Carmen and Sonia, both single and in their midthirties lived on the second floor, each with two children. Separated by a thin wall was tío Ricardo's small room. On the first floor, Sra. Flora's twenty-five-year-old daughter, Valentina, shared a room with twenty-four-year-old Margarita, an adopted niece with cerebral palsy. And in a room abutting that of Sra. Flora and Rodrigo, her thirty-year-old daughter, Florcita, lived with her partner, Kevin, and their two children.

Rodrigo's job loss had rippled through family relations. Carmen and Sonia worked in unstable jobs that often changed month to month: office cleaning, stocking supermarket shelves, selling pirated CDs. They would have to take on extra hours to pay the utility bills and the monthly quotas on debts until Rodrigo could find another job, but they faced the prospect with a mixture of resignation and frustration. The affects of working overtime also intensified anger toward Florcita and Kevin, who had begun to drink hard liquor again, stealing and selling household foodstuffs to purchase *pisco* (hard liquor). Florcita was in danger of losing her job as a teacher's aide. Kevin, just released from a one-month psychiatric internment for addiction to *pasta base* (cocaine base paste) and for manic depression, paced the house nervously and angrily all day long. In a confrontation between the three sisters shortly before I arrived, Sra. Flora had stepped in to defend Florcita. "You always paint her as the bad one in the movie," she said. Carmen and Sonia had walked out. Shortly after, Florcita left the house with Kevin and the children.

As Sra. Flora recounted the details of the argument to me that Easter, she crumbled cracker after cracker between her fingers. Rodrigo sighed heavily and went to the door to smoke a cigarette. The tensions, she said, were "eating my nerves." She pointed to a framed black-and-white photo hanging on the wall behind me. The photo was taken before she moved to Santiago in the early 1960s. With long, curly dark hair and a white apron tied around her slim waist, she stood smiling behind a table stacked with homemade bread. Comparing her body then and now, she said, "*Todo esto*"—the economic precariousness, the debts, the smoldering frustration with Florcita—"it makes me fat. If I eat, it's like I'm eating double." Protecting Florcita wove into the ongoing household economic pressures, and Sra. Flora embodied *all this*, literally speaking, through her nerves.

Sra. Flora's eaten nerves speak to intersecting dynamics of care, illness, and economic indebtedness within the domestic (see Arriagada 2010; Valdés et al. 2005; X. Valdés 2007). What are temporal and moral textures of this care? Let us move in time with Sra. Flora and her intimate relations. Can this movement in time attune us to care as a kind of "active awaiting" (Cavell 2005, 136)?[1] By this phrase, I mean a patience for the possible, which draws on the hope that relations could change with time. In this chapter, I consider how this "active awaiting" draws on a wider network of dependencies that provide the temporal and material resources for this care. Waiting reveals how domestic relations with neighbors and institutions of credit both mesh with and create cuts in intimate relations. It helps us flesh out the problem of responsibility for and to kin.

"TODAY, ALL OF US ARE SUBJECTS OF CREDIT"

In June 2005, the Chilean Central Bank published its *Report on Financial Stability for the Second Semester of 2005*. Charting the expansive progression of the Chilean economy, the report states in its principal summary: "This positive economic situation has ushered in a greater dynamic of consumption and investment during the present year. The interest rates continue stimulating the expansion of credit. The debt of households continues increasing at elevated rates, rates that are greater than the growth of their incomes" (Banco Central de Chile 2005, 7). Between September 2004 and September 2005, the level of household indebtedness from mortgages increased 17 percent and the level of indebtedness tied to department stores and bank loans increased by 21 percent. Meanwhile, disposable household incomes increased by only 9 percent (p. 38).

Chile's leading conservative newspaper, *El Mercurio,* publicized the figures, citing the combined generation of credit sources and increasing indebtedness as both "good and bad news" for the consumer. Attempting to dispel anxiety over these figures, Raimundo Monge, the chief of strategic planning at the Spanish-owned Santander Bank and the president of the Banking Committee for the Association of Banks in Chile, placed them within a narrative of national development based on the expansion of the market: "Indebtedness is natural in an economy that is growing and that has better prospects and more trust. . . . The greater the development of the country, the greater will be persons' debts. In fact, the report of the Central Bank notes that the indebtedness [in Chile] is less than in developed countries" (quoted in Rivas 2006).

The circulation of such numbers in the media—and the discourses in which they are rendered socially and politically intelligible—points to public anxieties and ambivalences over indebtedness, which has become a narrative linchpin in both left- and right-wing politics. Spurred by increasing income inequality, job insecurity, and state regulation favorable toward lending institutions, the consumer credit industry in Chile is one of the most powerful in Latin America. It has grown significantly since the democratic transition in 1990. In 1993, there were approximately 1.3 million department store credit cards in circulation. By 1997, this number had escalated to 5.2 million, and by 1999, when I began my fieldwork in La Pincoya, there were 7 million (PNUD 2002). As of 2008, there were approximately 29 million nonbank credit cards in circulation, averaging 3.5 cards per person (Varas C. 2008).

Department stores such as Almacenes París and Falabella not only offer credit cards but also have opened their own banks. Supermarkets, such as Supermercados Líder, as well as pharmacies, now offer their own credit and cash advances. Credit cards, according to Superintendent of Banks Enrique Marshall, make up more than half of the financial utility of department stores: "The cards of department stores have registered an unusual development, something that you do not see in other parts of the world where this business is purely in banking" (quoted in Fazio 2005, 180). By 2006, the national census showed that low-income populations earning between USD 110 and USD 300 per month were spending 36 percent of their monthly income on consumer debts (MIDEPLAN 2006).

Accompanying this credit expansion, however, are accounts portraying the dangers of indebtedness, the psychosocial causes of debt, and debt's psychological sequelae. For example, in June 2000, *El Mercurio de Valparaíso* ran an article, "The Risk of Living in Quotas," describing how a small-business owner had committed suicide because of his "overindebtedness": "Although suicide is not a generalized phenomenon, experts point out that this overindebtedness is inciting an increasing number of sick leave days because of depression" (*El Mercurio de Valparaíso* 2000). Responding to such dangers and risks, the National Corporation of Consumers and Users (Corporación Nacional de Consumidores y Usuarios), a nonprofit organization established in 2000, produced a two-part web-based video report titled *Indebtedness: Indebted or Overindebted Chileans?* A female reporter opens the report, remarking, "I have the impression that Chile, we Chileans, have changed. Today, all of us are subjects of credit. It doesn't matter how much we earn, where we live, they bombard us with offers to change the car, the television, the house, without caring about what income we have" (CONADECUS 2007).

While the mainstream media have tended to focus on the new consumer desires generated by the credit economy, among low-income populations credit has become a resource within the context of eroding and unstable wages, as well as of the privatization of public services. For example, political scientist Verónica Schild points out, "covering basic necessities such as health insurance, education fees and basic services through credit has become ubiquitous" (Schild 2007, 192). Yet accounts of economic indebtedness in Chile have hinged on the consumer subject and the control exerted through the credit system on workers, positing this neoliberal economic subject as either the starting point or the endpoint of analysis (Cruz Feliciano and Véliz Montero 2007; Moulian 1997). Attending to the difficulties in caring for kin, however, brings into focus how credit and experiences of economic indebtedness are mediated by "house relations" set within a wider field of domestic relations.

As I discussed in the introduction, the house is spoken of in terms of intimate kin relatedness—one's "house of blood"—and the obligations that come with kinship, "commitment to the house." The constant construction of the house, through renovation or mortgage payments, can be understood as a constant achieving of relatedness. These house relations are interconnected with intimate kin outside the house—through sisters, mothers, and daughters, as well as friends. This wider field of intimate kin and friends can be understood as domestic relations.

While domestic relations are not unique to Chile, the primacy of house relations and the extensive availability of credit to the poor give such relations a unique shape. For example, although Carol Stack's seminal work on domestic networks in poor African American communities resonates in part with these domestic relations, in Stack's account the spread of domestic activities shared across households and the constant movement of individuals among rented residences render "which household a given individual belongs to a meaningless question" (Stack 1974, 90). Such a tenuous relation to the house contrasts sharply with relatedness in La Pincoya, where domestic relations beyond the house can be thought of in terms of their pull toward house relations, in which women may be engaged in helping one another across houses, but with the hope of affirming a relation within the house itself.

It is in the positioning between these house relations and the wider field of domestic relations that care for the mentally ill and addicted within the home takes shape. I want to return to Sra. Flora and her family to trace out how struggles over this care pull women between kinship relations within the house, and how women draw on domestic relations and institutional credit to affirm a child's place in the house.

MAKING TIME

I met Sra. Flora in June 2000 on my second three-month stay in La Pincoya. Over eight years, I saw how constant economic precariousness often cast her affective stakes as mother and *pareja* (partner) against each other. The loss of Rodrigo's job in March 2004, however, sent the family into economic difficulties they had not experienced since the Pinochet era. Now, only one adult, Rodrigo's cousin, tío Ricardo, who continued to work in the same textile factory, had stable employment. With his lost wages and his difficulty finding temporary work, Rodrigo pressured Sra. Flora to address Florcita and Kevin's drug and alcohol use. Daughters Sonia and Carmen had also heard rumors about them: Florcita was going door to door asking for money from neighbors. Kevin had been seen in a drug dealer's car. In this context, Sra. Flora invited me to meet with her, Florcita, and Kevin together.

With her blue-gray eyes and long, curly brown hair, Florcita inherited the youthful Sra. Flora's looks. Indeed, Sra. Flora invoked this likeness, especially when reflecting on Florcita's drug use. "She looks like me when I was young. But I say now that she *was* really beautiful. Now, she is getting destroyed by drinking and drugs." Florcita sat in the corner, hand on her chin, sullenly looking at the floor. Sra. Flora pressed them to speak. "Go ahead, tell her about your illness, about the drugs," she said, pointing to Kevin and then to both of them. Neither immediately spoke. But just as Florcita raised her head, Kevin cut her gesture off abruptly, pulling his chair toward me.

Since suffering a stroke in 2001, Kevin had experienced multiple panic attacks, fear, and waves of anger. He hurriedly spoke of his first "attack":

> I had a stroke on the 22nd of December 2001. I was working late, going to bed late, getting up early. I was working as a bus driver [a city bus driver], arriving [home] at 2 A.M. and leaving at 4 or 5 in the morning. I was at the bus stop [in La Pincoya on the main street, Recoleta], and I felt a thing like *brrrrbrrrrbrrrbrrr, brrrbrrrbrrr* [he makes a twisting movement around his ear]. I was stuck there, and: "Ay, my God, what is happening to me?" I was taken to the emergency room [in the local primary care clinic] by my *compañeros*. They gave me an injection to calm me, and they said that I had depression, anxiety, and all of that stuff. Then from there they took me to the Psychiatric Hospital. They asked me lots of questions, and then they took me to a cardiologist. And then told me, Ya, you have a problem with your heart. This same cardiologist sent me to a neurologist, and they did a scanner on me, an electroencephalogram, a really complicated thing. And they found that my heart was bad.

After the stroke, Kevin acceded to a state pension for disability, which he called "retirement."[2] The slowness of life at home, however, made him nervous and agitated.

> I would like to return to working, but I have a bad [unfunctional] hand, a neurological damage that stays forever. They give me pills, but I walked around high, yellow [skin]—pure pills. You know, I will take pills for my nerves and nothing more. I am nervous. I feel like, how to put it, with what name . . . It's like when a ball is bouncing like this, like *papapapapapapa!* all this year. My aggression, my violence, augmented. More than anything it's made me more aggressive. As a human being, I don't accept it. Until today, I do not accept that this happens. I don't accept it because I am thirty-two years old. I have half of my life in front of me, so . . .

He paused. Bouncing his knee up and down, Kevin changed course. He recounted the circumstances that led up to his current state of illness.

> All of a sudden, I had many goals. When I was mixed up in drugs, I said to myself, "I will jump out of this [doing *pasta base*]. I will buy all this stuff for myself [*comprarme de todo*], I will buy myself [things] from here and there." And I had the desire [*tenía ganas de comparme un auto*] to buy myself a car also. Yes, I would buy a car. [He said this with a sense of wonder.] I would work for a car. So, I put myself to work, working, working, and working, and working, and working, and working, and working. I drove myself crazy working, but until even today I still have the desire to get up and go to work. But now, the rhythm that I have is very slow. Because I don't work, I can get up from bed at the hour that I want, and I don't have anything to do. Last night, I felt so alone, but I have the fear of being alone. And then, all of a sudden I got an attack [a panic attack] . . . But, I opted to retire.

For Kevin, the desire and the wonder for the car could not be dissociated from a desire to work and to have a working body. Sra. Flora interjected, "He is very aggressive. He will break a cup for whatever reason. There is no control. It's like . . . *pap!*" (She snaps her fingers).

"Does the illness affect your family?" I asked tentatively. "Not much," Kevin responded, leaning back in his chair. "Florcita is very tranquil. My woman, tranquil. She knows I am sick." Florcita shrugged her shoulders. Sra. Flora questioned him, contesting his seeming indifference. "Why were you working so hard? To reach the goals that you had?" Kevin responded, "Yes, because we lost everything when we were mixed up in drugs." Sra. Flora nodded. "And, this is when I began to gain weight," she said. She began to recount the damage that their previous addiction to *pasta base* had caused, as if to warn and remind them of what it could lead to in the present.

When Florcita and Kevin were involved in *pasta base* (*metido en la pasta*) in the late 1990s, the family's debts to department stores began to soar. Kevin and Florcita sold household possessions to buy *pasta base*. Cocaine base paste is similar to crack cocaine. Base paste is composed of the intermediary products in the purification of cocaine. Those products are cut with a host of available agents, such as neoprene and kerosene, and then can be smoked or snorted. Available national statistics report that the prevalence of base paste addiction comprises 0.6 percent of the total population (CONACE 2006). Yet such figures must be taken critically, given that the survey relies on self-reported use of an illegal substance. In La Pincoya, *pasta base* addiction has become a pervasive concern, provoked by a general sense that the number of neighborhood youth addicted to base is increasing.

"They sold everything," Sra. Flora said of Florcita and Kevin. "The TV, the stereo, a bed. They would steal when we were not in the house. They would steal if we did not have everything in the house under lock and key." During this period, they also fought with each other in the home. Kevin flew into rages, resulting in broken walls, doors, and windows. These cycles of theft, destruction, and debt in households struggling with addiction to *pasta base* were familiar themes in La Pincoya. During this time, Flora said, monthly debt payments took up half of Rodrigo's income. In an act of desperation, she separated Kevin from Florcita by locking Florcita in her bedroom to "rehabilitate." "I locked her in the room for thirty-one days, bringing her lunch, tea. But, I did not let her out until she was rehabilitated." The *separation*, Sra. Flora emphasized, is what ultimately allowed Florcita to rehabilitate. "You've never considered that you have a *toxic relation*?" she asked them.

While we listened, Kevin had grown noticeably restless. Finally, he stood up and left, knocking the chair to the floor. "See?" Sra. Flora looked at me as I winced, while directing her words to Florcita. "Even when he was making money as a bus driver, he didn't help pay off the debts. He never bought a car either, so what did he do with the money?" She intimated that he used the money to buy drugs. Florcita then stood up with a scoff. "Look, he was buying things for the children," she said. "He paid for the light and water too. You can't throw all the blame on Kevin. You make him more aggressive with your stories." Florcita left the room. Turning to me, Sra. Flora said, "See? She doesn't want to listen. She is in love with Kevin."

As each confronted the other, the question of what place, if any, Kevin had in the home bubbled angrily to the surface. But like many times before, it was not a question that would be, or perhaps could be, resolved. Indeed, for many families with whom I worked, confrontations and arguments over relations or one's place in the home were not aimed at resolution—as if the place of another were spatially and temporally discrete, and as if each argument could be read in terms of intention. Rather, through their force, they tacitly acknowledged the uncertainty and vulnerability of that place and staked a claim to it.

In the midst of these tensions, Sra. Flora still sought ways to address Kevin's aggressiveness that invited him back into relations in the home. Having maxed out her own credit cards, she borrowed her neighbor's card the next day to purchase Kevin a new stereo. We rode the yellow-and-white city bus to Santiago's center, getting off near the doors of the Almacenes París department store. As we pressed stereo buttons and twisted knobs, opened and closed CD racks, Sra. Flora told me, "Music helps calm his nerves. It tranquilizes him and distracts him." This purchase was also an enactment of care for Florcita. Listening to music might diffuse Kevin's aggression, holding his attention in a way that pills did not, while providing a time for change to occur.

Outside of Sra. Flora's view, Florcita too found modalities to care for Kevin. Alcohol and pills. Later that night, I was at a friend's home in La Pincoya when Florcita knocked on her patio gate. "Luz! Luz!" she called out. I recognized the voice and went out to greet Florcita while Luz put her infant son to bed. Florcita's two young sons accompanied her. She was carrying a backpack. As the children ran inside to play with Luz's older children, I asked Florcita how she was holding up with Kevin. Dark rings wrinkled under her eyes as she spoke. Kevin had run out of medication for his nerves. "So, I buy pills from Sra. Maria [owner of a corner store] to make him sleep. He's desperate and aggressive."

She unzipped the backpack. Florcita explained that she was selling foodstuffs to make some money. It was full of packs of spaghetti, marmalade, and a bag of rice. These were the same goods that Sra. Flora had bought in the local market earlier in the day. I asked her what she intended to buy with the money earned from selling these goods. "*Pisco,*" she said. "If we share a bottle of *pisco,* and I give him a pill, I know he will sleep." Luz joined us. Florcita sold her a pack of marmalade. We each gave her a tight hug and watched her walk up the street with her children. Luz looked silently at the marmalade pack in her hand, as if considering the possibility that it had been stolen. "Well," she remarked, "we don't really need marmalade; we already have two packs. But I see Florcita, and I know she needs the money. So I do what I can to help."

Exploring the moral texture of these acts of borrowing and buying allows us to appreciate subtle transactions of care between neighbors and kin that take place every day. Could these actions be interpreted as gestures of care that demonstrate how domestic relations are actualized in the home? We may think of domestic relations in the home as being present in their potentiality. When intimate kin take up domestic relations by borrowing, selling, buying, listening, or visiting, these relations are realized, made actual, within the home in specific ways. In this case, borrowing a credit card from a neighbor to purchase a distraction, or buying redundant goods so a neighbor can tranquilize her partner, makes the time to set a different tone in family relations or at least provides a time of respite in order to face them anew.

Uncertainty infused these diverse gestures of care. How much time would a distraction last? Would a family member reveal a different aspect of herself if the tone of family relations shifted? Would she, as many said, "show the other face of the coin"? As families waited to see loved ones show a different side, this "made time" rubbed against the temporality of monthly debt payments and the uncertainty of unstable wages that impinged on the home.

LIFE LOANED

Over the next three months, Florcita and Kevin were not at home when I came to visit. Rumors spread that Florcita was engaging in prostitution to buy drugs. Kevin was said to be spending time with friends on "the other side" of the *población,* a way of saying that he was consorting with *pasta basteros* (addicts to *pasta base*). On one occasion, I saw Kevin driving an old sports car with three men whom I did not recognize. He called out to me, "Clarita!" I waved to him, but his tone of voice made me fear approaching the car. Stopped in front of the house, he revved the engine repeatedly, laughed, and drove off. A dust cloud lingered at the door. Several evenings, I spotted Florcita from afar with her children, returning from her work as a teacher's aide. By the time I arrived at their home, she had already gone to other friends' houses, leaving her children in the care of Sra. Flora.

Sra. Flora developed a growing reticence about Florcita and Kevin. In contrast to her earlier attempts to talk about the state of relations as a way to address and diffuse their tensions, her silence suggested that the neighborhood rumors and Florcita and Kevin's friendships with *pasta basteros* had overrun her, leaving her little to say that would be listened to. When I inquired about them, she remarked, "What can I say. They don't listen. For now, I just eat it." Indeed, Sra. Flora was literally embodying the effects of this failure to listen. She had gained several kilos in the previous three months. Her ankles were constantly sore. She went to the general practitioner in the local primary care clinic, who suggested a diagnosis of hypothyroidism, but her thyroid tests were within normal limits.

Meanwhile, the house faced mounting difficulties in keeping up with monthly debt payments. Rodrigo found a minimum-wage, temporary job in construction, building chalets in Chicoreo. The hours were long, and the bus fare took up one-third of his income. As a result of his unemployment, the family got behind on their payments to department stores and the electric and water companies. They had to resort to cash advances from the Líder Supermarket to buy groceries. Debt collectors from the department stores had arrived at the home, threatening to take an inventory of household possessions of value that they could sell to pay off the debts.

Just over the northern hills bordering La Pincoya, Chicoreo was quickly becoming a location for "green," "natural," and "alternative" living for young professionals, hip actors, and TV personalities. As we sat outside in the evening chill, Rodrigo compared his lifeworld to those in Chicoreo: "There, they pay for the houses in cash. And here, I'm still paying quotas on this chair. So, this chair—the Hites [department store] still are the owners of it. Credit is for the poor." Rodrigo voiced a shared sentiment in La Pincoya. As long as one continued to make monthly payments on commodities, they were not one's own. Other neighbors linked the uncertainty of ownership to the uncertainty of life itself: "Tenemos una vida prestada" (We have a loaned life).

The "loaned life" was tied into the historical conditions of the credit system itself. As many adults who lived through the dictatorship told me, the Pinochet regime gave credit to the poor. Credit gave the poor access to material resources for a "dignified life." In reflecting on her family's history of debt, Sra. Flora elaborated on these historical conditions.

It started when Pinocho [Pinochet] came to power, because before, credit was for the rich, those same rich who worked in the government, in the same commercial houses. And I remember when Pinocho was elected [salió], he gave credit to the poor. Hites was the first store that offered credit to the working class. And you could arrive with your income statement and your identification card and the light and water bills, and you could take whatever you needed. And with this, the poor began to get themselves into debt. *Pppffff*. And now you will not go to any house, Clarita, where there is not a family in debt, because to have your things of value, you need to be indebted. I remember when tío Ricardo asked for a loan from Atlas [bank] for 100,000 pesos [USD 160], and was paying for three years, but gave back 300,000 [USD 500]. And that is how the rich financial businesspeople make their money off the poor.

"What were the consequences?" I asked.

Well [she paused], good, because before, no one could buy anything, and we were experiencing needs [*pasando necesidades*] much worse than before. Imagine, Clarita, entire families sleeping in the same bed. I with my husband and my three children slept in the same bed for years, but when the department stores began to give credit, we could buy a bunk bed and the children slept on top on the second bed and we slept on the lower bed. So, with this credit, families could live with more dignity, a dignified life. They had their stove, their refrigerator.

Yet, as she explained, such resources for a dignified life emerged in conjunction with new visibilities and social controls:

But with all of this, families began to get into debt, and there appeared DICOM [the private credit registry], because the businesspeople realized that the poor were getting into so much debt that they could not pay their quotas. Many people owed three, four, five times their monthly income. One owed in Hites, in Ripley, in Almacenes París. And with light, water, and something to eat, one did not make it to the end of the month. So, with computation, the computer, everything changed, because, for example, you could now be in Puerto Montt in Hites. And they could see in the computer there that you owed in Hites in Santiago. And they say, "You can't take out this TV, because you haven't paid your *letras* [monthly payments] and you're late." So now there is more pressure to pay the *letras* on time, or you have to do everything possible so as to pay the *letras* on time—work extra hours, look for small temporary work [*pololito*], whatever thing to not arrive in DICOM.

New temporal forms of surveillance arose with the development of extensive credit reporting systems that meshed the state-mandated credit registry of the Superintendent of Banks and Financial Institutions with the main private company for credit information, DICOM (Center for Information of Commercial Documentation; see Castel 1991).

In 1979, the National Chamber of Commerce and private entrepreneurs had established DICOM, four years after the initiation of the Chicago Boy's structural adjustment plan. Throughout the 1980s, it won public bids to provide private credit information to the Superintendent of Banks and Financial Institutions and made individual contracts with banks and financial institutions. Owned by the U.S.-based company Equifax since 1997, DICOM's database currently contains financial information on persons with a tax identification number and any credit history. This information ranges from a history of bad checks, overdue bills, consolidated debts, reporting registry, to one's credit score (Cowan and De Gregorio 2003).

As Sra. Flora emphasized, DICOM exerted a continual presence in everyday life, in terms of both the material constraints that came with a troubled financial history and the anxieties that being in it, or on the verge of being in it, generated. To be "in DICOM" meant that one could not accede to any form of institutional credit: bank loans, department stores, or state-financed loans for higher education. Further, those in DICOM were often subject to labor discrimination (Raczynski et al. 2002). DICOM was used as a character assessment, a screening for personal responsibility and discipline. And, with access to DICOM's database, employers often conditioned contracts to the worker's status in DICOM.

From 1979 to 1999, when the Senate passed Law 19.628, Protection of Data of Personal Character, popularly known as the "DICOM Law," one's financial history was not only available to all employers and financial institutions, but it also remained in the DICOM database even when debts had been settled (see Ruiz 2002). The persistence of this history was often called the "debtor's stigma"; it made life chances attenuate, as if one were in an interminable, invisible cage (see *La Cuarta* 2002; Raczynski et al. 2002). The 1999 DICOM Law was the state's attempt to limit the abuse of this database, but it can also be interpreted as a spur for consumer spending by facilitating access to credit by previously "stigmatized" debtors (Ministerio Secretaria General de la Presidencia 1999).

According to the law, employers could not discriminate on the basis of DICOM information. In addition, individuals who settled their debts would be removed from the DICOM database after three years. Those who did not would remain in DICOM for up to seven years. Nevertheless, even after the requisite number of years in DICOM, the debtor's stigma continued in practice. Many debtors remained in the DICOM database despite having settled debts several years earlier; many employers continued to screen workers through this database. While consumer credit provided access to a dignified life, DICOM's persistent biographical consequences bound this life to feelings of anxiety.

Nevertheless, while DICOM registered individual credit histories, in

La Pincoya this biography was experienced as an accounting not of the individual but of the family tied into the home: "We are in DICOM" or "Families are in debt." This displacement of the DICOM biography from the individual to the family mirrored the fear of repossessions by debt collectors, who inventoried any item of value within the physical boundaries of the home to satisfy the outstanding debts of any family member with that same address. Thus, family members said, "Van a embargar la casa" (They will repossess the house), not only when the house itself was threatened with repossession but also when any individual in the home had reneged on his or her debts. While debt is in the name of an individual, the enforcement of debt through repossession materially implicated the entire home and the relations constituting it.

In his essay "Postscript on Control Societies," Gilles Deleuze examines the transformation of disciplinary societies based in institutions such as the prison, school, and asylum into societies with open, continuous, and free-floating control through the synergy of the market with new technologies. "A man is no longer a man confined but a man in debt," writes Deleuze. "One thing, it's true, hasn't changed—capitalism still keeps three quarters of humanity in extreme poverty, too poor to have debts and too numerous to be confined: control will have to deal not only with vanishing frontiers, but with mushrooming shantytowns and ghettos (Deleuze 1997, 181). But the expansion of the credit system among families in La Pincoya challenges this homogenous view of the poor, as well as capitalism's supposedly obvious inclusions and exclusions. The mechanisms of control societies are not beyond the extreme poor. Rather, they are precisely the mechanisms through which the materiality and image of "extreme poverty" are destabilized. It is this destabilization of the image that was embodied and absorbed into family relations.

Shadowed by the threat of DICOM and repossession, families in La Pincoya worked to keep up with the temporality of monthly debt payments, what they called *manteniendo la imagen* (maintaining the image). A common phrase used to describe the work to keep up with payments to department stores, utilities, and banks, *maintaining the image* conveyed the transient, insecure, and uncertain nature of the dignified life made possible through credit. Is this life a life that I can own, that I can trust? Will it exist tomorrow? This sense of uncertainty pervaded everyday relations. Gossip abounded about those who were *aparentando,* who projected the markers of material wealth beyond a family's means, and those who were *marceros,* who wore brand-name clothing even as they struggled to get to the end of the month. Against this uncertainty, families engaged in a work of maintenance to avoid falling into DICOM, to get out of DICOM, or to make debt payments in the face of repossession. Families cut back on food costs, asked neighbors, friends, and extended family members for loans, worked for overtime pay, and took on extra jobs. In this way, the "loaned life," a fragile existence, was held together through, and often despite, the temporality of credit.

UNBEARABLE VOLUME

For Sra. Flora, this uncertainty knotted together with Florcita's addiction, generating a domestic struggle over time itself. By June 2004, the tension of intimate relations had reached a nearly unbearable volume, like the stereo that Sra. Flora had bought Kevin to calm his nerves and that now blared heavy metal day and night. Kevin and Florcita were consuming *pasta base* and had become increasingly violent with each other. Once while I had tea with Sra. Flora and Rodrigo, we heard Florcita and Kevin yelling and fighting. The sound of breaking glass and walls being punched reverberated through the corridor. Then Kevin ran into the living room holding a knife. His forehead was lacerated. Florcita had hit him with an iron bar. He called the police. When two policemen arrived, they first questioned Kevin in a formulaic tone, "How many times have you hit your woman?" Kevin laughed, saying "Look at me, she hit me." An argument ensued between Kevin and Florcita in which each accused the other of being a *golpeador/a* (beater). Despite our contestations and pleadings, the police ultimately sided with Kevin. They arrested Florcita and took her into custody for the night. Later, Sra. Flora and I learned from Florcita that the argument had been set off by a missing piece of pizza. Florcita had brought home a pizza from the school where she worked. She shared it with her sisters, setting aside a piece for Kevin. The piece disappeared, however, and Kevin accused Florcita of eating it.[3]

This eruption of violence set in motion a daily struggle between Rodrigo and Sra. Flora over Florcita and Kevin's place in the home. Rodrigo simply demanded that they leave. Sra. Flora, on the other hand, wanted to help Florcita separate from Kevin, which would take its own time. Gradually, this struggle over letting time do its work became cast in economic terms. Rodrigo told me his unstable wages were barely covering monthly bills, department store quotas, and food. Florcita and Kevin, he said, were not contributing to the home. They were leaving the financial and emotional responsibility for caring for their own children to him and Sra. Flora. Tired of spending his income on paying the bills, he used his end-of-the-month pay to buy a new shirt, sweater, pants, and shoes. When the light was cut to the home for nonpayment, Rodrigo argued that it was her excessive care for family members that produced this darkness.[4] His frustration with her defense of Florcita and Kevin bled into relations with her other kin. He said that she would "sit in the dark" until she "put limits" on her family visiting the home. As she told me, "How can I limit my own family members from coming here? I was not raised that way, and it's difficult for me to change at this point in my life." After Rodrigo lost his job, she said, "Se puso machista, muy machista" (He's become very dominating).

In our conversations, Sra. Flora moved between the affective registers of time and space when speaking about Rodrigo. Time as possibility, an enduring patience with Rodrigo: "Let us see everything in its time." Space as a declaration of the finitude of her relation to him: "I want him to leave the house!" Yet when she recounted how she met Rodrigo, she cast their relationship and their process of constructing a life together in the shadow of other intimate experiences of male violence. Sra. Flora had met her husband when she migrated with her family from Los Angeles in the south of Chile to Santiago in search of work. She was sixteen years old when she became pregnant with her first child, Carmen.

> I was dating my husband when I was sixteen years old, and I was very sick, very sick. I went to the doctor, and they did some blood exams, and then afterward they did not explain anything. They gave me a letter from the doctor. I went to a meeting with my friend. I had the letter in my sweater pocket, and left it there on the chair [at home]. I still had not read the letter. My mother read it, and arrived to the [friend's] house furious. My mother beat me up [me sacó la cresta], took a stick and hit me in the face, in the mouth. I did not know why. And afterward, my father came and he beat, beat, beat me in the face, breaking all my teeth. And then all of my brothers—imagine it, I have four brothers; there were only two women in the family. All of my brothers and my father went to look for my husband, and they beat him up. I was in the hospital for one month, and he was there for forty-five days. They operated on my mouth and had to take out all my teeth. But I did not lose the baby. This baby was Carmen. Afterward, there was so much pressure for me to marry him. And, we married in '66. He began to walk around with other women, drink alcohol. And my brothers saw him with other women, and they hit him, beat him. My father said to him, "You are walking around with another woman when my daughter is in the home pregnant with your child?" But when they beat him, he arrived to the house and hit me, saying that it was my fault that they beat him. And every time they beat him, he arrived to the house to hit me. And that went on for years.

In 1976, tío Ricardo came to live with her. Arriving in Santiago destitute and in search of work, by chance he saw Sra. Flora walking in the Plaza de Armas in Santiago's center. She had known him from her time in Los Angeles, and in Santiago she offered him shelter in the house she shared with her husband. He could stay if he worked and helped pay the bills. Some months later, Rodrigo arrived.

> When Rodrigo came to the house is when the problems started. Because during this time, my husband continued to beat me. . . . Rodrigo and Ricardo heard everything. Ricardo never dared to do anything, because he was scared of my husband. But Rodrigo, on the other hand, did not have fear of anything. And he said, "I can't stand it, that you are *sacando la cresta* [beating yourself up] working to maintain the house and this *desgraciado* [wretched person] is arriving to the house to hit you and harass you. I cannot bear it."

On New Year's Eve of 1977, Sra. Flora and Rodrigo threw a party. They waited for her husband, but he did not return home. After several drinks and much conversation, Sra. Flora woke up the next day in Rodrigo's bed.

> I was so ashamed. I could not look him in the face. . . . He left for a few days, but returned. He looked for me at my work. He was persistent. He told me that he was in love with me, that he did not have any fear of my family or my husband. That he could care less about them. He told me he wanted to throw my husband out of the house. But I told him I could not do it, out of respect for my family. He was angry. Then he came back to the house [and stayed] for months. . . . After having relations with Rodrigo, I separated from my husband. We had separate beds, and I did not let him have relations with me. But one night, I arrived to the house exhausted. . . . And because I was not vigilant, my husband searched for me [*me buscó*], and he obligated me to have relations with him again. Three months later, I felt really ill, and I discovered I was pregnant again. I told Rodrigo I was pregnant, and he left the house for six months. But, when he returned, he said that he continued to be in love with me. And my husband left the house, because he could not stand it. And I never asked anything from him. Afterward, Rodrigo and I started to move up [*surgir*]. We constructed the room where Florcita and Kevin stay. We constructed the second floor. Rodrigo says that Valentina is his daughter because he raised her. And she calls him *papá* because she does not know her father by blood.

Sra. Flora's narrative reveals that there are two different elements composing "house relations": blood and everyday labors of caring for another. In this case, these everyday labors "cut" blood relations, limiting the network of actual kin while producing new kin relatedness, paternity: Valentina calls Rodrigo "Dad," while her biological father is an inactivated memory (see Strathern 1996). Her narrative also shows the ways in which a break with a male partner occurs in an "unstated" register. In maintaining her family's respect, Sra. Flora married her husband and endured his sexual violence. She also maintained this respect in the way she recounted these experiences to me, by focusing on the actions and desires of the two men while leaving her desires unstated. "He continued to be in love with me." "He returned." "He left because he could not stand it." Yet, at the same time, she shows how her patience allowed for that break and allowed for new house relations. She took on this tone again with Rodrigo. She patiently absorbed the darkness of the home while protecting Florcita. Alongside this awaiting, however, she also asserted a determined ability to live without Rodrigo. As she told me after another argument with him: "But when we fought again last Saturday, I said, 'If you want to go, then just go' [said in a defiant tone]. Don't feel committed to me. I will lose weight and look for work. I don't need your contribution here in the house. I will not be here begging that you stay here."

Then in early October, Sra. Flora fell ill. After her return from the hospital, I visited her. Covered by an old blue quilt, she convalesced in their cramped bedroom. I asked her what had happened. The night she fell ill, she and Rodrigo had fought. Rodrigo had discovered department store bills that Sra. Flora had been hiding and paying *piola* ("quietly," or "without notice"). She had bought clothes for Florcita and her children. Rodrigo threatened to leave the home. Sra. Flora confronted Florcita, telling her to leave Kevin. Florcita refused. She loved Kevin, she said, and she hated her mother for bending to Rodrigo's demands. Sra. Flora felt a terrible pain in her abdomen and stabbing pains in her heart. She thought she was having a heart attack. Rodrigo took her to Hospital José Joaquín Aguirre. She had an acutely inflamed gallbladder and underwent surgery. When she returned home, Rodrigo had momentarily put aside his demands. "It seems that Rodrigo got more enthusiastic about the house [after I got sick]. He took pity on me, seeing me in this condition," she said. "He can't leave me now." Sra. Flora's surgery and recovery not only affected Rodrigo but also seemed to dampen family tensions. Kevin and Florcita, for their part, had turned down the music.

The damage Sra. Flora embodies through this waiting raises questions as to the limits of this mode of care. In circumstances of precarious employment, targeted state programs for those who do the work to qualify as "extremely poor" (see chapter 3), and a fragile and underfunded public health system, the sense of responsibility for kin can feel infinite.[5] Such a sense of responsibility is heard in women's differentiation of *la casa* (house) and *la calle* (street), in which the "street" is spoken of as unpredictable, faceless violence and scarcity—"He might be killed or stabbed; how would she survive?"—while in the "house," moments of scarcity and interpersonal violence are engendered in flesh-and-blood relations and can be mitigated, assuaged, and endured as part of life itself. Waiting, then, can be understood as a manifestation of the desire to be infinitely responsive (see Das 2010b).[6] Realized through domestic relations and credit, this desire orients subjects toward "the possible," the lived sense of indeterminacy in the present that provides hope for relational futures. But this sense of responsibility can become unbearable with, for example, the threat of deadly violence in the home. Indeed, when such a threat arose, Sra. Flora had to face the fact of her finite responsibility even as she held on to this desire for infinite responsiveness, a desire to continue waiting.

GIFT OF BREAD

December 28, 2004. Two months had passed since I had last seen Sra. Flora. When I entered the house, she was standing in Florcita and Kevin's room, cleaning up what she called "the disorder." She greeted me with a warm hug, telling me that she had "good news." Kevin and Florcita had left the house three weeks earlier, she said, and *"ahora estamos tirándonos pa' arriba"* (literally, "we are throwing ourselves upward," or "moving up in the world"). She seemed exuberant. We walked across Florcita and Kevin's room, where mounds of clothes lay strewn across the floor.

Leading me to a new interior patio, she said, "Look, I enclosed all of this. I put a little garden, and the grass is growing well." A cement walkway separated a patch of grass on one side from a small fruit tree and plants on the other. She led me back through the house. "We are repairing the house. We are moving the kitchen over there, and putting the bathroom here [pointing to where the kitchen was], because the kitchen and bathroom had rats. After thirty-four years, the wood bathroom had a terrible stench." The new kitchen would replace the passageway to Florcita's former room. As we returned to the patio, she said, "I am going to put floor tiles in all the bedrooms, and new ceramic tiles in the living room, kitchen, and bathroom. We have all this projected for this year 2005. It will be a good year."

Sra. Flora walked with more energy in her step. She projected her voice instead of guarding it closely in hushed whispers. She recounted to me the events that led up to Florcita and Kevin's leaving. Shortly before they left, Kevin got high on *pasta base*. "He was walking around aggressive," Sra. Flora said. "All of a sudden, he took an iron bar and hit her and hit her. Florcita was underneath the covers [of the bed]. If she had not been, he would have killed her. With blood coming out on all sides. We had to take her to the emergency room. I told them to leave after that. 'If you can't leave Kevin, *I won't have you die here like this*. Please. Just leave.' And finally, they did. They just got up and left."

Sra. Flora's narrative was not one of abandonment or social death. Rather, by telling Florcita to leave the home, Sra. Flora reaffirmed her life within it. At the same time, however, by marking out the home as nonviolent, she established a boundary around this spectacular violence and the everyday, unaccounted-for violences through which the home was being produced (Price 2002). As we talked further about Florcita, Sra. Flora justified to me why she told Florcita to leave the home: "It gives me pain and rage [*rabia*], but now I leave her, I leave her, because I did everything and more than I could do. It's like, how do I say this to you? Like a woman—" She called out to her daughter Sonia in the other room. "Sonia! How do you call this [kind of] woman that likes to be beaten?" "Submissive?" Sonia replied. "No, that's not the word. It starts with an *m*," Sra. Flora answered. "Masochist?" "That's it!" Sra. Flora replied. "Masochist! Masochist is she! It gives me pain because I never hit her. I only hit her three times when she was eighteen years old and was going out with this *desgraciado* [referring to Kevin]. And I thought she would change, but it all went worse."

Then, in a seemingly hyperbolic fashion, she told me how they would now pay their debts *ahead of time*. Rodrigo had just secured construction work with a fixed contract, and with Florcita and Kevin gone, they had fewer costs. "Rodrigo earns 180,000 liquid [disposable income] and Ricardo 140,000. I have planned it that I will pay the monthly payments ahead of time. I want to finish paying in August. I know that I can do it, because the children [Florcita, Kevin, and their two children] are not living here. Imagine it. I am saving so much because I am not using so much light, water, and now I don't have to make so much for lunch."

Sra. Flora's search for the word *masochism* and her new accounting of their debts seemed to reveal her painful awakening to her relation to Florcita. By searching for the word *masochism*—and not *submissive*— she articulates the complex weave of intimacy and violence that Florcita embodies, a weave in which Sra. Flora finds her own limit. She cannot will Florcita to separate from Kevin. Then, in her new accounting of debts, she finds a way to voice that limit: that she is finite and separate from Florcita. She suffers finite responsibility. Notice how a discourse of cost-effectiveness is taken up in a *moment of retrospection* on events in which a relational future is at stake.[7] Rather than conclude that a calculus of cost-effectiveness is mechanically shaping decision making within the home, we may consider how this discourse might voice the difficulty in caring for others. Through such discourses, separateness is voiced. At the same time, they deflect the difficulty of recognizing the denial of another while furthering the grip of such discourses within the home. Such a move is what Stanley Cavell has called the scandal of skepticism: "With the everyday ways in which denial occurs in my life with the other[,] . . . the problem is to *recognize* myself as denying another, to understand that I carry chaos in myself. Here is the scandal of skepticism with respect to the existence of others; I am the scandal" (Cavell 2005, 151).

In the next moment, Flora's voice changed tone. Waving her finger, she said, "But, I still do not let the little children [Florcita's two sons] go hungry. They come here for food, and I also still pass them coins." She continued: "I got into debt, 300,000 pesos for Christmas, buying gifts for them. Sonia also got into debt. It's just that the children don't understand, and ask [*piden*]. You need to buy gifts for children. But, that's OK."

As our conversation drew to a close, Sra. Flora asked me where I was heading. I told her I was interested in finding Florcita and would look for her in the Plaza Pablo Neruda (a frequent meeting ground for drug deals) and then visit the houses of Florcita's friends. As I gathered my things, she told me to wait a moment. Walking into the kitchen, she returned with two warm canvas bags. Each held a homemade loaf of bread. "Here, take one for yourself, and give one to Florcita." Connecting mother, daughter, and anthropologist, this gift did not constitute an act of reciprocity. Rather, it was a thread of sustenance between Florcita and life within the house. A labor of Sra. Flora's own hands, it delicately materialized a gesture of care, inviting her back home.[8]

Later that afternoon, I found Florcita. She and Kevin were renting a one-room shack attached to a friend's house. Estrella, their friend, lived with her mother in a run-down wooden house on the opposite side of the *población*. She and her mother both worked in piecemeal sewing at home. She led me to their room, saying, "You know, their mom threw them out of the house." Kevin and Florcita were in a deep sleep. I wrote a small note to Florcita about my visit and her mother's gift and left it with both bags at their feet.

"IT'S LIKE MY SISTER"

I have visited Sra. Flora's family every year that I return to La Pincoya. Even with monthly debt payments, they fixed the house incrementally. Ceramic tiles on the floor, one by one. A new sliding screen door for the patio. A fresh coat of paint on the walls. Three months after Florcita and Kevin left, their two children asked Sra. Flora if they could live with her. She took them in. Kevin attempted to take the children back, but both Sra. Flora and Rodrigo stood their ground. In late 2005, however, Sra. Flora found Florcita unconscious in the neighborhood playground just a few houses down from their home. She had been raped by a group of bus drivers as she sought to sell sex for *pasta base*. Rodrigo carried her back to their home. Upon hearing about the rape, Kevin was enraged. High and angry, he yelled at Florcita and blamed her. Sra. Flora called the police. Kevin was interned again at the Psychiatric Institute. Florcita joined a community treatment program run by one of the many Pentecostal groups in La Pincoya.

After his internment, Kevin came back to live with Florcita in Sra. Flora's home. I spoke to Florcita in January 2006. She had gained some weight, but her face bore the strains of addiction and physical abuse. "I'm getting better," she said.

> My mom keeps telling me to leave Kevin. She doesn't trust me now, because of Kevin. But I tell her. "He's been with me all the time. He'll be with me." My mom doesn't understand how I can be in love with him. She never understood, since I was young. But, we've changed now. She has to accept that, acknowledge it. There's a before and an after. I go to the meetings, and they make me feel better. I'm going to look for work. I want to move up. I want to live in our own house, get a municipal subsidy [for a house], have our things.

Over time, however, more things went missing in the home. The TV went one day. A few weeks later, the stereo. In the following months, a couple of dining table chairs. Sra. Flora bought a new TV, a new stereo, on credit. Rather than demanding that Florcita and Kevin leave as he did before, Rodrigo resorted to drinking beer in the local canteen. He spent less and less time in the home, arriving drunk late at night. Meanwhile, Florcita would leave the house for days.

In July 2007, I returned to La Pincoya, this time with my husband. We had just gotten married a few months before, and I was making rounds, introducing him to friends and neighbors. It had been a year and a half since I had seen Sra. Flora. We walked to her house for a visit. The house was stripped bare. The floor, where there was once ceramic, now was concrete, blackened with dirt. Where once was a sofa, there were two wooden stools. The new stereo, broken, after Kevin had thrown it across the room. Tío Ricardo had lost his job in the textile factory. He was now looking for temporary construction work but, at his advanced age, finding work was difficult. Sra. Flora's brother Diego, who lived one street up, had died of a heart attack in his home. A quiet and dark stillness filled the entire home.

Daughters Sonia, Valentina, and Margarita came to greet us. But the air seemed burdened and pained. Sra. Flora invited us to sit on the wooden stools. She said, "All this, they broke everything. And I am still paying the quotas on the things they broke. See. Look, look, I don't have anything for us to take tea in, see. I can't even invite you and your husband to tea. I'm sorry. See, this is how it is now. And it pains me. It pains me so much." She repeatedly apologized for not having anything in which to serve us tea. "No, no, it's OK, it's OK," I said, trying to reassure her.

Sra. Flora recounted to me the events leading up to the present: about Florcita and Kevin's drug use, Florcita's selling of sex for drugs, their parties that now overran and destroyed the home, the debts that she could not pay, Rodrigo's resignation. "It's like my sister," she suddenly said. Her sister, she continued, had been a militant for the democratic movements. "She was tortured. She was in Villa Gremaldi.[9] They burnt her up into her uterus. She was burned from the inside. Then, they dumped her on the street. We found her unconscious and took her home. We tried to take care of her. But six months later, she died of cancer of the uterus, from all of the burns. The burns kept eating her uterus." She stopped. "I had not told you this before." It was true. In the eight years that I had known her, never once did she tell me about her sister's death. "So, you see, I am not well. I spend a lot of time now, thinking about my sister, how she died. I don't know why I took out the theme now. Just now. Look, you with your new husband. He seems quite *tierno* [sweet]. These times, they've been very difficult, much worse than before."

Three months earlier, Sra. Flora had had a stroke. "Look at my eye, it's *desviado* [off-track]. The doctor said that it would not come back, and that there is nothing I can do now." Her right eye was deviated laterally. She was short of breath as she spoke. It seemed that she experienced a pressure to find words, as well as a difficulty breathing. The doctor, she said, also told her that her heart was not working well. But she had sensed this herself. "I'm broken. My body is broken. The house, everything is broken."

My husband does not speak Spanish. He attempted to understand through my translations and through bodily gestures and tones. But when Sra. Flora began to tell me about her sister, I stopped translating. Receiving this pain took its own time. Sra. Flora's evocation of her sister at this juncture in her life might help us attend to the feelings of violence she may be embodying as she tries to respond to her kin but is faced with the limits of their responsiveness. As such, Sra. Flora's memory of her sister and the political conditions that produced her pain affectively resonates with conditions in which she experiences her own body as "broken," Florcita's body as violated, and "the house, everything is broken": fractured between the multiple relational ties that produced the home itself.

A LOAN FOR ANOTHER LIFE

To leave you with this scene of destruction would obscure how the use of the credit system can also provide different relational futures. In August 2008, I returned again to La Pincoya. On a bright, chilly afternoon, I stopped by Sra. Flora's home. The blue-painted patio gate was wide open, and the sound of hammers rang out into the street. The facade of the house had been completely renovated. An oval front step covered with salmon-colored tile introduced a carved wooden antique door. This new front door was framed by new rectangular, mottled-glass windows. Rodrigo emerged from inside the house and greeted me with a big hug, sweating from the renovation work that he was completing. Sra. Flora then appeared and also gave me a tight hug. "Look, we are renovating the house. Beautiful, you see," she said. Surprised, I asked her to give me a tour. We walked through the house. It was almost unrecognizable. The kitchen was enlarged and decoratively tiled in black and white. A long wire was strung across the kitchen with hanging bunches of onions, peppers, and garlic. There were now two sparkly bathrooms on the first floor with deep tubs and shiny shower heads. Florcita's former room was transformed by a large sliding glass door that opened onto the interior patio of the house, where a few white chickens and a large black-and-green rooster pecked the grass. "See," Sra. Flora said, pointing out the details of the renovation to me.

As we stood in Florcita's former room, I told Sra. Flora how struck

I was by the changes. "How did . . . ?" She interrupted me, answering, "I took another loan on the house." She refinanced the house in order to afford the renovations. "But, how . . . ?" My voice trailed off. Sra. Flora responded, "Well, Rodrigo was drinking, drinking all the time. And I said one day, 'Ja, ja, no more. No more. Never.' I confronted him: 'Look. You are going to change or you leave this house. I can't bear you like this.' I took out the loan, and I said, 'We are going to renovate the house. We will have a new life.' He got enthusiastic, and went out with the money and bought all the materials. So now, he is working in construction, and we save a little at a time to be able to renovate the house just the way we want. With a different style than everyone else." This time, the loan provided the materials to hold Rodrigo's attention and allowed time to work on relations.

I asked her about Florcita. Florcita, she said, was now living three houses up, renting a room from a neighbor with Kevin. Sra. Flora had used a portion of that loan to help pay for their rent. After several months of *pasta base* use, Florcita had joined another Pentecostal meeting to regulate her addiction. Kevin, on the other hand, continued to consume, but Florcita persisted in a relationship with him. Sra. Flora asked Florcita to move out of the house but made arrangements with the neighbor. She brought food to them each day, and Florcita occasionally stopped by the home but did not stay long. With the move, Sra. Flora and Florcita had, for the moment, crafted a new way to maintain proximity while distancing Kevin from the home. In this way, they forged a new lease on life—in a different style—staking the everyday again in an uncertain future.

Attending to the tensions between waiting and the ongoing demands of debt, scarcity, and multiple kinship obligations reveals how intimate relations of the house are simultaneously constructed, made possible through, and also threatened by the mechanisms of credit. Moving with these relations in time helped me attend to the force of possibility within intimate relations. We might call it a sense of hope that another can reveal a different aspect of herself in time, and the sense of obligation that arises with it. Care-as-waiting relies on that hope, which is actualized within the house as illness and momentary renewal. In the face of disappointment with this hope, such caring can become conditions through which the past of state violence are made available within one's present and within the ordinary itself.

CHAPTER 2

Social Debt, Silent Gift

LOWER THE POINTS

We sat in the living room on a couch covered with thick plastic. Paz's two-year-old daughter, Felicidad, sat in the lap of her grandmother Sra. Ana. As she combed her hands through the child's blond hair, Sra. Ana told me how Paz had begun smoking *pasta base* again two months earlier. Paz had started intermittent *pasta base* consumption six years previously. She had stopped consuming when she became pregnant after selling sex to a fifty-year-old neighbor. Paz's return to *pasta base* had palpable effects within the home. She sold her daughter's formula, received from the local primary care center, as well as the child's diapers.

Sra. Ana was sixty-five years old and widowed. She lived with her two daughters, Paz and Pamela, on a housing site comprised of a two-room house and a provisional shack. Pamela worked in subcontracted office-cleaning, and her husband worked in construction. They had three children and lived in the shack. Sra. Ana worked as a security guard in the women's prison in the municipality of San Joaquín in the southern zone of Santiago. Her other daughter, Paz, had had a number of temporary jobs, the last one working for the municipality in park maintenance, picking up trash in the plazas and parks in the neighborhood.

Woven into these difficulties were Sra. Ana's feelings of shame produced by Paz's thefts from one neighbor's *almacén* (shop) and another's liquor store and, just recently, from Susana and her husband, Antonio,

Sra. Ana's friends across the street. Paz had broken into Susana and Antonio's house while they were visiting relatives on the coast. She passed their DVD player, their son's PlayStation, and Susana's heirloom clocks to a youth in the neighborhood who sold stolen goods in other neighboring *poblaciones*. The next-door neighbor's son, Miguel, noticed the door open and found Paz lying on the couch asleep. He called the police. She was arrested.

Sra. Ana recounted, "Paz robbed my purse that had 28,000 (USD 46). She is stealing from the neighbors. I don't even want to walk in the street and show my face. The others say, 'She is the *mamá* of this girl who walks around robbing.'" Sra. Ana's husband had died of pancreatic cancer eleven years earlier. She commented that, after his death, she thought, "Now we can have a happy family, all tranquil. But, no. One son of mine has been in prison for the past six years for the same *porquería* [filth]. He walked around robbing, and was jailed for robbery with intimidation. And I say, What *mamá* has so many bad children? We have a big cartel [*media cartel*] here in the house. I think I did what I could. I don't know how I failed."

Sra. Ana apologized "a thousand times" to Susana. She bought another PlayStation for her son on credit, the only item left that they had not been able to recuperate through neighborhood channels. On top of monthly utility bills and food, which she shared with her daughter Pamela, Sra. Ana was paying for replacements for the stolen powdered milk for her granddaughter and monthly quotas on the PlayStation, as well as monthly payments to the neighbors for stolen goods and money. She and Susana usually relied on each other when faced with a "critical moment," moments when they would not make it to the end of the month. But, in the midst of the gossip over the thefts, she told me that she had "shame" (*vergüenza*) to ask Susana for a loan.

Sra. Ana applied for a municipal subsidy to offset her water bill, money that she could then use for covering monthly costs of bread. At the time of my visit to her house, she was waiting for a social worker to conduct a household needs assessment, which, she hoped, would provide her with a point score low enough to qualify: "I have to lower the point score" (Tengo que bajar el puntaje). She recounted that, on a visit one year earlier, the social worker had seen three old televisions in her home. None of them worked, she said, "but, the social worker wrote something down on the piece of paper, and I didn't get the point score." This time, "I heard from friends that if you walk around dirty, make the house dirty—if you look poor, like animal, then they lower your points. This is why I will not shower. I will not shower until after the social worker comes," she remarked to me defiantly and angrily. She said she was *pasando hambre* (experiencing hunger) but always made sure that her granddaughter had enough to eat. "How do you bear it?" I asked. She responded, "I grew up with cow's milk. I am strong. At times, I think that God is testing me, but then I think, how long the test. I would never wish this to happen to another person, not even to my worst enemy."

Sra. Ana's desire to make good on her obligations to her neighbors, her sense of shame in asking a friend for help in the face of a theft that betrayed their intimacy, her experience of hunger, and her resentment of social workers' criteria for need reveal potent frictions between a moral fabric of neighborhood life and official assessments of poverty: between a "living with dignity" that is contingent upon neighborhood relations and their boundaries and the state's criteria for poverty.

In the previous chapter, I explored an "active awaiting" as a mode of care for the mentally ill and the addicted made possible through institutional credit and through domestic relations beyond the home. The availability of credit has also significantly altered the nature of poverty itself, providing access to consumer goods typically outside the low-income monthly budget while extending a temporality of debt payments that may not be matched with stable work and incomes. The very dynamics of economic precariousness generate what men and women call "critical moments," when temporary work is cut short, wages unpaid, or illness episodes generate more expenditures than can be handled by families.

This quality of economic precariousness has, however, emerged alongside the state's own debt to the poor: the "social debt" to the poor accrued during the Pinochet regime's market reforms, a debt that would be paid through expansion of targeted poverty programs. In this chapter, I bring into focus the critical moment as a way of considering the moral dimensions of poverty in relation to the social debt: what those critical moments reveal about the boundaries of speech and silence tied into a living-with-dignity and the frictions between this living-with-dignity and the visions of the poor embodied in official assessments of need.

EXTREME POVERTY AND THE SOCIAL DEBT

On May 21, 1990, President Patricio Aylwin gave a speech to the National Congress marking the beginning of democratic transition in Chile and outlining the temporal and moral contours of that government's vision of transitional justice. Addressing poverty would be one crucial aspect of reconciliation. "I think that if we want to strengthen national unity, we need to set our eyes on a common future that unites us, more than a past that divides us. Let us leave history to judge that which has occurred and put our zeal toward the tasks that the *patria* [fatherland] now demands of us in order to forge the future. But this healthy proposition cannot be an obstacle to taking on with courage the problems inherited from the past, like those in relation to human rights and the so-called 'social debt'" (Aylwin Azócar 1990, 7–8). Effecting a vision of national consensus, his speech not only oriented the country to the future but also rendered the past as debt, one that could be empirically accounted for and paid through, in his words, "a process of democratization and modernization and the payment of the social debt contracted with the most poor" (p. 41).

The social debt was to mark a new phase in the relations between the state and its population. The payment of this debt would contrast with the regime's doctrine of "pure growth," in which the state addressed only "residual" poverty that could not be absorbed by the economic system. For the Pinochet regime, "extreme poverty" was the necessary remnant produced by the market. And the role of the state—indeed, the only role of the state within the population—was to technically eliminate extreme poverty through the provision of selective direct monetary subsidies and targeted programs for those families who fell below an economic level considered indispensable for basic subsistence, that is, for biological survival.

In 1975, Minister of Planning Miguel Kast produced the "Map of Extreme Poverty," which laid out how extreme poverty would be assessed: with a new means-testing tool called the Ficha-CAS (Comités de Asistencia Social) to be administered by the municipalities (Kast Rist and Molina Silva 1975). The Ficha-CAS used "home equipment"— defined as a television, refrigerator, washing machine, and stove—and housing conditions as proxies for income (Vergara 1984, 1990). These crude measures worked at the level of both the household and the population. First, households were assigned a point score. Second, all point scores were aggregated in the population and mapped according to municipality, thus allowing for a focalization of resources in specific municipalities. Households falling below a specific score would be qualified as "extremely poor" and receive direct monetary subsidies, as well as subsidies for housing units, milk and protein mixes for children under six years old, and access to free health care. The Ficha-CAS was launched on the national level in 1980 and was not revised to include income until 1987. For the regime, showing a technical reduction in "extreme poverty" would legitimate the "success" of military rule.[1]

The first government after Pinochet, comprised of a coalition of democratic parties called the Concertación, sought to mark a political boundary with the dictatorship through its approach to poverty. The state's "care," however, was not a return to the welfare apparatus that had developed from the 1950s to 1973. Rather, concerned with maintaining "growth with equity," the Concertación government strengthened the regime's focalization and decentralization of poverty programs and subsidies (Ffrench-Davis 2004; Raczynski 2008). Increased social spending accompanied an expansion of selective subsidies and programs for the poor, most of which were decentralized to the municipalities.

Modified in 1996, the Ficha-CAS II included more discriminating variables, such as widened criteria for the kinds of wall material used in home construction and the kinds of flooring, to allow for an expansion of those included within the programs. However, the means-testing tool continued to rely on the presence or absence of "home equipment" as a factor in needs assessment. Unadapted to new economic realities of the poor, it did not include data on personal and household indebtedness. Further, the Ficha-CAS II was generally administered every two years by municipally based social workers, assuming a stability of conditions that did not cohere with the precarious reality of most families. With the increase in social programs and subsidies, however, the Ficha-CAS point score gained a ubiquitous presence in the lives of the poor. Government social programs, municipally run social programs, monetary subsidies funded by ministries—such as the Ministries of Planning, Labor and Social Provision, Housing and Education—and by the National Fund for Health, all used the point score as part of their assessment of need.

While the Ficha-CAS can be critically appraised for its accuracy, it can also be understood as an instrument that disentangles material objects from human lives and thus takes them as objects denoting a stable economic status, a reading of objects that is transportable and generalizable. But the point score itself became entangled in lives as it was differentially used across ministries and municipalities. Access to each program or subsidy depended on how each ministry used and weighed the point score, as well as on the discretion of the municipality (Larrañaga 2005; Teitelboim G. 2001).

Such continuities in social policies toward poverty could be understood within the political climate of the first democratic government, but also in relation to this government's and subsequent governments' commitments to maintaining Chile's image of "economic success" by deepening neoliberal reforms (see Paley 2001). Right-wing parties and Pinochet's shadow cabinet imposed strict norms of fiscal discipline on the Concertación government, which the new government took on as its own method to address social ills while promoting economic growth.

Thus, during the 1990s, the increased funding for social spending was largely made possible by the 1990 Tax Reform, which derived most of its revenue from increasing the *impuesto de valor agregado,* or value added tax. The 1993 Tax Agreement made between the Concertación parties and the right-wing Renovación Nacional Party stipulated a fixed ceiling on social spending, so that the growth of budgetary spending for social policies would by law always be lower than the growth of the gross domestic product (Fazio 1996). In terms of real pesos, public spending rose progressively during the transition. Notably, when measured as a percentage of the GDP, social spending actually decreased in relation to economic growth during the transition.[2]

What have been the consequences of the "growth with equity" principle for the poor? Notably, poverty, as measured by the monthly income required to satisfy basic necessities, has declined, from 45 percent of the population in 1988 to 13.7 percent in 2006, while indigence, as measured by the monthly income required to satisfy basic alimentation, has decreased from 12.9 percent to 3.2 percent (Raczynski 2008).[3] With national statistics showing a significant decrease in poverty, and after official acknowledgments of human rights violations and the institution of constitutional reforms, President Ricardo Lagos declared on a state visit to Australia in 2005 that the "transition" had concluded: "Twenty years ago, there was a national accord/agreement to achieve a more democratic country, 15 years ago the democratic governments started and now we can say that the Chilean transition has concluded" (quoted in Agencias 2005).

Yet in poor urban neighborhoods, this now-paid social debt continues to generate questions about the "actual justice" of the transition. That is, the justice that is empirically accounted for through poverty programs and statistics on poverty. In the everyday workings of poverty programs, the criteria to gain entrance into such programs, and social workers' visions of the poor, obscure the dynamics of pervasive economic precariousness. Experiences of poverty are shaped by the irregularity of cash flow produced by temporary and unstable forms of labor. Yet, in these programs, women contend with an assumption that recipients of state aid embody a certain kind of moral subject, as well as contend with a reading of material objects as denoting economic status abstracted from concrete circumstances. Let me turn to Valentina and Pato.

CRITICAL MOMENTS

Valentina was thirty-seven years old and Pato thirty-eight years old when I met them in 2004. Valentina stopped me outside the primary care center, where she sold used clothes strung from a rope between the trees. She wanted to sell me a pair of jeans. We ended up chatting. Her husband, Pato, was a taxi driver. The week that I met her, they were late on their dividend for their house and had withdrawn a cash advance from Líder Supermarket to buy groceries. She explained the situation to me: "It gives me despair, but one doesn't walk around crying for pity." She resorted to selling off their clothes. Valentina had recently been diagnosed with depression and was receiving free fluoxetine and group therapy in the local primary care center. (This program is discussed in chapter 6.) I asked if I could interview her, and she invited me to her home for tea.

When I arrived at their house, Valentina came out to greet me. Through the front window, I could see her husband turning off the TV. The silver fifty-inch Panasonic TV extended from the living room's corner to its center. It rested on a table, under which a large silver Sony sound system flashed its red and green lights. Two overstuffed tan armchairs sat close to the TV. Valentina guided me past the living area to the dining table, where teacups were set out. While Valentina prepared tea in the kitchen, I asked Pato about his work history. Pato had been a taxi driver for the past two years. Fifteen years earlier, however, he had started working at the Machasa textile factory.[4] During that time, he said, he was earning well. His monthly income was 250,000 pesos (USD 410). Machasa provided the basis for this house, he explained, because it was a "time of *stable work*. . . . The company treated the workers well. There were benefits to working there, respect for the worker. Machasa was a Chilean company, but it went bankrupt."

After eight years of employment, Pato moved to Sodimac, a manufacturer of transformers and lighting fixtures. There, he worked in a part-time trucking job, transporting goods from warehouse to stores. His starting monthly income was 60,000 pesos (USD 100). "From 250,000 to 60,000, just like that," he told me. "It was virtually impossible to live during this time. We were paying dividends [on the house] of 25,000, then paying for school for the children, and the rest of the bills. No alcance para comer." (It isn't enough to eat.)

Then, after six years of working for Sodimac, Pato renounced his work. The company had hired an external subcontractor to find workers, "*un contratista* [subcontractor] who receives his income for each worker that he brings to work, 5,000 pesos per worker, but pays the worker the minimum 115,000 pesos. Two months before I left work, the *contratista* came up to me and asked me to work with him, but for half the income, and it wasn't acceptable to me [*no me convenía*], so I left." He told me that work is like this "everywhere now. You have to work for a *contratista,* who can tell you to sign a contract for two months, then two months more, afterward another month. And if you work for a while, you pass to an indefinite contract without signing anything, but when they throw you out, they pay a smaller indemnity, because all of those months when you had a definite contract do not count. The system now is like this. *El mano de obra* [manual labor] now is very cheap."

Pato analyzed how labor laws generated new labor hierarchies and everyday instability. As an outcome of Pinochet's Labor Plan, as historian Peter Winn discusses, regimes of flexible labor continue to exert one of the most detrimental effects on the livelihoods of the poor (Winn 2004). Consisting of a series of decree laws designed primarily by Pinochet's labor minister, José Piñera, the Labor Plan worked in three broad directions.[5] First, Decree Law 2.200 (1979) and Law 18.018 institutionalized new forms of unstable labor by giving the employer the power to terminate contracts with thirty days' notice, without justification, and to unilaterally change the nature of the work or the actual work site (Silva 2007; Winn 2004). Second, Decree Law 16.757 (1979) amplified the role and scope of subcontracting to all areas of a company's labor, allowing companies to subcontract out labor inherent to principal production, such as equipment maintenance and repair (Silva 2007, 4). Third, Decree Laws 2.758 (1979) and 3.648 (1981) severely restricted collective bargaining by allowing companies to replace striking workers after fifty-nine days and by abolishing specialized labor courts (Winn 2004).

Starting with the Aylwin administration, successive Concertación governments attempted to reform the Labor Code. As sociologist Volker Frank has pointed out, however, the Labor Code has produced "an ever increasing tendency to substitute permanent contract workers with temporary and subcontracted labor, a lowering of income for the total labor force, a decrease in fixed individual incomes for Chile's workers, and an increase in incomes tied to productivity gains, bonuses, and other 'incentives'" (Frank 2004, 74; see also Henríquez and Riquelme 2006). For historian Gabriel Salazar, this "logic of employment," in which "no work contract should be permanent and every worker, according to business interests, is dispensable," has become "the third vertex of the 'social pact' of neoliberalism" (Salazar Vergara 2005, 88).

Indeed, by 2005, the Decree Laws' legacy in the current Labor Code produced an extremely precarious labor situation in which more than 93 percent of new work contracts lasted less than one year, and 50 percent lasted less than four months (Riesco 2005, 59). In La Pincoya, this high turnover and limited lifetime of the work contract tied into new hierarchies between local *contratistas* and their neighbors. These *contratistas* reap substantially higher incomes through subcontracting neighbors on "definite," or time-delimited, contracts that last less than twelve months, typically two to three months, depending on the type of work. For the urban poor, the state's regulatory environment has institutionalized work as discontinuous and unpredictable.

Valentina returned to the table with bread, margarine, and cold cuts. Pato continued talking, spreading margarine on a piece of bread. After Sodimac, he decided to become a taxi driver. His family lent him money to buy a car. But, he told me, this work is even more unstable. "I don't know if this day will go well or badly for me. During the week, I can earn 20,000 to 30,000 pesos, and this is not sufficient for the house. So, I go to work on the weekends, Friday at night, Saturday at night, to equilibrate the week." Pato returned to commenting on labor and politics. "In Chile, *factories* have turned into *warehouses*. I can say this because I *lived it* [*lo viví*]. In a factory—before—one worker painted the cup, the other made the cup, the other put the stamp on it, the other packaged it. But today, the cup arrives here made. The only thing that the worker can do is put the stamp on it that says 'equis' [X] country, and packages it. And they throw out the ten workers that before made the cup. The CUT [Central Unitaria de Trabajadores, the national union organization], which supposedly should protect the worker, does not want to do anything, because it does not want to criticize the government now. But, I say, if Lavín [then mayor of Santiago, and a member of the Unión Democrática Independiente party, backed by Opus Dei, an ultraconservative Catholic organization] were president, then maybe we would have a change with the CUT, because we would have to *fight against something*."

Valentina yawned. The discussion of the CUT did not seem to be holding her attention. But as I turned the conversation back to the home, she became animated. "Do you make it to the end of the month?" I asked. Valentina answered, "We use the [credit] cards—Falabella, Ripleys, Almacenes París—because you have to buy materials and clothes for the children to go to school. We can't pay with money, so we have to use cards." She continued: "You know, I went to the municipality to do *trámites* [paperwork]. I spent the whole day *tramitando* [doing paperwork] to get the subsidies, but the *asistente* [social worker] there said that they would use the same information, the same paper [*hoja*, literally, the "sheet of paper"] that we had in 2002, and now it's 2004. Las cosas han cambiado" (Things have changed). Right now, she said, "we are passing a *critical moment.*"

She told me about the social worker's visit two years earlier, in 2002. She had petitioned the municipality to have the social worker assess their household for a water and electricity subsidy when Pato was out of work. "He only looked at what we have. Our TV, our stereo system, refrigerator, and he gave us a point score that was higher." Pato latched on, with frustration in his voice: "The most grave is that I am without work *now; now* I have unstable work. For that, I ask for help *now.* They see the tele and think that we are well, but they do not understand that I beat myself up [*me saque la cresta*], almost going crazy, working to buy this tele, working twelve hours a day. But it was because of this, because I could do it with overtime."

Pato and Valentina sketched out the temporal disjuncture between discontinuous work patterns and needs assessments materialized in social workers, paperwork, and point scores. This temporal disjuncture took on moral intensity with respect to specific material objects—televisions, stereos, and more recently, computers and laptops. Pointing to the TV, Valentina joined in: "But, they do not understand *this* achievement. That we achieved buying this tele when he was working well, overworking, more hours because we wanted to buy the tele. And, now, what do I do? Like most people around here, take the tele to the house of a friend, hide this table [pointing to the table on which the TV sits], hide the stereo system and the refrigerator, to show that, yes, *we are poor.* Today, things are so bad. It's bad will" (*la mala voluntad*).

Pato and Valentina illuminate a few crucial observations with respect to the experiences of economic precariousness. Let us first consider the unpredictability of wages and work. On the one hand, working "extra hours" has become one way to save money in order to buy large consumer goods. These consumer goods, then, are taken as part of household assets in needs assessments, without consideration that "extra hours" and "almost going crazy" in fact allowed for their purchase. On the other hand, working "extra hours" may be necessary just to cover monthly expenses, or may be insufficient to cover the month. Second, institutional credit through department stores and supermarkets is often necessary in order to "make it to the end of the month." Yet, as we also have seen in chapter 1, the unpredictability of work is at odds with predictable monthly debt payments, but this unpredictability also means that credit must be relied on.

Third, there is an intense moralism articulated around the relations of the poor to consumer goods. This moralism may be related to an image of the poor as nonmodern or precariously modern. In this view, consumer goods bring the poor into modernity, and being deprived of consumer goods then qualifies a household to be a recipient of state intervention and aid. But, at the same time, many households do have consumer goods, and it is the plethora of consumer goods that feeds arguments that the poor are engaged in profligate spending: that they are not being "responsible" consumers. Thus, we can understand Valentina's gesture of pointing at the television and her vehement remark that it is an *achievement*. The argument about profligate spending not only forecloses a consideration of the multiple demands and desires that the poor experience but also asserts and demands a hyperausterity and hyperrationality of the poor that those who are not poor—and who do not struggle to get to the end of the month—could simply never live up to. It grounds decision making in the division of reason and emotion. And it limits poverty to survival, but in doing so, forecloses careful attention to how need might be enmeshed in a whole range of relations.[6]

GOVERNMENT OF THE POOR

Curious to hear a social worker's perspective, I contacted the municipality's office for Programa Puentes (the Bridges Program) and was able to fix an interview after several months of persistence. In 2000, the Lagos government (2000–2005) developed the social policy ChileSolidario. Ostensibly breaking with the earlier paradigm of focalizing resources to vulnerable groups, ChileSolidario would direct its resources toward the integration of "families and not individuals" into a social protection network. The foundational model for ChileSolidario was Programa Puentes, a program developed through the Fondo Solidario e Inversion

Social (Solidary Fund and Social Investment), which stimulated collaboration between nongovernmental organizations, private companies, and the state to fund targeted programs to build "human capital" through microenterprise. Families who qualified as extremely poor signed a document upon their entrance into the program. Called the "Family Contract," this document was a pledge to "improve their life conditions" with the assistance of the state and to "work to overcome those aspects of greater precariousness and necessity defined by themselves" (Palma and Urzúa 2005, 22). The family, primarily through the woman, would be expected to achieve increasing "autonomy" from this state social protection network over time.

The program worked by means of interlocking mechanisms: (1) an initial *bono de protección* (protection voucher), which functioned as seed money to begin a microenterprise, and (2) twenty-four months of "psychosocial intervention" entailing monthly visits from a municipal social worker who would not only monitor the economic progress of the household but also verify that family members were complying with a range of social interventions, from courses in "family dynamics" (such as learning domestic communication skills and prevention of domestic violence) to birth control to medical checkups for children.

A series of direct subsidies in decreasing amounts were disbursed to single mothers in their capacity as head of household, to the women partners of male heads of household, or, in the absence of the female partner, to the eldest female child—even over the male head of household—over the length of the program. These decreasing subsidies over time assumed that as the program proceeded, the family—and particularly the mother—would become increasingly autonomous and "self-responsible" (MIDEPLAN 2004; Palma and Urzúa 2005). Poverty was conceived of as a fact that could be progressively solved—through the woman—rather than as contingencies to be absorbed. A family-centered policy such as this, focused on the mother, has a long genealogy in the liberal Chilean state. Historian María Angélica Illanes has closely examined how, during the emergence of the "social question" in the late nineteenth century, the reassertion of the Catholic figure of the mother through marianism had powerful consequences for the orientation of state policies toward the poor. Simultaneously, the "woman-mother" of the popular classes became the point of intervention for a scientific and philanthropic approach to poverty (Illanes 2007).

Programa Puentes exemplified what Michel Foucault called "governmentality": disciplinary regimes that hook the individual with population. Family here becomes an instrument in the government of the population, which is inseparable from fields of knowledge dedicated to "the improvement of its condition, the increase of its wealth, longevity, health, etc." (Foucault 1991, 102). How was this "government of the poor" taking shape on the ground?

A social worker, Ximena, met me in her small office in a rundown building separated from the mayor's offices. A long line of women stood outside her door. Her short gray hair and wire-framed glasses were set within a stern and commanding disposition. She ushered me into the office, leaving the door open to the outside. As women leaned against the door frame, I started with the basics. "Can you describe a little bit about the goals of the program?" I asked.

To my discomfort and surprise, she described the program's goals by using the women as examples. "This program is to satisfy basic needs. Last year, we gave out forty-five *mejoras* [*mejoras habitacionales,* or home improvements; here she is referring to two-room shacks to alleviate overcrowding] to people in this *población* to satisfy the minimum requirement for habitation. We give blankets, sometimes clothes. Some families of seven have two plates to eat from. The roofs on their houses are made of plastic, or they are not insulated. So we give them material for iron roofs. There is a problem of education here. The people here need education to get out of their poverty." Pointing to a mother standing at the door with her toddler she said, "Some mothers do not understand that their two-year-old children should not be in diapers. These [she pointed at the women in line] are the extreme poor, the people who fall below the line."

A woman entered the office. "Excuse me, excuse me. Señora, I didn't receive a blanket last month. What happened?" Adjusting her glasses, Ximena asked her name and national identification number. Finding a file on her desk, she said, "Look, what happened is that you're in a program that has goals. You have to reach those goals. So if you do not reach them, we do not give you the things, *te fija* [get it]? It's all a process. It's not for *everyone*. It's for the people that go on advancing in the work that we are doing, with the support of you all." The woman interjected, "But I had the paper, that little paper [*papelito*]. It's just that my boy was sick . . . " I could not tell if Ximena knew what this woman was referring to. Ximena interrupted, "So now, just maybe there is a possibility, because we are entering a new phase of giving out blankets, and so if they see you have advanced, then they will give you one."

Leaving, the woman nervously and confusedly responded, "Ja, ja."

Ximena used the program's disbursements of money and materials in a system of punishments and rewards pegged to the state's time line for family "development" and "autonomy." In this time line, families were punished for contingency and, at the same time, a moral subject was generated. Remarkably, Ximena never told the woman what she had "failed" to achieve. I asked Ximena what "goals" the woman had failed to reach and if the woman knew what those goals were. Ximena answered that the woman knew well what she needed to do, which was to make sure she was present when the social worker visited her home: "She has to learn responsibility." The woman was not upholding her end of the "Family Contract" with the state.

Resuming the conversation, I shifted the focus to Ximena's own history, mainly to deter her from using the women as examples. Ximena had started as a social worker in 1978, working in Macul, then moving to Cerro Navia and, finally, Huechuraba. "Has poverty changed since you started," I asked? She responded, "Oh yes, very much so." Before, more people were in hard poverty, she remarked, but now there was more violence and drug addiction. "The people are much more deteriorated now than they were before," she said. "Let me explain this well. Before, there was an economic deterioration, a social deterioration. But not a psychological deterioration. But now there is less deterioration in the economic part, in the social part, but today there is a psychological deterioration of those who are below the poverty line. It's a deterioration in the human part" (*la parte humana*). I asked, "How so?" She continued: "The persons are very deteriorated. They are depressed, anguished, desperate. Because the truth is, when you are embedded [*metido*] in this poverty so, so hard, you cannot dream of anything. So it is a poverty more of the soul that, in those years, was not seen. We saw, before, material scarcity or, better yet, social scarcity. But not this, what we are seeing now."

I wanted to know more about this vision of the poor she was laying out. "What were the causes for this change?" I asked. She responded, "I personally think that it's from the media and what comes through the television. Everyone, everyone, everyone has a television, and the poor see these marvelous things. Everything so pretty. On the other hand, in this epoch—I'm talking about 1978, 1979—not everyone had a television, not everyone had access to the media. So, then, the people were, like, more *clean* [*limpia*]. On the other hand, now the people have access to television; and the resentment that they have [emerges from] not being able to accede to everything that is changing [to the latest commodities]. [It is based in] 'what others have and what I don't have.' [This resentment] sums itself up in a huge consumption of drugs, alcohol, and violence, which is tremendous, absolutely tremendous; in [comparison to] that epoch, you did not see this." She continued, "So the deterioration of the human being is very strong, in comparison to fifteen years ago [notably, marking the end of the dictatorship]. I would attribute it principally to the media and the theme of drug addiction and alcoholism. It's very strong the change, we could say."

My face must have betrayed my thoughts. Ximena remarked, "Don't get me wrong, I work for human beings to change. It's the work that I do. If I didn't believe in change, I would go home and close the windows. Yes, it is difficult. There are families that we will never change. They will continue to be a burden for the state. Because, first of all, they are persons who are intellectually deteriorated. More than their souls," her voice rising, "*they are stupid, they are stuck*. I say that they are 'stuck' in quotation marks because they will never exit poverty. We will continue to have to support them. And then there are people that, yes, with our help they advance." I was baffled and disgusted. Was this a show of power?

The emphasis on the poor's burden on the state and their obligation to uphold the goals of the Family Contract—complying with monthly social worker visits, birth control, and child checkups—illustrated how the state's social debt to the poor had transformed. Through the systems of verification and disciplinary technologies designed to generate the self-regulating citizen-subject independent of the state—and through this social worker's stance toward the poor she sought to "help"—the state's social debt to the poor had morphed into the poor's debt to the state. That is, in receiving aid, the poor owe it to the state to become "autonomous" from any state intervention, to absorb and manage difficult economic and social realities themselves.

Ximena laid out familiar differences between the deserving and undeserving poor; I would like to call attention to the way she also outlines a "moral narrative of modernity" (see Keane 2007), and how an idea of the poor figures within this narrative. In her account, it is not that "the poor" desire modernity but rather that they have not learned the self-mastery to survive modernity. Unable to contend with the attractiveness of material objects—those marvelous things—that come with modernity, the poor become enmeshed in other (dangerous) material objects such as drugs and alcohol, which deform and impoverish their once pure, or "clean," souls.

Unlike anthropologist Webb Keane's discussion of the Calvinist whose moral imperative might be to disentangle himself from material objects, this social worker's concern is *how* subjects are enmeshed in material things. The discipline required of the modern subject, then, is to modulate the desire engendered by the attractiveness of objects. Through this modulation, or self-regulation, the subject as a citizen becomes autonomous from the state. For the social worker, such discipline is what the poor must learn but almost always are failing at. With a "poverty of the soul" that has already deformed them, the poor as deteriorated human beings do not have this capacity for living well with material things and thus do not have the regulatory will required of a citizen.

This conversation can be posed against the way women speak about having to fulfill an image of poverty for the social worker's visit through dissimulation. As women remarked: "You have to be animalized to get subsidies." "They are only concerned with the image." "Deshumanizante" (Dehumanizing). Their remarks that one must be "animalized" draw attention to the actual scandal of such programs. The everyday dealings with such poverty programs are not marking a boundary between the human and the animal; rather, *animalized* points to how such dealings, in which poor women are considered "stuck," are constantly marking a difference *between* humans (see Cavell 1979, 372–378).

Such marking of difference is voiced through the tones of rage, resentment, and frustration as women speak about social workers' visits or travails in municipal offices endured in the hopes to secure subsidies that have become necessary for families faced with pervasive economic precariousness. In these concrete encounters, these programs assert that the poor pay their debt to the state by achieving dignity, but this dignity is opposed to and only possible through a progressive exit out of poverty.

Within neighborhood life, however, a different set of ideas and practices informed a living-with-dignity. This "living with dignity" is neither formalized nor publicly pronounced; it is neither isolatable nor pinned down as a moral code. Rather, its outlines emerge through sustained engagement with everyday life in the *población*. By paying attention to how critical moments are acknowledged in everyday life, we appreciate both quiet forms of solidarity and the boundaries that give dignity its local intelligibility. That is, a lived dignity can be appreciated through close attention to *who* responds to critical moments and *how* they respond, to the boundaries between different kinds of social relations.

ACTIVE SOLIDARITIES

Consider *la polla*. It's like a hen taking care of her chicks, Susana explained to me. Susana ran two *pollas,* rotating neighborhood credit associations primarily organized and employed by women. Wearing pink flip-flops, cutoff sweatpants, and a tank top, Susana sat on the shaded front step of her patio. It was December 2004. I accompanied her as women dropped off their payments, stopping for a few minutes to chat while Susana ticked off their names on a large sheet of ruled paper. Susana ran two *pollas,* one on a weekly basis and the other on a monthly basis. For the weekly *polla,* members paid two thousand pesos a week for ten weeks into a collective account held by the head of the *polla.* Women drew numbers, and the woman with the first number in rank order could choose which week out of the ten total weeks she would use the funds. For the monthly *polla,* the logic was the same. Women paid five thousand pesos a month for ten months. This rotating credit allowed members to buy commodities typically outside the range of the monthly household budget, pay a portion of their credit card debt, pay late utilities, or settle debts with family members and neighbors.

Susana and her husband, Antonio, were in their midthirties. They, and their two children, ages five and eight, lived in a house inherited from Antonio's mother, who had passed away several years earlier. Susana had taken over the *polla* five years ago, when the previous leader had left the *polla* in what Susana called "a disorder." During that year, two women had stopped making their monthly payments after receiving the collective funds. Since Susana became the leader, however, no woman had missed a payment. If payment were late, Susana went to the woman's home, inquiring about payment and "catching the vibe" of the situation. If the woman really could not pay, she said, she would put in her own money or mobilize through her (Susana's) sisters, mother, and aunts to make that woman's contribution. The woman would then have to pay Susana back at the end of the month.

Through her leadership of the *polla,* Susana was privy to all sorts of gossip and hints about domestic problems. Neighbors asked her about other neighbors, yet Susana took great care in speaking of others and knowing when to stay silent. Susana evinced this orientation toward others when I asked her how the *polla* came to receive its name. Susana responded with a laugh, "You know, I don't know; maybe La Polla [the national lottery]? For me, what I think of is a hen that brings together

her little chicks underneath her feathers and takes care of these little chicks."

In her patio, Susana introduced me to the ten women in the monthly *polla*. Still curious about how the *polla* became named as such, I asked these women the same question, "Why is it called *la polla?*" Sra. Ana C. and her daughter Joanna suggested, "It's like La Polla on the tele, because, all of a sudden, you get a lot of money at once." This association with La Polla de Beneficiencia, the national lottery, was reiterated to me by the other women as well. Signed into law in 1934 by President Arturo Alessandri, La Polla—translated as a bet on a horse race or specifically as the sixteen-hundred-meter flat race for three-year-old colts and geldings—was originally established by the Central Committee of Beneficence and Public Health of the University of Chile's School of Medicine. It destined funds derived from horse-racing bets to hospital services and social programs for the poor.[7] Today, La Polla is a public-private gaming company that by law must donate 5 percent of its income from each lottery to government services geared to the poor.[8]

Playing La Polla was ubiquitous in La Pincoya. Both adults and youth, men and women, bought numbers at neighborhood *almacenes*. La Polla generated legendary stories about the fortunes and misfortunes of neighbors. Don Gabriel, the brother of Sra. Flora, had won "millions and millions of pesos" from La Polla several years earlier. With the money, he bought a yellow-and-white Metalpar bus, the common city bus of Santiago, and a house for him and his wife. But, it was said, there was nothing more that don Gabriel loved than a good barbecue. Each weekend, he shared his fortune with the neighborhood. Neighbors pleasantly recalled the smell of grilled meat wafting down the street. The patio gate would be open, and all would be welcome. "It was like Fiestas Patrias [Independence Day celebrations], but every weekend for don Gabriel," a neighbor remarked. Within a year, most of his money was spent, and his wife, it was rumored, swindled him out of the house. He ended up having to sell his Metalpar to settle other debts, and moved in with his brother Diego.

As the quintessential game of chance, La Polla was a potent element in a social imaginary geared toward the play of fortune. As Jorge, an unemployed carpenter, told me, "Finding a job is like playing the lotto: everything by luck." La Polla, however, condensed not only a pervasive sense that life hinged on accident and wager but also a sense that neighbors and kin relations could transform luck's adventure and give it a different course. As women threaded *la polla* to La Polla, they differentiated the two through their relationship to "the system" (the neoliberal system) and to neighborhood life. "It's illegal," Sra. Elva, a member of *la polla,* stressed to me. Surprised, I asked, "How so?" She responded, "Because it's *outside the system.*" I asked for clarification through examples: "So could the police take you prisoner, give you a fine?" Sitting next to her, Sra. Gabriela responded, "No, no. Understand. It's not like that. It's outside the system, it's illegal."

Sra. Ana explained further. "Look, *la polla* is illegal, not like La Polla that comes on the tele, which is legal. It is illegal. Here, if a woman, a *pollera,* wants to take all of the money and run off, then you can't go to the police and say 'Look, this woman robbed me,' because there is no documentation. There is no paper, only the word. So, you have to trust a lot in the woman who runs the *polla,* because she has to be really responsible; she has to go to the house of the person who did not pay and demand that this person pay as it corresponds, because all of us [*nosotras*] depend on the *polla.*" The emphasis on the document showed the extent to which the dealings with the state were actualized and imagined through papers (see Poole 2004). But speaking of the "illegal" in relation to this economic form also conveyed the extent to which the state and market had experientially melded since the Pinochet regime.[9] Here, "illegal" marked the outside of "the system"—*el sistema neoliberal*—and the contractual guarantees and arbitrariness that this system presupposed.

"Outside the system," on the other hand, the obligation to make one's *polla* payments—to keep one's word—was cast in oblique relation to everyday religious vocabularies.[10] The money that women set aside for the *polla,* women said, was "sacred money" (*plata sagrada*).[11] "Sacred money" thus is "a material part of and participant in a moral world of social agents" (Keane 2008, 30). In the context of the *polla,* this money indexes interdependency. This interdependency meant that women could count on the *polla* money in a context where little, contractually speaking, was held constant. As Paloma explained to me, "You can miss paying *las letras* [the monthly debt payments] one month, but *la polla* you never miss. It is because others depend on you and you on them." She continued: "It's like the saying 'Dios te aprieta, pero no te ahorca'" (God squeezes you, but does not hang you.)

As I continued these interviews, I was curious to hear how *la polla* related to historical forms of popular economy. During the dictatorship, "spontaneous economic organizations" emerged across Santiago's *poblaciones.* Similar to the "kaleidoscope" of popular economic forms in Atlantic Africa that Jane Guyer explores in relation to a context of structural adjustment and currency fluctuations (Guyer 2004), these organizations embodied collective efforts to survive the consequences of the military regime's market reforms (Hardy 1987; Razeto M. 1990). Primarily organized by women, and often with the support of ecclesiastical institutions, they sustained a range of life necessities and possibilities, from overcoming starvation to organizing rotating credit. For example, in *ollas comunes* (communal cooking) women contributed available household ingredients into a neighborhood pot that would then provide meals for their families. In *comprando juntos* (buying together), women contributed a set amount of money into a fund that was used to buy foodstuffs at bulk prices. These foodstuffs were then equally divided among the women's households. *Grupos de ahorro* (savings groups) were rotating credit organizations with the same structural form as *la polla.*

So extensive were these organizations during the dictatorship that sociologist Cristián Parker remarked at the time that they created an "informal social security net" for the poor. This net was closely articulated with grassroots ecclesial organizations advancing a liberating popular Christianity that worked against the authoritarian regime (Parker Gumucio 1991, 56). Documenting the emergence of these "new networks" over the course of the dictatorship, sociologist Luis Razeto has suggested that they constitute an *"economía de solidaridad"* (economy of solidarity), an alternative to "the predominant capitalist and statist models of economics"(Razeto M. 1986, 86). This "economy of solidarity" was based in an alternative value system, one in which "mutual aid, cooperation, and community or solidarity" were not seen as "something accessory or secondary but as inherent in the way that they [the poor] seek to face their problems" (p. 90).

Solidaridad, in Razeto's view, was an ethical discourse grounded in everyday religious values that gave priority to the collective good over individual gain, values he sees as advanced by the Catholic Church, despite Pope John Paul II's condemnation of liberation theology and Christian Base Communities in Latin America. Indeed, in writings after the 1990 transition, Razeto cites the pope's speech at the Economic Commission for Latin America and the Caribbean during his visit to Chile in 1987 as evidence of support for an "economy of solidarity." In this speech, the pope proposes an "economy of solidarity" that divides the materiality of economic mechanisms from the spirit of solidarity:

"The most appropriate economic mechanisms are something like the body of the economy; the dynamism that gives it life and makes it effective—its internal mysticism—it owes to solidarity. . . . No other thing signifies, over all else, the reiterated teachings of the Church about the priority of the person over structures, of moral conscience over the social institutions that express it" (John Paul II 1987, 249).

Could such an ethical discourse of solidarity be practiced in *la polla,* one that presumes the division of matter (economic mechanism) and spirit (transcendent values)? I asked Sra. Ana if *la polla,* or something like it, had existed decades ago, previous to or during the dictatorship. "I don't think so," she said. "Well, during that time, we had money but nothing to buy—that is, the money was visible. But now, there are things, but there is no money. It is invisible. You see the things that you can buy, but the money is not enough to buy them. So, *la polla* helps you to buy things that you need." I asked her, "So it's not related to *las ollas comunes, comprando junto*s, and *grupos de ahorro* . . . ?" She responded emphatically, as others afterward responded to me, by referring to the historical moment, and not the form itself: "No, no. *La polla* has nothing to do with that time [during the dictatorship]. It was a time of solidarity. Nowadays solidarity doesn't exist."

I tried to clarify my question: "But, the form of *la polla,* in which women put money each month—it's the same as the *grupos de ahorro?*" She responded, "Yes, but no, no, no. It's something else. The vibes are different." Invisible money—credit and its consequences of pervasive indebtedness—were now the conditions through which historical forms of solidarity took on life, in contrast with the political conditions of economic scarcity under structural adjustment. In *la polla,* money was visible or tangible as effective cash. This rotating effective cash helped women mitigate indebtedness "in the system"; it retained "indexical links to its sources and owners" (Keane 2007, 242). On the other hand, invisible money, or credit mechanisms, were dematerialized; however, as we saw in the previous chapter, this form of money too invited possibilities while also generating a discipline of debt payments.

The "different vibes" of the *polla* suggest this form's potentiality within actual concrete circumstances. Today, it makes possible unnameable interdependencies that contend with present conditions of pervasive institutional indebtedness. Experientially distant from historical forms of popular economy under the Pinochet regime, *la polla* did not easily inhabit an ethical discourse of solidarity. We might think of *la polla* as the "becoming minor" of La Polla, similar to Deleuze and Guattari's writing of a "minor literature" that emerges from the major language (Deleuze and Guattari 1986, 17). Unlike in a major literature, which would stay within a regime of individual concerns, in a minor literature the individual concern "thus becomes all the more necessary, indispensable, magnified, because a whole other story is vibrating within it" (p. 17). While La Polla promises individual fortunes, *la polla* advances an "active solidarity in spite of skepticism" (p. 17). *La polla* took what was now a quintessential emblem of the market—the lottery of luck and individual fortune—and magnified the individual concern into interdependence.

Such "active solidarities" were also seen in bingos organized by extended family members and neighbors when loved ones were diagnosed with catastrophic illnesses. Such was the case with Sra. Mariela, who, after six months' waiting for a referral to a tertiary care institution, had been diagnosed with metastatic uterine cancer in August 2008. Unable to afford morphine for palliative care, her extended family and neighbors organized a bingo to raise funds. A next-door neighbor offered to print out fliers and put them up on street lamps. Another neighbor two streets down offered to hold the bingo in her home. Sra. Mariela's sisters, cousins, daughters, and nieces bought hot dogs and buns to make *completos*. Other neighbors came with boxes of wine.

About forty extended family members and friends arrived. Alternating *kumbia, reggaetón,* hip-hop, and folklore played in the background as teenagers took turns putting on different CDs. Sra. Mariela's daughter led the bingo. People played for hours, each time putting in six hundred pesos to play another round, buying *completos* for five hundred pesos, and glasses of wine for two hundred pesos. Packs of cigarettes were opened and passed across tables. We played all night, until the morning hours, with the hum of story- and joke-telling punctuated by occasional cries of "Bingo!," the winner receiving applause and a glass of wine. "Don't worry, it's not like bingo in the movies," one woman remarked to me as we joked that I had not won a single round. "Here, we don't play to win."

SHAME, RECIPROCITY, BOUNDARIES

Women also turn to their domestic relations in mitigating critical moments. As we have explored, domestic relations are those relations with kin and friends made intimate through time in the daily activities of living: child care, cooking, and visiting. Asking for small loans or food, or borrowing a credit card, however, is not a smooth and unproblematic act. Rather, there is a deep sense that women should *aguantar,* or endure hardship, contending with it quietly and persistently: "Lo arreglo piola" (I sort it out quietly). "Rebusco y rebusco por una luca" (I scrounge and scrounge for a thousand pesos). Shame (*vergüenza*) often shadowed such acts of asking.

This sense of shame was evoked by Susana as she confronted a moment of economic scarcity. It was a hot day in late January 2005. Susana was quietly leafing through a newspaper when I walked by her patio. Antonio, her husband, leaned on a half-painted taxi that was partially taped in newspaper and parked in the covered patio. "Hey, Clarita!" he called to me. Antonio turned off the roaring industrial paint blower. I had met them in June 2001, when they were "moving up." Then, Antonio had a stable job painting cars in the Jaguar factory and had just been promoted. Susana stayed at home, having given birth one year earlier to their second son, Ian. In 2003, however, the Jaguar factory closed. With his skills, Antonio quickly found another job in a small car shop in the neighboring municipality of Quilicura, but he quit after six months. As Susana explained to me, "Antonio was getting up at six in the morning to go to work and not coming home until ten at night. He spent more in bus fare than he earned." Susana began to search for work, although she wanted to stay at home with the children. When I visited her in June 2003, she had recently been hired by a sub-contractor to work in food preparation in a private Catholic school of the *barrio alto* (wealthy sectors). "The day that I entered work," she told me, "I took breakfast with the other women who worked in the school. And I cried, and I don't know why, but I was crying taking my coffee."

Susana rode her bicycle each day to work and back, up the winding highway over the hills, Los Pirámides, that connected La Pincoya to La Dehesa, one of the wealthiest sectors of Santiago. She earned minimum wage, 120,000 pesos (USD 200) per month. Antonio began to work painting cars in the patio of his home. He took out a bank loan to buy his own equipment and called his former bosses at the now-closed Jaguar factory to spread his contact information. Soon he was receiving commissions. But the work was unstable. Some months, he would have two or three jobs that would generate from 200,000 to 300,000 pesos (USD 300 to 500). In other months, he would barely earn 50,000 pesos (USD 80).

While Susana's income was stable but minimal, Antonio's fluctuating income meant that they swung between months of relative wealth and scarcity. When school was closed for summer break, Susana too was without income. As she explained it, she was "fired" from her job in December, and would receive one unemployment check of approximately 90,000 pesos through the state's public-private unemployment insurance, the Administradores de Fondos de Cesantía that was established in 2002. She would then be "rehired" by the subcontracting company in March. In this way, the company would not have to pay health or retirement benefits to its employees, since none of the employees had indefinite contracts. Thus, each year, Susana had to go through the same job training she had undertaken in previous years, as if she were the new employee that she technically was. As Susana remarked, "Every year, it's a new year."

January 2005 was turning out to be a month of scarcity for Susana and Antonio. With Susana out of work, Antonio tried to secure more paint jobs. The prospects were glum. The neighbor's half-painted taxi would bring in 30,000 pesos. Antonio's silent cell phone meant no new jobs were scheduled. As I approached the house, Antonio, who had stepped indoors, came back out to the patio with three homemade popsicles. As he handed me one, I asked Susana how she was doing. "Surviving," she answered. It was Thursday, and they had only 1,000 pesos to last them until the next Thursday, when she expected her check from the Administradores de Fondos de Cesantía—neither enough to buy groceries at the local outdoor market held on Friday nor to cover a week's worth of bread. On Wednesday, the electric and water bills came, and they had to be paid in five days or the electricity and water would be cut.

I asked her what she would do. She reflected on how she turned to her friend Sra. Ana during times of crisis. "I'm not like others," she said. "I don't have any shame [vergüenza] in asking for help. I can go to Sra. Ana and ask for a little bit of sugar or spaghetti noodles. But I always give it back. That's the idea. You always have to give back what you ask for. So we will not go hungry." Susana sketched out the vulnerability of a moral boundary between the two senses of pedir—asking and begging. To avoid a slip from asking to begging, "asking" is taken up into reciprocity, temporally tied into domestic relations of friendship and kinship.

Women often commented on the vulnerability of this boundary when scenes of "asking" came up in everyday neighborhood life. For example, as I was standing with a few women in a neighbor's almacén, they gossiped about a woman, Rosita, who was rumored to have asked for money from several neighbors. One woman remarked, "Qué vergüenza, andando llorando, pidiendo la lástima" (What shame, walking around crying, asking/begging for pity). The conversation spiraled outward to other women who cry and "beg for pity." Another woman remarked, "It's that . . . ayyy, that they need to understand, we are human beings. We do not walk begging in the street, like little dogs. We have dignity. One devalues oneself." The exclamation of "shame" here is a remark on the woman's voice, a woman whose "crying" is not heard as a human cry for help but verges dangerously on a whine. It is an exclamation of the shame generated by conditions that produce that voice, a failure of domestic relations, tied into where that voice is heard and by whom—in neighborhood life and by neighbors. The sense of threat attached to begging powerfully echoes Illanes's portrayal of the repugnance toward the kind of dependency that the subject of charity embodied in receiving alms (*limosnas*), a repugnance that grew in the late nineteenth century amid the tensions of a budding socialism and a Catholic Church that advanced charity as the glue between poor and rich in relation to the divine (Illanes 2007, 78–109).

Instead of confirming a picture of an autonomous liberal subject, however, this repugnance reveals *how* women are enmeshed in *different* kinds of relations. It reveals the difference between neighbors and domestic relations, those relations with friends and kin. An asking that crosses the boundary between neighbor and friend/intimate kin makes more vulnerable the boundary between asking and begging. We could think of shame as an affect that shadows moral boundaries. Boundaries, in this discussion, are not lines drawn around sociologically defined sets of actual people. Rather, as Marilyn Strathern discusses, they are in relation to *ideas*. Thus, the specific ideas of neighbor and friend in La Pincoya have "boundary-effects" (Strathern 1981, 82; see also Addo and Besnier 2008). We can therefore think of neighbor and friend as different relational modes. Women inhabit these relational modes every day. Through acts of reciprocity that constantly stabilize a woman's ability to endure, critical moments are quietly contended with and contained among kin and friends, "shoring up" moral boundaries when faced with hardship's corrosive potential.[12]

Among friends and intimate kin, a time of *shared intimacies* makes possible an explicit recognition of critical moments through acts of reciprocity that sustain mutual obligation. That is, unlike neighbors, friends and kin have an evolving knowledge of the intimate personal difficulties of another and develop a sense of a life story through such knowledge.

It was through such "sharing of intimacies" that Susana spoke about her friendship with Paloma, her "catching" or comprehending the moments when Paloma was going through hardship, and the way in which she acknowledged such hardship:

> Paloma will never say that she is doing badly. She will never arrive and say, "Pucha, Susana, I am in bad shape, can you loan me two lucas?" No, *yo lo cacho* [I comprehend/capture it] that she is in bad shape when she cannot pay for the *polla*. And I say, "I don't have money, but I can pass you a luca [a thousand pesos] in the meantime." Or I will hear the little girl [Paloma's daughter] crying because she does not have milk, and *cacho* that she is in bad shape. I offer her a cup of rice, she takes it and eats it. Or, if I loan her money for the *polla*, she is always thankful, but always gives me back the money. She scrounges and scrounges for *una luca*. She never walks around crying. She does cleaning for Sra. Ana [a neighbor], and Sra. Ana pays her. . . . I see with her, really, there are worse cases than mine. . . . Her husband is a vagabond. He works for two months and vagabonds the rest of the year. And really, it gives me pain, conversing with Paloma. *Me caga la onda* [It shits on the mood]. Antonio says to me sometimes, "You have to stop listening to Paloma, because it gives you pain, it makes you sick." But I feel that she needs to speak to me. I listen to her intimacies.

Later, when I asked Paloma who her friends were in the *población*, she said to me, "Friends? I don't have many friends. Susana is my friend. We share our intimacies. Friends are few, neighbors are many." Indeed, such a sentiment was echoed to me by many women in La Pincoya. Only upon meditation over the boundary between neighbors and friends did I begin to realize that the crucial difference between inhabiting friendship and neighborliness lay not in the perceptive activity of catching those signs of critical moments, such as the cry of Paloma's hungry child, but in how that catching would be or could be addressed.

In friendship, gifts are given in the modality of reciprocity—of mutual obligations that carry a relation forward in time and in which personal intimacies are shared. But neighbors are those who might hear gossip of each other but know little of the personal intimacies as they unfold over time. How would these critical moments be acknowledged by neighbors if neighbors are expressly *not* supposed to know of these critical moments, and if in explicitly acknowledging them they might jeopardize the delicate work of domestic relations in enduring and containing those critical moments? As a relational mode that works through gossip, dissimulation, and pretending, "the neighbor" helps us consider a silent kindness that occurs in everyday life. This silent kindness occurs despite the rancor in neighborhood life.

GOSSIP OF NEIGHBORS, ILLUSION, BAD PAY

While acts of reciprocity among friends and kin attempt to shore up and contain hardship within specific bounds, gossip about neighbors abounded. Consider gossip about being a "bad pay," *mala paga,* a person who took advantage of others by delaying or avoiding paying back a loan from a friend or to a local store. To describe the effects of such gossip to me, Paloma recounted the story of Sra. Isabel. Sra. Isabel had taken money from several *pollas* (local rotating credit associations), but when her turn came she did not pay her share. Gossip (*pelambre*) spread that she was a *mala paga.* "Neighbors talked. 'She took advantage of others; she doesn't realize we're all facing the same needs; she's selfish, a swindler.'" Paloma described how neighbors stopped helping her, saying, "No fue solidaria con nosotras" (She wasn't solidary with us). *Almacén* owners made up excuses so she could not make purchases *al fiado* ("on trust"; payment at the end of the month). Unable to depend on others, Sra. Isabel and her family had to leave La Pincoya. "Where did she go?" I asked her. "Don't get me wrong," she replied, "I never knew her; I just heard the story."

Gossip about a *mala paga* generates an atmosphere that corrodes a woman's relations with her neighbors and has the potential to threaten the fabric of domestic relations between those accused and those circulating the gossip. Susana underlined the force of this gossip in explaining how she chose the members of the *polla.* "I ask for recommendations if another person wants to belong to the *polla.* I ask the women in the *polla,* 'Do you know her?' And if a woman says, 'No, no, she is a bad pay, and she is not trustworthy,' then I tell her that we don't have enough numbers." I asked Susana if she ever directly confronted a woman with this gossip. Denying entry into the *polla,* she responded, was a delicate task, worked through excuses. "Look, you can't say 'You're a bad pay' to someone's face. These are your neighbors, or your cousin or aunt, sister-in-law . . . You live with them, greet them in the street, sometimes have to depend on them. It's like the saying, 'Pueblo chico, infierno grande' [Small town, big hell]. You say, 'Look, I'm sorry, we already have so many people in the polla this time.' Could you imagine saying, 'Look, *huevona* [idiot], you're a bad pay'? Caradura [With such nerve]? Nada que ver" (The sense here is that one just would not do such a thing; literally, "Nothing to see").

Susana's remarks show not only the delicate work involved to avoid acknowledging rancor, disappointments, jealousies, and hateful feelings for neighbors and one's kin but also the pervasiveness of those feelings in everyday life. Gossip (*pelar;* literally, to peel) effects that pervasive uncertainty about neighbors' feelings for each other, coloring those relations with profound ambivalence. The resulting avoidances and evasions, combined with face-to-face courtesies, are expressed in what many called the *doble sentido* (double sense/meaning) of everyday life. "Todo tiene un doble sentido" (Everything has a double sense/meaning): the necessary illusion that sustains a life subject to precariousness.[13]

CONTEMPORANEITY OF GIFT

Anthropologists have explored the jealousies and rancor manifest in this "double sense" of everyday life (Ashforth 2005; see Das 1998; Evans-Pritchard 1976). That is, jealousy and rancor manifest most acutely with those whom one depends on most, precisely because one cannot just have transparent access to another's mind. Perhaps less explored is how kindness could be possible next to, and indeed intimate with, such seething feelings of jealousy, hatred, and rancor. The kindness I explore below is distinct from those face-to-face courtesies and excuses that achieve that "double sense." Working through the subtle and indirect ways in which women perceive and acknowledge their neighbors' critical moments provides one way to consider the kindness that, along with the rancor, is concealed through this illusion of everyday life.

Let us recall Susana's remark about "catching" the moments of hardship as they occur. In the *Real Academia Española,* the verb *cachar,* deriving from the English verb *to catch,* is defined as "to comprehend" or "to suspect." *Cachar* as colloquially used might express "Get it?" or "Understand?" But in relation to the critical moment, the traces of etymology seem significant: women are catching small but significant details of an intimate neighbor, friend, or kin as they are occurring in time. Such perceptive "catching" of the critical moment by friends as well as neighbors suggests that signs of hardship still seep out beyond boundaries despite one's desire to *aguantar* (endure). A child's cry from hunger, a visit from a debt collector, the electricity cut, a domestic fight over bills spills out into the street, all signal to others, despite oneself, that one is in need and needs the help of another. For neighbors, how to respond to this seepage or to the gossip about another's critical moment involves subtle performances that conceal the critical moment as well as the act of giving. A contact for temporary work is passed to another neighbor, whose electricity has been cut, on the pretext of "just in case";

a neighbor's hungry children are invited to lunch with the excuse that there was too much food prepared; children are invited to play at a neighbor's house, and an offer to pick them up from school along with her own children is extended.

Such performances occur in a manner that is barely noticeable. Here are a few scenes. One afternoon, Ruby asked me if I could also pick up her next-door neighbor's children from school, since I was already going to pick up Ruby's son for a few weeks. Maca's husband was a salesperson for NutraLife, a company that sells health supplements in middle- and upper-class neighborhoods. I had met him once when he stopped by Ruby's house during the coldest months of the winter of 2005 to learn how to rig the electricity meter from her husband, Héctor. At the time, Maca's husband had just started working for the company. He had impeccably cut chestnut brown hair and was wearing a yellow fleece sport jacket embroidered with the NutraLife logo. He asked me where I was from. I answered, "The United States." "No, I mean what city," indicating a kind of cosmopolitanism that moved beyond identifying nationality. "Oh, Boston," I said. "Good, good," he said approvingly. "We have offices in Los Angeles."

In the course of the next few months, neighbors said that Maca's husband had become *arribista*—a social climber—doing this work, that he got used to talking to the *chicas cuicas* (upper-class ladies). Then rumors circulated that he was beating up Maca and had stopped paying the bills. "He's so well-dressed, and gives Maca *una miseria* [a pittance, or a miserable amount of money] for the house." A few months later, Ruby mentioned she had heard that Maca's husband had left her for some woman in the *barrio alto*. Maca, she said, was now left with two small children. "I heard they are going to repossess the house," Ruby said. "She's going to have to look for work *afuera*" (outside the house). The next day, when we saw Maca cleaning her patio, Ruby went out to tell her that I could pick up her children from school for the week. "Don't worry about it. Clara's picking up Héctor chico" (her son). Afterward, Ruby remarked to me, "I hope she finds her *príncipe azul*" (prince charming).

On another occasion, Anita, a neighbor married to a distant cousin of Ruby, stopped by while Ruby was doing piecemeal sewing in her home. Ruby said, "Come in, come in, but I can't stop to talk. We'll talk while I work." Anita rarely stopped by Ruby's house. Yet this time she stayed for a couple of hours, first mentioning that she was starting a bicycle club for youth and asked if Ruby's sons might be interested.

Ruby vaguely answered that one of her sons might be interested. Then, they gossiped about others. Anita brought up having heard that Centro Restaurant—a company that subcontracts food preparation workers to restaurants and schools—was looking for workers. Meanwhile, she started to help out with the blouses, using a knife to pull out small stitches in ones that Ruby had not done well. A few days later, a shop-keeper, Sra. Maria, stopped me as I was buying some sliced cheese for evening tea with Ruby. She asked me how Ruby was doing. I answered without exposing Ruby's acute financial problems to her: "I think she's OK. Busy as usual, why?" Sra. Maria said that she had heard rumors that Ruby and her family were on the verge of losing their house. "She's a hard worker. It's a pity."

A final scene: As Susana and I were walking up the street, we heard a heated argument coming from a neighbor's house. We caught only a couple of phrases: "And we don't even have a peso for bread!" Jorge yelled. "Shut up! Shut up! You, you passing the days in the street, yell-ing cuss words like an idiot *flaite*," Sara yelled.[14] Two days later, I ran into Susana on the street as she came from an early workday. When we passed by the neighbor's house, she called to Sara through the patio gate. When Sara arrived, Susana asked her if she had made lunch yet. She hadn't, she said. Susana said that she had made too much food—Sara could send the kids over: "I have some things to do, but send them over in a bit." But when Susana and I arrived at her house, it was appar-ent that she had not yet prepared any lunch. She set herself and me to making a large pot of spaghetti noodles with a sauce of tomatoes and pieces of hot dog.

Throughout these scenes, concealed acts of kindness—such as provid-ing lunch, helping with sewing, passing a work contact, picking children up from school—acknowledge these critical moments without explicit recognition. Such hidden or concealed gifts might be understood as a symptom of what Jonathan Parry calls an "ideology of the free gift," which is particularly acute in "market societies" and, more importantly, in Christian ones. Thus, "free gifts" are "ideally given in secrecy without expectation of worldly return," since such acts are determinative of indi-vidual salvation: "The notion of salvation itself devalues this profane world of suffering. The unreciprocated gift becomes a liberation from bondage to it, a denial of the profane self, an atonement for sin, and hence means to salvation" (Parry 1985, 468).

In an insightful engagement with Parry's analysis, Fennella Cannell discusses how anthropology has to a great extent relied on a Christian theology that is "only ascetic in character" (Cannell 2004, 341). And further, she notes that anthropology in its claims to be a secular discipline has "incorporated a version of ascetic and Augustinian thinking in its own theoretical apparatus" (p. 341).[15] Here, I am concerned with what happens to kindness in accounts that assume a Christian theology as denying this world. This-world denial has implications for what is cast aside in investigating the gift: kindness is cast aside as that sentimentality or artifice that sweetens an action, geared to getting real results, namely, salvation or climbing a social ladder. Turning to the parable of the Good Samaritan in the New Testament's Gospel of Luke, for example, yields other possibilities for kindness within Christianity itself. Luke sets up the parable with the lawyer's question to Jesus: "Master, what must I do to inherit eternal life?" Jesus says to him, "What is written in the Law? What is your reading of it?" (Luke 10:25–28). The lawyer answers, but then asks Jesus, "Who is my neighbor?" Jesus offers the parable as his own reading of the love commandment "Love thy neighbor as thyself," but interprets that commandment by throwing into question not only who is a neighbor but also to whom that question would be directed.

While there is a considerable theological literature on this parable, I will limit my discussion to Jesus's act of asking the counterquestion "Which of these three, do you think, was a neighbor to the man who fell into the hands of the robbers?" Theologian Ian McFarland suggests that Jesus's question "redirects attention from the status of others to that of the lawyer himself. . . . 'Neighbor' is not a category that the lawyer is authorized to apply to others; instead . . . it recoils back upon him as a moral agent capable either of being or failing to be a neighbor to someone else" (McFarland 2001, 60). In responding to Jesus, the lawyer then must respond to himself: "The one who showed him mercy." To further unpack the word *mercy* in relation to the neighbor, I turn to the Latin etymology of the Spanish word used, *misericordia*.[16] *Misericordia* is derived from *miserēre* (to have piety), which itself derives from *misero* (wretched, deplorable), which itself is a transliteration of the Greek *mīsos,* or hate, in relation to *cordis,* "heart" (Barcia 1889, 372).

An intriguing insight that comes from this etymology is that the "love for the neighbor" might be inseparable from hate. We might consider such ambivalence in relation to Jesus's questioning, "Which was neighbor?," which involves answering to oneself, or the possibility that one might fail oneself in relation to others. "Loving kindness" or loving one's neighbor, would be neither "sentimentality nor nostalgia." Rather, as Adam Phillips and Barbara Taylor assert, "Kindness split from hatred breeds a fundamental loss of contact with oneself and others that leads to a prevailing feeling of unreality, or being unrecognized. There could be no intimacy without hatred, and no enduring pleasurable contact between people without surviving the hatred that always exists in relationships" (Phillips and Taylor 2009, 88).

The delicate concealment of kindness in these ethnographic descriptions, however, makes us return from statements about kindness in general to a consideration of the specific threats that critical moments pose in this world, and the possibilities for thinking about and living a this-worldly generosity that these concealed responses might offer. To further elaborate, I draw from J.L. Austin's essay "Pretending" (Austin 1958).[17] Austin's discussion of pretending helps me shift my attention on the gift in three crucial ways, all of which entail shifting from investigating the performative aspects of the *gift/countergift* to attending to the contemporaneity of the performance of *giving*. By contemporaneity, I mean the co-occurrence of acts and circumstances.

First, the discussion of pretending focuses attention on the co-occurrence of acts, or their contemporaneity, rather than on expectation or futurity. In pretending, Austin remarks, "I must be trying to make others believe, or to give them the impression, by means of personal performance in their presence that I am (really, only, etc.) *abc* in order to disguise the fact that I am really *xyz*." Thus, "*contemporary behavior* misleads as to *contemporary fact*" (p. 276, emphasis in original).

One example that Austin provides is that "I" may pretend to have been furious by "emerging from the conference room breathing hard and making derogatory remarks about the proceedings: but not by leaving traces in the conference room—bitten carpets, maybe—designed to make you think that I was furious at the time." Contemporary behavior—my pretending to have been furious—misleads as to the contemporary fact that I am not "recovering from or still suffering from the after-effects of fury, or mulling over fresh memories of fury" (p. 276). Leaving traces in the conference room of bitten carpets and smashed chairs might deceive you into thinking that I was furious, but this deception is not the same as my pretending to have been furious. Pretending requires the pretender to be "present and active in person to effect the deception by dint of his current behavior," but also, as Austin seems to implicitly suggest by addressing his reader, that I, the pretender, must be present to another—or another must be in my present—to effect this deception. Pretending therefore has us reorient ourselves from the temporality of gift and countergift to consider a performance (an act) concealing another act (the giving), in which both pretender and audience are in each other's present continuous. If I could draw a picture of this reorientation, it would be a picture of slicing through a layer cake: through the multiple layers that are composing an instant—those co-occurring acts. Or, as a single drop of water that has different layers of sediment.[18]

Second, attending to the performance of concealing "something else" helps us consider what concealing might allow and protect in everyday life. As Austin remarks, "If there is no sort of urgency to hide what we elect to hide, we may prefer to speak of a leg-pull or of an affectation or a pose" (p. 276). For example, in pretending to wash windows, I am "really up to something other than cleaning the windows," like casing the valuables in your house. Or children who are "pretending to play chess" are really "up to some mischief." In La Pincoya, what is concealed is not only the giving but also the neighbor's "catching" of the critical moment. Concealing allows for the enduring to endure. It protects a "living with dignity" by *not* explicitly recognizing the critical moment and one's act of kindness, since as a neighbor one should not have personal knowledge of such critical moments.

Such concealing differs from Bourdieu's elaboration of the gift within games of honor. In precapitalist societies, acts of kindness occur in face-to-face relations and are cast as "collective misrecognition" of the "objective truth of the game" of social interests: "the moral obligations and emotional attachments created and maintained by the generous gift, in short, overt violence or symbolic violence, censored, euphemized, that is, misrecognizable, recognized violence" (Bourdieu [1980] 1990, 126). In contrast, capitalist societies rely on "objective social institutions" to perpetuate dominance. In seeking to explain that "lasting hold over someone," Bourdieu quickly explains away kindness in terms of the player's interest. Generosity is understood through "modes of soft domination," foreclosing thought on other modes of relating that might also be occurring. Taking pretending seriously, however, allows us to attend to that "mischief," which we could think of as impersonal kindness. But it also shows how that kindness must be concealed to protect a living-with-dignity.

And a third and related point: pretending reveals the force of words and the moral energy in remaining silent. Thus, the animated silence to make it appear as if nothing is happening at all suggests investigating the moral along the "threshold of perception" of illusion (Deleuze and

Guattari 1987, 279). As Austin remarks, "A pretence must be not merely like but *distinctively* like the genuine article simulated" (Austin 1958, 274). Thus, if one is pretending to pass by, one passes by. One would not pretend to be "just chitchatting," by greeting someone and running off.

Focusing on pretending, or concealing, as a way to engage the moral in everyday life can be compared to anthropological work that focuses on ritual contexts in which the formalism of acts of reciprocity distinguishes them as "reciprocity" rather than "exchange" (Keane 2010). And, it can be compared to anthropological work that marks out the ethical from everyday life: those acts that have public consequences and that "stand out from the stream of practice" (see also Lambek 2010; Lambek 2011, 3). Rather, by staying at that register of the "stream of practice" and instead exploring that stream's layers—that contemporaneity, a "slice" through those layers or a "drop" of time—we might elucidate how words have the potential to destroy the delicate concealment crucial to enduring the critical moment, an essential aspect of "living with dignity." Thus, pretending helps us attend to a quiet moral striving that happens every day, the achieving of illusion.

Pretending brings into focus again the boundaries between the relational modes of friendship and neighborliness, specifically with regard to the personal and the impersonal. As we heard from Susana and Ruby, friendship involves sharing intimacies, a knowledge of those personal dramas that are occurring within the boundaries of a domestic, which includes intimate kin and friends. Keeping critical moments within such bounds is crucial to shoring up the moral boundary between asking and begging, a boundary that is constantly in danger of being corroded by economic precariousness. In domestic relations, giving occurs through personal knowledge not only of the critical moment but also of the ways in which this critical moment emerges from and enters into a life story. It occurs as an explicit recognition of this moment, but only within the bounds of this domestic and in order to keep such moments within it.

In the relational mode of neighbors, however, acts of kindness that acknowledge the critical moment cannot rest on that past and future of shared intimacies. Rather, such acts of kindness seem to rest on a different kind of sharing. While gossip and seeping signs might betray the critical moment despite one's desire to "endure," they also bring into focus a lived vulnerability—that slip between asking and begging—informed by the forces of economic precariousness (see also Povinelli 2006). Giving in this relational mode is premised not on sharing personal intimacies but on a vulnerability that is a shared condition.[19] In distinction to friendship, giving in this mode involves an impersonal "catching" and responsiveness—through gossip, seepage, and pretending—that helps enduring to endure. At the same time, pretending conceals that vulnerability.

That this vulnerability is so concealed and is only hinted at through gossip and seepage, and that the response is also concealed, points us to the limits of understanding these acts of kindness in terms of certainty and knowledge. This giving evades a sociological "pinning down"; it cannot be assessed and evaluated through technologies of verification that presume to get at a truth. On the contrary, uncertainty is its medium. The uncertainty entailed in this giving—Is this a critical moment? Have I failed to respond? Will I just ignore it?—returns us to the discussion of Jesus's counterquestion in the parable: "Which was neighbor?" This question is turned back on the one who asks it. What might this uncertainty teach us about the acknowledgment of the other?

In discussing what expresses acknowledgment in theater, Stanley Cavell offers further insight: "We are not in, and cannot put ourselves in, the presence of characters; but we are in, or can put ourselves in, their *present*. It is in making their present ours, their moments as they occur, that we complete our acknowledgment of them. But this requires making their present *theirs*" (Cavell [1969] 2002, 337). Cavell continues: "And that requires us to face not only the porousness of our knowledge (of, for example, the motives of their actions and the consequences they care about) but the repudiation of our perception altogether" (p. 337). Repudiating our perception and facing the porousness of our knowledge of the other involves a risk of exposing the self to the fact of separateness. The problem posed with this risk is *not* how to live with the fact that everyone is commonly vulnerable, but rather that *that* vulnerability is mine to respond to: "We are endlessly separate, for *no* reason. But then we are answerable for everything that comes between us" (p. 379).

Concerning the boundary between neighbors and friends, the difference is not between the "presence" of the friend and "present" of the neighbor, but rather the difference lies in *how* being in another's present and acknowledging those critical moments can occur: they occur through explicit recognition made possible through "shared intimacies" or through pretending that rests on a shared vulnerability and impersonal responsiveness. Such "being in another's present" might be contrasted to the poverty programs of the "social debt" in which women must sign a Family Contract, promising to improve their conditions over time despite economic precariousness, or to the social worker's view of poor families as a "burden" to the state. One implication, then, is the violence of this time of debt; another implication, however, is that such violence displaces moral and political thought of what *could possibly* be shared.

VIVIR CON DIGNIDAD

As performances of "living with dignity," such gifts in everyday life are tangential to anthropological conceptions of life that hinge on the dualism of bare life and qualified life. In his essay "Ethics of Survival," Didier Fassin powerfully critiques anthropology's extension of *homo sacer,* or "bare life," across contemporary societies. Such an extension generates a "hierarchical conception of lives (physical life being reduced to bare life) which is also a hierarchical conception of human beings (between those who only have their bare life left and those whose life is qualified)" (see Agamben 1998; Fassin 2010, 87–88). Focusing instead on "life as survival," Fassin draws from biographical fragments produced through interviews to suggest that physical life and qualified life come into subtle articulation. Exploration of the existential intertwining of biological life with qualified life in subjects' "telling of stories" could allow for a more "democratic" politics of life, not in terms of the "rights-bearing subject," but in terms of the speaking one.

Attending to these performances in everyday life stands adjacent to the life of this speaking subject. Such gifts do not enter into biography as discrete and recountable moments, since they were never to have happened at all, quietly occurring within that "stream of practice." Faced with punctual moments of economic scarcity, and with respect to governmental discourses on poverty that cast dignity in opposition to poverty, both neighborliness and friendship in their different ways aspire to a dignity within poverty and not opposed to it. And, women strive to achieve this dignity along the lines of speech and silence.

This line between speech and silence recalls Veena Das's attending to men's and women's "obstinate turn toward the ordinary" in relation to the violations of life itself: that ethnography might attend to the "extreme hesitation" in putting that which violated the "whole principle of life . . . back into words," and thus the "deep moral energy" not to speak of that which so violated life itself (Das 2007, 90–92). Considering the performance of giving in everyday life likewise helps us attend to the deep moral energy in silence, but within the ordinary itself. Such silent shoring up of a dignified life helps us appreciate how speech can jeopardize the very fabric of other's lives. Indirect modes of talk, such as gossip, provide the suspicion to others that another needs a hand while also foreclosing acts of kindness to others; an explicit recognition of giving has the capacity to betray that critical moment, depending on the relational mode.

In ethnographically attending to the shoring up of moral boundaries that are constantly made vulnerable by the forces of economic precariousness, the force of words in making and threatening a living-with-dignity is revealed. However, the contemporaneity of giving—this pretending—reveals a different aspect of living with dignity. That is, the mischief that sneaks in during pretending: the act of kindness that is allowed and made possible, a generosity that can neither be registered as a debt nor accounted for solely through the expectations of otherworldly salvation in a future. Could such "mischief" of impersonal generosity and kindness open anthropological imagination to a *possibility* of justice in this world as it silently persists alongside the accounting practices of the social debt (see Constable 2005)? Justice that cannot be empirically pinned down by the state's accounting, but is instead heard in its silences? As Marianne Constable acutely remarks with respect to modern law, "To face the threat of the disappearance of justice . . . is to hear a voice that heeds and speaks of possibilities of law that are neither the articulations of power nor the powerful discourses of positive law. It is to hear in the air the silence of modern law as the necessary voice through which human beings sing of their earthly encounter with the world that is given them. . . . Justice lies in stillness, awaiting the silent call to it that comes out of the human need to act and judge in a world that is *not* of one's own making" (p. 177).

The social debt demands an empirical accounting both in terms of poverty reduction and in terms of technologies of verification through poverty programs, which in their everyday dealings assert that dignity is achieved only through a progressive exit out of poverty. Through the accounting of such "social facts," the state can claim that justice is indeed being pursued, even as such programs generate differences between humans and, with such differences, profound resentment and frustration. Yet in staying with, or being immersed in, a "drop of time," anthropological inquiry can attend to those kind acts—those presents of this world—a responsiveness to the lives of others that can neither be named nor instrumentalized as social policy in the service of actual justice. To name this responsiveness "popular justice" in opposition to the state would therefore miss the point. It is not an explicit articulation of "justice" that can be latched onto with certainty and that can enable one to strike out with a claim to empowerment. Such a rendering evades the medium of this responsiveness—uncertainty—and imposes an empirical knowing on the revelations of acknowledgment. Rather, as a scene of instruction, this responsiveness teaches us how to listen to this uncertainty and, thus, to the possibility of justice.

CHAPTER 3

Torture, Love, and the Everyday

A WORLD'S WITHDRAWAL

In August 1999, I met Ruby. She knocked on the door of Julieta's shack one afternoon to charge her for an unpaid debt. (We will meet Julieta in the next chapter.) Ruby did piecemeal sewing for a local workshop that produced sweatpants sold in Patronato, the textile sector of Santiago. A few months earlier, she had sold several pairs of sweatpants to Julieta, with the agreement that Julieta would make weekly payments on them. Julieta, in turn, sold them to various neighbors but was delaying her payments to Ruby. Ruby began to visit Julieta's shack at least every other afternoon and delicately probe for payment, but instead received a cup of tea and entertaining conversation. It was during those visits, made possible through a debt that to this day remains unpaid, that I came to know Ruby; her husband, Héctor, a former communist militant who had been detained and tortured under the Pinochet regime; their children; and their extended kinship network.

At that time, Ruby, Héctor, and the children, Davíd and Emilio, were living as *allegados* in the house of Ruby's mother, Ana.[1] They occupied one of two shacks attached to the original house. Ruby's two older sisters and brother, and their partners and children, also lived in the house. With extended family living on several conjoining streets, and because of her outgoing and warm nature, she was greeted by neighbors in her comings and goings in the street. In contrast, Héctor was hardly known among the neighbors. Julieta gossiped to me about his history of torture and detainment, remarking that it made him "reclusive" and "solitary." Ruby, however, offered a different account of his reclusiveness. It was not only that he withdrew from the world, but also that the world withdrew from him.[2] "The world has failed him," she said, remarking that this failure "gives me rage, gives me so much pain. With this *democracia entre comillas* [democracy in quotation marks], his grand faith in the world died," she remarked to me. "I and the children are his only world now."

In the previous chapter, I explored how the state's attempt to pay its social debt to the poor through targeted poverty programs might be considered alongside silently living with dignity, shored up by acts of kindness. Now I turn to the "moral debt" owed by society to those who suffered human rights violations under the Pinochet regime. The state's official acknowledgment of torture under the Pinochet regime came to life in La Pincoya among neighbors and within Ruby and Héctor's domestic life and extended family.[3] This official acknowledgment took place in 2004, fourteen years after Pinochet's handover of power, and thirteen years after the National Commission for Truth and Reconciliation produced the Rettig Report.

An official discourse of reconciliation advanced an ethics of pardon, dissociated from market reforms, to acknowledge past human rights violations. Yet the reception of this official account of torture tied into the ways in which families and neighbors attempted to secure livelihoods in an economic system—*el sistema* or *el modelo*—that many said "*nos duele*" (hurts us). For those who suffered state violence waged in the name of market reforms, reinhabiting an everyday life materially shaped by these reforms means that state violence resulting in human rights violations and ongoing economic precariousness, while not identical, must be held together, as they are lived by many in La Pincoya.

In what follows, I describe scenes of Ruby and Héctor's everyday life between 1999 and 2006, moving between their domestic life, neighborhood meetings, and public and official accounts of human rights violations. Rather than recount their lives as a *trajectory,* as if their lives could be charted like a brick path laid out in advance or retrospectively traced with clarity, I write domestic *scenes,* starting with our initial meeting, scenes that do not presuppose what should come of relations, but which attend to those "intimate aspirations" (Das 2010a) that, if imagined as music, might be heard as improvisation. I hope these scenes convey the difficulty in, and hopes for, an awakening to relations with intimate kin, relations imbued with disappointment in this actual democracy. We might then hear Ruby's words—"I and the children are his only world now"—as an expression of both aspiration and disappointment.

MORAL DEBT

I first arrived in La Pincoya several years after the National Commission for Truth and Reconciliation released the 1991 Rettig Report.[4] Emphasizing the establishment of "consensus" and "moral healing," the report provided a temporality to political violence. Casting violence as an aberration in Chile's history of democratic rule, the report sought to identify the ideological bases that generated human rights violations while advancing ethical practices of forgiveness in the constitution of the self (see Grandin 2005). In effect, it generated an official account of democracy dissociated from the historic struggles for economic justice and equality that would implicate the actual institutional arrangements of the state while, at the same time, displacing moral responsibility for "healing" state violence to the self. This dissociation took place as the Concertación governments sought to pay their social debt to the poor, as I described in chapter 2.

President Patricio Aylwin (1990–1994) invoked this temporality in a speech on March 12, 1990, at the Estadio Nacional (the National Stadium, which had been a detention center from September to December 1973). Advancing a specific temporality to moral healing, he remarked, "I consider it my duty not to let time slip through our fingers, looking at the past. The spiritual health of Chile demands that we find ways to carry out these tasks of moral healing in a reasonable period of time, so that earlier, rather than later, arrives the moment in which, reconciled, we all look with trust to the future and join efforts in the task that the Fatherland [La Patria] demands of us" (Aylwin Azócar 1992, 13).

Aylwin's emphasis on a reconciliation that turned toward an ideal future must be understood within the constraints of the political and judicial context. According to the armed forces and supporters of right-wing parties, human rights violations fell under the rubric of an "internal war" against Marxist elements. As former Army General Manuel Contreras Sepúlveda remarked in a 1991 televised interview: "In a war, there are dead, wounded, missing and prisoners, but there are no detained disappeared. . . . There are no disappeared detainees in a subversive war, and this was a subversive war" (quoted in Brown et al. 1991, 9).[5]

Such negations on the part of the armed forces, as well as the continued presence of Pinochet as commander-in-chief of the armed forces, created enormous political stakes in how human rights violations would be revealed. Restricting the investigation of violations "to the extent possible," Aylwin delimited the scope of inquiry to the cases of the detained-disappeared, executions, kidnappings, and assassinations motivated by political reasons, including within the Rettig Report investigations of those who lost their lives promoting the regime itself. Only those violations that, in Aylwin's words, "resulted in death" were included in the investigation. In excluding both individual cases of torture that had not resulted in death, and collective tactics of repression, human rights were cast as those natural rights protecting the body from death.

On March 4, 1991, however, having read the Rettig Commission's report documenting 2,279 cases of political execution and disappearances between 1973 and 1990, Aylwin gave a televised address to the population that demonstrated a subtle shift in public discourse on how past violence related to the present. Rather than sealing the past, Aylwin emphasized ethical commitments necessary for national unity and reconciliation, in particular the individual's ability to pardon. Such ethical work on the self in relation to others would be the necessary condition for living the past as past.

Many compatriots think that it is time to put a *"punto final"* [final period] to this theme. For the good of Chile, we should look toward the future that unites us, more than toward a past that separates us. There is much we have to do to construct a truly democratic society, drive development, and reach social justice that we would waste our efforts in inquiring into wounds that are irremediable. We recall the words of Pope John Paul II on his visit, "Chile has a vocation of understanding and not of confrontation. The divisions cannot keep deepening. It is the hour of pardon and reconciliation."

Who would not share those aspirations? To realize them, there is, nevertheless, a need to specify those offended who are called to pardon, and those offenders who have to be pardoned. I cannot pardon for another. The pardon is not imposed by decree. The pardon requires repentance from one part, and from the other, generosity.

When it was agents of the State that occasioned such suffering, and the competent organs of the State could not or did not know how to sanction them, and neither was there the necessary social response to impede it, the State and the whole society are responsible, either through action or through omission. It is Chilean society that is in debt to the victims of human rights violations.

Because of this, the suggestions about moral and material reparation that the Report formulated are shared by all sectors (Aylwin Azócar 1992).

Aylwin advanced several prescriptions for reparation, including the establishment of free health care for those exiled and exonerated, and for family members of the politically executed and detained-disappeared, through a system of benefits called PRAIS, the Programa de Reparación y Atención Integral de Salud (Program of Reparation and Comprehensive Health Care). He also established a system of monetary reparations in the form of monthly pensions to living family members, including spouse, father, mother, and children, up to 140,000 pesos per family. He prompted the judiciary to take up pending criminal cases in light of new evidence, in spite of the 1978 Amnesty Law that provided amnesty in criminal cases that occurred during the state of siege between September 11, 1973, and March 10, 1978 (see Stern 2010, 113–135).[6]

As several scholars have discussed, human rights discourse embedded in the rhetoric of reconciliation constituted a central axis along which the Concertación governments consolidated democratic rule while continuing to deepen economic policies instituted by the Pinochet regime (Moulian 2000; Richard 2000; Ruiz 2000). For example, anthropologist Julia Paley argues that the Rettig Report "emphasized the healing and reconstitution of the nation, through the burying of the past. The nation and its future became the centerpiece of identity" (Paley 2001, 128).[7] But a closer reading of Aylwin's discourse renders not an image of "burying the past" but a casting of the *past as debt,* inflected by both Catholicism and a discourse of human rights (see Fassin 2007a). Through appeals for pardon, an ethical work on the self forges a specific relation to the past as a moral debt; the self, as well as society, achieves perfection through pardon, through reconciling defined sets of victims, perpetrators, and witnesses. That which happened in the past is accounted for through this labor of *coming to an agreement over that past*—a reconciliation—assuming that the events of violation and of dictatorship were arranged in successive order from past to present.

Within such a normative framework, struggles over memory can be understood as *assigning meaning* to this violence in which competing "emblematic memories" confront each other in the public sphere, as historian Steve Stern suggests. Notice that in such a conception of memory, an *actual* form of life, or actual relations, are not held up as questions. Rather, public debates, or "memory knots," over the justification of political measures to save, protect, or dispose of life inform a national memory. Memory knots "awakened" the "social body" from "reflexive everyday habits that foster numbing" by "bringing the charged issues of memory and forgetting into the public domain. . . . One responds even if the purpose of response is merely to find 'relief' and return to normalcy" (Stern 2004, 120–121).

Stern's conception of memory relies on narration and public acts: anecdotes, reports, spectacles, speeches, media events, and street demonstrations. We could ask, then, how a conception of memory changes in the register of everyday life: for example, in the quiet ways individuals receive the pain of others, in the moral energy in remaining silent about those acts that violate life, or in the expressions of disagreement that are not registered in public discourse. Moving from a conception of memory in terms of public discourse to practices of memory in everyday life in La Pincoya involves a different attentiveness to both the experience of time and the self. With Héctor and Ruby, awakening was not an awakening *from* everyday habits but *to* the everyday itself—to one's relations with intimate kin—in the face of political aspirations that staked the self's existence to future generations, and in the face of economic realities that provided the basis for disagreement about whether democracy had yet arrived.

EL CERRO

After several impromptu conversations in Julieta's shack, Ruby invited me to take a walk with her to a canal in the hills bordering La Pincoya. We met outside the front gate of her shack, which faced the hill's slope. But, to my surprise, and contrary to neighborly customs, she did not invite me inside her home. Instead, she apologized for the gate's sad appearance—spare planks of wood of varying sizes hammered together and ill fit within the frame.

Climbing the hill with her small, flop-eared dogs, Indy and Laico, jumping and barking behind us, we reached the canal crosscutting its steep face.[8] Brown water and garbage floated by, a smell of pig manure was strong in the air, and farther up sheepherders were guiding a small flock to a green patch in the distance. "This canal," she told me, "my mother told me the day of the *golpe,* corpses were floating along the canal. My mother hung heavy blankets on the windows for months afterward to block out the images. Tengo grabada esta imagen" (I have this image recorded). I sensed that she might continue, but she stopped.

Instead, she turned to speak of her father and his illness. "Schizophrenic-alcoholic," she said. Returning again to the day of the *golpe,* she said, "On the day of the *golpe,* he ran through the streets, crazy, shouting, 'Allende lives, Allende lives!' A military officer was going to shoot him, but a neighbor said, 'No, he is just crazy, he does not know what he is saying.' The officer told him to go home. After that, my father started drinking and did not stop. He has been in and out of the Psychiatric Institute ever since." Her father was now severely disabled. Several months before I met Ruby, her father had had a stroke, sustaining severe brain damage, which left him in a vegetative state. In the same month, her mother had undergone surgery for a large benign brain tumor. Her home was not "welcoming" to visitors, Ruby explained. "I don't like that others see my father in this condition, *decaído* [deteriorated]. It's something very delicate for the family."

Ruby recounted that her father was the illegitimate child of a French aristocrat and a Chilean-Spanish woman. After the two married, they had several more children. Yet her father was treated more as a servant, and he often sustained his father's explosive temper. He ran away from home, she said, and lived with several children underneath a bridge over the Río Mapocho. Through gritty persistence, he made a living running a small snack stall outside La Vega, the large outdoor market in Santiago. There, he met Ruby's mother, Ana, and they started a life together in the *tomas* of La Pincoya. They had four children: Soledad, Lorena, José, and finally Ruby. The children and their partners and children continued to live in the same house.

Although her siblings also lived in this house, Ruby had assumed the primary responsibility for her father's care. José, her older brother, was "light," according to Ruby, meaning that he could not be counted on in difficult moments. Soledad and Lorena were struggling with their partners' addictions to *pasta base*. Ruby eventually gave up her outside job in subcontracted office cleaning and began work in piecemeal sewing at home. From office cleaning and lifting her father into a wheelchair, Ruby developed a herniated disk in her lower spine.

We arrived at a bench made of two tree stumps and a halved log. As we sat looking at the view of the *población*, she asked me about my parents. My mother had died two years earlier, also after suffering a stroke and remaining in a vegetative state for several years. I recounted a tiny fragment of how my family had cared for her at home. In response, Ruby said, "Hemos cruzado una frontera" (We have crossed a frontier/border). She invited me to take another walk.

During those conversations on the hill, Ruby told me about the sacrifices Héctor had made for democracy and the effects of his disappointment on his intimate relations. Yet the hill became woven into the conversation. As we walked, she told me how he isolated himself from neighbors and maintained a distance from his family, who, except for his estranged brother, moved to La Florída, a municipality in the southern zone of Santiago. But when we reached a particular view of the neighborhood below, she told me how "the *población* was surrounded by *milicos* [military]. From the hill, the military shot any person in the street." She recounted how the Communist Party had granted Héctor, who was then in hiding, a scholarship for university studies in Cuba. At the time, Ruby was pregnant with their first son, Davíd. Héctor decided to stay. As we reached a particular tree, she stopped. "I think this is where we buried a pot of books." She told me how several families hid contraband books and magazines in cooking pots and buried them on the hill. "But, after so many years, we forgot where we left them."

Noticing how she steered between speaking of Héctor and the hill, I asked her, "But how was it for you, living with Héctor in hiding?" She said, "*Bueno,* I was his *amortiguadora,* like the hill with its pots." An *amortiguador/a* is a mechanism, material, or solution that absorbs and compensates for shocks, jolts, the brightness of light, and the intensity of sounds. To *amortiguar,* according to the *Real Academia Española,* is to "make it so that something is less alive, efficacious, intense, or violent, tending toward extinction." At the time, I could not appreciate how deeply that remark sketched out the affective horizons of their everyday life: how, during dictatorship, Ruby absorbed violence done to Héctor and thereby transfigured it, made it less "alive," and how, under democracy, she absorbed the life of this death of a part of Héctor.

The following year, Ruby invited me to her home to meet Héctor. During my absence, Ruby's father had passed away. He was buried in a plot next to Héctor's father, a militant of the Movimiento de la Izquierda Revolucionaria (MIR), in the Parque de los Recuerdos (Park of Memories) within the bounds of the municipality. Ruby had returned to work shortly after the funeral. She spoke little of the funeral. Instead, she showed me photos of family events—Fiestas Patrias barbecues, birthday celebrations, Christmas—pointing out her father in each scene. She now worked as a nanny in La Dehesa, one of the wealthiest sectors of Santiago. She told me that her *patrona* was "nothing new. There are seven of us working for her, and she pits one against the other. All those rich people, they have different morals." Héctor, on the other hand, was working as a parking lot attendant for a private hospital, earning minimum wage.

When I arrived at their home, Ruby was cooking chopped-up meat seasoned with salt and oregano in a pan on top of their paraffin stove. Their home was cramped yet inviting. The living room fit a round dining table, four chairs, and a worn armchair. Two bedrooms came off the living room, each with a single bed. They shared one bathroom among the four siblings' families living in the site. On the walls hung multicolor banners of Cuban folk singer Silvio Rodríguez, the late Chilean folk singer Víctor Jara, and John Lennon.

Opening a large cabinet, Héctor showed me his extensive collection of tape cassettes, most of which were dubs from LPs: Chilean singers and bands, including Inti-Illimani, Víctor Jara, and Violeta Parra; jazz; Silvio Rodríguez; North American heavy metal bands; and especially Frank Zappa. He asked me if I knew of this band or that band, only to discover, to his amusement, my limited knowledge of the U.S. rock scene. Music, he said, was one of his "therapies." "When I keep my mind busy, it serves as therapy, so I don't have time to think about the other things. I repair the house, save money for our new house, and listen to music." Ruby then described how he sometimes put on headphones when he arrived home and sat listening to music for hours. He responded quickly, "At times, I isolate myself [*me aislo*], I isolate myself. But, when I assumed the responsibility of having a family, I assumed it 100 percent. I continue in another fight now. It is the fight to maintain a family." Héctor's emphatic assumption of his responsibility—100 percent—in quick response to Ruby's words indicated that a different responsiveness to his family might be eluding him. What was he not seeing that Ruby felt was right in front of him? And, what was Ruby, in her remark about the earphones, calling him to see?

BIRTH

In late July 2002, I visited Ruby again. I knocked on the door. "Ruby! Ruby!" I yelled. There was no answer. I yelled again, and there was still no answer. After several minutes, I heard feet shuffling in the house. Ruby opened the door. She looked pale and ill. Her long chestnut hair was cut short and covered with a knit wool cap. Her eyes were puffy and bloodshot. "Come in, come in," she said, and asked me if I would like some tea. She sat down, slowly and painfully, telling me that she felt nauseous. "I'm pregnant," she said. "Three months." She showed me the ultrasound pictures. The pregnancy threatened their aspirations and sent both Ruby and Héctor into despair, but in different ways. "All of our plans to buy a house, to have our own space . . . with a baby, our economic situation . . . ," she said. "Héctor won't even talk about it. He walks around feeling down [*bajoneado*] and doesn't talk. He doesn't even want to touch me. But I think to myself, it's not my fault. I went to the *matrona* [at the local primary care center] and put in the injections [contraceptives]. But it didn't work." She told me she had been vomiting every day and had lost her appetite. "It's as if I want to vomit out the baby. My body, my being [*ser*], is rejecting it."

Before the pregnancy, Ruby had switched from her work as a nanny to assembling shoes in a Hush Puppies factory. She told a trusted supervisor on the factory floor about the pregnancy, knowing that in time she would be unable to hide it. Working on a fixed contract, she feared she would be fired. Her supervisor, however, urged her to "hide the pregnancy," and in the meantime she would recommend Ruby for an indefinite contract. She could then take maternal leave. Ruby attempted to work for the first two months of the pregnancy, but with her nausea she could not withstand the smell of the leather and toxins. She renounced the work, although it signified giving up a stable, minimum wage income.

She returned to piecemeal sewing in her home, assembling parkas and vests to sell in Patronato. Boxes of half-sewn jackets filled the living room. Shards of fabric and long black zippers littered the floor. She was working nearly twenty hours a day. She described herself as "*aperrada a la máquina*" (working like a dog at the machine) to earn enough money to cover their daily costs and the costs of a baby and to continue to save money to qualify for a home loan.

In the midst of this work to secure a future, and of Héctor's turning away from her, a kind of limit to her sense of being human emerged. Perhaps sensing this condition, her younger son, ten-year-old Emilio, called her to his present. "Emilio tiene el alma sensible" (Emilio has the sensitive soul), she said. "He is the only one to give me *cariño* [affection/ love]. He lays his head on the *guata* [abdomen], and gives it *cariño*. He says, 'Mamá don't cry. This is my little brother.'" Through love, he tried to bring this baby, which her being rejected, into his realm of kinship, to which she belonged.

The baby was born premature, in the thirty-fourth week of gestation. I had returned to Cambridge, Massachusetts. I checked in with them through phone calls, relying on the phone lines of Ruby and her sister

Soledad, which were sometimes disconnected for up to three months. Ruby lost a great deal of blood with the birth and was hospitalized for two weeks, along with the baby, who had difficulty when he was born.

Héctor also occasionally sent me e-mail letters. In April 2003, he wrote me:

> Hi Clara,
>   Sorry for not having written in so many days. What is going on is that various things have happened to us that have us worried.
>   In any case, I begin by telling you that the child is doing very well. He already is two months old and fat like a ball; he weighs almost five kilos and measures 52.5 centimeters. The good thing is that he is receiving milk from the mother, and also milk from the bottle.
>   Ruby is doing very well, although she has much work at home with the children and with the tasks of the house.
>   Davíd and Emilio are studying and doing relatively well.
>   And, I, although my health is good, have problems from the point of view of work. Lamentably, I was left without work and the things have put us in quite a bad spot; I am looking for work, but things are quite ugly. As if the problems were adding up for us, the effect of Bush's war with Iraq has meant an increase in the prices of almost all the articles of basic necessity. . . .
>   In spite of this, I and the others are doing very well and happy principally with the baby, who came out healthy for us.
>   Well, Clara, I say good-bye to you, leaving pending a commentary on what is happening in Chile and the world, principally that of the war.
>   Bye,
>   *Héctor*

After two months, Ruby found work once again as a nanny. Héctor dedicated himself to housework and caring for the two children and the new baby. He remained unemployed for six months, until Ruby had "feeling" with her *patrona*. A general manager of an Argentinean CD and DVD factory, she gave Héctor a job in warehouse inventory. Such acts of charity by *patronas* on behalf of their domestic workers were grounded in the *patrona's* feeling of intimacy with the worker, often through confiding personal fears and frustrations. Yet such charity often came at the cost of a host of favors—an occasional overnight stay to watch the children as the parents attended social engagements, working overtime a few days, and so forth. Such was Ruby's debt to her *patrona*.

When I returned in January 2004, Ruby told me of another dimension of the baby's arrival. During the pregnancy, Ruby and Héctor had not discussed the baby's name. When Ruby returned home from the hospital, she had gone straight to the civil registry and named him Héctor.

"Héctor was angry," Ruby recounted. "He said that the child should not have a name that carries with it such a dark past. And I said to him, 'Well then, maybe you will be reborn.' And, I tell you, Clara, since that creature, that little earthquake, forced itself into the world, something changed in Héctor, like he was discovering the world again. Lleva sus cosas bien pa' dentro [He carries his things well inside]. But I tell you, something changed inside. I'm content that I named him Héctor. Maybe Héctor will have a second life. Not like the Pentecostals, *cachai* [get it], we're communists, but something different, in his being" (*ser*).

Ruby's naming was not the playing out of a cultural script. Ruby, it seemed to me, was hoping that naming the child Héctor would awaken her husband to their everyday life, to a "second life" of these flesh-and-blood relations. Not that he would forget his past and be born again, but rather that he might attend to the details of their lives with as much concern as with the distant events of war.

HUMAN RIGHTS

During this time, the possibility of an official report on torture, along with individual reparations, emerged. In the face of pressure from right-wing political parties and human rights organizations, in August 2003 President Ricardo Lagos proposed the creation of a national commission to establish a list of those who had suffered torture under the Pinochet regime and provide them with "austere and symbolic" reparations. By November 2003, the *Diario Oficial* (the state institution that publishes laws, decrees, and other juridical actions) published Supreme Decree 1.040 creating the National Commission on Political Imprisonment and Torture, known informally as the Valech Commission, after its president, Monseñor Sergio Valech. The commission's mandate was to "determine, in accordance with the antecedents that they present, who are the persons who suffered privation of liberty and torture for political reasons, by State actors or persons in its service, in the period understood between September 11, 1973, and March 10, 1990" (CNPPT 2004).[9] The commission had six months to solicit and validate testimonies and prepare its report.

When the state released the official report, along with monetary reparations for victims, this acknowledgment took on a different life in La Pincoya. Neighbors drew explicit continuities between state violence and ongoing economic insecurity; nongovernmental organizations offered alternate sources of compensation for those excluded from the official list. The word *torture* gained a second life, beyond the state's criteria. And with this emerging reality came new tensions between Héctor and Ruby over how to acknowledge Héctor's "things within."

Did the commission's mandate shape this second life? Shadowing the commission's work was the fact that all testimonies provided were to be held under "lock and key" for fifty years, thus blocking human rights lawyers' and judges' access to this evidence in criminal investigations. Yet the very definition of torture, the exclusion criteria, and the scarce public knowledge of the commission also shaped its local reception. Drawing from both the United Nations Convention against Torture and Other Cruel, Inhuman or Degrading Treatment or Punishment, as well as the Inter-American Convention to Prevent and Sanction Torture, the commission defined torture as

> any act in which severe pain or suffering, whether physical or mental, is intentionally inflicted on a person for such purposes as obtaining from her or a third person information or a confession, punishing her for an act that she has committed or is suspected of having committed, or intimidating or coercing that person or a third person, annulling her personality or diminishing her physical or mental capacity, or for reasons based in any type of discrimination. Always and when said pains and suffering have been committed by a State agent or another person in its service, or who acted under its instigation, or with consent or acquiescence (CNPPT 2004, 19).

By this definition, collective forms of coercion or mass repression were excluded, such as *allanamientos,* the widespread military practice of surrounding *poblaciones,* sacking houses, interrogating, menacing, and threatening family members, and holding the men within cordoned public spaces, such as a soccer field, for days and subjecting them to degrading treatment.[10] The commission also marked temporal boundaries by technically excluding short-term arrests and detentions of individuals—under a period of five days—which were frequently associated with *allanamientos* (CINTRAS n.d.).

Individuals in the metropolitan region of Santiago had a window of six months, between November 13, 2003, and May 31, 2004, in which to provide their testimonies.[11] But diffusion in the mass media was limited to one week of notice on television and radio, along with notices in state offices and the metro (the subway system, which was not widely used by the urban poor).[12]

On November 28, 2004, President Lagos publicly acknowledged the widespread use of torture by state agents during the Pinochet regime in a speech titled *Para Nunca Más Vivirlo, Nunca Más Negarlo* (To Never

Live It Again, to Never Again Negate It). Out of 35,868 persons who presented testimonies and documentation, 27,255 individuals complied with the "strict requirements to be accepted by the Commission" (Lagos 2004). Those who qualified as victims of torture would receive what President Lagos had earlier called "austere and symbolic" reparations: a lifelong pension of 112,000 pesos (USD 188) for the victim,[13] equivalent to 1.5 times the minimum pension; guaranteed access to continued studies; free health care through the Program of Reparation and Comprehensive Health Care, and housing subsidies.

Human rights organizations regarded the Valech Report as an important symbolic step in the official narrative of human rights in Chile. The report, however, also inspired critical reflection on the part of some human rights organizations, such as CODEPU (Corporación para la Defensa del Pueblo; Corporation for the Defense of the Pueblo) and CINTRAS (Centro Integral de Derechos Humanos y Salud Mental; Comprehensive Center for Human Rights and Mental Health), who were sensitive to the limitations of the official report, not only in terms of the commission's process of diffusion, solicitation, and validation, but also because of the continued impunity with regard to human rights violations. These organizations estimate that between two hundred thousand and three hundred thousand individuals had been tortured under the Pinochet regime.

The report also generated concerns that the field of human rights itself had been restricted to an all too narrow view. Within an authoritarian context in which the threat of death was immanent, human rights had been exercised for the defense of biological life. Yet this concept of life, as the underpinning of human rights work, now seemed inadequate. As Simona Ruy-Perez of CINTRAS remarked to me in an interview in July 2005, "Human rights work in Chile is like a dog chasing its tail. We go in circles, trying to catch something we cannot catch. . . . The neoliberal system is what turns society." The executive secretary of CODEPU, Vicente Espinoza, went further in his reflections to me:

> The field of our work [human rights] has a visuality of failure. We work on the level of symbolic reparation, which is not to say that this register is not important, particularly for national memory. The issue of human rights as the defense of life was an articulating theme during the social battle of the 1980s. Eighty percent of those who occupied positions in the first Concertación government were all linked to the defense of these human rights. It was something fundamental. Now, this concept generates a certain conformity. Santiago is a city with foci of extreme poverty, which was created during the dictatorship, and this continues to become more extreme

each year. Now, if you do not have a credit card, you do not exist. Your life is structured on debt and credit. This is what permits you to survive.

THE HURTFUL SYSTEM

These critical reflections resonated with an animation of the word *torture* in everyday language in La Pincoya. In the wake of the Valech Report, I noticed that, in my interactions with neighbors in La Pincoya, the word *torture* was peppered throughout conversations: "Debt is a torture," "The system is a torture," "I can't find work; it's torturing me." The use of this word in ordinary language intrigued me. It was not typically used to express the anxieties over work and debts, which were expressed as "agony," "desperation," "dragged in the dirt," or "eating my nerves." Could the use of the word *torture* have indexed a past continuous, a shimmering that might in a moment pass across a threshold of everyday perception?

In conversations in La Pincoya with neighbors belonging to the Communist Party, the word *torture* was used to emphasize the past continuous in the present. In June 2005, Ruby and I were invited to a dinner in honor of the late Gladys Marín organized by Communist Party members in La Pincoya. Several had experienced torture under the Pinochet regime; others had lost partners to the sequelae of torture.

When we arrived, M, a social leader in his midforties, was speaking about those who did not receive reparations. He did not qualify because he could not remember the date that he was tortured. He recounted, "It's complicated. When I went, I forgot the date. And I said, 'I'm sorry, but I don't remember.' And they said to me, 'But how?' 'It's that I don't remember.' The only thing that I remember is that they beat me, they hit me, but the date? I forgot. And I was denied, but many did not give their testimonies for psychological reasons or for disinformation" (lack of information about the commission's existence). J, a well-known labor organizer in his fifties, interrupted him with rage in his voice.

> What can they do to me? What more can they say to me than "Kill him!" To me, what more can they do to me than kill me! It is the last thing left that they can do. Lo otro, lo entregamos [Everything else, we offered it]. We did the things we needed to do. Here we have it. He, as I, is fighting; we are here, continuing, continuing our political belief that we have, our ideology. And we will continue until we cannot anymore. This is what I said to the woman [*mina*, in the Valech Commission]: What would be gained if they killed me; just go ahead and kill me! I don't have any problem [*rollo*] in saying what happened. That I was tortured, that I was persecuted throughout the whole

dictatorship. *Tortured* [his emphasis]. Until today, I am tortured, because no one gives me work. No one gives me work.

M followed quickly.

The system hurts us, Clara. In this [the Valech Report], we are not in agreement with the government, not at all [*para nada*]. It's that, you know, they say that if the affected [tortured] passed away, there is no benefit [paid out]. What happens with the family that also suffered? Really suffered ill-being [*malestar*].[14] They suffered as well, the children, the woman, they *suffered* [his emphasis]. Because they were not well. In terms of human rights in Chile, in one way or another we were all tortured, psychologically, of life, of health, and already from direct cases [those who had been subjected to detention and torture]. For them [the wealthy], it is natural [to achieve well-being]. For the worker, it is more difficult to arrive to this place. Others who have a lot, they will never recognize what to us hurts us. That is the difference. How much does it hurt us to pay for education, how much does it hurt us to pay for health.

R, the current partner of M, whose husband died of torture-related sequelae, continued:

And your milieu [*entorno*] is to live paying the debt and the interests on it, and not to grow [*surgir*] as a person. So, you do not have any guarantee that, yes, there will be the promise of being another person [other than the indebted person]. Lamentably, this government has been a farce for us, because as communists we fought for equality for all. But when this government—we need to call it "the democracy," within quotation marks—that we've never had a democracy. And no one can negate that this government has been a transition to the right—and not to the poor of this country. I say to you, we continue indebted, we live for debt. And I say to you, 100 percent of the persons are psychologically ill [*psicológicamente mal*], because we are thinking, "What will happen this month, with what will I pay?" . . . I tell you, lamentably, personally with all my debts, I am left with forty thousand pesos, and I have to survive—where [how]? And pay for light; and if I pay for light and water, then I don't have enough to eat. And you know how much forty thousand pesos is worth in this country. Nothing. My *compañero* fought so that this "democracy" would arrive, and it was for nothing, not for me, not for my children. . . . In this terrible country, they want to show a country that is not what it is. Nothing of what they say that we are—a country free and democratic, that everything is fine, all is one. It bothers me. It embitters me to see the news on television.

I want to pay close attention to their use of the word *torture* in its indexing of *actual* life conditions: of not finding work, the hurt of paying for health and education, debt. Torture is *both* a violation of the individual body that occurred in the past and the pain of actual life conditions in the present (see Das and Addlakha 2001). Their words require an understanding of the specificity of state violence—in this case, what the state wielded violence in the name of—as well as an acknowledgment of political commitments in the making of the self. Such specificity shapes the ways in which past and present relate in everyday life, depending on how one is inserted into the present. For these men and women, economic precariousness is intertwined with the experience of state violence. The very dailiness of unemployment and debt constitute a past continuous of state violence transfigured, made present in and as the everyday.

Delineating the use of psychic evidence in the validation of torture among French asylum cases, Didier Fassin and Richard Rechtman elaborate how a global moral economy of trauma identifies legitimate victims and provides "a language in which to speak of the wounds of the past" (Fassin and Rechtman 2009, 280). Trauma, as ambiguous evidence of torture, "is a tool used in a demand for justice," in which political subjects come to identify themselves with the figure of the victim. "Survivors of disasters, oppression, and persecution adopt the only persona that allows them to be heard—that of the victim" (p. 279), even as it obscures social relations and "violates historical reality." Yet in their use of the word *torture* to speak of actual conditions, these men and women, as political subjects, are not identifying with the figure of victim. Rather, they enact their own political commitments by saying that torture *continues as the system,* and by disagreeing with the government not only about the criteria for reparation but also about the arrival of democracy.

Democracy continues as an aspiration, not an actuality: their historical reality. As J put it: "We are here, continuing, continuing our political belief that we have, our ideology. And we will continue until we cannot anymore." Or, as R says, "We've never had a democracy. And no one can negate that this government has been a transition to the right—and not to the poor of this country." Attending to these political commitments means acknowledging that these men and women have staked their existence on these commitments. That, in their words, their "sacrifice" was a condition of an eventual community. Rather than evaluate such commitments, I am interested in how the ethical and the political articulate through memory.

A week later, Ruby and I attended a celebration for the inauguration of new local cell of the Communist Party. Neighbors were discussing the ethical implications of accepting reparations. Held in a neighbor's home, a small gathering of neighbors enjoyed *empanadas* and mulled wine. M invited us to join the conversation at the dining table, where a group talked about the "large quantity" of people remaining "outside the law."

> *M:* Many *compañeros* remained outside when they opened the law. A law opens and is closed. Whoever remained outside, remained outside, whether it be for disinformation or for psychological reasons.

> *P:* It's really complex. They are superficial laws. They are only doing something for outside [the global view], to say that Chile is settling the thing [*arreglando la cosa*], but in reality they are not doing it [settling it].

> *M:* I agree with what you are saying. That the state, the government has a false quantity [*cantidad falsa*, of those tortured]. It limits, and opens a law, and a large quantity are remaining outside. This is convenient for the Lagos government.

Laws did not figure as a set of bureaucratic rules. Rather, they were political forces, generating temporal conditions to minimize the damage and producing a "false quantity" that could be projected to the exterior. This minimization, however, had an effect of "inverted magnitudes," creating a proliferation of associations between the arbitrariness of the state, and suspicions and moral judgments about those who were named on the list and were receiving benefits (see Brown 1981). As we conversed further about the individual indemnifications, the conversation turned corrosive as fingers were pointed at neighbors who received benefits.

> *Ruby: Pucha,* it is awful. I fucked myself up [*me saque la chucha*] to arrive to democracy, and *chucha* [fuck], they are going to pay me because I fought? It is also ethical [Giving one's testimony raises ethical questions].

> *V:* It's that there are people who have not done anything and are receiving benefits.

> *Clara:* Why?

> *V:* Because they are *opportunists* [her emphasis].

> *L:* There were people who were not detained, and they are receiving money. The people who really sacrificed, they are not receiving money.

> *M:* The people who are receiving benefits are receiving because one does not have any more commitment [*compromiso*] than go with the document and start to receive money. But what happens with one who works with a political conscience [*conciencia política*]? It psychologically stays with you, and it is not so simple to just go and arrive [and give your testimony].

> *V:* There is a Chilean saying—"El chileno es fácil para olvidar." The Chilean easily forgets.

Such accusations of opportunism point to a deeper threat that came with reparations—not the way that monetary reparations operate in an audit culture (see Nelson 2009), but how accepting the state's terms of reparation itself threatened one's moral and political commitments, the self's political conscience. Memory appears here as an ongoing activity and orientation in the present: the very relations one has with oneself.

ASPIRATIONS

Héctor did not attend these meetings and dinners. In January 2004, Ruby and Héctor moved into a neglected two-room house one street from her mother's house. They had saved enough to make a down payment and qualify for a home loan from Banco del Estado. When they moved in, Ruby imagined various scenarios: hosting meetings of the Communist Party in their own home, holding neighborhood social events. Ruby was becoming more involved in local social organizing and envisioned their home as a nexus for such gatherings. But Héctor's vision was different. He took out a loan of 100,000 pesos from the bank Bansolución and constructed an imposingly tall, thick, gray concrete wall around the house, with an equally heavy wood-and-metal gate. The neighbors were bothered and disturbed. The wall broke an implicit sociality. Neighboring houses had open metal fences that allowed for conversations and gossip between home and street and between neighbors. Ruby found herself both apologizing for and defending the wall.

This wall between Héctor and his social world also carried into his response to the work of the Valech Commission. When the Valech Report was released, I asked Héctor if he had considered providing his testimony. He responded, "The fact that people know what happened to me does not sit well with me. . . . I don't like it. . . . That form of being does not attract me." He said he would rather pass "unperceived." To be singled out and known, perceived through an individual testimony based in one's injuries, rubbed against his political convictions but also threatened his everyday sense of security: "I take it from this point of view. To be a little more secure in my walking [*mi andar;* my everyday life], in my living. . . . In the personal [*lo personal*], I have it always well inside [Lo tengo siempre bien pa' dentro]. And most likely that is because I suffered, and I achieved knowing very well the awful [*nefasto*], the harmful that could be for one and for others if they found out one's things. . . . So, to take care of all of these consequences, I just simply preferred to not speak."

Interwoven with this fear inherent in speaking of one's involvement was Héctor's fear that narrating the violence done to him would deform his children. As he told me, "I do not tell the kids what I suffered. I want my children to be normal. I want them to grow up in a normal milieu" (*entorno*). As when Ruby named little Héctor, he worried that, in his words, *"lo tóxico"* (the toxic) would pass to his children. When Ruby, Héctor, and I talked about life under dictatorship, he recounted experiences of being detained, quickly switching the topic when his children entered the room.

But, this lived silence around his involvements and detentions also articulated with his aspirations for future generations, and he treaded close to those activities and injuries in order to voice these desires. One long night, Héctor and I were helping Ruby remove stitching from a pile of silk blouses. We sat in the living room with Davíd and Emilio, who were half watching television and half annoying each other. We chatted about various neighbors' children who had become addicted to *pasta base*. Héctor said that Pinochet was responsible for this addiction in the *poblaciones*. During his youth, he said, police under Pinochet "sold the drug to the kids to make them manipulable [*manejable*], to kill social commitment." I asked him how he became involved in politics. He then recounted his ethical and political awakening (*tomando conciencia*) under dictatorship and how his actions related to "the personal."

> *Héctor:* A dictatorship that had been so atrocious, so atrocious, with so many disappeared, dead, and so much persecution. This is what made me *tomar conciencia,* and I realized that things happened that were, that were . . . that we cannot permit. And what can I say, what do I think with respect to now [today]? That it would be lame [*fome*] that my grandchild or my great-grandchild, or perhaps that a generation afterward, would read the history of Chile and think that "my great-grandfather lived during that period. How would he have acted? If there were such atrocious things happening in this country?" It would be lame if they said, "Oh, he lived a normal life. He never dared to do anything." For me, that would be lousy [*penca*]; it would be lame; it would be disagreeable personally if they said something like that about me. I would not prefer that my grandchildren, my future relatives, that no *po*. I lived a dark period of this society, this country, but I did something to change it. I did something to change it, and I think that what I did was the most correct. Now, lamentably, that one does not arrive to getting what one aspired to [*pretendía*], that is another thing. But, we managed to obtain the minimum reachable, which was to arrive to democracy. That does not mean that in the country a more social politics would be achieved, more concerned with the people. Well, in that, it has still been in "we'll

see" [veremos], still has been in working for that [en trabajar para eso].
But at least we achieved arriving to democracy, a thing that is basic and
fundamental.

Clara: So, when you say *democracy,* what do you mean by that?

Héctor: Actually, I don't like that word. It's to say, it doesn't attract me
today, the way it is used now by political parties and companies for the
rich.

Héctor then turned to the subject of receiving reparations, speaking
of the "not personal":

So, it is not that I was fighting for personal ends. After I did everything I
needed to do, I took myself out of political contacts. It was to achieve something for everyone, the best possible for everyone. I have never been so idealistic to think that we could achieve everything at once. . . . It's now the case that
I don't continue in politics. One never asks that one does super well, but that
the incomes are more dignified. But, one asks why I fought, so that I would
have a better income? No, not at all. I don't like that others know what I did
and what I do. No, I want to be, and pass for, anyone [una persona cualqui-
era] who walks in the street. . . . I am not fighting to achieve a good title, that I
deserve a good income, a good post. I can't leave to the side someone who has
not been able to study for reasons that are the same as mine, and this does not
mean that this is an undignified person. He is another human being. In order
to be, he has to have the same basic things, in order to live a life as it corresponds. So, for that I fight. For that, I am always criticizing things, because
he should be respected and live in a normal form, not like those who live
in pomposity with everything, with everything within their reach. . . . We've
talked about inequality before. That so much wealth could be stretched a little
bit, so that those who are lower can achieve living in a more dignified form.
This is what I criticize [for]. So, coming back to that theme [of reparations].
I did not fight to have an income. I fought so that the things in this country
would turn out better for everyone. I, fighting in order to have benefits, as if
I retired because I was a combatant—I don't want this. I desire that my fight
has been to achieve something for this society. And that society affects me as
well. Better the society, better am I. It is not something personal. So, if there
were not such a difference between those who earn more and those who earn
less, we would achieve everything. Those are my aspirations.[15]

Héctor's personal and impersonal aspirations differ both temporally
and relationally. For the personal, he imagines an inheritance received
by his future generations. This inheritance is Héctor's account of himself
as a subject of action: that, in his words, he did "something to change
it," and that his grandchildren could speak of his actions in their life
with a sense of "the correct" (Foucault 1997, 217).[16] The temporality of the personal, therefore, connects his actions with future children

through an imagined act of reading and of being written. I might venture that Héctor may also be aspiring for his grandchildren's inheritance of this political subject, this subject of action who would act in dark times and in the face of "atrocious things." Regarding the impersonal—a relational mode of fellow humans, of a someone, an "in order to be," that is also himself as a "person like any other"—Héctor aspires to an equality among all humans, a continuous presentness between society and the self: "Better the society, better am I."

Listening to Héctor, I am struck by resonances between the *form* his aspirations take with me and the genre of *testimonio*. As a form of writing that grew from Latin American grassroots movements during the 1960s, and that is expressive of the experiences of the popular and marginal, *testimonio* can be understood as a practice and performative speech, at once personal and collective, and at once testifying and bearing witness to violence (Beverley 2004; Yúdice 1991, 17).[17] As Doris Sommer aptly elaborates, the "I" of *testimonio* seeks neither to represent his or her community nor to identify with the reader through metaphoric substitution, but enacts "a lateral move," a metonymic "identification-through-relationship" in which readers are "invited to be (*estar*) with the speaker rather than to be (*ser*) her" (Sommer 1991, 39). *Testimonio*, as a practice of being with others, not only can inspire the possibility of political community but also can be understood as an ethical practice of the self, a self that is woven into these potential relations—those metonymic moves in and through speech and writing. Thus, in *testimonio*, the self bearing witness to violence *grows in lifeworlds* and is not reducible to the self implicated in psychiatric or legal testimony (see Warren 1998, 113–132).[18]

With Héctor, these personal and impersonal aspirations seemed to be at a certain remove from his children, who sat next to him on the sofa as he spoke of being read by future generations and of equality for all. Writing of these aspirations today, I am accompanied by Ruby's uneasy feeling that such writing-to-futures also carried with it Héctor's difficulty in *seeing* his children, that to limit desire might be a way to inhabit everyday life.[19] Even as he voiced an aspiration *next to* his children *for* future generations, I hear Ruby asking me the following day, with a hint of exasperation: "But what are his aspirations for *sus propios hijos* [his own children]?"[20] Ruby might be pointing to a different modality of living a moral life, in which one's account of oneself is not in the form of a subject of action, that subject of action who recounts what one did in one's life. Rather, a different modality might involve attending to one's relations: an account of one's relation to oneself, a relation constituted with intimates. But then, we might consider the energy and care with which Héctor remains silent about that which violated life itself. Such silence, he hopes, will protect his own children's normal lives.

A few days later, I was watching over little Héctor while Davíd did his homework after receiving a harsh talking to from Héctor before he left for shift work. Davíd was at risk for failing a grade. I commented to Davíd that he took care of his little brothers a lot. He responded, "It's because my mom and dad are working so much. We don't see them."

Clara: How does it make you feel?

Davíd: It bothers me. So, I bother them. I pretend that I don't understand, but . . . Getting up early. Life is just purely for working [*pa' puro trabajar*]. Even the old, they die working.

Clara: But do your parents tell you why they have to work so much?

Davíd: Because the system is like that. They work for little money. My dad has to work every day because the bills need to be paid. He's not seen in the house. We don't have enough money to eat if my dad is only working [referring to the fact that his mother also has to work].

Clara: That's frustrating.

Davíd: Sometimes I get angry, for example, if we want to buy a candy for Emilio but don't have the money.

Clara: Has your dad talked to you about what he experienced during the dictatorship?

Davíd: He hasn't told me much. They killed a few friends of his, and that made him go crazy.

Clara: What did you feel when you heard this?

Davíd: Equally, it gave me pain. [Igual me dio pena]. They hit him, they hit him, and I imagined it was happening in my gymnasium [at school]. . . . Someday, I want to earn a good income. I want to send my parents to the countryside.

PINOCHET'S MONEY

Although Héctor remained outside the Valech Report, by March 2005 an unexpected constellation of governments, courts, and nongovernmental organizations opened up an alternative possibility for indemnification for those excluded from the official list. This time, the indemnifications would not come from the state, but through the complex international case against Pinochet involving the Spanish courts, the United States government, and Riggs Bank, called the "Riggs Case."

News of "Pinochet's money" circulated by word of mouth in networks of social organizations and among local Communist Party members. These new funds, however, presented a different struggle between Ruby and Héctor over official acknowledgment.

Let me briefly sketch out a few threads. In 1996, the Spanish lawyers filed criminal and civil lawsuits against Pinochet for crimes of genocide, terrorism, and torture between September 11, 1973, and March 11, 1990.[21] Interpreting Spanish domestic law as having universal jurisdiction, Judge Baltazar Garzón opened the possibility for crimes against non–Spanish nationals to be included, and for a "customary definition" of genocide to be upheld in the Spanish courts. On October 16, 1998, while Pinochet was in London undergoing back surgery, Judge Garzón ordered his arrest and extradition to Spain on this basis, and three days later ordered his assets to be frozen. Over the course of a year and a half, Pinochet remained under house arrest in London while British courts decided whether or not he had sovereign immunity. Finally, Home Secretary Jack Straw decided in March 2000 that Pinochet was mentally unfit to face trial. Pinochet returned to Chile to face criminal charges.

The Riggs Bank case began in 2004. On July 15, 2004, the United States Senate's Subcommittee on Investigations released the report *Money Laundering and Foreign Corruption: Enforcement and Effectiveness of the Patriot Act, Case Study Involving Riggs Bank*. This subcommittee had the task of investigating money-laundering activities in the U.S. financial sector. Its report uncovered how the U.S.-based Riggs Bank, owned by the Allbritton family, had assisted Pinochet in concealing and moving his assets while he was under investigation and subject to a worldwide court order freezing his assets. Pinochet, through Riggs Bank, had hidden more than $8 million in shell accounts in the United States and the Bahamas (Coleman and Levin 2004).

The revelation of Pinochet's embezzlement and hidden assets opened up expanded legal proceedings against Pinochet and bank officials. On September 16, 2004, Spanish lawyer Joan Garcés petitioned the Spanish courts to add the Riggs Bank's directors, Joseph and Robert Allbritton; board member Steven Pfeifer; and bank officer Carol Thompson as defendants in the criminal and civil lawsuit under Judge Garzón for their role in concealing Pinochet's assets. According to Garcés's legal reasoning, the concealment of assets threatened the creditors' (the victims') ability to receive their rightful indemnification from the debtor (Pinochet) when the debtor would be convicted of crimes at a future date.[22]

In February 2005, the Allbritton family settled with the Spanish courts by agreeing to pay $8 million to the Spanish organization Fundación Presidente Allende, which represented the victims of Pinochet's crimes, and $1 million for legal costs, and to present all evidence of movements of Pinochet's bank accounts. This organization established the Assistance Fund (Fondo de Ayuda) to provide indemnifications to victims of torture, disappearances, and assassinations in Chile, as well as to those living in exile. Forty percent of the funds would be destined to those included in the Rettig and Valech Reports. The remaining 60 percent was designated for *those not included* in the reports. With assistance from the Chilean-based nongovernmental organization CODEPU, the Fundación Presidente Allende opened solicitation between March 1, 2005, and December 15, 2005. Those who had not been included in the earlier reports were asked to fill out a form and list approximate dates of imprisonment and torture, and to provide any documentation supporting these claims. Testimonies were not solicited. The forms and supporting documentation would be reviewed by a nongovernmental executive commission.[23]

By June 2005, Ruby had heard about the funds through the network of social leaders and Communist Party members. She brought it up to Héctor during evening tea, who responded, without interest, "Well, I would know the least about this theme." Frustrated, she turned to me, asserting that Héctor had a right to the indemnification, and she tied this into their current economic difficulties. At the end of May, Ruby had had to quit her job as nanny, giving up a stable income of 160,000 pesos per month. Little Héctor had developed unexplained rheumatological symptoms. The two-year-old repeatedly broke out in a rash of purplish spots and lost weight, in spite of medications given to Ruby by the pediatric rheumatologist at the public hospital, which I later discovered were appetite stimulants. She took Héctor out of the neighborhood day care financed by Catholic charities and returned to piecemeal sewing at home so she could care for the child herself. This cut their monthly household income in half, which fluctuated between 170,000 and 180,000 pesos (USD 285–300).[24]

> If in this moment we are experiencing many needs, then I say, Well, if a part of these necessities could be covered ... Because in the end, if Héctor actually is how he is, then it was because his dedication was for other things. As his mother has said, "Héctor only dedicated himself to politics. He forgot about his studies. He forgot about his parents. He forgot about all of us, and he dedicated himself only to this, and what did it leave him?" His mother always criticizes him for that. ... As I said, if it results or not, we need to go

for it [*jugársela*]. Go for it because, in reality, this is not something you have to beg for [*limosnear*].[25] This is a right that corresponds to Héctor, understand? Like all the other persons. But Héctor is not of this personality. He's not one of those people that likes to take advantage of such circumstances. As I said to you, his uncle from Romania also said it to him: "Héctor mobilize yourself!" Because the consequences that Héctor has are a product of a government that damaged him. And if there is a form to indemnify that, then he should do it!

Héctor remained silent.

We might be tempted to interpret Ruby's demand for indemnification in light of her newly forged engagement in neighborhood social organizing and politics, marking a shift from her (feminine) waiting and patience with Héctor. But hearing Ruby's words as vindication of a middle-class liberation from a gendered domesticity seems mistaken to me. Ruby's words do not strike out from a "private sphere," claiming and gaining a life "on the street" as a political subject of victimhood. Indeed, never once did she use the word *victim*, not even in relation to gaining "benefits"; rather, she used the verb *dañar* (to damage), indexing an act of physical damage and emotional hurt, as well as an infringement on rights, the consequences of which are lived through Héctor's relations with others (see Fassin and Rechtman 2009). Thus, I hear her expressing a hope that this domestic would be inhabited differently: she was calling Héctor, in various ways, to the flesh-and-blood relations constituting this domestic. That her social organizing and political commitments tracked into the house through her words—"Héctor, mobilízate! These are rights that correspond to him"—might, however, suggest the multilayered ways in which politics and the state are present in people's lives. Here, a language of rights is a medium through which intimate relations are addressed. Thus, this language is not an escape from a domestic but rather a medium through which this domestic is transfigured.

TONES OF LOVE

Over the next two months, I accompanied Ruby as she wove her way between institutions, social networks, and family determined to have Héctor's injuries and sacrifice acknowledged, juggling her movements with the demands of work. Héctor, on the other hand, just let Ruby pursue it, for the most part, neither inhibiting nor actively helping her. Through this process, I began to hear Ruby voice a different tone of love for Héctor. Rather than emphasize the absorption of his pain (*amorti-*

guadora), she sought to awaken him to their life together. Calling him into this quest for indemnification seemed to me to call him to account for himself in relation to her and the children.

The shift was perceptible in ordinary conversation—for example, when Ruby and I chatted about relationships. I was single at the time, and Ruby would alternate between teasing me about interested men in La Pincoya, seriously warning me not to trust them, and reassuring me that I would meet someone "who shares the same values." One afternoon, swerving around some tough advice she was giving me about boyfriends, I asked her to recount to me again how she met Héctor.

Ruby said, "Ah, it's a really beautiful history." She narrated a detailed account, alternating between past and present tense, between seeing and being seen by Héctor.

I met him when I was thirteen years old. We [she and her friends] were going to a party. I dress myself up well [Me arreglo bien]. I was really thin at the time. In this party, here [I was] timid, but here a guy comes up to me, and his name is Juan. He took me out to dance [Me sacó a bailar]. But I see a thin hippie guy [*un flaco hippy*] with long hair [she points to the corner]. He walks in, in a sky blue crinkled cotton shirt. What I like the best was his smile. There were so many girls chasing after him. He didn't pick me up [No me agarró]. That same day, I dreamt about the thin guy [*el flaco*], the pretty hippie [*hipito lindo*]. I didn't see him again. Then, there was a huge protest. The young guys [*los chiquillos*] are running, and I see Héctor there. They hid in my house. He returned! The next time I see him, we are in a party. I was with my friends. They put on the song "Hotel California," and Héctor asks me to dance with him. He asked me for a kiss, and I said no, the issue is not that easy. But then he gives me a kiss. I say to him, "I recognize you, but I don't know you." But afterward, a kiss left from me [de mi salió un beso].

I remember that about Héctor. There were tremendous conflicts happening in school. I cried a lot. My parents obliged me to work [to drop out of school]. But you know, one noted that he walked in something else. I absorbed [*amortigué*] everything that was happening. So, I don't say anything, just laugh, always really positive. Afterward, things [persecution] became more intense for him. I continued waiting for him, waiting without limits. In a party, I meet his mom for the first time. He appears. They hugged, but it felt that he was a bit separated from the family. I began to *cachar* [notice/ figure it out]. Héctor began to stay in my house. Then, a trip to Cuba was arranged for Héctor [for university study in exile]. He said that he would come back and look for me. I don't know. I cannot respond. I knew what was happening to Héctor. "I see your tears. Your shining eyes" [as if Héctor were talking to her]. One lived so much with that. I have never had a partner that got so attached to me [se encariñó]. It changed my whole milieu [entorno]. "Héctor, if you had had a pretty family over there, I would stay for you [be with no other]." And now it's even more, until today. Now we are nineteen years together and I find that the love continues the same [*igual*]. I have learned to understand Héctor's situations, and I always stayed quiet. Now, no! Now, I say to him, "No po huevón! [No fool!]."

Ruby spoke of love as patiency (see Carrithers 2005): "From me left a kiss." "I continued waiting for him, waiting without limits." But now she expressed this love not only as a quiet absorbing (*amortiguar*) but also as its limit: "Now, no!" This shift, however, generated tensions between them as she sought further details of his arrests and detentions. Ruby asked him about dates. He would respond that he did not remember. She asked if she could talk to his mother. He responded that he didn't want to be bothered.

Frustrated, Ruby would turn to me while Héctor sat within earshot. "He is stuck," she said, pointing at him. "It's personal for me too," she said, remarking in a harsh tone that he was unable to find work himself. Instead, she was the one who went out *"tirando curriculos"* (throwing résumés) for him, evoking an image of throwing cards in gambling. Indeed, since I had known Ruby, she had found Héctor work either through work contacts passed to her by her relatives or neighbors or by *patronas*. She remarked how he would sit for hours with earphones on, listening to music when he returned from work instead of helping the children with their homework. But in the face of their son Davíd's need to repeat a year in high school, Héctor yelled and chastised him. "What does he expect, when he doesn't even help in homework!" Ruby said. "I don't have my primary school [have not completed primary school]. He has his *cuarto medio* [high school degree]!"

In these moments, Héctor sat with a tightened face. A feeling of the unbearable crept into Ruby's tone. If a condition of their love was her absorption, then that love might have its limit. The responsiveness that Ruby asks for, however, is not one that casts Héctor as a moral agent accountable for certain actions or compromises he made with his life in the past. She saw that responsibility as lying elsewhere: "He could have been a grand professor of sociology. This is what this government has done to him." Rather, she is asking him to see what is in front of him, to try to arrive at her present.

After much insistence, Ruby persuaded Héctor to take a weekend family trip to visit Héctor's mother, Sra. Laura, in the municipality of La Florída in the southern zone of Santiago. I was invited along. Sra. Laura had moved to La Florída from La Pincoya in 1985, five years after

Héctor's father had been killed in a bus accident. Sra. Laura and her late husband had lived in La Pincoya since 1969, when they secured a housing site through President Frei's Operación Sitio, one year before organized groups of the poor began massive land seizures (see the introduction). Sra. Laura lived with her partner, Jorge, who had a tendency to get drunk and sometimes belligerent at family gatherings. Jorge was only ten years older than Héctor, and their relationship was strained. Jorge's family did not have a history of political engagement, and he often belittled the ultraleft movements, of which Héctor's father and Héctor were a part. Ruby wanted to speak to Sra. Laura about Héctor's detentions, but raising the theme was delicate. Sra. Laura suffered from anxiety, and Héctor was particularly protective of her.

Amid this mix of affects, evening living room conversation was kept "light," talk about recently pirated movies, comical stories about children, and so forth. It was surprising then that Héctor suddenly began speaking of the *tomas* that gave rise to La Pincoya and the day of the *golpe*. The conversation moved back and forth between Sra. Laura and Héctor. One started a story, and the other would pick up a thread. Ruby and I listened.

> *Héctor:* I was commenting to Clara about the time that we were walking in the hills. It was crazy. I see bursts of gunfire below. And everyone is throwing themselves on the ground. It was an *allanamiento*.
>
> *Sra. Laura:* Yes, I was in the patio of my house, and I saw you coming down the hill, and the military was firing.
>
> *Héctor:* That was terrible. I was arriving from school, and the sector was filled with police. It was another *allanamiento*. My dad left.
>
> *Sra. Laura:* But what happened there. It was that anyone who was of the ultraleft, they killed them right away [al tiro]. It was terrible, filled with military. But Freddy [Héctor's estranged brother] had put his foot in a pot of boiling water, and your father had to take him up in his arms. It was pretext [to get out of there, to not get killed], but also to take him to the hospital.
>
> *Héctor:* Dad made a kite that said "MIR" in red, and he flew it in the *población*. The military fired on it.
>
> *Sra. Laura:* The day of the *golpe* was terrible.
>
> *Héctor:* My dad had so much rage that it was as if nothing mattered. They came burning cars. There was nothing more to do.
>
> *Sra. Laura:* Your dad went to Alameda [the central street in Santiago's center, where the presidential palace is located]. It was like an obligation he had: to defend his government. It was terrible. It was just too

terrible. . . . We found Jorge [a friend of her brother]. They shot him and then threw him in a trash can. The dogs were eating him. They were eating his body. So much hate, and they would not stop. . . . You would not imagine such terrible things. We fought without wanting to. We fought so much. And then, they detained Héctor. They had him in a storehouse [*galpón*] over there. It was psychological torture. I had to stay out there day and night so they wouldn't disappear him. "Where could they have taken him?" All the moms were staying outside.

Héctor: What? I had no idea that you were there.

Sra. Laura: Yes, and it turns out that Patricia [a young woman and friend of the family] remained there, and those [detained and remaining in the storehouse] were the first ones that resulted in death [*salieron a morir*; within their intimate circle]. And one by one they were tortured. I remember I had to go to the Vicaría [Vicaría de la Solidaridad, an institution of the Chilean Catholic Church established by Cardinal Raúl Silva Henríquez to provide assistance to victims of the Pinochet dictatorship's violence] a lot. They presented me with a lawyer when you were detained. Ruby, you need to just bring his name to the Vicaría.

Héctor: I try not to talk about those things.

Sra. Laura: Yes, we all lived with this fear. It was pure terror, terrorism. Héctor did not have to tell me he was involved. I knew when I saw him in his bedroom. He was seated, listening to Silvio Rodríguez. He got up and said, "Bye mom." "Bye Héctor." Ah, that day . . . [She begins to cry.] I was there alone, waiting for him to come back. The little girls [her daughters] were in school. I try not to see it.

Héctor waited as his mother cried, then he shifted the tone. "But we also lived beautiful moments too."

A week later, Ruby and I went to the Foundation for Documentation and Archive of the Vicariate of Solidarity in Santiago's center to ask for a certificate of Héctor's records of detention. A young woman was sitting at the front desk as we came up the stairs to the third floor. "How can I attend to you?" she asked, looking back and forth between us and her computer screen. Ruby nervously tried to explain that she needed documentation of Héctor's records because they were applying for the "funds of Pinochet." She gave the woman his full name. The woman gave her doubtful look, saying, "But he presented himself to the Valech Commission?" Ruby answered, "No, no. What happened is that Héctor sustained a very tremendous action [*tuvo una acción muy tremenda*]. It was so tremendous, and he was disappointed. So he dedicated himself to working."

Another woman walked in. The receptionist interrupted Ruby, saying: "I will attend to you after her." Ruby continued talking about the consequences that Héctor had faced in giving up his studies and his inability to hold down stable employment. The woman continued to look at the computer screen, and started typing. She was not listening. "Ja, we will ask for a certification. But, it takes a long time, two months." She started filling in a form by hand. "What do you need it for?" Ruby answered again, this time saying, "CODEPU." She continued: "He was really damaged, do you understand? Since then, Héctor has not wanted to have a political commitment with anything. He lived clandestinely. He was tortured, he lost everything. And that affects me and our children." The woman nodded. "Your address?" "Your telephone number?" "Ok, we will call you." The phone rang. The woman picked up. We left the office.

As we walked down the stairs, Ruby seemed frazzled, looking at posters on the bulletin board and reading them mindlessly out loud. I was disturbed. I commented that the woman seemed surprisingly apathetic. She responded by contrasting the rippling of pain and memory through the family with the woman's indifferent registering of the individual case: "The more registered you are, the more they make you disappear."

HEADACHE IN THE EYE

Simultaneously with her attempts to secure indemnification for Héctor, Ruby also began a search for stable work and a higher income. I want to pick up and follow this thread of economic precariousness in Ruby and Héctor's lives to trace its bodily expressions, to show how the sporadic nature of their work made regions of the past materially present. The instabilities in their daily lives manifested in unpredictable cash flow, irregular work patterns and tasks, and erratic shift-work schedules. Table 1 shows Ruby's and Héctor's employment trajectories up to June 2005.

The trajectory, however, does not allow us to appreciate the texture of daily instability. Let me turn to the layers of daily activity that made and unmade their everyday routines. In June 2005, Ruby began piecemeal sewing work in *la rueda* (the wheel). *La rueda* is a form of labor common in piecemeal sewing in which one person is responsible for only one task—for example, attaching the collar to a fine silk blouse. Contracted by a clothing company, the leader of *la rueda,* who most often lives outside the *población,* finds the workers through neighborhood connections. Workers are often not given contracts. The leader drives from

TABLE 1 RUBY'S AND HÉCTOR'S EMPLOYMENT TRAJECTORIES, 1999–2005

Ruby	Héctor
July 1999: office cleaning	August 1999–March 2003: work as a
August 1999–February 2000: piecemeal	hospital parking lot attendant
sewing	April 2003–September 2003: unemployed
February 2000–April 2002: nanny work in	October 2003–June 2005: DVD/CD
La Dehesa	warehouse inventory work
May 2002–July 2002: Hush Puppy factory	
work	
August 2002–June 2003: piecemeal sewing	
July 2003–May 2005: nanny work in	
Nuñoa	
June 2005: piecemeal sewing	

one house to the next, picking up a completed batch to give to the next woman in *la rueda*. The tempo of *la rueda* depends on the pressure exerted by the leader, but also on the women themselves. The women are paid according to the number of units finished. If one woman finishes several units, this puts pressure on the next woman to finish her task for those units within the same amount of time. If she doesn't, her piecework may be divided between herself and another woman.[26]

Ruby's first assignment was to put zippers in fuzzy pink baby jumpers, for which she was paid 100 pesos (17 cents) for fifty jumpers. Between taking care of little Héctor and other housework, she made 6,000 pesos (USD 10) in three weeks. She was then switched to sewing very fine frills into the chest darts of silk blouses. For this work she received 200 pesos (33 cents) for thirteen blouses. But, the work was painstaking, and it was new: the fabric, the type of stitching, and the placement of the stitch all required the building of experience. It took Ruby three hours to do thirteen blouses. The leader of *la rueda*, Sra. Teresa, returned the sample unit Ruby made. The frills were not done correctly. Ruby had to remove the extremely fine stitching without ruining the material, or she would have had to pay for the fabric. This task was nearly impossible. Sra. Teresa switched Ruby from sewing the frills to collars and cuffs. Ruby aimed to make 20,000 pesos (USD 33) each month, but she ended up making only 8,000 pesos (USD 13) in four weeks of work with the blouses.

Economic pressures started to build. Héctor's income of 160,000 would not leave enough money for food after covering the household expenses: the mortgage payment of 40,000, Héctor's daily bus fare, department store debts, the quotas on the sewing machine, the utility bills, and the private medical visits for little Héctor's persistent weight loss. Exacerbating the situation, the leader of *la rueda* was late in her bimonthly payments. Héctor and Ruby skipped making the June dividend payment. Ruby drank black coffee and sewed. The hum of the machine pervaded the house, beneath the *Toy Story* video that she played repeatedly for little Héctor. The child, however, often preferred to sit in Ruby's lap and cried when he could not. Hunched over, seated in the same position, looking so closely at tiny seams—sewing is extremely fatiguing, particularly on the eyes. She said, rubbing her eyes, "I can't get a rhythm."

After one month, Ruby decided to look for work "*afuera*" (outside the house), hoping that she could find a job close to home, but she feared work as a nanny. She could not imagine caring for other children while Héctor continued to have little appetite and was underweight for his age. "A daily agony," she said. I accompanied her to the Municipal Office for Labor Information (Oficina Muncipal de Información Laboral, OMIL). There she received the *tarjeta de cesantía* (unemployment card) that gave her access to the unemployment subsidy (described in chapter 2) and to the "database" of job opportunities: a bulletin board and Rolodex. Companies also called the OMIL to ask for names of those looking for low-paid, subcontracted, and temporary labor. As we walked in the street, I asked Ruby what OMIL stood for. "OMIL, OMIL. I don't know for sure. Something to do with emergency. Because not having work is an emergency, so they must deal with crisis situations."

The office was small and run down, with dim yellow lighting and several chairs. The chairs were empty, but several men and women were standing around a glass-covered bulletin board that had lists of potential employment. "Looking for domestic employee [*empleada doméstica*]. Live in [*Puertas adentro*]. 160,000 monthly [USD 268]." "Office looks for employee for cleaning, Monday, Tuesday, Wednesday, at night. 90,000 monthly [USD 151]." Ruby wrote down several telephone numbers, the amount paid, and the schedule. She made phone calls; a month passed, but no answer.

In the meantime, Héctor too faced daily instability, but because of his schedule. Héctor worked shifts. In June, he was working nights, waking up at 2 P.M., preparing lunch for himself and the children while Ruby continued working, then getting to work by 7 P.M. He did warehouse inventory until 7 A.M. and arrived back home by 9 A.M. and promptly went to sleep. The last weekend in June, he had no time off. The warehouse needed people working extra hours (*horas extras*), but the extra hours began in the morning. Héctor came home for two hours and returned to the warehouse, working until 7 P.M. The following week, he was assigned mornings again. But the assignment was interrupted when his boss suddenly moved him to nights in the middle of the week. "Me descompagina" (It unsettles me), said Ruby. With Héctor's schedule in flux, routines could not be maintained. Héctor looked tired and was unshaven. He had a perpetual spasm in his neck. Compounding the physical toll, Héctor was told to do manual labor, unloading immense wooden shipping crates of primary materials used to make compact discs. This work was not part of his contract. Three years earlier, he had been diagnosed with osteoporosis, rare for a man of his age, and suffered from a chronic lower back injury. Now he began to have severe back pain.

By the end of July, Banco del Estado sent its next mortgage statement. Ruby and Héctor owed 40,000 plus another 13,000 for interest and the late fee, and the next 40,000, making it a bill of 93,000. Other bills arrived. Bills from Johnson's and Hites department stores, Líder Supermarket, and Bansolución added up to 65,000 in monthly debt payments. Ruby said, "If I pay these bills, there will neither be money for the bus, nor money for food—nothing. So, I need to look for *pitutitos* [contacts for little jobs or work], selling music [pirated CDs]." She decided to pay one dividend and half of the monthly debt. Her sister Lorena lent her 10,000 for the month.

One week later, Ruby had a terrible headache. I met her at her house. "I have a stabbing in my eye," she told me. "I have a headache. But all in the eye. I think I will vomit. The stress has me *embarrada* [covered in mud/dragged in the dirt] from the nerves. All the time, you're with this pressure. I go to bed thinking; I get up thinking. The organism is angry with me because my mind doesn't allow me to be tranquil [*no me deja tranquila*]. The pressure is so much. There are so many people in the same situation as me, and so it's so difficult for one to fix one's situation, because all of us are in the same situation. This evil system has all of us poor people screwed" (Este sistema maldito nos tiene cagado a todo los pobres).

When the headache subsided somewhat in the evening, Ruby told me that it came from the images "recorded" (*grabada*) in her eye. These were the thoughts that raced through her mind at night and did not let her organism rest. I asked her to describe the images. She began with the image of her father suffering a stroke. "My dad began to rock forward.

It was so tremendous. He could not move. I have this image so recorded. My dad was everything." Other images followed. Her mother's vision: dead bodies floating down the canal on the day of the *golpe*. Héctor's vision: Ruby's "shining eyes" when he invited her to take a walk on the hill and told her that he had decided to stay with her rather than go to Cuba. She was nineteen years old and pregnant with their first child, Davíd. As she described the images, she pressed her hand over her eye. Through her elaborations, Ruby's "typical symptom" showed how the regions of *a* past—the violence of the *golpe*—are actualized in the present as an individual's bodily pain (Freud 1966, 335–337).

A TIME TO CRY

Two weeks later, Ruby received a call. She was offered employment as a nanny in the house of a wealthy young couple. The couple had moved into the new "suburbs" in Huechuraba, which was now being marketed as idyllic and close to rural life. The pay: 200,000 pesos (USD 336), with the promise of a contract after a test period of three months. Héctor would have to go back to day care, which, she said, "will destroy me inside."

At this point, Ruby felt that there were no other options. She took the job "*ojos cerrados*" (with eyes closed). A week into her work, Ruby awoke with swollen eyes. I arrived early in the morning to accompany her to her *patrona's* house. Her hernia had inflamed anew from the demanding work schedule and the lack of consideration on the part of her *patrones*. She recounted, "Clara, I was all dressed and ready to go home, everything was in order. I climbed the stairs to inform Sra. Nicole. She was lying in bed reading, everyone was in bed. From the bed, she points to the corner of the bedroom, and says, 'Ruby, I told you to vacuum over there.'" Ruby moved the heavy wooden armoire to reach behind with the vacuum cleaner.

After the thirteen-hour workday in her *patrones'* house, Ruby awoke with swollen eyes. She told me it was because of her dream.

> First, I saw Héctor drunk. He told me that he wanted to sleep with another woman. I said, "If you have so many necessities, then, go do it." And Héctor got up from the chair and walked out of the house. I watched him turn the corner, and thought, "This is the last time that I will see Héctor," and I began to cry. I began to walk down the street. I walked and walked until I encountered a woman and her child in the middle of the street. She said to me, "My child has died." She was sobbing, and I too cried for the woman. Crying, I

closed my eyes, and when my eyes opened, I was in a factory, where all the women were talking about an abusive boss. They worked without contracts and worked in fear. I cried with those women.

The dream evokes the breaking of the natural and the social. Contracts are ruptured. Love is betrayed. The natural generational order is undone. The historical, political, and intimate merge in allusions. The woman holds and mourns for her dead child in the street and not in the home. Can Héctor's drunken desire to sleep with another woman be read as his political involvement, and his turning the corner, the threat of him being disappeared?

Listening to Ruby's dream and seeing her swollen eyes, I do not ask *where* the real resides, nor do I position the dream as a "threshold" between wakefulness and sleep, as in the frame of a door, or see it as the image of entering an "outside" (see Pandolfo 1997). I am not prompted to conduct a work of interpretation that starts from the manifest dream to discern the latent dream that lay within her psychic being. Rather, I worry how my writing can acknowledge that dream and Ruby's tears. To find my way, I listen to what Ruby says about her swollen eyes: "Perhaps it is because all the crying was done in the dream, and not in reality, where it should be done."

What did the dream itself allow or open?[27] My sense is that it opened a time to cry, to mourn with others. In the dream, Ruby, the mother, and the workers—in contiguity—mourn this actual everyday shadowed by doubt and precariousness. They mourn an everyday in which the investment of love in a world—that aspiration for an eventual world—is not returned. Such a mourning *of* aspiration suggests how the economic and the political are deeply implicated in the possibility of a break with and betrayal of one's intimate relations. Ruby's virtual tears might be the drops of precariousness and doubt sprinkling her actual everyday.

ADAPTING

In April 2006, the Fundación Presidente Allende published a list of those who qualified to receive the indemnification. I called Ruby and Héctor from Cambridge, Massachusetts. They had not received word from CODEPU, and I offered to check the web site for them. Indeed, Héctor was listed under the victims of torture and relatives of forced disappearance and executions who did not figure in the Valech and Rettig Reports. Héctor would receive an indemnification of USD 1,206. Ruby did not bring up Héctor's pain as evidence of being vindicated. There were no dramatic gestures or words. Rather, she said, "Good, at least we can use the money to finish the *pieza atras*," their own separate bedroom that they had slowly been constructing, brick by brick, since they had moved into the house.

Héctor received the news by steering away from the topic entirely. This time, however, he focused on Ruby's election as president of the Junta de Vecinos (the Neighborhood Council) and the meetings and social events that now took place in their home. Héctor's speaking of Ruby's neighborhood activities and hopes with such care struck me, as if something indeed had changed in his *ser*. Héctor seemed to also be struck, pausing and saying to me with a bitter but also hopeful laugh, "But one must keep adapting," as if by attending to his immediate relations—Ruby and the children—an everyday life might also hold some promise.

Living next to Ruby, Héctor is finding a way to live his disappointment with this democracy, "adapting"—but not conforming—to a world that he wages his dissent in, but one that his wife now makes her own political engagements with, and one he hopes his children will lead normal lives in. The scene here is one of neither destruction nor redemption. Héctor is not disavowing this world, refusing its existence, but finding a way to live in it by the work to attend anew to Ruby and the children. Meanwhile, he hopes that he, or the grandchildren—those future generations—might one day use the word *democracy* again, that he might one day speak it in friendly accord with his world, or that his grandchildren might speak it in accord with their world.

It is in these minute shifts of a life that we might appreciate the doubt and promise shadowing intimate relations. When we move from the transcendent values of reconciliation, to the everyday, the nature of acknowledgment changes: from forgiveness for a past act, such as the accounting of a moral debt, to arriving at another's present. This arriving at another's present can be understood as an awakening to oneself and others, in which times for mourning are created and attempts are made to live together again: through absorbing death for a life together, and in acknowledging another's desire, even if doing so means a bitter compromise with oneself. With such labors of self-revelation come fragile promises for an eventual everyday.

CHAPTER 4

Neoliberal Depression

MOTHER MILITANT

"*Depresión neoliberal*" (neoliberal depression)—this is how Leticia describes her bodily pains, racing thoughts, and sleepless nights. It was June 1999, four years after Leticia had returned from exile in Buenos Aires, and four years into her state of "exile in my own country." Leticia was fifty-two years old, a former communist militant who had been exiled to Argentina in 1987. She had returned in 1995 to La Pincoya, where she had arrived as a child with her mother as part of a *toma* (land seizure) and where her children had remained during her exile. Leticia called herself a "single mother." She had been separated twice and had six children. Julieta, the eldest, was thirty-one years old at the time. (Leticia had informally adopted Julieta from her own alcoholic sister.) Julieta was married to Emilio and had three of her own children. Leticia's sons Sebastián, age twenty-nine, Jonathan, twenty-seven, and Oscar, twenty-two, were the children of her first partner, Pepe, whom she separated from in the late 1980s. Gonzalo, age twelve, and Mario, age ten, were born in Buenos Aires when she was with her then lover El Negro, a communist militant who, along with Leticia, was exiled after being labeled a "terrorist" by the Pinochet regime.

Leticia and her daughter, Julieta, were the first persons I met in La Pincoya when I arrived for preliminary research. Our meeting had been arranged through the feminist nongovernmental organization Movimiento Pro-Emancipación de La Mujer Chilena. Originally established during the 1930s to advance women's rights, it culminated with women's suffrage in 1947. The organization was reestablished under the dictatorship in 1983 as a coordinating body for several feminist organizations, with the objectives of advancing democracy, protecting human rights, and promoting equality for women. Under democracy, it was reorganized as a nongovernmental organization (see MEMCH 2010). At the organization's offices, Rosa had flipped through a yellowed Rolodex of names of *pobladoras* who had worked with the organization. She came upon Leticia's name. Later that afternoon, I called Leticia. We agreed to meet at a bus stop on Recoleta, the long, straight road that traverses the city from south to north and ends in La Pincoya.

The yellow-and-white city bus made a grumbling halt across the street from the community center. I stepped out of the bus. A plump young woman with curly, light brown hair, fair skin, and an amused smile leaned against a green iron fence across the street. She said to me, "Now tell me, you must be Clarita. My mother told me that a *chinita* was coming to visit us." She winked. As Julieta explained, Leticia had "a meeting" and did not have time to meet with me. Instead, she had sent Julieta. We walked up the street where Leticia lived. Children kicked a ball back and forth in the narrow street. A few dogs ran along the sidewalk, sniffing the ground.

Julieta unlocked the black iron gate, inviting me into her wooden shack adjacent to the main house. The afternoon fell into evening. Julieta asked me about my life in the United States. I asked her general questions about the history of the *población*. Julieta gave me more pâté on bread with cups of coffee. Then Leticia opened the gate and called to Julieta, who rolled her éyes and said, "Come." As we stepped outside to meet her, Leticia greeted me with a flood of words, barely acknowledging Julieta, who promptly turned around and went back into her shack, closing the door.

The main house had burned to the ground three months before. Several months prior, with the electricity cut because of missed payments, Julieta had asked a neighbor, Sra. Maria, to share electricity by throwing over a long cable from their house to hers. Julieta would pay a percentage of Maria's monthly bill. But exposed electrical wiring had sparked a fire, consuming the entire house and most of their belongings. Sootstained walls and a patched corrugated iron roof framed the remnants of blackened furniture. Leticia offered me tea. We sat on chairs amid the rubble. She began speaking about her children. I was pulled into knots of betrayal. "No one listens to me in this house. I speak in a language that the others do not understand; not even my own children understand me. I work for the social, and here is pure *consumismo* [consumer society/consumption] and individualism. I have *depresión neoliberal*" (neoliberal depression). With her back to the window, she did not see Julieta peeping into the living room from the patio. Julieta shook her head, rolled her eyes, smiled, and winked. I tried to concentrate on Leticia's words.

"What do you mean by neoliberal depression?" I asked her. "Ha," she said, "that takes time to explain. Do you have the time?" Over the next eight years, at times living with Leticia and her children, I began to appreciate this neoliberal depression, crystalized in that moment between Leticia's entrance and Julieta's closing door.

In the previous chapter, I explored the hopes for and difficulty of awakening to one's intimate relations in the wake of state violence, a disappointment with democracy, and ongoing economic precariousness. While Héctor made a bitter compromise with himself to "adapt" in relation to Ruby's persistence and patience, Leticia's attempt to live within the conventional world of kinship relations effected further feelings of exile. Her relations with her children not only were full of everyday slights and insults but also were pervaded with a deep sense of betrayal of the very relations of mother to children. Militancy and exile seemed to cut against the fact of Leticia's maternity. Leticia and Héctor's different struggles in reinhabiting an everyday life outline complex relations between family, sexuality, and the life of liberal political community.

Feminist scholars of Chile have extensively elaborated how reliance on women's roles in reproduction and domestic labor has been a central aspect of imaginations of political community since the emergence of the liberal Chilean state and throughout dictatorship.[1] This work complicates Carol Pateman's focus on women's exclusion from politics: that the social contract—the creation of contracts between men that establish the sovereign—is contingent upon and opposed to the sexual contract (male sex-right over women as wives; Pateman 1988). Thus, historian Heidi Tinsman's study of agrarian reform in Chile (1950–1973) provides a dynamic account of patriarchy as a "multiplicity of arrangements derived from broad principles legitimating men's authority over women" that eroded some forms of male dominance (landowners' sex-right over rural women) while strengthening others (*campesino* men as breadwinners) (Tinsman 2002, 12–13).

As Tinsman argues, Christian Democrats under Frei advanced agrarian reform both by promoting "family-centered strategies" that cast *campesino* men as breadwinners and by promoting male class militancy, thus championing male-headed families and men as political militants. Women were brought into the national process through their domestic role as mothers. While the socialist Popular Unity party of Salvador Allende sought to widen the scope of women's political mobilization, socialists still contended with "the endurance of a strong maternalist and family ethic" that figured women as future mothers. Thus, Popular Unity advanced a "double celebration" of women's class militancy and their unique roles as mothers. "This implied a double strategy of praising the ingenuity of female workers while insisting on women's primary roles as mothers and homemakers with unique capacities for love and tenderness" (p. 238). Thus, for example, *La Nación*, the state newspaper, "reserved special praise for the fact that women had 'become leaders without abandoning their home and children'"(p. 238). Such a double celebration, Tinsman argues, split women between mothers and future mothers (or female youth) who could be exempted from such "natural duties," while still perpetuating male authority over women. Thus, the failure to institute more "egalitarian and gender-inclusive policies with regard to women's productive labor, youth education and political mobilization" encompassed both the Christian Democrats and the Left (p. 285).

Tinsman's incisive critique focuses on the complex ways in which women were created and constrained as agents in relation to politics, understood as participation in political mobilization and inclusion within the labor force. I want to slightly shift this emphasis to explore how liberal imaginations of political community hinge on sexuality. Examining such liberal imaginations can help us understand the common tensions of different political parties in Chile.[2] And, further, exploring men's and women's different attachments to political community might help us see limits to an understanding of women either as being divested of agency within the domestic or as exercising it as political and social actors "beyond" the domestic. That is, it also highlights the limitations of defining agency solely in terms of a "masculine" sensibility: as a gesture of acting on the world (see Richard 1993). In light of liberal imaginations of political community, the fact that Popular Unity advanced women as militants *and* mothers is striking in contrast to, for example, providing a social category in which a woman might *renounce* her capacity for reproduction in order to pursue a (masculine) political militancy. We might then appreciate Leticia's experience of coming apart as a mother militant in relation to this complex holding-together entailed in Popular Unity's double celebration of women, as militants and mothers.

Examining child custody cases in the colonial archive in India, Veena Das elaborates how nature had to be built block by block in colonial situations. Judges' appeals to "common sense" regarding the "natural rights" of the father and the welfare of mankind rely not on a given natural body but on the normatively configured order of the family (Das 2006). These cases reveal how the symbolic weight of the father remains pivotal in liberal imaginations of political community and the place of the family within it. Within the liberal imagination, reproduction articulates rather than separates the public and private: "Once the idea of God as author of nature and time is displaced and the political body is seen as subject to death and decay, secular means have to be crafted in order to ensure that the sovereign receives life beyond the lifetime of individual members" (p. 84). Such secular means hinge on the reproduction of the population of legitimate citizens who are sexed individuals. Thus, in Rousseau's *Emile*, men and women give life to the sovereign in different, but conjoined, ways. For a man, one must be a head of a household and must know for whom one ought to die in order to be a citizen of the state. Marriage, paternity, and mortality are key aspects of citizenship.

On the other hand, "a woman's duty as a citizen is confounded with her duty to her husband" (p. 108). The woman figures as a seductress who may make the man too attached to life, but also as a mother who may prevent the man from being a proper head of household by giving him illegitimate children. Reproduction is a duty of citizenship: bearing legitimate children who "are willing to both reproduce and die for it [political community]" (p. 109). Thus, women provide life to political community through the natural means of reproduction within marriage, while men must be prepared to die, or sacrifice their lives, for the life of the sovereign. The certainty of paternity becomes a crucial aspect of political community in relation to women's duty as citizens: "the citizen's investment of affect in the political community is attested by his desire to reproduce and give the political community legitimate, "natural" children . . . [and] a woman's infidelity is an offense not only against the family but also against the sovereignty of the state" (p. 211). Das's argument helps focus us on the problematic ways in which family and state relate in the liberal imagination, complicating simple oppositions of public and private. Sex is implicated in how the citizen is attached to the life of the sovereign and, thus, attached or detached from his or her own life and death. The figure of the mother militant is tensely posed in this constellation of life, death, and the sexed citizen. How would her readiness to risk life, or die, for an eventual political community be received: as sacrifice or as abandonment?

Let me return to Leticia to consider the ways in which this liberal imagination might haunt her intimate relations. I am concerned with how the fact of Leticia's militancy and exile renders existentially uncertain the fact of her maternity: her relationship as mother to her children. And, I am concerned with *how* she attempts to relate to her children again after exile. Turning to her adopted daughter, Julieta, I then consider how and when the uncertainty of paternity surfaces in intimate relations. Throughout these descriptions, the existential uncertainties of maternity and paternity arise in the midst of enormous economic pressures and in a delicate weave of relations. Thus, rather than consider liberal imaginations of sex and political community as providing norms that are followed robotically, we may attend to the acuteness with which they emerge in life and the ways in which individuals experiment with these norms in reinhabiting everyday life. Individuals are not understood as autonomous beings arising from nature, but rather as beings already born in social relations. Individuality, then, might be understood as that singular weave of relations in which the problem of the other is planted in the self: "individuation with respect to the one upon whom my nature is staked" (Cavell 2005, 146).

LETICIA

I lived with Leticia and her family for several months over a period of three years, between 1999 and 2001, and then regularly visited Leticia and her family for the next five years, spending time with her in her home and joining her at protests, marches, funerals, and weddings. In 2002, Leticia was asked to present her biography of political involvement in La Pincoya for a cultural event sponsored by the municipality. The event, however, was cancelled. But Leticia saved the text, which she shared with me in 2004. I share excerpts of it to outline the chronology of her political involvement and the events leading to her exile. This chronology helps convey how politics shaped her subjectivity over time, but it also sketches out the dangers she experienced and the material difficulties of her return.[3]

Leticia joined the Juventud Comunista (Communist Youth) in 1954, when she was seven years old. Her mother and father were members of the Communist Party. Born in the port city of San Antonio, Leticia moved with her parents to Santiago. She married her boyfriend, Pepe, at the age of fifteen. When she was twenty-one years old, she became one of the leaders of a *comité sin casa* in the municipality of Conchalí. In 1969, she helped coordinate a *toma* (land seizure) that led, one year later, to the Allende government's provision of land titles to those families occupying the land. Between 1960 and 1973, Leticia lived what she called "an eternal spring," working as a kindergarten teacher in the national day care system. But then the *golpe* arrived:

> The happiness lasted for a short time. September 11, 1973, changed my life. I listened on Radio Magallanes to Compañero Allende[, who said] that we should present ourselves at our places of work. I with my children—Julieta, of five years; Sebastián, of three years; Jonathan, of one year—I went to the bus stop. There were thirty state buses. The day had begun with a clear sky and with sun, but slowly appeared in the sky various helicopters from the direction of Colina. One of those hit a *cerro* [hill], producing a strange and thunderous sound, but this echo did not detain me. I was clear in my commitment to the government and to the children who stayed with me in the day care.

After the *golpe*, Leticia began to face persecution in her work. She had been denounced by a coworker as a "Socialist" and was detained, along with her children, for several hours in a military office in Providencia, an upper-class municipality. After this detention, her supervisors accused her of not doing her work well, and she was reprimanded several times.

> The military officer who attended me gave me various bits of advice: "Señora, don't trust people, because the communists take advantage of good people like you, and they are violent and financed by the Russians." He told me that if I continued to carry out my work well, then I would not have any problems with the authorities. I left there with a lot of fear. I took my children out of the guard station. They let me go to my house after ten at night, although there was a curfew. With "lies," I was able to get to Alameda [the main thoroughfare in Santiago] by car, where there was a post of military officers, who, seeing me alone and with three children, gave me safe conduct. I could return to my house, although with much fear, walking from Mapocho [River] to the end of Recoleta. . . . When we were in meetings or in the office, she [the supervisor] reprimanded me because, according to her, I did not know how to do my work. . . . One day full of everything, and with rage and impotence, I walked out crying and did not come back. So that they paid my income, I had to sign my termination of contract. I already had four children.

By 1986, Leticia had joined the Frente Patriótico Manuel Rodríguez (FPMR), the armed Left movement that had been established in

1983. Through a Catholic-run polyclinic and leftist physicians, she was trained in minor surgery, or "the surgery of war." She worked in clandestine posts. At this point, her two eldest sons had also joined the FPMR. On June 15 and 16, 1987, the Centro National de Informaciones (CNI; National Center of Information), the regime's intelligence gathering agency, undertook Operación Albania, or the Massacre of Corpus Christi, an organized and systematic assassination of FPMR members that left twelve members dead. Since the "pigs" were rounding the *población,* she could not return to her house. Leticia had to begin living clandestinely, unable to see her husband or children. During those months, she fell in love with her *compañero* El Negro and became pregnant. "I remember that it was two degrees below zero. I did not return to my house; since that moment I had to constantly change locations. Portraits [of Leticia and El Negro] with the names 'Víctor and Susana' [the regime used photos for identification paired with false names] made it impossible for us to leave together." Waiting to escape, she discovered she was pregnant with their first son, Gonzalo. He was born four months after her arrival in Buenos Aires. In Buenos Aires, she and El Negro had another son. They participated in solidarity movements for Chile and experienced death threats and one assassination attempt.

In 1995 Leticia returned with El Negro and her two small sons to La Pincoya. "Upon my return to the country, I discovered with darkness that, when I wanted to go back to work, the harassment continued, and upon searching for my certificates of study and title to apply to work, I found that they did not exist in any place. For that reason, it was impossible for me, and I had to start over again, take the exams of first through eighth grade and then take the license exam in order to be able to work." By 1999, she had finished her high school requirements. But alongside these difficulties, she faced rejection by her children, who felt that she had abandoned them.

Always the Spring

"I am not a conventional woman," Leticia said to me, not with pride, but with a sense of guilt. It was 2004, and we were in her kitchen, drinking tea and eating the leftover bread that she had brought from the subsidized primary school where she worked as a kindergarten teacher's assistant. Crying, she said, "Look at all my children. Julieta did not finish high school and has remained here for ten years, and what does she do? Breathe. Jonathan lost everything and is now walking around with a girl from the municipality offices [right-wing bureaucrats], and I think he is involved in drugs. Sebastián did not finish high school and is stuck. Oscar, at least, changed. Yes, he changed. Maca [his girlfriend] has been very important for him. He is more tranquil. But the two little ones (Gonzalo and Mario), there is no case to be made. They had to repeat a year in high school. And I see all of this, and I ask myself, Why? And the only thing that unites all the children is the mother, and I say, perhaps, it was I who was the cause. I failed."

Leticia had just had an argument with one of her sons, Jonathan, who had swindled her other son, Sebastián, out of his truck, using it as collateral for a bank loan. He had defaulted on the loan, and the bank had repossessed the truck. He had called her to provide his side of the story. But Leticia told me she had already heard enough, and she chastised Jonathan: "How could you have done this? Swindling your own brother? I am your mother, and I tell you to get the truck back for Sebastián." Jonathan yelled at her through the phone: "Chhh, and now you think that you are my mother? You were never a mother for us." He hung up the phone.

His denial of her maternal relation to him affirmed her self-doubt: "If I had been a traditional mother, a conventional housewife taking care of the children, with an alcoholic husband who beat me, maybe things would have turned out different. But I fought for the social, sacrificed my children for a social fight. And moreover, it did not result. All of this fight was for nothing. I was not a conventional mother. I am a *madre soltera*" (single mother). What did "single mother" mean for Leticia?

She picked up a packet of papers on the table. While addressing me directly with her eyes, she directed her voice toward Mario. "I want to write my *testimonio*, I am writing my *testimonio*, my *testimonio* for my grandchildren, to leave something for my grandchildren." She began to cry. She shook the pages, "Son los cuentos, pero no son cuentos. No son cuentos. Es mi vida. *Mi* vida" (These are the stories, but they are not stories. They are not stories. It is my life. *My* life"). She stresses the *mi*.

She was about to begin reading to me and Mario, but she stopped. She told me to bring my computer the next time I came. She would dictate the words to me while I typed. When I arrived the next afternoon, she decided that I should first listen to her narrate. She would then have me type as she narrated the second time. Such a writing of *testimonio* differs from other testimonial narratives in which the activist, anthropologist, or journalist initiates the dialogue through probing questions (see Beverley 2004). Leticia had already handwritten her *testimonio*.

She seemed to desire a listener for her narration, or performance, a listener who would also take the time to type it into a computer and save it on a disk. Her son had just bought a secondhand computer, and she wanted an electronic version so that she could edit it herself again and again. I was both audience and scribe.

I felt overwhelmed trying to listen and type at the same time. I asked her if I could record her narration. She responded, "Ay no!" This reading of the text was supposed to be lived, not captured on tape. Leticia wanted me to listen to her voice and appreciate the feel of the words, the way in which she slid from one line to the next, and to feel the sounds and the images she evoked. I tried to both appreciate and type, sensing my failures in both. Now, I try again. Sitting at the spare wood table in the living room, she read out loud to me in her smoke-roughened voice, starting with scenes from her childhood:

> The memories hit me as if they all want to leave at the same time. After many days of intense rains, from my window I contemplate the clean sky of an intense blue, the imposing mountains with a white that blinds the gaze and gives me a sensation that runs over all of my body, like a purified energy from the soul. What first arrives to my memory is a big carousel that goes round and round without stopping. When it finally stops, from a height I contemplate the port and the sea. I feel the breeze coming toward me, I look down and see the small people that smile happily, I see cotton candy, candies, caramel apples, and my mother so beautiful with me, with her jet-black hair. Her skin is white and eyes the color of honey. I feel the unmistakable noise of the sea that I recognize even with my eyes covered, so bound to me with its green-blue color, its boats, its ships and rock piers, that today still I feel the same emotion when I contemplate it.
>
> I am full of pain and happiness because I go on a journey with an unknown destiny for me. This produces in me a grand emotion. I will get to know the city, in a bus full of people who are talking to each other. I look through the back window and how the landscape grows distant. It is night and I sleep in the arms of my mother, dreaming of the adventure that has already started. I do not have to be scared, because I am big. I am six years old, and that is many years. The arrival of the spring: with the melodious chirping of the birds that accompany me in my path, with my white dress.

In this segment, Leticia and her family were moving to Santiago. She paused in her reading, pointing out the allusion to her First Communion in the Catholic Church—the white dress.

> And the church, it is a day of festivity for me. I walk through the green vines, collect flowers, and later, with a butterfly, climbing the fig trees to collect herbs and figs. Señora Anita, friend of my mother, cared for me because

my mother needed to work. Around the brazier with charcoal lit to red, I live with oranges roasting, which she gave me for the cold of the nights, in the cold nights of the winter. The charcoal launched sparks that I felt, [the charcoal sparks were] like an accomplice in the history that sang to us: [it sang] of the long street with fig trees, that on the Night of San Juan appeared snakes, that the fig tree flowered at midnight, that there appeared a gentleman dressed very elegantly in black, and a top hat, and it was said that he was the devil in person—that, of course, was something I could never prove.

Her story ends with the Night of San Juan, celebrating the birth of Saint John the Baptist, which is observed on June 23 and 24. On these nights, the devil walks the earth, and mother earth can demonstrate unexpected powers. As the myth goes, if one can capture an ephemeral fig tree flower blooming exactly at midnight, without turning away for fear of the walking devil and snakes, then one will be happy for the rest of one's life. While the Catholic Church established the date for commemorating Saint John to coincide with the European summer solstice, the Night of San Juan coincides with the winter solstice celebration We Tripantu, or Mapuche New Year. At this time, members of the community prepare themselves for the new year by cleansing the body of the negativity of the preceding year (Foerster 1995; Traverso 2007).

For Leticia, this reading was enough for one day. She asked me to buy a pack of Nescafé. When I returned, she was asleep in bed. Several weeks later, she read the next section, which marks a different chapter in her life. Leticia wrote of the experience of her sexuality, the difficulties of moving between being a child and being a woman:

The arrival of the spring—so beautiful as always, with the peach and plum trees in bloom, with new dreams, illusions, and thinking about new adventures—also brings changes that I do not comprehend. I am very scared. I think that I will be sick, that it has hit me. What will I tell my mother? They tell me that I am a woman, that I have to take care of myself. I stand in front of the mirror and contemplate myself for a long time. I arrive at the conclusion that I am the same. I am eleven years old, and I want to be able to play and dream of stories of fairies and princesses. Between herbs and wild flowers.

Between so many laughs and happinesses, I, along with my friends, prepare a party for the spring. With costumes, floats, paper flowers, serpentines, and balloons. Mamá, I am the queen of the flowers. Along with this comes my first illusion of love. I discovered my blue prince [*príncipe azul,* or Prince Charming], more elegant than the prince of Cinderella, but the reality was much more crude. He considered me to be something like his little sister. These illusions were my first pains of love.

> A group of friends playing and growing together, we were discovering that values important to our lives united us—like loyalty, solidarity, and love above all else and for those who surrounded us, especially for the children.

As I mentioned earlier in relation to Héctor's aspirations, the *testimonio* genre can be understood as an ethical practice of the self, at once personal and collective, testifying and bearing witness to violence. Leticia's *testimonio* departs from this form of self writing in three ways, although she still calls her form of writing *testimonio*. First, her claim to her writing is that it is "*my* life" rather than a testimonial account that enacts the unique individual but also performatively extends as an account of a collective struggle. Second, the narrator's agency is not posited as a subject relating events but rather is oriented to relating impressions. Recounting her memories of being a child, Leticia relates *impressions* rather than actions: the white of the mountains that blinds the gaze and runs through her body, the unmistakable noise from the sea, her mother's eyes the color of honey, the feeling of sickness while becoming a woman. And, third, she recounts these impressions primarily in the *present tense*, as a child, in contrast to *testimonios* in which events are recounted in the past tense from the perspective of an adult.

In his elaboration of forms of self writing, Michel Foucault distinguishes between the different moral selves implicated in the epistolary account of oneself and the monastic notation of spiritual experience. Both are correspondences, but Cicero's correspondence is a decipherment of the self by the self, whereas the epistolary account of Seneca and Marcus Aurelius "constitutes a certain way of manifesting oneself to oneself and to others. The letter makes the writer 'present' to the one to whom he addresses it" (Foucault 1997, 216). This making present is very different from a correspondence in which information is conveyed *about* the writer's life and activities; instead the writer is made "present with a kind of immediate, almost physical presence" (p. 216). Thus, letters between Seneca and Lucilius relate "the interferences of body and soul (impressions rather than actions)," "the body and the days" that testify "in this way not to the importance of an activity but to *the quality of a mode of being*" (p. 218; my emphasis).

Foucault's distinctions help me consider Leticia's *testimonio* as a distinctive writing of the relation to the self. The moral mode of an "opening one gives the other onto oneself" (p. 217) in this writing presents new relational possibilities distinct from those presented by the subject of action who bears witness to violence. Leticia's writing shows the creative potential of subject and genre in a world in which *testimonio* is an available genre of the narrative of the self.[4] In reworking conventions of *testimonio,* Leticia makes herself present as a child, testifying to the quality of a mode of being-child or becoming-child. Through her words, the child's world is almost physically palpable and has a sense of shimmering, brimming potential: a vitality. Indeed, through this writing, Leticia's impressions relate a discovery of a world and self again, as a child discovers a world and self together. Who are those others whom Leticia, as a child, makes herself present to? Who could receive this *testimonio?* That Leticia reads her *testimonio* to me while writing it for her grandchildren suggests to me who Leticia imagines might allow her that "congruence" of writer and reader—that being present as a child— and with whom such being-present would have a difficult reception: her own children, whose relation with her was pervaded by betrayal.

Leticia's reading and my typing continued at a halting pace. Some days, I would arrive and Leticia would not be in the mood, lying in bed under the covers. Some days, I would arrive and she would not be at home, instead volunteering as a teacher's aid at a night high school for adults, or gone to a meeting at one of the many neighborhood organizations. Some days, she would not like the words she used and, sitting next to me facing the screen, would say, "What is the word!? What word to use!?" Other days, we would manage to enter two sentences before she would tell me to stop typing and just listen.

Without sense or reason, I found myself married at the age of fifteen. Behind, stayed my girlhood toys. They are illusions now, I am a señora; also my dreams and fantasies were reality. There was no honeymoon, neither the dreamt white dress, nor the walk down the aisle toward the altar of the church on the arm of a wished-for father. Only the love for children has remained, which grows like flowers every day. My commitment will be forever and can complete their dreams and the fantasy of offering them love and values, so that their future can be better than ours, which all of us have a right to. Hoping to have my own children, I strengthen myself, studying, making myself capable, offering the best of myself. Finally, I will be a mother. A dream long hoped for. My children arrived converted into little visiting angels, and later embark on a flight without return, like a breath that went, leaving me very alone and sad. The separation was made less difficult when I offered myself entirely to the children of my *barrio.*

The time passes without stopping, and loneliness returns to be my inseparable companion. I am a separated woman; I feel like society has hung a sign around my neck that says, "Vacant."

As if all of the feelings, the values, did not count, working without resting, fortifying the organization to achieve conquest for a society more just.

Because the sun shines everyday to give warmth to everyone, because there are no rich or poor—all of us are human beings.

The arrival of a new year brings my life the most precious [thing], my long-hoped-for dream, my son, a mountain of fat love, pink, with eyes full of light, discovering this world. He is the first of six children that arrive in different epochs of my life, filling me with happiness.

1970. At the coming out of the sun again, bigger and more brilliant than ever with its warmth that covers everyone, is the arrival of a new spring of the year 1970. Carnaval, laughs, sobs of happiness. We are respected and valued in our work, and we have rights; a New Man is born [an allusion to the Popular Unity's vision of education embodied in the New Man, a student who, through education, awakened to social problems and engaged in collective action for societal change].

My neighbors go into the street from their houses; we hug, laugh, sing. Alameda de las Delicias [the main street of Santiago, which was renamed Libertador O'Higgins after the *golpe*] is transformed into a huge carnival of costumes and dances that confuses itself with the multitude. I in my dress of Madame Spain, with the happiness on my skin, my children converted into a beautiful butterfly and a little yellow rooster with a large, colored crest. His Tata tells him, after battling a lot, that he should not let it fall, "Te voy a sacar la cresta" ["I will hit you"—a pun on the "cresta" of the rooster costume that her son was wearing and the popular expression "Sacar la cresta"]. The laughter was heard in the bus; it was a beautiful day of spring.

1971. Those were almost three years of work with twenty-five hours each day, with happiness without stopping. In this time I enjoyed marvelous things that I never imagined, like going to the cinema for the first time, entering a soda shop to serve oneself a soda "alone," buying myself pretty underwear, only for me, like those that the artists of cinema wore, having a special perfume.

The happiness did not last long.

As Leticia leaves herself as child to become mother and militant, the tone begins to oscillate. The physical intensity of relating impressions of becoming a mother flits among phrases that have an almost rote feeling when she speaks: "so that their future can be better than ours, which all of us have a right to." I notice that when she cannot find words, she finds them in ghostwritten phrases that, when spoken, have an almost wooden tone: "Because there are no rich or poor—all of us are human beings." Chronology makes its appearance—1970, 1971—indicating a successive orientation to time distinct from the temporality of relating impressions in *a* day. Being present as a mother in writing might suggest the difficulty of being present as mother in actuality, and how that being present is tied to her political commitments.

Let me return to Leticia's claiming herself as a single mother. In her *testimonio,* the male partner is absent. The single mother appears not as an image of the mother *with* her children *separate from* the absent father, as construed in the cultural symbol of the Madre-huacho, which, as anthropologist Sonia Montecino elaborates, is the syncretic symbol of the Virgin-Mother emerging from the mythic union of indigenous mother and Spanish father. This union "divinized" the mother while absenting the father and construes women as mothers whose natural duty is to care for their *huachos* ("orphans," or more specifically, "illegitimate children"; Montecino 1996). Rather, in Leticia's account, the mother appears as separate from the children themselves. Recall her words: "The time passes without stopping, and loneliness returns to be my inseparable companion. I am a separated woman; I feel like society has hung a sign around my neck that says, 'Vacant.'" I hear *separated woman* not as her marital status but rather as voicing the doubt shadowing the fact of her maternity. And when she writes that society has hung a sign around her neck that says "Vacant," I appreciate this phrase in light of her writing that her children have left her figurative womb, the "little visiting angels" who "embark on a flight without return": a picture of a breaking of relations between mother and children. Thus, loneliness becomes her "inseparable companion."

The tensions inherent in the double celebration of mother and militant are acute in her writing. As a militant, Leticia risked her life—was ready to die—for the life of an eventual political community. Yet, for her as a mother, this readiness to die—manifested in living clandestinely and exile—made it impossible to care for her children. In his genealogy of community, political philosopher Roberto Esposito suggests that community should be interpreted neither as a property or possession nor as a "mutual, intersubjective 'recognition' in which individuals are reflected in each other" (Esposito 2010, 7). Rather, community can be interpreted as a debt, "a gift that is to be given, and that therefore will establish a lack" (p. 6). Esposito suggests that what unites subjects is their gift of their subjectivity, which he defines as "their initial property" (p. 7). Considering Leticia's experience, I might take Esposito's insight and cast it differently. Instead of taking subjectivity as an initial property of a subject, we might take subjectivity as that singular weave of relations. How then might we understand the gift to be given? Returning to La Pincoya, Leticia experienced both the broken promise of community and her children's feelings of betrayal. Her children did not receive her exile as a sacrifice, a gift of one's ready death to sustain the life of political community. Rather, they experienced what was given to community as abandonment.[5] At the end of 2005, after the death of Gladys Marín, the general secretary of the Chilean Communist Party and an icon of the Chilean Left, Leticia decided that the few pages I had copied were enough. She named those fragments "Always the Spring."

Internal Conflict

In 1999, when I first met Leticia, she told me that she was living "an emotional crisis." We listened to a tape cassette of Víctor Jara, the renowned singer-songwriter who was tortured and executed by the military regime five days after the *golpe* on September 16, 1973. Leticia wiped away tears after singing along with the lyrics, remarking, "In this epoch, we were all family, to be a *compañero* was like . . . like to be I myself; we were all one, and one was all. It was a climate of solidarity, commitment, and companionship that I will never see again before I die. . . . My dreams, my hopes, my memories are all linked to an epoch that permits you to survive this emotional crisis." Four years had passed since her return to La Pincoya from exile in Buenos Aires. She said that she returned to find her children as adults, with her oldest daughter, Julieta, now married and having given birth to her first daughter. Julieta acted as a mother to her three younger brothers. And instead of returning to a more just society, Leticia returned to a Chile that had become the "model" for neoliberal economics. "Everyone lives in their own nucleus. We lived in an atomized society," she repeatedly said.

While completing her high school degree, Leticia did piecemeal sewing. El Negro found temporary work in construction. There was hardly enough cash flow to cover the monthly bills for electricity, water, and gas. They fought continually, and El Negro began to drink hard liquor and cheap wine. He beat Leticia and the children, and after one year in the house, he had an affair with a new lover and left Leticia. They separated one year after they returned to Santiago. Leticia remained alone but continued to be in love with El Negro. "He's a *machista*," she said, "but he is intelligent and *consciente*. He's made a *compromiso social*." In the face of bitter rejections from her children, she turned toward *lo social*—a commitment to grassroots social organizing and community-building—founding a neighborhood children's education organization.

By the time I met Leticia, her life was unraveling. She worked as primary school teacher's assistant by day and attended cultural and political groups at night. She spent more time in community organizing with *compañeros* of her generation than with her two younger children,

Gonzalo and Mario. Her neighbors and older children commented to me behind her back that she was "running away from her house," which had turned into "chaos" and "disorder" with her return. Even her *compañeros* began to tell her to "stay at home" rather than participate in evening meetings, after seeing her two youngest children malnourished and neglected. "Be a mother to your children," they told her.

When she arrived home late at night, she experienced shooting, prickling pains that radiated down her spine and arms. The pains were so intense that she yelled at Gonzalo and Mario when they came to embrace her. They shouted back: they hated her, they wanted her to die, and they wanted to live with their father, El Negro. They attempted to hit her, and she angrily yelled back, "Cállate!" (Shut up!), and sometimes she hit them back. Often, the two children were so frightened by Leticia's anger that they would seek help from their older sister, Julieta, hiding in the provisional shack that she and her husband, Emilio, had built next to Leticia's house.

When I stayed with Leticia, they sought my protection as well, yelling, "Tía Clara, help!" when they feared that Leticia would hit them. Grabbing Leticia's shoulders, I told her to stop, blocking her from reaching the children. Once I returned to her home to find Leticia shaken after a particularly violent outburst. She said to me, "You know, I never was beaten as a child. Now you have seen me hit Mario, but hitting him also hurt me. I never was a *golpeadora* [a woman who beats her children], and I was not brought up to be a *golpeadora*. At times, I do not know who I am."

She continued: "I feel *un conflicto pa' dentro* [an internal conflict]. Perhaps if I had not left the country, if I had been a mother to the children, then they would not fight with me. And maybe they would be more committed to remembering. Of course, I feel guilt, but they also mistreat me. Just today, Julieta mistreated me. Mario mistreated me. Oscar mistreated me. Julieta thinks only of her family (her husband and their three children). They don't share. And look at Oscar, he's twenty-two years old and he acts like he is fifteen." She then asked me: "Do you see a *familia integrada* [a close-knit family] here?" I responded, "Here? Here, in this house?" "Yes," she replied. I hesitated, hoping to forestall judgment, not knowing quite what to say. She replied impatiently, "Obviously, no. Look, everyone here is *en su lado* [off on his own]. I work for *lo social* [the social] and here, in my own house, everyone is alone."

A few months after that explosive outburst, Leticia and I took a bus trip to the *cordillera,* the Patagonia mountain range separating Argentina and Chile. We sat on a snowbank that looked toward Argentina. She told me then that she continued to look toward the *cordillera,* somehow hoping that her former life of political commitment, a life that to her "made sense," would return to her from "over there."

Disorientation

In 1999, Leticia was diagnosed with severe depression in the local primary health care center. She was referred to the Psiquiátrico (Psychiatric Institute), where she was given a prescription for fluoxetine. She did not take the medication, but hoped to "rebuild" her relationship with her two younger sons through family therapy sessions offered at the local Center for Community Mental Health. She reflected, "Perhaps if there is someone who helps us to communicate with each other, we would understand each other better. And my children would understand why I fought and why I keep fighting for the social." After waiting several months for an appointment, she finally met with a young female psychologist. The prescription: stay at home with your children and act like a mother. Leticia again fell into an "abyss of guilt," and this guilt further amplified her hold on the idea of "the social."

This inner experience of conflict could be understood as an incongruity between the inner life and her outer world. Neighbors, *compañeros,* and psychologist offered a vision of healing as returning to oneself as a mother: she should invest affect in her children. Yet her children had difficulty receiving that affect. Recall her son Jonathan's words: "You were never a mother to us." In her older children's eyes, she had abandoned them through her exile. This abandonment put the very fact of her maternity in doubt. And her attempts to relate to her children as their mother were met with fighting and anger, denials that threatened to destroy her very sense of self. Let me emphasize: seeing Leticia as somehow "failing" to be a mother, as disregarding her children to pursue a fantasy of "the social," does little more than assert normative assumptions of what a mother should be, and it unwittingly asserts a givenness to men and women's different attachments to political community. In a fissure between the demands of the everyday and the loss of a political project, Leticia's despairing attempts to rectify "the social" and "the family" led to a multiplication of everyday violences (Kleinman 2000). Such violences amplified her feelings of perpetual exile, and she reached the threshold of losing herself.

In 2004, when she was writing her *testimonio,* Leticia began to experience bouts of disorientation when walking in the city. She would not know where she was or how she got there, and could not remember her name. Leticia's sense of self was foundering. It was as if the once significant markings of her life's sensibility were lost, and she wandered without the means to acknowledge the here and the now. Her memories seemed to form a "virtual being" (see Bersani and Phillips 2008, 86), but they threatened to exile her from her actual everyday: "The memories hit me as if they all want to leave at the same time."

On one occasion, Leticia recounted that she had been walking in Santiago's center. "I was so submerged, thinking and thinking, how could things have turned out so differently. I felt the joy, the happiness, the sun's rays of that time on me. And then, I looked up to the buildings, and it gave me panic. My heart was beating fast. I was sweating. So much sweat. I was thirsty. I turned around and around, and I was looking at the stores, standing in the middle of Paseo Ahumada [a central, pedestrian-only street lined by stores]. A policeman came up to me and said, 'Are you OK, do you want some water?' He bought me a bottle of water and told me to sit down on the bench. He asked me my name, and I could only say, 'I am lost . . . Where am I? Who am I?' He said, 'Calm down, señora, calm down, you are here.' And he put his hand on my shoulder, and I started to cry, and then I began to remember that I am Leticia, and I am from La Pincoya." The once life-threatening policeman had now turned into a figure who helped her remember this world.

Domestic Economies

But even as her sense of self was unraveling, Leticia remained tethered to it through the domestic economy: the need to pay bills, loans from *compañeros,* and debts to department stores and supermarkets. These economic demands were shaped by the affective configurations of the domestic.

After she financed a local children's cultural group on her income of 90,000 pesos (USD 150) per month, Leticia's money vanished before she could buy bread for her two youngest children. She gathered the remaining leftover and discarded bread from the public school where she worked to feed herself and her children. She assumed the monetary debts of a communist *compañero* as an act of loyalty, although this meant her own debts went unpaid. To cover them, Leticia asked her ex-lover, El Negro, for a personal loan to buy a sewing machine. She told him that piecemeal sewing work could add 30,000 pesos a month to her budget. Instead, she used the sewing machine to start a microenterprise to sell girls' sweatpants in the local market, and bought the fabric on credit. However, her partnership with two other women in La Pincoya fell through. Between her other work and her political commitments, Leticia did not have time to sew her quota of sweatpants. Bolts of fuzzy material in blues, greens, and yellows littered one corner of the house.

One month later, Leticia joined another microenterprise, selling liquid detergent from her home. Plastic bottles full of green liquid filled the front windowpanes. She put a can on the windowsill to keep track of the money earned from selling detergent. But soon she lost track of the earnings, drawing money out of the can whenever she needed to go to the corner store for bread or milk. When she had finished selling off the last of her detergent, Leticia found that she did not have enough money saved to buy the supplies necessary to produce and sell her product. And without this source of income, she was unable to pay back the loan from her ex-lover.

Leticia never directly mentioned the extent of her indebtedness to me, and when I did manage to ask her about her monetary debt, she would answer by criticizing *"consumismo"* (consumerism) and the political economy of facile credit that was "suffocating" the *población*. She would point to her children, "Look at Julieta, spending money on cable television when she herself is out of work. And Oscar, who cannot pay his monthly quotas on a new camera that he did not need."

During my previous stays with Leticia and her family, I was able to gather only a partial account of her debts from her son Oscar and through my role of warding off repeated calls from various creditors, who told me how much she owed them. Oscar too was uncertain of the depth of Leticia's indebtedness. He underscored the gravity of the situation, however, by observing that her income seemed to disappear the minute she received a paycheck, even as monthly bills remained unpaid. In 1999, he remarked to me, "Where does the money go? No one really knows. But I am sure that she is struggling *pagando las letras*" (paying the monthly quotas). I asked Oscar why Leticia would not tell me about her debt. He responded, "It gives her shame. Imagine, she cannot even tell me, Oscar, her own son, how much debt she has. Can you imagine how it would be to tell you? . . . It gives me shame, too, to tell you about her debt." For Oscar, the confusion over these debts tied into his sense that Leticia was not capable of being a mother.

While Leticia and Oscar experienced shame over her debts, Julieta expressed a mix of resentment and loyalty. Leticia's debts hung over the house like "the witchcraft of bad vibes." With water, light, and telephone bills outstanding, the debts that hung on Leticia had Julieta, her daughter, "hanging by the neck." When Julieta was two years old, Leticia had found her starving and abandoned by Leticia's sister. Leticia had raised her since then. Julieta told me that she was "the only poor fool who will stand with her mother until the day she dies." Nevertheless, to Leticia, Julieta was a disappointing, apolitical consumer. As she said, Julieta wore ideology like trendy clothing bought in the market. She participated in protests against Pinochet only when they were *"de moda"* (in style), and she was more interested in *aparentándose* (creating an image of wealth above one's material means) than in improving the situation of herself, her family, or the community. Leticia told the neighbors that her daughter walked around with *"la cabeza lavada"* (brainwashed); and she chased Julieta's friends away from the house, calling them *ordinario* (coarse, ordinary) and *consumista* (consumerist). Leticia remarked numerous times that Julieta "never pays the bills" and, instead, spent her money on toys for her children. "Imagine, Julieta bought a toy for 12,000 pesos [USD 20] and is paying weekly quotas. The man from the department store comes to the house to collect the payments, but Julieta has not paid in weeks, and I am the one to lie and tell him that she does not live here." She sighed. "But what can I do Clara? She is my daughter."

Yet, despite these slights and insults, Julieta said that she owed her life to Leticia and was indebted to Leticia's vision of the social for her own existence. Julieta paid rent to Leticia for occupying the one-room shack that she and Emilio had built on Leticia's site. Nevertheless, despite the rent payments, Leticia had on several occasions demanded that Julieta pay the monthly utility bills or leave the house with Emilio and her children. Julieta had scrambled to find extra money. In the winter of 2000, for example, Leticia asked Julieta once again to leave the house if she did not pay the outstanding electricity and water bills. Julieta sat on her bed with tears in her eyes, telling me that she felt "trapped" within these four walls. She was frustrated that Leticia gave away her own income and Julieta's rent payment to "all things social" before paying for the family's basic necessities. In contrast to her brother Oscar, Julieta attributed Leticia's vanishing income not to her perpetual indebtedness but rather to her overcommitment to, or compulsion for, *"lo social."*

Yet, even with the added burden of monthly bills, Julieta told me that she did not feel *"rabia"* (rage) toward her mother. Rather, she felt *"culpable"* (guilty) and said that "Leticia gives me pain." Julieta believed that her mother was advancing these monthly ultimatums not only out of economic desperation but also out of a desire to test her loyalty. As Julieta said, "She knows that I will always be by her side; she knows that she can always depend on me. So she does this only to bother me."

When Julieta could not manage to pay the outstanding bills, the water, electricity, or telephone was cut. Gossip about Leticia having "gone crazy" ran up and down neighboring streets. Among her neighbors, some said that Leticia cared more about "the social" than her own children, much to Julieta's shame. After days without either electricity or water, Julieta, at her wits end, reluctantly would ask her mother-in-law, Rosa, who lived across the street, for a loan. But, Rosa too was struggling, with two of her daughters addicted to *pasta base* and no other source of income save her son's work as a cook. Rosa frequently offered to bring lunch for Julieta's children. She remarked to me that the children should not go hungry at the cost of paying the bills, but she could do no more.

When all else failed, Julieta would visit Don Alejandro. A local butcher and shop owner, he was the local campaign point man for the municipality's right-wing mayor. In exchange for a promise to campaign for the right-wing party, Julieta got a meeting with the mayor. As a result, Leticia's bill payments were postponed and basic necessities reconnected. To Julieta, the exchange of local political support for debt relief posited neither Julieta's nor Leticia's leftist political views against the mayor's conservative politics. "No estoy ni ahí" (I couldn't care less), she told me. In distinction to her mother, Julieta evoked a popular saying, "Today for me, tomorrow for you" (Hoy por mí, mañana por tí), and argued that this was the only politics one could live by in *today's* Chile.

JULIETA

Julieta's account of her relation to herself took shape through this complex mix of resentment, loyalty, guilt, and care for Leticia. "Leticia *talks* about exile, *hueveando* [making nonsense], but she never *really* was exiled," Julieta told me. Throughout the time I spent with Julieta, she repeatedly told me "not to believe Leticia's suffering." She warned me: "Leticia was not a mother. She left me to be the mother, and then she comes back here, crying, and I pay all of her debts?"

Julieta told the story of Leticia's exile in an entirely different light: in light of the domestic damage extending from Leticia's absence and return. According to Julieta, Leticia fell in love with El Negro while she was married to Julieta's father, the father of Julieta's three younger brothers. Before their exile, she had an affair with El Negro and was pregnant with their first child, Gonzalo. During this time, El Negro was arrested and tortured. He was forcibly exiled to Argentina in 1987. Leticia decided to leave her family and follow her lover. Julieta says that she was the only one in the house who knew about the affair and Leticia's pregnancy. When Leticia did not return home from work that day in 1987, Julieta knew that she had "left us abandoned" and took it upon herself to tell her father the news of her mother's affair. Leticia's abandonment and Julieta's knowing silence so angered Leticia's husband that he stormed out of the house, never to return.

The children were left to manage on their own and only heard about their mother through her *compañeros*. There were promises that she would send for her children, but none were fulfilled. As the eldest, Julieta found work as a live-in nanny to support her three brothers and herself. She recounts her work, *"puertas adentro"* (live-in employment), as degrading and dehumanizing, a time in which the *patrón* (boss) attempted to rape her and then violently beat her for resisting his sexual advances. During this time, the oldest of her younger brothers, Jonathan, became a leader of a Frente Patriótico Manuel Rodríguez cell in La Pincoya, and after Leticia's departure, their house became a site of intense police vigilance. Under this extreme political and economic pressure, Julieta took responsibility for the economic and moral well-being of the home. As she said, "I paid the bills, and *saque la cresta* [beat up] any of my brothers who got into trouble." She compared herself to Leticia: "When I was running the house, none of the *cabros* ["kids," referring to her younger brothers] were taking drugs. If they did, I would beat them up, and they knew it. But now, look, Oscar is addicted to *pasta base*, and Leticia just turns a blind eye. This *huevón* [idiot] is *medio loco* [crazy], and Leticia says nothing."

When Leticia returned, she could not accept Julieta as mother of the younger children. Leticia attempted to reinstate herself as the moral authority of the home and to make the children accept her lover, El Negro, as their own father. When Leticia told Julieta to call El Negro "father," she refused and told her younger brothers to refuse as well. "Leticia kept slapping my face, telling me to say 'father,' but I refused, just stayed silent. Is this *huevón* related to me? No. He's only her *com-*

pañero. It's her business. I would not say it. She gave up, and my cheeks, they were red, red from the slapping, for days."

The housing site was then physically divided in two, with Julieta and Emilio in a provisional shack constructed on the site's patio, and Leticia, El Negro, and the three older boys and their two half brothers taking the primary house. But the affective divisions were more ambiguous. Julieta said that she still maintained her position as moral authority. As she said, "All of my younger brothers, they come to me when they need advice. Jonathan came to me with all his worries before he was going to marry his wife, Fanny. Did he talk to Leticia about his worries? No, he came to me because he trusts me. And Oscar, he comes to my side of the house when he loses another job and is in trouble. Does he talk to Leticia? No. None of them depend on Leticia. They all know that she is *media loca*" (crazy). Julieta then went on to negate Leticia's relation to her as a mother. "Look, I never saw Leticia as a mother. She is more an *egoista* [selfish person] than she is a mother. She expects everyone to give to her, crying about how she has no money, how she is so depressed, but she gives nothing to us in return. If I could, I would live apart from her, *cada uno pa' su lado*" (everyone in his place).

Since Leticia's return, the house had been filled with suspicion. Julieta remarked that Leticia's abandonment of the children and her desperate commitment to *lo social* had corroded their relation. "How could she just leave us *botados* [thrown out] and come back and lie about her exile?" Although she said that she still felt indebted to Leticia, she could not be receptive to her stories of suffering.

Let us turn our attention to the ways in which paternity, seduction, and militancy emerge in Julieta's narrative. First, the intensity with which Leticia desires her older children to call her lover "father" seems to express a desire to secure paternity when paternity itself is colored by betrayal. Second, embedded in Julieta's denial of Leticia's pain is her denial of Leticia's militancy. In Julieta's narrative, Leticia abandoned her children because of the seductions of a man, a lover with whom she bore illegitimate children. She did not abandon her legitimate children because of a readiness to die to give life to political community. Rather, the man was both seducer and militant. Leticia did not suffer exile, only he did. As militant, he made his sacrifice. However, as seducer, his claim to paternity in *this* domestic had to be enforced rather than embraced. In Julieta's account, the mother militant is written over: "Always crying about her exile. You have to get used to it and don't let it affect you. *Me acostumbré* [I got used to it], and now I let her talk and talk."

Julieta's narrative of Leticia's exile bears traces of the articulation of sex and political community in the liberal imagination. In her narrative of intimate betrayals, paternity, reproduction, and mortality emerge again as key aspects of the troubled relations between family and state. Julieta's lived relations to her husband, Emilio, and her children, too, bore traces of this articulation. But these traces manifested differently. These differences suggest attending to the problems of sexuality and political community as they emerge in actual lives. Therefore, this ethnographic engagement is not *about* how paternity and maternity figure in Chile in general; instead, it responds to the uncertainty of *this* mother and *this* father. Let us consider the weave of relations in which Julieta's subjectivity took shape. Julieta's relationship with Emilio was itself shadowed by betrayal. Emilio, she said, was a *"sinvergüenza mujeriego"* (a shameless womanizer). Friends and neighbors urged Julieta to leave Emilio. Leticia urged Julieta to "kick him out of the house." "This is a woman's house, Julieta, not a man's," Leticia remarked. Yet Julieta continued to stay with Emilio. When I asked her once if she loved him, she hesitated, then replied, "Look, I do not love him. I cannot say that I love him. I can say that I have *cariño* [affection] for him. . . . You know that his mother, his sisters, and brothers live across the street. If I leave him, what would I do? All of them would be against me."

Monthly Psychosis

"It's a *psicósis mensual*" (monthly psychosis), Julieta told me, speaking of her worry over the arrival of her menstrual period each month. It was March 2004. Her period was a few days late. She was anxiety-ridden, hoping that she was not pregnant. Julieta had four children, three of whom lived with her; the eldest lived with her grandmother in the port city of San Antonio. Julieta and Emilio had been married for more than a decade, and their relationship had become embittered. As she said, "He has done nothing in the house. The only thing that he does well is breathe."

Their domestic life suffocated her, even as she attempted to maintain it. And she challenged it by running up against everyday habits of female decorum. Julieta dragged a bench to the gate of their patio and drank beer in plain view of the street. She used cuss words liberally between puffs of smoke. She told lewd jokes and scolded her husband in front of others. Neighbors were both frightened of and drawn to Julieta. With her sharp wit and even sharper tongue, she told things as they were.

"Al pan pan, vino vino" (As bread, bread; wine, wine), they said. Julieta fantasized about leaving Emilio. She wanted to someday save enough money to leave him and take the children with her. She spoke of going to France as a domestic worker and earning enough to buy a house for herself and her children in Santiago upon her return. She watched French films on cable television, associating Spanish subtitles with the spoken words.

At the time, Julieta was working as the caretaker of an elderly woman in an upper-class sector of the city and earning minimum wage. She had a small wooden box where she hid money. She showed me her reserve of 60,000 pesos (USD 100), the amount she had saved for a plane ticket to France. But with Leticia constantly demanding money to cover the monthly bills, Julieta would lose the little money she could save from her work. She told me that the house was a "black hole," where one entered and was trapped in a "mental paralysis." "I don't know, Clara," she said. "It's as if we were all in a boat, and I am the only one who is rowing; but I row and row, and we get nowhere." I asked her why she did not just leave Emilio, reiterating what her friends and neighbors said to her. "It's not so simple, Clara. Who would take care of the children if I go out to work? Right now, I depend on my mother-in-law. Leticia does not take care of the children, and I cannot leave them at home *botados* [thrown out] like she left us. Anything can happen here. Daniela [her oldest child] could get abused. If I leave Emilio, then I lose that support."

She added, "My mother always tells me to leave Emilio. She tells me that he is a good for nothing. But at the same time, she tells me to pack up, and leave the house. So I am trapped. What do I do? Sometimes, I feel that there is a spell cast on this house, a spell so that you cannot escape. There is no exit from this house. It's always the same: going in circles in the same space." Indeed, the house itself had an agentive force. The complex matrix of debt, guilt, and resentment was the house's atmosphere, which was palpable to all who entered. As Ruby, their neighbor, once said to me, "It's awful in Sra. Leticia's house. I feel like the house is choking me. I try not to stay long." Julieta said that, in reality, she would only be able to leave this house—to escape this thick glue of affects—when her children were grown. Another pregnancy was out of the question, unimaginable but nevertheless feared every month.

Julieta nervously waited for her period to arrive. A week passed, then two weeks, and then three. She bought a home pregnancy test. She was pregnant. Devastated, she told me, "Me cortó las alas" (It cut off my wings). With her youngest child out of diapers, she was finally feeling "a taste of freedom." She remarked, "I cannot go back, cannot go back to being caged in the house," referring to the time when her three younger children were infants. Through her tears, she told me she would still go to France, and would *juntar plata* (save/accumulate money). "I will study," she said, "and travel." She told her mother-in-law, Rosa, who advised her to *tirarse pa' arriba* (keep going, keep moving up). Her sisters-in-law said, "Didn't you take care of yourself?" blaming her for the pregnancy. "I didn't do it with my finger," she remarked. "It takes two; why are they just saying, 'You, you, you'?" She mentioned that she was taking birth control pills and feared that the antibiotics that she had previously taken could have limited their effect. But "no one believes me," she told me. With sadness and rage, she said, "And in this country of shit, *machista,* you cannot even have an abortion. They make you have a child if you are poor. Country of shit." I asked her how Emilio reacted to the news of the pregnancy. "He didn't say anything, just shrugged his shoulders and said, 'Bueno.'"

Abortion constitutes a "crime against the family order and public morality," according to the Chilean Penal Code, and a woman who "authorizes or consents" to one can spend one to three years in prison (Herrera Rodríguez 2008).[6] While therapeutic abortions were legal beginning in 1930, as designated by the Health Code, the Pinochet regime revoked this law, specifying in the 1980 Constitution that the "life that is about to be born" also has rights and guarantees as a legal person. Simultaneously, the Chilean Catholic Church, responding to Pope John Paul II's conservative agenda, increased its involvement in politics, putting direct pressure on legislators to make decisions based on their faith (Blofield 2001). Because of abortion's illegality, the only statistics available on the prevalence of abortion in Chile is based on postabortion hospital admissions. From this sampling, it is estimated that between 40,000 and 150,000 abortions take place per year. The maternal mortality rate from abortions since 1990 has been estimated at ten deaths per year (Szot M. and Moreno W. 2003).[7] While upper- and middle-class women can pay for an illegal abortion in a private clinic, many low-income women resort to backstreet practitioners who may have little or no medical training.

Julieta told her *patrona* that she was pregnant. She was a wealthy elderly woman with ailing health, and Julieta took care of her at night from 8 P.M. to 8 A.M. At first, her *patrona* wanted to fire her. But because Julieta had already signed a contract, her *patrona* could not fire her without infringing on the *ley del embarazo* (a law that protects women from being fired on the basis of pregnancy). Julieta explained, "But she's going to try to bother me, *me huevea* [fuck around with me], over and over until *me aburre* [I get bored] and I leave. She's already started." She said the worst consequence of losing her job would not be the money, but rather the loss of freedom, that freedom from the "cage of the house." Julieta was supposed to have the baby in late November or early December 2004.

Silent Debt

One week later, I was with Leticia. We had just finished taking evening tea, and I was going to accompany Julieta to Santiago center, where I rented an apartment. Julieta would continue to the *barrio alto* (the rich sector of the city), where she worked. As we walked to the door, Leticia told me in passing that her daughter "lost her baby," intimating that Julieta had had an abortion. We stood in the street outside the patio's black gate. Manuel, Julieta's middle child, was hanging onto his father's arm. Emilio was obviously drunk and was trying to shake off the child in order to grab Julieta. Leticia and I had just stepped into a fight. Leticia grabbed Emilio. "Let her be, *huevón!*" He ripped his arm from her. She grabbed it again. "You stay away from my daughter. You stay right here, and let her go to work," Leticia yelled at Emilio. Emilio pulled his arm away and shook his fist at her. "Chhhh. Leave us." Julieta began to walk down the street, and I followed close to her. Emilio followed both of us. Leticia yelled from the house, "Leave her be, Emilio!" Manuel cried, and I turned around to see Leticia scoop him up and take him into the house.

> *Emilio:* I will drop you; no, I will drop you off at your work. You are cheating on me.
>
> *Julieta:* I am not what you think, I am not a slut, you are drunk. No, go to the house, go, go.

Emilio's eyes were bloodshot. His shirt hanging out of dirty black jeans, hair tousled. His breath and his body smelling of beer.

> *Emilio:* No, I will drop you off.
>
> *Julieta:* Cree' que te pongo el gorro, eso es que cree' tú, huevón. [You think that I cheat on you, that's what you think, idiot.]

We walked in silence to the bus stop on Recoleta, the main street that runs to the center of the city.

Julieta: Go to the house. Go and take care of the kids, go to my house.

Emilio: No, no, you are cheating on me, I will drop you off.

Julieta: No!

Emilio: Why?

Julieta: Because you are drunk. You are drunk, Emilio; you give me shame. You cannot walk with me in this condition, fucker.

Emilio: I will drop you off. I know it, that you are screwing with [cheating on] me.

Julieta: You have to respect me. I am not your child, I am not your child. I am not cheating on you. You are drunk. You will not get on the bus. You will not. I will call the cops.

She crossed the street to where there was a police truck and stood in front of the truck, but did not talk to the police officers. I tell Emilio, "Talk about this tomorrow, Emilio, when you are tranquil. You can't talk now. Why are you thinking this way?"

Emilio: Clara, one realizes, one knows when you are being screwed with. Why does she not tell me? Why does she not tell me that she is with someone else? Why does she not tell me now?

Clara: I don't know, I don't know, Emilio.

Julieta crossed back to us without having spoken to the cops.

Julieta: You will not get onto the bus with me, *huevón.*

Emilio: I saw you, I followed you in the truck, and I saw that you did not get off the bus, you did not take the other bus.

Julieta: What? And when you screwed me over [when Emilio cheated on her]? I didn't follow you. I am not a slut. I am not your child.

Four buses passed. We took the next one. Julieta boarded the bus with Emilio right behind her, but she paid only for her own ticket. I boarded after Emilio and paid for my ticket. The woman collecting the money said to me, "He needs to pay," pointing to Emilio. I replied, "But he's not with me." The driver stopped the bus, saying, "Compadre, you have to pay." Emilio said to Julieta, "Pay for my ticket." Julieta refused. Emilio reached for Julieta's bag, but she held it against her chest. The driver intervened. "Hombre, you have to pay or get off." The woman collecting the money said, "She's a woman, you have to respect her."

Emilio replied, "She is my woman; she has to pay." Julieta said "No" firmly, eyes directed forward. "We'll go to the cops, then," said the driver. He returned to driving. With the bus speeding, we fast approached the police station on Recoleta. Emilio again demanded that Julieta pay the bus fare. Julieta said, "They will put you in jail, Emilio." "Clara, give me three hundred pesos." I replied, "No, I won't do it, Emilio."

When we arrived at the police station, the bus stopped. The driver, his friend, and the woman came to the rear of the bus where we were seated. The police officers signaled: "Open the back doors." The driver said, "OK, amigo, you have to pay or get off." Emilio again replied, "She is my wife, she needs to pay." Two officers boarded the bus, saying, "Pay or get off." Emilio reiterated, "She is my wife, she has the money." The two cops replied, "But if she does not want to pay, you have to pay. Pay or get off." Emilio attempted again to grab Julieta's bag. Again, Julieta held on tightly. The two officers grabbed Emilio. One of them put him into a headlock, the other was pulling his torso off of Julieta. The friend of the driver was trying to wrench the bag out of Emilio's hands. The driver pushed Emilio out of the bus. Finally the bag was wrenched out of his hand. The bus driver returned to driving. I switched seats to sit next to Julieta, and we watched as the officers dragged Emilio into the police station.

The bus rumbled toward the city center. Julieta spoke softly. "Huevón. No estoy poniendo el gorro [Idiot. I am not cheating on him]. . . . Y tener otro cabro chico con este huevón, tú sabes, tú cachas [And to have another child with this idiot, you know, you understand]. La vieja me pagó para hacerlo, pero tuve que encalillarme por un año con ella. La vieja pagó todo. No podía." (The old woman paid me in order to do it, but I had to go into debt with her for one year. The old woman paid for all of it. I could not do it.) My gaze shifted from the street to her face. She had teary eyes, continuing: "Me siento tranquila" (I feel tranquil). She looked out the window, wiping away tears, saying, "Un año no es nada en comparación con una vida" (One year [of debt] is nothing in comparison with a life.) I winced as I reached for her hand, and held it until we reached the stop where she switched buses. She waved goodbye, telling me to visit her again soon.

A week passed. I visited Julieta. She and Emilio were sitting around the table in their shack, smoking cigarettes and drinking tea. She joked wryly with Emilio about what had happened. Now, rather than sitting around with no job, she remarked, he would have to work two jobs to pay off the fine levied by the police. They laughed and continued to joke that Emilio now was *"encalillado"* (owed a debt) to the police. Emilio said, laughing, "Tengo que firmar todo los días que estoy pagando mis cuotas" (I have to sign everyday that I am paying my quotas). Emilio had to go to the police station periodically because he was paying the fine for public disturbance in installments. This scene revealed the different domestics experienced within the house. While Emilio and Julieta could talk about and joke about the economic pressures generated by his debt to the police, Julieta's debt to her *patrona* silently circled between Julieta and me through exchanges of knowing glances.

As Julieta and Emilio continued to joke about debts, the conversation shifted to Leticia. Julieta showed me some bills in Leticia's name that they had found: 50,000 pesos (USD 90) owed to Almacenes París department store, 30,000 pesos (USD 50) owed to Líder Supermarket. "And she tells you, Clara, that I am the one who is spending the money. All the bills from the department stores are in her name. And at the end of the month, the same *hueveo* [ridiculous situation] will occur, and she will make me pay the bills," Julieta said with an ironic laugh. "Who is the most indebted here?" she asked.

Only several months later, in November 2004, did Julieta again mention the abortion. She had just finished paying off the debt to her *patrona's* husband. Three months earlier, her *patrona* had died. Julieta had attempted to revive her through CPR, but to no avail. And with her death, Julieta was again unemployed. But she still had to pay monthly quotas to the *patrona's* husband for the remaining debt. She began to sell off old clothes from her household, calling it "spring cleaning" (in English), and made enough money from that and from selling their stereo to pay off the debt. She spoke while ironing her children's school uniforms on a yellow-felt-covered board. Although she had tears in her eyes, she laughed, saying, "You know, it's ironic, I paid off the debt nine months later. I would have had the baby now." She turned silent and continued to press a pair of pants, lifting them up, neatly creasing them, and smoothly turning the iron over them again and again. She asked me to hand her the next pair of pants. Then, together, we folded the ironed clothes into neat piles for the next school day.

Exploring women's testimonies about abortion in Chile, anthropologist Susana Herrera discusses both the disjuncture and intensified relations between institutional and ecclesiastical judgments, and the complex affective knots women experience after undergoing abortion (Herrera Rodríguez 2004; Herrera Rodríguez 2008). "For many this experience is their enormous secret and their enormous affliction, because many experience abortion as something contradictory, so that they hide it in their private histories in order to protect themselves from aggression, stigmatization, shames, and judgments of which they could be an object, since this is a situation they never thought they would live—an extreme and violent situation in which they assault and are assaulted. Victims and perpetrators of an action that many cannot forget or pardon" (Herrera Rodríguez 2008, 606).

But framing experiences of abortion in terms of victim and perpetrator itself discursively inscribes abortion solely within a particularly circumscribed legal and ecclesiastical imagination. This imagination relies on an opposition of public and private, and on agency construed in relation to a willful autonomous subject who must take responsibility for actions. Responsibility is interpreted as an interiorized sense of guilt and shame, and these feelings become "private histories" sealed off from a public sphere. This framing becomes acutely problematic when attending to the experiences of abortion within a weave of relations. And further, it may obscure other ways in which a liberal imagination might be haunting Julieta's experiences.

Let us return to that difficult scene in the street. I want to draw attention to the nature of Emilio's accusations. For Emilio, the abortion provoked uncertainty about Julieta's fidelity: he accused her of cheating on him. I might venture that what was at stake in this uncertainty, and in the rage that was manifested, was Emilio's paternity. Paternity was itself rendered uncertain, and this uncertainty could potentially extend to his relation to his children. The liberal imagination haunting these affects is not one of men as autonomous beings who emerge from nature and have authority, or sex-right, over women, but rather one of men as fathers, a scene of social relatedness.

The stakes for Julieta, however, were different. Julieta could not imagine having another child. This despair was articulated in relation to Emilio and his kin. While she desired to separate from Emilio, she depended on her mother-in-law and sisters-in-law across the street, who helped her in moments of economic scarcity and in caring for her children when she went to work. Her despair was also colored by the fact that she felt she could not rely on her mother, Leticia, whose exile and militancy made her experience of maternity existentially uncertain. In this ethnographic description, abortion can be displaced from a liberal discourse that posits it as a fight over choice, and over ownership of one's body, and instead can be understood as the struggle over relations: a bodying forth of relations in which those relations are at stake.

Following the abortion, suspicion fell over Julieta's fragile domestic relations. Julieta's silence and remarks can be understood in light of this suspicion and the need to keep her world intact. Keeping this world intact meant a delicate work of inhabiting the everyday: folding the laundry, picking up the children from school, while silently paying off the debt to the *patrona*. Moved to abortion by her intimate relations and her aspirations, she now lived in an atmosphere of suspicion that made vulnerable her place within those relations. Neither a trope of resistance nor an assertion of male domination seems helpful in acknowledging her silence. Rather, I receive her silence as a heightened attentiveness to the relations that her existence was staked upon, relations that the abortion shadowed in doubt.

THE NEST

In March 2005, I received a call from Leticia asking me if I would like to accompany her to the funeral for Gladys Marín, the secretary general of the Chilean Communist Party during the dictatorship, who had gained respect from many sectors of the population for her commitment to the working class and her unyielding fight for social justice. In La Pincoya, people of both the Left and the Right mourned her death.

In September 2003, Marín had been diagnosed with a brain tumor, and she had passed away on March 6, 2005, after several rounds of experimental therapy in Cuba. Two days later, the government, the Communist Party, and several other leftist political parties organized a public funeral and procession for her. Leticia and I met in the center of the city, in the mass of more than half a million people who were mourning Gladys Marín's death. The largest public march that the country had seen since the end of the dictatorship, the procession was a collective outpouring of both grief and discontent. Leticia was in tears and barely able to speak. Like many others, she was dressed in black, and we walked down the street holding hands. We were accompanied by her son Gonzalo, who tied blue-, red-, and white-striped ribbons marked with a small black band around our upper arms. We reached the Cementerio General, where her body was buried, and where Guillermo Tellier, the vice president of the Communist Party of Chile, and several representatives of Cuba and Vietnam made speeches.

The sun beat down on us, and familiar faces walked through the crowd. Leticia saw her ex-lover, El Negro, who was standing nearby with his wife. We walked farther down the street and sat on the curb while listening to the speeches. Leticia turned to me. "Something in me has died. Our *compañera* has died, and we have all died with her too." She was exhausted from the sun and from the tears. I accompanied her back to her home, where she climbed the stairs to her bedroom and laid down in bed. I made her tea. On her desk, I noticed boxes of alprazolam and fluoxetine and asked her if she was now taking medication for depression. She told me she had seen a new psychiatrist at the Psychiatric Institute, who had given her the prescriptions. The psychiatrist, upon looking at her medical file, had remarked, "You have quite a file." Leticia said, "I sometimes think, does everyone see me as crazy? And then this doctor points out my file . . . " Written on the prescription was the diagnosis "chronic depression with anxiety." I asked her if she would take the medication, or if, as she did six years earlier, she would seek psychotherapy. "I don't see a psychologist, because things have not changed in the family, so what can I do? I only take the pills to sleep sometimes, but I forget most of the time." The medications provided little solace for her existential pains.

A few weeks later, Leticia called me again and asked me to accompany her to San Antonio to meet her mother, Mama Ana. Mama Ana and her husband, Tata, lived with Leticia's oldest son, Sebastián, his wife, and their two children, as well as Julieta's oldest daughter. "You have never met my mother, in all these years, and you must meet her before she dies. She is very sick, I told you that before," Leticia said. We agreed to go over the long Easter weekend. I arrived at Leticia's house and saw Julieta packing up her belongings. "What is happening?" I asked her.

Leticia had decided to sell the house in La Pincoya, Julieta said, and return to San Antonio to take care of her ailing mother. "But where will you go?" I asked her. Her eyes reddened. "I talked to my mother-in-law. She has a room in her house, a small room, where we will have to stay for a few months. After that, I do not know." I was shaken. Leticia heard my voice. She yelled out that we should hurry up and catch the bus. I said good-bye to Julieta, hugging her. I so hoped to see her when we returned from San Antonio. En route to the bus station, I asked Leticia about selling the house, and she confirmed that she was indeed selling it. I asked her about Julieta: "But what will happen to her?" She responded, "I can't keep Julieta in the house forever. She needs to *independizarse* [become independent], and maybe the only way is for her to get out of this house as well."

We arrived in San Antonio, a port city looking out onto the Pacific

Ocean. Mama Ana and Tata lived in a small wooden house seated on the top of a hill.[8] Their street curved to a view of the ocean. The air was clean. The streets, full of sand. Small wooden houses with wood fences lined the street. Occasionally the sounds of a puttering car punctuated the ocean waves and the wind from the hilltop. There was no sound of large buses roaring on city streets. Instead, rickety buses painted blue, green, yellow, and red moved about San Antonio's center. We were out of scorching hot, dry Santiago.

We took the bus up the hill to Mama Ana's home. Leticia spoke of moving to San Antonio and noted that she was moving to the ocean instead of looking to the *cordillera* (which signified her exile). By coming back to live with her sick mother, she remarked, she would live her own final days in peace. She told me that, if her own children had negated her, and if her dreams for a just society had failed and died with the death of Gladys Marín, then at least she could take care of her mother during the last years of her mother's life. Once we entered her mother's humble wood house, I sensed that Leticia had indeed changed. She still spoke in the same rushed way, with a similar overflow of words, filling the space. But there were more pauses. She stopped to watch a movie. She laughed more. She took a nap. She drank five cups of tea in the afternoon and played with her grandson Diego. She told me to go to the waterfront with her son Sebastián and grandsons Diego and Javier.

I remarked that she seemed much more tranquil, and she agreed. "Is there a time when we want to come back to the *nido* [nest]?" Leticia asked me. In the years that I had known her, this was the first time that I heard her speak of changing her relationship to "the social." "It is the difference between looking toward the *cordillera* and looking toward the sea. And the waves that continue to go out to the horizon, a different horizon," she said to me. We sat on the bank of the road that offered a view of the ocean. The breeze lifted her short gray-brown hair. She continued:

> I think that I have a debt with my mother for having abandoned her for so much time. . . . I did so many things for other elderly ones; I did so many things for other neighbors, for other people, but I did not do the same for my own as I should have done. And now I do not know if I will be able to remedy the bad that I did. I do not think so, and this makes me feel very bad. I wish I would have given my children a family that I did not have. . . . I think that coming back to San Antonio is like coming back to the nest after a whole life of being far, not only to be with my mother, but also just to be . . . to feel the noise of the ocean, feel the breeze, the tranquility. . . . I think that I still have things pending in my life, wounds that I have to heal and things that I have to do.

Inhabiting a world seemed imaginable for Leticia here, with San Antonio's different horizon. I am reminded of her *testimonio*. The quality of a mode of being-child that her writing made present, a mode of relational possibilities. In this turn to the nest, Leticia found herself as a daughter rather than as a mother. Her relation to her children remained a disarticulating experience. In a repetition of the question she had asked me when I first came to live with her, she said, "I do not know. You, knowing us, for the time that you have known us, what opinion do you have of us as a family? I think that for you, we are not a family." "Why?" I asked her. "Because we all walk on different paths in all directions; no one is concerned for the other, and a family is a whole. It is not only to share the good moments but also the bad ones." I paused and responded, "I don't know what to say . . ." She looked out at the ocean.

Several weeks passed after our magical trip to San Antonio. I visited Leticia again in La Pincoya to see when and if she was still going to sell her house. At the door I yelled, "Leticia! Leticia!" The house was quiet. No children were running around behind the black iron fence surrounding the patio. I entered the house with the extra pair of keys that Leticia had given me years ago and climbed the stairs to her bedroom. She was lying in bed, and her breathing was labored. She greeted me, telling me that she had "bad news." "I'm sick," she said, and related to me how one of her lungs had "collapsed" shortly after our trip to San Antonio. She had woken up at night, unable to breathe. For one week, she had lain in bed with no assistance, without her children noticing that she was not well. Her son Oscar was spending more time with his girlfriend, Maca, and was rarely at home. Her two younger children, Gonzalo and Mario, now teenagers, had decided to live with their father, El Negro, after Leticia told them that she was going to sell the house. Julieta, Emilio, and their three children had stayed in their shack and had not visited Leticia since she had told Julieta to move out.

A colleague from the primary school where she taught had discovered Leticia, unable to get out of bed. The colleague had been sent to find her and ask why she had not appeared for work for the past week. Leticia was taken to the hospital, and she stayed there for several weeks. She felt she was at the end of her life. "I feel it," she said. But now, ailing, she would not spend her final days with her mother, and she would not sell the house. She remarked that she now wanted to live out the rest of her days "alone in my house and in peace." When I arrived and noticed that the house was so still and quiet, I had thought that perhaps Julieta had indeed moved. When I saw Leticia, I asked her if this was the case.

She responded, "I don't know. She can stay here if she wants, as long as I am alone in this house. I do not want to fight anymore."

Later that week, however, her son Oscar and his girlfriend moved back into the house to take care of Leticia. As Oscar said, "I am trying to change my relationship with my mother. Before, I escaped with drugs. I was out on the streets. I cannot say that my mother was a good mother to us. You understand what happened, Clarita. . . . You know"—he paused—"it's complex. I have so many *sentimientos encontrados* [conflicting feelings]. But Maca told me that we should go back and take care of her. Maca is good for my mother. She is not like us [the children]. She listens to her, but she can listen because she does not have our history. It's difficult. I don't know what more to say. Leticia is my mother."

PASSAGE OF TIME

Months later, Oscar and Maca got married at the civil registry. A wedding celebration followed at the house. I helped Leticia in the kitchen as we prepared *cazuela,* a soup of chicken, carrots, potatoes, corn, garlic, and cilantro. Leticia worked slowly, leaning on the counter when she felt fatigued. But even with her ill health, she said she was content, laughing and smiling while the others took pictures of our cooking preparations. Leticia's mother and stepfather, Mama Ana and Tata, arrived, despite Mama Ana's ill health. Oscar's brother Sebastián and his wife, Dani, along with his younger brothers, Gonzalo and Mario, brought boxes of wine.

Oscar's father, Pepe, Leticia's first husband, also came, much to Oscar's surprise and happiness. This was the first time that Leticia had seen Pepe since 1987, when she had boarded the bus to Buenos Aires. Oscar insisted that I take a picture of himself between Leticia and Pepe, both of them awkwardly half-smiling. Despite their awkwardness, they hugged and joked about how aged the other looked. It was as if there was nothing more they could say. Time had worked itself into their separation. We toasted the couple in the patio with champagne.

Yet, while the festivities went on, the uncomfortable presence of Julieta's closed door framed the scene. Leticia told me to knock on her door and tell Julieta to join the celebration. In her pajamas, Julieta opened the door and ushered me inside. I asked if she wanted to join the celebration. She said, "No estoy ni ahí [I couldn't care less]. I was not even invited. Oscar did not invite me, because I accused Maca of stealing my money. Maca does not sit well with me. She spends all of her time with Leticia, listening to her. And I ask myself, why does she do that?" But, just as she invited me to sit down, Oscar knocked on the door, pleading with Julieta to come out and at least greet her grandmother. Sighing, Julieta opened the door and stepped out into the celebration in her pajamas. Oscar handed her a glass of champagne, which Julieta held in her hand without drinking. She sat down next to her grandmother for the next few hours, holding her hand, in silence.

CHAPTER 5

Community Experiments

MUNICIPALIZATION

2001. I am taking the yellow-and-white city bus from Santiago center back to La Pincoya. The bus is stuffed full of people returning from work. A young woman invites an older woman carrying a large plastic sack to take her seat and rest. Tired bodies and sleeping heads bump against the bus windows for almost an hour. We cross Américo Vespucio, the highway that encircles the center of Santiago, and continue down Recoleta, the main road to La Pincoya. As we enter the *población*, to our right is the old police building, widely remembered in La Pincoya as a site where torture was carried out. To our left, the Consultorio La Pincoya, a primary care center, and the Centro Comunitario de Salud Mental, the Center for Community Mental Health, or COSAM.

The walls of the buildings are covered with graffiti. Broken windows and an unhinged main door at the COSAM speak to years of under-funding and neglect. Physicians at this center are mainly from Bolivia, Ecuador, and Cuba and are aided by a few Chilean interns who rotate through for educational purposes. They attend patients who wait for hours in line for an appointment. Primary care physicians refer the patients with complex medical cases, such as cancer, severe mental illness, or a need for a surgical procedure, to secondary and tertiary institutions. But patients often wait months or even a year to see a specialist. Stories are commonly told of a relative, friend, or neighbor who "died waiting for a referral." In the COSAM, psychologists—who burn out rapidly and are replaced year after year—attend patient after patient with depression, anxiety, drug addiction, and alcohol dependency. The COSAM is so understaffed and serves so few in the *población* that many families I work with in La Pincoya do not know of its existence. And if they do, they have waited several months for an appointment. The inequality of access to timely medical care and mental health services established as a result of previous state violence seems concretized in the two rundown buildings opposite the police station.

Since the Pinochet regime municipalized primary health care services in 1981, local health care institutions have become sites where municipal needs, constraints, and local political interests meet the technical norms and political interests of national health programs. Under Pinochet, the municipalities, which were governed by appointed mayors, and the Ministry of Health bore uneven administrative, technical, and financial roles. The Ministry of Health effectively handed down technical guidelines and norms that were to be fulfilled by primary care workers. These health care professionals were no longer considered civil servants but were contracted by the municipality and were considered, under the Labor Code, to be private employees.[1] Municipalities were reimbursed for services rendered based on a fee-for-service list that privileged curative over preventive services.[2] Because the real costs of operation often exceeded reimbursements, municipalities had to make up the deficit with their own funds.

In 1992, as elected mayors assumed their posts, the Concertación government sought to both expand and contract municipalization. The Ministry of Health attempted to reassert its central supervision of health services, at the same time that municipalities continued to be largely responsible for fiscal deficits under a new system of per capita payments (Gideon 2001). Primary care workers were placed under a labor code different from that of other municipal employees. As political scientist Mary Rose Kubal remarks, municipalization yielded a "hybrid decentralization" entailing "limited political decentralization, no fiscal devolution, and increased administrative centralization" (Kubal 2006, 127). Yet even as municipalities had to respond to the demands of central government and depended to a large extent on the centralized disbursement of funds, municipalities developed political cultures and allegiances that conditioned the local life of national programs.

Ethnographic engagement with specific lives can reveal how state institutions and discourses of the social and moral debts of dictatorship are folded into everyday life. In the previous chapters, I described the difficulties and hopes entailed in being present to others, and how the self is simultaneously enmeshed in multiple relational modes in everyday life. I have also attempted to consider lives in their singularity. Thus, rather than make general claims about neoliberalism or liberalism, about men and women in Chile, I argue that engagement with specific lives reveals both traces and subtle reworkings of conventions and norms. I also argue that the ways in which we attend to lives in time is important. Thus, rather than take discrete moments in a life and generalize them over the course of a life, and rather than make general statements about decision making within poor families, I have sought to attend to process in life—to moments in their specificity—and what such different moments might reveal about care and its limits amid economic precariousness.

Now I turn from an engagement with specific lives to an exploration of the national rollout of a community mental health program for depression. This national program for the diagnosis and treatment of depression was part of a broader effort to pay the "historical debt" to the population after dictatorship. But, much like the engagement with specific lives, ethnographic description of this program's unfolding in La Pincoya reveals the singularity of community mental health experiments and the variability of intervention. Rather than take for granted that national programs progressively standardize diagnosis and treatment and thus respond to (and create) common problems, we might instead consider historian Harry Marks's insight that standardization is a *problem* precisely because variability is the norm (Marks, personal comm.). What forces are revealed in engaging this experiment in La Pincoya?

Over the course of the democratic transition, mental health researchers and state officials sought to epidemiologically map the inequalities in mental health care produced during the dictatorship. And, in response to these inequalities, they designed a randomized-controlled trial for the treatment of depression in low-income populations, which became the basis for the National Depression Treatment Program. Integrated into primary care, this program advanced community participation and decentralization. The life of this program within the municipality gives us a lens through which to view the paradoxes of decentralization and the conditions for community that yield divergent therapeutic trajectories.

MENTAL HEALTH'S HISTORICAL DEBT

In 1993, the Mental Health Unit of the Ministry of Health released the National Plan for Mental Health. This plan advanced a decentralized and community-based mental health care network to address the psychological sequelae of political and economic repression that the Chilean population had experienced in the previous two decades. According to the Ministry of Health: "The social and political changes that lead to the recuperation of democracy in the country carry with them a sharp perception, by the whole of society, of the interaction of political, economic, and repressive situations and the interaction of social coexistence with the manifestations of psychological suffering and psychosocial problems" (Ministerio de Salud 1993, 3).

This national plan resonated with regional and international mental health policy, but was not necessarily defined by it. In 1990, the Pan American Health Organization's Caracas Declaration called for "the restructuring of psychiatric attention to Primary Health Care and under the framework of alternative models centered in the communities and within their social networks" (PAHO 1990, 3). Ministry of Health officials explicitly drew from this regional emphasis on decentralization and community mental health initiatives to further epidemiological research on common mental disorders in the Chilean population. The specificity of this historical moment and international health policy converged.

In a review of epidemiological studies published in 1993, epidemiologist Rubén Alvarado points out that no large-scale epidemiological studies had been performed between 1967 and 1991. Indeed, the scarcity of epidemiological data on the mental health of the population during this period went hand in hand with the almost total debilitation of community mental health, or intracommunity psychiatry, under the dictatorship. Under the leadership of Dr. Juan Marconi of the University of Chile, intracommunity psychiatry had gained a foothold in the university from 1968 until 1973, and had a lasting influence on a generation of psychiatrists who trained with him, including those psychiatrists in the state mental health unit and the academy.[3] Its core concept was "cultural relativism," which drew from anthropology, social medicine, and sociology in treating alcoholism in the community. It challenged traditional psychiatric practice by moving outside of the psychiatric hospital and into the community, and for that, it was sometimes charged with being "unscientific" (see Mendive 2004). Community leaders, psychiatrists, social workers, and epidemiologists would address together the psychosocial problematics identified by the community itself.[4] This incipient movement in community mental health ended abruptly with the *golpe,* at which point psychiatry returned to being a hospital-based practice.[5]

By 1993, only one epidemiological study had been published on common mental disorders in the southern city of Concepción. Alvarado concludes by outlining the challenges facing epidemiological research in mental health in Chile:

1. The necessity to use actualized diagnostic criteria, based in current classifications (DSM III-R or ICD-10), along with methodologies that permit an assurance of greater integrity of the information (techniques of sampling; standardization of instruments, in particular their validity, which would assure their good verifiability); and a well-done statistical analysis.
2. The utilization of instruments of international use for studies of population prevalence, which would permit a transcultural comparison (Alvarado 1993, 137–138).

Such standardization and modernization of epidemiological research would permit the planning and evaluation of systems of mental health services throughout the country. These systems were, at the time, "characterized by their scarcity." Their "development was not governed by long-term planning, [they were] disarticulated from the rest of medical attention, provided little coverage, [were] oversubscribed by the population, had low efficacy for an important portion of the problems and little evaluation of their interventions" (p. 140).

Indeed the use of internationally accepted epidemiological methods and disease criteria was crucial in providing a scientific basis for renewed community mental health programs and assessing their efficacy. This scientific basis would counter claims that community models for mental health were "ideologically motivated" and therefore not based in sound medical or public health practice. As psychiatrist Carlos Madariaga reflected in 2005: "The community model in psychiatry and mental health is supported in a solid joining of premises coming from the biomedical sciences as much as from the social sciences, and has contributed direct benefits to the clinic, to epidemiology, to psychosocial interventions, to prevention programs and rehabilitation, etc. We reinforce this concept because of a recurrent critique of its social and community focus, coming from a biomedical perspective, that this only deals with ideology, and that it lacks a scientific basis" (Madariaga 2005, 52).

In 1995, psychiatrist Ricardo Araya conducted an epidemiological study for the Ministry of Health that measured psychiatric morbidity in twenty-three primary care centers in Santiago, the first of its kind in Chile. Previous studies, he argued, had not used "internationally accepted epidemiological instruments and methodologies to measure the levels of mental disorders in primary care," and thus "the estimated prevalence has fluctuated between 14 and 60 percent, depending on the methodology used and the population studied" (Araya 1995, 4). Employing internationally accepted instruments, Araya found that the prevalence of mood disorders in the population who used primary health care services was 52.5 percent with the General Health Questionnaire, a screening tool for mood disorders, and 57.3 percent with the Clinical Interview Schedule—Revised, a diagnostic tool for mood disorders. Women were found to have a much higher prevalence of mood disorders than men, and the probability of suffering a mood disorder was "intimately linked to situations of marginality, unemployment, low income levels and education" (p. 10).

Such research led to larger studies of the prevalence of common mental disorders in the population, using international diagnostic criteria and epidemiological methods. Between 1996 and 1998, a team of Chilean researchers based at the University of Chile led by Araya and Graciela Rojas undertook the largest epidemiological survey of common mental disorders in Santiago to date, surveying more than eight hundred thousand people in Greater Santiago. Using ICD-10 diagnostic categories for comorbid depression and anxiety disorder, anxiety disorder, and depressive disorder, the researchers found a 25.1 percent prevalence of psychiatric morbidity, with the prevalence of women twice as high as that of men. The prevalence was significantly higher in groups of men and women with low income, unstable or no employment, low educational levels, and low-quality housing conditions. The results were published in the *British Journal of Psychiatry* in 2001 and again in 2002, in Chile, by the National Service for Women (Araya et al. 2001).

The epidemiological data provided ample scientific evidence to argue for intervention at the population level. In April 2000 the Mental Health Unit of the Ministry of Health released the National Plan for Mental Health and Psychiatry, remarking, "The State has a historical debt with the mental health of the population; because of that, to make the National Plan for Mental Health and Psychiatry progressively a reality is a challenge that the country and its authorities [will] assume through the sectorial actions by public health [agencies]—and, as it corresponds to a modern and commonly shared and committed state, it will combine resources and intersectorial actions together with the active commitment of the whole society" (Ministerio de Salud 2000, 7). The Ministry of Health's Mental Health Unit, in conjunction with academic psychiatrists and epidemiologists, had mapped out the "historical debt" with rigorous methodologies, using internationally accepted criteria that would allow for comparisons with other countries.

As a pillar of this mental health care network, the Ministry of Health's Mental Health Unit had launched a pilot program for depression to improve detection, diagnosis, and treatment in primary care centers. Based on a community intervention study carried out by psychiatrists at the University of Chile and the University of Bristol, the program integrated the treatment of depression into primary care services. Psychologists, social workers, and nurses were trained to lead "psychoeducational group intervention" sessions for patients diagnosed with depression according to ICD-10 categories. In six such sessions, patients were to learn about the causes and symptoms of depression, as well as learn cognitive behavioral skills to cope with depressive symptoms. Primary care physicians were trained to adequately manage basic pharmacological treatments consisting of fluoxetine, imipramine, or amitriptyline. Patients were given a free supply of antidepressants for a minimum of six months.

In 2001, the program was under preliminary evaluation by researchers from the University of Chile's School of Public Health. By 2003, the program was initiated in La Pincoya. When I returned to La Pincoya in January 2004, I hoped to track women longitudinally through the program. What I discovered, however, was a tense entanglement of municipal politics and health services, made even more acute by the fact that it was a municipal election year. Insecurity, fear, resentment, and frustration circulated among the local mental health workers and municipal health officers, affects in which I too became caught up.

MUNICIPAL ELECTIONS

"The elections are coming," my friends in La Pincoya told me. It was February 2004. In nine months' time—in October 2004—municipal elections would be held throughout Chile, and the political campaigns of the center-left Concertación parties and the right-wing Alianza parties (an alliance between the Renovación Nacional and the Unión Democrática Independiente [Independent Democratic Union]) were already apparent on the street and in the media. In La Pincoya, the current mayor, Carolina Plaza of the ultra-right-wing political party, the Unión Democrática Independiente, had already set in motion a populist campaign that involved visible markers of "civic progress." Palm trees were planted at the entrance of the *población* and outside the old police station. Hanging above the almost completed police station—a five-story green-and-white building that would house an additional two hundred police officers—was a banner with a picture of Carolina Plaza wearing a hardhat and carrying a shovel. Alongside the picture: "Inversión 1.000.000 pesos. Cumplido." (Investment 1 million pesos. Finished.) Underneath, the slogan read: "Huechuraba te quiere a tí" (Huechuraba loves you).

The primary care center was repainted, the graffiti covered over. A new, bright white illuminated sign hung above the main entrance with overlaid pictures of a physician looking through a microscope and a physician examining a child. Along Recoleta, the main road, the mayor had begun a "beautification campaign," planting grass and rose bushes along the sidewalks, where previously there had been only dirt and scattered refuse. Billboards of Carolina Plaza's smiling face were placed every few blocks. Referred to as "Lady Di" by many in La Pincoya, she was called the "media picture of beauty": blond hair, slim, and a smile with perfect teeth. And she was intensely popular in La Pincoya. Many had banners of her hanging above their houses; others wore yellow T-shirts printed with "Carolina te quiere" (Carolina loves you). At the same time, rumors and resentment fed rancor between neighbors of opposing parties: "She is giving people who vote for her a box of food"; "She put 50,000 pesos (USD 90) into every savings account of those who are applying for municipal housing"; "bribery"; "buying votes"; "The people are so manipulable"; "She is only concerned with the visual; to her it's all about images."

In these circumstances, my proposal to observe group sessions in the primary care clinic—which was accompanied by supporting letters from the Ministry of Health's Mental Health Unit and the director of the Health Service of the Northern Metropolitan Region (SSMN)—stalled in the municipal bureaucracy. My follow-up phone calls to the director of the health area (the director of all health services within the municipality) were not returned. I could not undertake the work unless I had site permission. In the meantime, I attended a meeting of local health activists and health promoters at the SSMN, which oversaw the implementation of health programs and services in the municipalities.

In a large conference room, health monitors and activists discussed the tensions between the state and municipalities. A health activist from La Pincoya stood up. "What we can say is that, in Huechuraba, and in many other places, the municipality is run like a small dictatorship! We think that we are in democracy, but the state does not reach the people. In the field of health, the municipality controls everything, instills fear in the people, because they depend on the municipality for health!" "But what can we do?" asked another activist from across the room. "We complain and complain, and yet we propose nothing!" The room fell silent, and after a strained and awkward pause, the subdirector of the SSMN suggested we take a break.

"SCHIZOPHRENIC SYSTEM"

After several weeks, I received a phone call from a psychologist who directed group sessions for the depression treatment program in the Consultorio La Pincoya. By chance, while discussing her late paycheck with the municipal director of the health area, she had seen my proposal on his desk and had quickly written down my number. She had heard "rumors in the primary care center that there was this student from Harvard who had been blocked from doing her research." She asked to meet with me in her apartment.

Paula was a young and energetic woman in her late twenties. She lived in Las Condes, a wealthy sector of Santiago, with her husband, who worked as an investment banker. Greeting me at the door of their fourteenth-floor apartment, she lit a cigarette. She was petite and thin. We sat down in her living room. On one wall was a framed print of *The Last Supper*. Next to it hung a dark-wood-and-gold crucifix. Leaning down to the coffee table, she lit a stick of incense perched on a porcelain Buddha figure. She told me, "Well, I don't know what to say. But I saw your proposal and heard the rumors, and I wanted to help. Tell me, what do you want to know about the program?" Surprised, I told her I had assumed that most municipal health workers would not want to speak to me, given that it was an election year. She answered, "It's paranoia, Clara. The director of health runs things like a dictator. He's authoritarian. You know, the directors of the primary health care centers and the COSAM are scared. They are scared of losing their jobs, because he keeps his eye on them, and he hires and fires at will. . . . Paranoia. What I see is that there is much rancor between the organization of health care workers with a leftist tendency and those in the municipality who are on the right. . . . To me, what do I care of politics? But, in your case, politics has much to do with it, Clara. That is what I think. My reasoning—really my own. I have not spoken to anyone about this."

She laughed ironically and put out her cigarette. "So, if they fire me for talking to you, then they fire me. I earn nothing there and receive no help. The only reason I do this is because I want to do something good for the people. I am not doing this for the money and not for politics either." Paula had been working in the program since March 2003, when it was extended to La Pincoya. Although frustrated and resigned, she continued to work in the program. "Every day when I come home, I think of quitting. But then I think to myself: I am the only psychologist there [in the primary care center]. The patients know me, trust me. I can't leave them." It was her Catholic conscience, she said.

Turning the conversation away from my own difficulties, I ask how these tensions affect the program itself. Her discontent was obvious as she paused and lit another cigarette. "I have a lot to say about this." She began by criticizing the lack of continuity in the staff, and the "bureaucracy" within the municipality. "There is a lot of rotation. I am one of those who have stayed, and I began only one year ago. The program started three years ago in other primary care centers. So, what happens with this program—if there is in fact a program—you need to adapt it to the primary care center, to the reality of the primary care center and the reality of the director, and those municipal officials, and the culture of the people, and whatever political current is the priority in that municipality. . . . The hierarchical part is not easy, because I arrived with the assumption that the director of the primary care center would be in charge of making decisions [*cortar*] and had an opinion. But you have the mayor, this director of health, there is a technical chief and another director in the municipality. So it turns out that you have to go through all these other people, understand? I am not so ambitious or idealistic as when I arrived. One is accustomed to the private system, where things function—you know—with money. But here, it cost me much to understand that there was much bureaucracy, that there were personal interests, political interests, and ta, ta, ta."

Paula expressed a view that was frequently expressed to me by conservative elites, that the market is value neutral and operates autonomously from the state. She saw herself as working in the public system for a few years while she established her private practice. Yet her remarks on the payment schedules and visible goals of the program elucidate challenges to the program's municipal life. As she remarked,

"I feel that I am involved in an absolutely schizophrenic public system, absolutely schizophrenic, this whole system." I asked her to describe what she meant by this "schizophrenia," and she described her first year:

When I arrived, I isolated myself a lot. I heard, "Not much money here," and I had to make the photocopies [of group session materials] for my patients from *my* [home] computer, with *my* ink [she emphasized]. Do you understand me or no? In this period, cautious. Later, I came to know more and said, "No, this does not correspond to me." [Printing materials for the program at home is not something I should be paying for or doing.] They don't have any idea. No one has any idea, no one has any idea. The basics, understand me? I tell you something: they have not paid me. January, February, not even March [for three months of the year 2004]. Well, I went to complain various times, and today, because I was firmer and arrived *con la pluma parada* [a coarse phrase that means "fight like an Indian"], I got an explanation: "Well, this happened when you entered the program." I entered in March of last year, and it was June, and still they had not paid me. And let me emphasize to you, I had recently arrived and didn't comprehend much of how things functioned, how things go here. It turned out that the money passes from the government to the Health Service North [the SSMN], the Health Service North passes it to the municipalities, the municipalities pass it to the primary care center—and that can take a lot of time. And yes, well, the Health Service North demands that you meet three goals. It fixes a goal in June, another in September, another in December. This means: "I don't know how you will do it, but meet the goal that I asked for. You find a way to reach the goal." For me there were a million obstacles.

At the beginning they [the municipality] kicked me around from one primary care center to another, from one side to another. [They would say,] "No, it's that there is no place for a psychologist here, or because there is no psychologist there." Kicking me around this way and that way.

Paula vented her frustrations one after the other. First, she was baffled that the local primary care center did not have the "basic" capacities for photocopying and printing available for the psychology staff. Second, she was frustrated by the delays in her pay. She sought an explanation from the director of health, who responded somewhat wryly by telling her that she should expect such delays: "This is what happened when you entered the program." Finally, when she first arrived in the municipality, she was punted between different primary care centers, which meant that she had no continuity with patients.

In other words, I went through a lot, Clara, but now I have blocked it out, and I have forgotten about it. But the municipality asks, "Have you reached your goal?" And if not, good-bye. So in the first months things got delayed, and [I was told,] "No, what is happening is that we have just started the program, so the money this and that, I don't know." But now, we are reaching a year [the program has been going on for a year], Clara, and so what happens? My contract is from March to December, and then they will determine whether I continue or not, depending on the goals. Principally, [they're interested in] quantity because they could care less about quality. Because they care about the quantity of people. But for me, I worry a lot about the quality. But, I am also pressured for the quantity. To them, they could care less. . . . Do you think that at any point a person has entered [my group session office] and said to me, "What are you doing, what do you need?" Or: "Consider, perhaps, that you are making a mistake in this"? No one has any idea. I could be doing something barbarous with my people, with my patients, and no one has any idea. Only the goal interests them. Beyond that, they do not pay the money for the year [that is, she will not be guaranteed her income for the year, even if she has a yearlong contract, as her pay will be contingent on performance]. They pay in partial amounts. That is, they pay money until June, and if you comply with the goal, they pay you until September. And if you comply with the goal, they pay you money until December. It is madness.

As Paula unpacked the tangled relationship between the municipality and the state program, I began to see how their differing political agendas and bureaucratic practices conspired, potentiating an atmosphere of precariousness and demoralization for the health care workers themselves. If the government assigned periodic goals for the numbers of patients treated, the municipality pegged the pay of health workers to reaching these goals. Between the internal politics, an overbearing focus on the number of patients treated, and job instability for health workers, the question of patient care itself was obscured.

To compensate for such frustrations, Paula devised alternative strategies for treating herself and her patients: "Sometimes, I burn incense in my office, and I think to myself, 'This incense is covering the office, protecting the office from the bad things here. This is a protected space.' Then, I can start my group sessions in this protected space." At the end of our meeting, I thanked her for her openness. She invited me to observe her group sessions despite the lack of site permission. But, concerned about putting the director of the *consultorio* in an awkward position, I decided to wait. I did not feel as immune to politics.

Meanwhile, I scheduled a meeting with the SSMN mental health officials in charge of directing and coordinating the state's mental health programs throughout the northern zone of Santiago. Primary care physician Estrella Gutierrez and psychologist Marco Barrientos met me in a small, cramped office at midday. Dr. Barrientos, a soft-spoken man in his midforties, displayed considerable caution while speaking to me. They were interested in my work in La Pincoya. I suggested that debt and unstable work might be conditions for depressive symptoms, and I elaborated several cases. I asked them how they thought the program related to these complex realities. Dr. Barrientos responded in a somewhat threatened tone: "Look, we have no control over the processes that you describe. We, as health workers, can only do so much. The goal of this program is the remission of symptoms. And, we are complying with this goal." But he was interrupted by Dr. Gutierrez. Also soft-spoken and kind, she was in her sixties and had short gray hair and round glasses. She said:

> At the heart of it, Clara, is this. The program is more a tranquilizer for the health system than it is for the population. So the health system, and therefore the state, feels that it has done something to address all of the issues that you have laid out. But, conscience and ethics interpellates you. In thinking about mental health and the marginality of the city, is it possible to design a program that addresses both the conditions that give rise to these symptoms and the symptoms themselves? This program was created with psychiatric categories and diagnoses as a guiding concept. Pure depression. But you will not find pure depression in La Pincoya. Rather, contaminated categories, contaminated by the social and economic situation in which these people are living.

After our conversation, Dr. Gutierrez invited me to her office, where she pulled out a thin document that she had authored, a support manual for group psychosocial interventions in alcoholism. Published by the SSMN, the manual was titled *Seamos Realistas, Soñemos Lo Imposible* (We'll be realistic, we dream the impossible). Rather than a series of group exercises, the manual was a reflection on the intimate effects of urban economic and social segregation in daily life. Dr. Gutierrez raised concerns regarding the multiple etiologies of depression, concerns that I think many psychiatrists would share. But I was ambivalent about judging the program's success or failure on the basis of disease etiology. The specific way clinical categories and therapeutic interventions are taken up are tied to actual contexts. What were the productivities of this program, and in what contexts could the program thrive?

AFFECTS OF EXPERIMENT

While I talked to local health workers, officials at the SSMN, and families, I attended psychiatry grand rounds at the University of Chile's Department of Psychiatry. There, I met Dr. Graciela Rojas, who was the chair of the Department of Psychiatry and, along with Dr. Rodrigo

Araya of the University of Bristol, one of the principal investigators of the community-based intervention for the treatment of depression. Dr. Rojas was warm, critical, and evinced an inspiring commitment to teaching and research. She ran a closely monitored and scrupulous research agenda that was joined to the training of psychiatrists, and she remained concerned for research subjects well after an intervention study had been formally closed.

In light of my continued difficulties in accessing La Pincoya's primary care center, she suggested that I visit the primary care center in the *población* La Bandera, one of the research sites for the community intervention study that eventually led to the National Depression Treatment Program. "The group sessions turned into a self-help group of almost fifty women who participated in the study," she told me. "They even applied for *personalidad jurídica*" (legal status as an organized group that would enable them to apply for state funds for social programs). This group and the evolution of the program's sessions epitomized to Dr. Rojas the potential of the community-based intervention: low-income women could identify sources of support through the program and become the managers of this support themselves, acting "independently" of expert knowledge.

What experimental conditions informed the formation of this self-help group? Let me briefly turn to the methods and results of the initial study. In 2000, Drs. Araya and Rojas led a study of a low-cost, primary-care-centered treatment program for depression for low-income women in Santiago. Designed as a randomized controlled trial, the researchers chose three primary care clinics in poor areas of Santiago and divided a sample of 240 female patients diagnosed with major depressive disorder according to DSM-IV categories into two treatment regimes.

The experimental regime was a "stepped-care improvement program." The women in this regime who were diagnosed with severe or persistent depression according to the Hamilton Rating Scale for Depression (a scale commonly used in psychiatric research to assess the severity of depressive symptoms) were given a combination of antidepressant medication (fluoxetine, amitriptyline, or imipramine) and seven consecutive weeks of "psychoeducational group intervention," along with two "booster sessions" at weeks nine and twelve. Social workers or nurses, who had been trained and observed by the researchers, covered a range of topics on depression, including, "the symptoms and causes of depression, available treatment options, scheduling positive activities, problem-solving techniques, and basic cognitive and relapse-prevention techniques." The patients were each given a manual on depression that covered the content of each session and listed examples and exercises (Araya et al. 2003, 996).

Primary care physicians were also given training by the researchers to administer a pharmacotherapy protocol including structured assessments at initial and follow-up visits for the patients with severe and persistent depression. In addition, the leaders of the group sessions monitored the adherence to medication regimes for the patients receiving pharmacotherapy. The patients in the control arm were given usual care at the primary health care center, which included antidepressant medication or referral to specialty services. The patients were evaluated at three and six months.

The results were published in *The Lancet* in 2003 in an article titled "Treating Depression in Primary Care in Low-Income Women in Santiago, Chile: A Randomised Controlled Trial." Comparing the two groups after six months, the researchers showed that those in the stepped-care program had significantly lower points on the Hamilton Rating Scale for Depression. After six months, 78 percent in the experimental group had scores at least 50 percent lower than their initial scores on the depression scale. At the same time, 34 percent of the control group had a 50 percent decrease in their depressive symptoms. The researchers underscore that the "main innovative element was the role enhancement for the non-medical group leaders, most of whom were available in the clinics and were often closely connected to local neighbourhoods." Thus, "modest interventions" within the scope of existing limited structures of care can have significant effects: "The combination of high rates of depressive illness, poverty, and scarce resources can easily induce nihilism in physicians and policy makers. Our findings should offer hope that modest interventions can have a substantial effect on depressive symptoms and functional impairment" (Araya et al. 2003, 999).

But these "modest interventions" also rested on an affective and ethical ethos of patient care. Such an ethos had been built into the community intervention study through the careful attention to patients and the training of primary care physicians and nonmedical staff by the investigators themselves. These were their ethics of experiment as well as the conditions of "community" set forth by the study.

I took a bus from La Pincoya to La Bandera, traversing the city from the northern to the southern zone. From the green hills surrounding La Pincoya, the plants and trees that residents cultivated in their patios, the children playing in the narrow streets and buying *calzones rotos* and *berliners* (two kind of donuts) from the donut seller's mobile cart, we passed through the smog-filled busy center. Finally, we arrived at the flat, dry southern zone and the *población* La Bandera. La Bandera, like La Pincoya, has its own history of collective action and social movements (see Paley 2001). And in 2004, the mayor of the municipality was Pedro Isla, a Christian Democrat and part of the Concertación coalition. When I arrived at the primary care center, I first introduced myself to the director and then went to observe the self-help group called Alegría de Vivir (Happiness of Living) that met in one of the large rooms of the center. Previously contacted by Dr. Rojas, the director greeted me kindly. This primary care center had been chosen because the director had previously worked with Dr. Rojas. The director told me, "The implementation here has been very fluid. We have social workers and nurses who come from La Bandera, grew up here, and still live here. They are the ones directing the group sessions."

We walked to the room where the self-help group's weekly session had already started. Women, primarily in their fifties and above, sat in a circle around the room, introducing themselves to each other. Some spoke of the group as the "most important meeting of the week, something that gets me out of the house." Others, shy to speak in public, smiled and just said their names. After introductions, they engaged in a variety of activities: role playing in which women acted out situations of domestic tension and machismo and cultivated skills for dealing with it; reading a self-help list of "twenty-five steps to be happy," each woman taking a turn to read a "step." Then, women shared stories about personal dramas in the home: pressing debts, domestic violence, going hungry from lack of income, inability to find stable work. The group leaders reiterated a point: "What is said in these meetings is strictly confidential and stays within these walls."

Afterward, over tea and cookies that some members had brought, I spoke to the group's leaders. They were longtime members of the group and had participated in the community intervention study. I asked them what the group meant to them. One leader answered, "Meeting people who are going through the same as you, who have depression, and who have the same problems in their houses. So, we find ways to deal with this together. We laugh, we cry a lot. It is a space to talk and feel comfortable. You don't have to say anything, or you can say a lot. You have a space here. This is self-help."

Afterward, they gave me a card they had made for Dr. Rojas and her colleague Dr. Fritsch thanking them for "their care and their support." One woman remarked, "The doctors are so loving. So caring." Some told me as I waved good-bye: "Tell them to come and visit again soon." The group was a mixture of affect, identification, allegiances, and intervention. Formerly an "experimental" group in the strict sense (a linking of the community and the clinical), the group had become a new test site for the formation of an affective community that employed "depression" as a proxy for multiple conditions that women struggled with in their everyday lives. Depression as an experience was reworked in a way that could articulate the interconnections between domestic troubles, debts, insecurity, unemployment, and scarcity. Considering this group solely as a biosocial association irrespective of lifeworld would, however, obscure the crucial point here: *the ethos of experiment invited neighbors to become friends.* Self-help, then, grew from relational modes of "the self."

The expansion of the randomized controlled trial to the community and the taking up of and transformation of identifications based on disease categories made this an exemplary case of decentralization as community participation. In her ethnography of the democratic transition, Julia Paley points out that "community participation" advanced by the Chilean government was one way for government officials to abdicate the state's responsibility in matters of community development and, thus, their acknowledgment of social and economic inequalities. Assuming their "democratic responsibility" through "community participation," *pobladores* would have to identify and solve local problems, become formally recognized through the governmental bodies, and continue their work with little or no resources from the state (Paley 2001). This institutionalization of community activism, Paley argues, established a contradictory space for neighborhood health promoters who were tied to government discourse while critical of it. Further, Paley criticizes government discourses of participation, pointing out that professional knowledge is the only conduit through which community participation could be enacted.

The flourishing of this self-help group was one example of an articulation of science, community participation, and decentralization in the service of a larger democratizing project. Paley's insights into the interface between technical and local knowledge are salient but do not consider the dimensions of how subjects take up and transform professional knowledge to generate something else. Such a transformation of knowledge also speaks to a new, shifting line in the objects of experiment within the medical sciences: namely, community as an object of experiment itself. How are experimental conditions established in community settings, and what happens to experimental conditions outside of the social and affective parameters generated among research subjects and with researchers? Community interventions were "social laboratories" where new techniques could be tested for their efficacy and cost-effectiveness, as well as "testing sites" by research subjects for the mingling of medical and social identifications—in this case, depression invites new sorts of connections.

In her work on the social, political, and biological management of the Chernobyl disaster, Adriana Petryna discusses how Chernobyl has become "valued as a kind of 'experiment,' allowing scientists to corroborate or refute biomedical data concerning the long-term health consequences of nuclear exposure" (Petryna 2002, 26). She challenges a narrow view of experiment as that "singular, well-defined instance embedded in the elaboration of a theory and performed in order to corroborate or to refute certain hypotheses" and takes a wider view of experiment as those technical interventions that are productive of new uncertainties in scientific and social arrangements (p. 26). Technical interventions realized within the population are "experimental systems"—"machines for making the future"—that "produce new and unanticipated resources in environments where little if anything is held constant" (p. 26). In the post-Socialist era, Chernobyl sufferers were integrated into a novel, centralized welfare system through documentary evidence of biological damage.

After I was granted permission to observe the group sessions in La Pincoya, I came to see the extent to which decentralization affected the experiment of community intervention. The study conducted by researchers in La Bandera was a highly controlled intervention in a context where social and political "variables" facilitated the intervention's efficacy—the reduction of functional impairment and the increased "participation" of subjects in addressing their own health care needs. But further, through the commitment to patient care, the researchers and social workers shaped an affective ethos of experiment. The so-called intangibles of medicine—such as a respect for and responsiveness to patients (which are thoroughly concrete)—play a crucial role in a community intervention's evolution.[6] This ethos laid the groundwork for a new site of experimentation in affects, disease category, and connections.[7] A different kind of experimentation evolved in La Pincoya.

SURGERY OF THE SOUL

After four months and multiple phone calls from myself and the director of the SSMN, I met with the municipal director of health education. I arrived at the Municipal Health Department offices located in a different primary care center of Huechuraba, where a secretary escorted me to a conference room. The director of health education, the director of the health area, and the chief technical officer were seated at a square white table. The first director looked stern and serious, the other nervous, while the chief technical officer smiled at me. The latter was wearing a jumper with embroidered lettering: "Huechuraba loves you." On the table lay my proposal marked up in yellow highlighter. Some parts were marked with green pen. Other parts were underlined with red pen. I sat down nervously with a feeling of dread.

The director of health education told me that the mayor had approved my study. He leafed through the papers on the table and showed me a small form with her signature and the municipal seal. A conversation ensued about the role of the municipality in my work. The director of the health area remarked, "The problem is this: When this plan for depression started last year, there was a lot of trouble with the SSMN and the Ministry of Health. There was a lot of resentment between the doctors and the psychologists, because they each have their own visions, their own ways of doing things, and we got caught in the middle." The director of health education interrupted, saying, "The problem is this. Everything and everyone in this municipality—the doctors, psychologists, and the directors of the *consultorio* and COSAM—everything and everyone, I repeat, are funneled through us. So the mayor made her report about your study, and the director of the health area made his prereport about your study. I made a prereport, and the chief technical officer made a prereport. What we need is to see how your work progresses each month, the results." I agreed to meet them, if they would make arrangements to meet with me. Yet neither the director of health education nor any other official contacted me after this initial meeting.

By the time I began observing the group sessions, I had met with Paula several times. During our conversations, Paula spoke to me about her strategy for the group sessions, which she called, "a surgery of the soul." "I work with women who have so many problems. Their husbands beat them, their son is a drug addict, and it's as if they haven't developed as full persons because they haven't had a chance," she told me. "And the doctors, they seem to think that our job is to make sure the women take their pills. It's so medical. But they do not pay attention to the problems of the soul. It's as if they do not take psychology seriously. If doctors say that they operate on bodies, we are doing much more delicate work. I tell doctors, when they look down on psychology, 'Look, you do surgery on the body, what I am doing is surgery of the soul.'"

Paula's therapeutic discourse was infused with her Catholic faith and a growing interest in mysticism, finding inspiration in the writings of Carl Jung. Focused on self-improvement of the soul, she explained her therapeutic vision as we had coffee in a café near her apartment.

> Philosophy enchants me, and a mountain of these things I have tried to insert in therapy. . . . I change the "switch" and tell them [the patients], "You have a piece of God in you. You are half animal and half light. You are functioning with the animal. The animal is he who feels pain, he who feels anger. The animal is he who becomes desperate. The animal is he who needs to eat, etc." "But," I tell them, "the animal serves to move you through the world. If you did not have this physical body that is like the animal, how would you move in the world? How would you walk? How would you eat? How would you wash? For this is your animal. The animal," I tell them, "is like a small, poorly raised child. So he who has to command is not the animal. The animal always wants more, always wants more, never is content, always desires something." So I tell them, "Where is your piece of God, your light, your *vieja sabia* [wise old woman]? Your *vieja sabia*," I tell them, "is what has to lead you forward, solve your problems, invent alternatives, occupy your head, occupy your heart."
>
> And there I go, pulling them in further until I feel that I have changed a concept, from this omnipotent God that is almost a capricious God—because he could either want to help you or not—to: "You have to occupy your piece of God, your *vieja sabia,* that is wise, that is perfect, that knows how to make decisions, that knows how to take the reins of life, your life. No one will do it for you." And I try to awaken this side. At the bottom of it, Clara, what I try to do is not to tell them what they need to do. I am not the one who can say to them: "Separate, if he has been hitting you for the past thirty years. Separate!" I am not the person to say that. The person herself has to make that decision. . . . This is what I say: "I give you a tool for cake . . . and you will make the cake in your house. I will not make the cake for you, nor will your husband, nor your children, nor your neighbor, nor God. You have to do it." This is a little bit of my philosophy.

"The *vieja sabia*?" I asked. "Yes," she responded. "It's the wisdom that we women have, our intuition, our conscience." She explained that the *vieja sabia,* or "crone," was a Jungian archetype: the wise older woman who seeks balance and compassion as well as peaceful and harmonious relationships to family and others. The *vieja sabia* is contemplative and acts on herself through meditation. In her discourse, Paula split the human between a world of utter, concrete baseness and a world of spiritual nobility: one half "animal," characterized as both infantile and purely biological; and the other half "light," defined as the *vieja sabia* or, as she sometimes called it, a "piece of God," a spiritual half that "makes decisions," "takes the reins of life." On the noble side were found "tools" for self-improvement, and such tools were used to walk better on the "animal side."

Paula's "surgery of the soul" entailed a new fusion of these halves: an initial splitting between the mundane concreteness of the "animal world" and the "world of light"; sustained therapeutic work in this "world of light"; and finally the return to the concrete animal world as a self-improved woman. At first blush, this "surgery" bears resemblance to Jung's elaboration of the psychological aspect of alchemy as a process of psychic integration (see Jung 1958). But her understanding of the self is strikingly different from Jung's idea of the self, which does not have content defined a priori but rather "carries the whole living past in the lower stories of the skyscraper of rational consciousness" (p. 40). Thus, the self is a process of individuation between personal (conscious) and nonpersonal (collective unconscious) forces. The individual as "unique, transitory, and imperfect" crystalized primordial ideas or archetypes (p. 63). Paula's idea of the self, on the other hand, emphasized a decipherment of the self by the self and, as I discovered later, work on the self that entailed a purification of memory.

I asked Paula how her philosophy and therapeutic approach related to the program's guidelines, pointing to the Mental Health Unit's manual for treatment of depression. The manual provided themes for each of the six group sessions. In session 1, the social worker or psychologist was to provide information on the symptoms, causes, and treatments of depression. "What is depression?" the manual asked. "A very frequent disease that has treatment. . . . What are the causes? We inherit genes. Chemical changes in the brain. Vital crises (pain and losses). Family, economic, and employment problems. . . . How does it affect us? Physical symptoms. Affects the emotions. Affects thoughts. Affects our conduct. . . . How can we combat it? With medical and/or psychological treatment. Keeping ourselves active."

In each following session, the group leader was to emphasize cognitive skills to assist in the identification of thought processes, attitudes, and behaviors that stimulate depression as well as alleviate depressive symptoms. The central message: "Keeping myself active." The patients are asked to complete "homework" for each session to consolidate the knowledge and insights they have gained in group therapy. For example, in the homework for session 1, the patients are to list five symptoms of depression that they have experienced. Following this, they are to write the symptom and identify which category the symptom falls under: body, emotions, thought, or conduct. The human and her symptoms, according to the manual, were already parsed into four categories, separating the materiality of the body from the cognitive realm: emotions, thoughts, conduct.

By the final two sessions, the emphasis switched. Titled "Plan for the Prevention of Relapse," session 5 included the formulation of a "plan for self-care" and a "plan for self-observation." Under the "plan for self-care," the women were to write down "five or six activities to fight against depression." Such activities were to be "the most realistic as possible. The more concrete the activities the better." Under the "plan for self-observation," the women were to "recognize the first symptoms of depression." These symptoms, the manual stated, "are very personal, change from person to person." A cognitive behavioral approach introduced the person's ability to recognize and identify symptoms rationally and then design concrete activities in the management of her symptoms. Patients, as such, were trained to know and act on themselves, but only along the grid of identifiable depressive symptoms and according to "realistic" or rational management.

This approach, Paula pointed out, did not address "the careful work of the soul" that was needed to "overcome depression." She was addressing "something different: spiritual fulfillment." And besides, she pointed out, "this program in La Pincoya does not work. You see it with the Municipality and with the Health Service North [SSMN]. They are not interested in how we do our work, if we have the tools. As I told you, they are just interested in numbers, getting people diagnosed and supposedly treated. I am just doing my best, doing what my conscience tells me. . . . Numbers are too easy," she remarked. This recourse to the spiritual could be understood as Paula's response to less-than-adequate resources, municipal politics, and a technocratic state. Yet her therapeutic vision can also be set within the complex cultural matrices of "rationality and religiosity, technocracy and faith" in contemporary Chile, in which spiritual dimensions of a neoliberal state are problematized, either through the opposition of the technocratic and the religious, or by experiencing religious faith—La Obra—through a faith in the market itself, expressed through consumption, wealth generation, and quantitative measures of success (Cárcamo-Huechante 2001, 156).[8] For Paula, a science of depression—either through neurotransmitters or cognitive psychology—blocked an investigation of the soul as a psychic reality.

GROUP SESSIONS

The group sessions I attended began at the end of September 2004 and lasted through October. The sessions were in the morning. In front of the center, women sold handicrafts and secondhand clothes to make it to the end of the month. A kindly old man, Orlando, greeted me each Wednesday morning and offered me a steaming cup of Nescafé. He ran a kiosk selling sweets and soft drinks to those waiting in line for medical attention. One of the *fundadores* ("founders," or those adults who took part in the *tomas*) of La Pincoya, he told me that his sons were out of work, his daughter had been waiting for a kidney transplant for "years" while on dialysis, and the income he earned from the kiosk went to help pay for her medications. He had started the kiosk in front of the primary care center to "meet a doctor who could help my daughter," but soon he realized that "I only sell to the other suffering and sick people. They spend their time, like my daughter, waiting in line, another number on the list." He was widowed and lived on a state pension for the elderly of 38,000 pesos per month (approximately USD 50). "In Chile, the working class has been crucified. And I don't even believe in God," he told me.

In the group sessions, however, transcendence became the key to self-improvement or progress. Paula's small office was decorated with plants. In the background, she played a tape of trickling water for "relaxation" while waiting for all of the women to arrive. Six women, from different parts of La Pincoya, none of whom I had met before, came to the group session.

We were seated in a circle. Paula briefly introduced herself, having met with each of the women individually before the group session. I then introduced myself and my research and asked the women if I could observe the group sessions. Honorina said, "We are all fine with that, but you cannot just observe; you have to also share your experiences. So we want to hear about your depression too. In Chile, everyone is depressed. You sound more Chilean than beans [remarking on my Chilean accent] even though you look like a *chinita* [little Chinese girl], so I include you as Chilean." Everyone laughed, and I agreed to share my experiences and feelings as well. But, throughout the sessions, it became apparent that there was very little space for words, other than Paula's words, and the occasional interjections and contestations of the women who were struggling to understand how Paula's therapeutic discourse fit into their own struggles and realities.

Macarena was in her early thirties and ran a kiosk near a primary school. She was married and had two small children. Several months before, she had attempted to commit suicide because of her overwhelming debts to department stores, the supermarket, and neighbors. Alejandra was in her late sixties. Disabled by severe back pain and loss of hearing, she lived with her daughter, with whom she had a tense relationship. Margarita was in her midthirties. She had taken care of her ailing mother until her mother had passed away in her arms, six months earlier. She sold cigarettes and sweets from her house to make ends barely meet. Her husband was addicted to *pasta base* and had beaten her several times. Gladys was in her late sixties. She lived with her husband, who was a construction worker but currently out of work. She did piecemeal sewing. The weight of her and her husband's debts made her "unable to get out of bed." Honorina was in her midthirties. She lived with her husband, now a taxi driver, and said that she had organic depression. Carla was in her early forties and lived with her husband. She strung tennis rackets at a country club in Vitacura, one of the wealthy sectors of Santiago. She worked days. Her husband worked from 9 A.M. to 10 P.M. selling tennis-racket-stringing equipment at various clubs, and also stringing rackets for sports stores. They rarely saw each other during the week, and she was worried that her husband was having an affair. These biographical details were never shared in the sessions, however. I was able to hear their life stories only when I made home visits.

Paula started the first session by asking, "What do you hope for in therapy? What do you want to get out of this?" Silence. Gladys responded tentatively, "That you heal us, take us out of our pain. That you help us. And that God protects you so that you can help us." Paula responded at length, using this to segue to the introduction of the group sessions.

> I'd like to complement a little bit of what you said. Here we are a team, *chiquillas* [a term normally used to refer to young girls, but often used in woman-only support groups] to treat depression. Here there are four very important elements in the treatment of depression. If one of those four elements fails, it is very probable that the treatment will fail. The first element has to do with you all, your motivation, your energy, your wishes, your wishes to heal yourselves, your wishes to move forward. . . .

The second element of this great team work is those who take pharmaceuticals, everything that is medical is *fármacos* [pharmaceuticals]. If they gave you a treatment with antidepressants, you need to finish them.

Third, we have therapy. If you come to one or two therapies, and then come back here to the psychologist, it is because you have not completed the treatment. You have to complete the treatment, at least six sessions of therapy. And come on time, and do not arrive late, and do the homework, and come with heart and mind open to listen, to understand, to learn.

And lastly is the faith in you all. You haven't heard that faith moves mountains? I tell you this. I don't care who you believe in, perhaps in the sun, perhaps your God is the sun—well, from there you grab on. Or perhaps he's called Buddha: there you grab with teeth and nails. Or maybe he's called Jesus. Now we will try to change the concept of God that we have, Jesus, for those who believe. We are not so spoiled that we wait until God knocks on our door and says to us: "Here it is, the gold platter; here is the solution." No *chiquillas,* you all will take the first step, and God, or who you believe in, will give the second step. First is your motivation, and after that is the help. Yes, yes, it will not be easy, you need to move yourselves, motivate yourselves. For that, we have four elements in the treatment of depression. It is not easy, like taking a pill and that pill will solve the problems. Who has solved a problem with a pill? I would like to know. No one . . .

Margarita interjected, "It does not solve problems; it just tranquilizes one." Paula responded, "This is the important part of the medication, the medication tranquilizes you a bit. Because of that, the other part that is done is therapy and work on yourself. What solves what—the pill? No. You all. That is it." Margarita then changed the topic. "I am here because I am concerned about my children. I want to be there for them." Paula interrupted: "For others, always for others. Look. And where is the space for you? It's as if you do not exist. Put on some makeup, feel good, just for yourself." Carla interrupted her: "But that is why my husband gets angry. I work all week, I come home tired. On the weekends, I don't want to put on makeup. I don't want to fix myself up. I just want to be at home and wear my sweatpants, be at home disorganized, relax, but he doesn't like that." Paula responded, "OK . . . here, there are no formulas. Not everyone is the same. But we are all here for the same thing. Depression." She elaborated on her vision of therapy, folding the women's ambivalence back into an affirmation of her therapeutic discourse:

> *Paula:* I would like for all of us to have a concept more or less clear today that will accompany us and will help us through all of the sessions. First, above everything, we must have very clear that the human being is composed of two things, of two elements. One is your animal part, the

physical, that which has hunger, that which has thirst, that which has the appetite for sex. The animal serves to move us through the world, we could say, to walk, to run. Do you understand what is the animal part? Yes? . . . But we have another part that is superpotent, that is our divine part, our part of light which differentiates us from other animals, that is our conscience. Here in this part of light is where your *vieja sabia* is. Your *vieja sabia* is this half of light, that is divine, that is perfect, that is intuition. This is the perfect part in all of us, the part that has clarity. It is the part that, when we make decisions, does it for us. Have any of you ever had an intuition? And when you have listened to your *vieja sabia,* when you have listened to your intuition, have you made a mistake?

Gladys: Sometimes. Things don't always function the way that one thinks.

Paula: So you are not listening to your *vieja sabia.* Our *vieja sabia* is our perfect part, it is our little piece of God. For that, what part of you all is going to help you move forward? Your animal or your *vieja sabia?*

Gladys: [looking confused]: My *vieja sabia.*

Paula: I will tell you something about how the animal functions and the *vieja sabia,* because they are two characters inside of you all. If you all, for example, have to get up early because you have to go and drop off your children at school—let's suppose—at 6:30 in the morning, and your animal part says to you, "Don't get up, what a pain, stay lying in bed, warm, good." What gets you up from bed? Your *vieja sabia,* if your animal wants to stay lying in bed. . . . It gave more than a few people a pain to come here, or they had problems in coming here. Obstacles were presented to those who came here. Yes or no? Am I speaking stupidities? Did anyone have a problem coming here?

Macarena: I had to run all over to get here, because this morning I had to be at the bank.

Paula: Who ran?

Everyone: The *vieja sabia.*

Paula: Now we will not look at the animal as if it were an evil, bad thing, like a bad angel. No. What happens is that the animal wants to get into everything, like a poorly raised child. What happens is that you have to use it for what it serves, with spirituality or with love, or with other types of things. There are things which it should not get into, and that you all should not permit it to get into.

Paula closed the session by turning to the manual. She quickly went through the symptoms of depression, the causes, and the treatments. Then, she ended with prayer. We sat in a circle holding hands and closing our eyes. Paula said, "God, or whomever you believe in, help us through the group sessions and connect with our *vieja sabia.*" We opened our eyes, and Paula asked the women how they felt. Some replied, "A little tired; it was a lot in one session." Others replied, "Relaxed. It tranquilized me a bit."

As I listened more to Paula, I was struck by the incredible self-mastery—or will—that the *vieja sabia* asserted: an intuition that was perfect, transparent, and which, if listened to, could avoid "mistakes" and even concrete circumstances. The cultivation of the self entails listening to the *vieja sabia,* which is the achievement of self-mastery. Nevertheless, although Paula had been asking the women to connect with their true intuition and act upon that with certainty, the contestations voiced by the women instilled some doubt in Paula herself. She expressed this doubt through ideas of reincarnation.

After the session, she reflected on her work: "Sometimes it's difficult, Clara. Please tell me if you think there are things I can improve, because I don't have an outside opinion, and I value that. I work with these women, and you see how they are. You see how difficult their lives arc, that they sometimes don't even have the money to take the bus to get here, and that they live in tremendously terrible conditions. And, I think, well, I have a friend who is Buddhist, and she told me about reincarnation. And I have thought to myself, how does the world perpetuate this? We have so much—I live with my husband in Las Condes, you are studying at Harvard. And then, I think about reincarnation and wonder, Were we all just reincarnated? Was it just their bad luck?" I responded, "But don't you think that it has more to do with economics, politics, and history than reincarnation? You yourself have pointed out the problems with the municipality." She paused, looked at me, and said, "Perhaps, but such differences, how can you explain that?"

"WE ALL HAVE TO PAY OUR DEBTS"

Each woman missed at least two sessions. They cited daily demands—looking for employment, caring for a sick child—or they simply "did not have the time." "I enjoy it," Margarita told me. We sat on the benches outside of the office before one of the meetings. "It's like a fantasy," she continued. "I come here and do not have to think about what is happening in my house. Here, we listen to the psychologist talk, and I can turn the 'switch' and relax. It's almost like being *in* the television, rather than watching it." I responded, "But does the fantasy help you when you go home?" Gladys responded, "It is a fantasy. And one hour of peace does me good. But no, it doesn't help at home. Has it given my husband a job? No. I do feel bad for the psychologist. She is so young.

She is trying, but she hasn't lived our lives. It's almost as if I feel that we need to protect her."

By the fourth session, Paula had taught us several techniques of "protection" and "safe ways to act out." One such technique was "the golden bubble." As she explained, "When you are in your house, and your husband, your son, your neighbor makes you feel bad, puts you back on that animal side, what do you do? Do you want the animal to come out? Or do you listen to your *vieja sabia?*" She told us to close our eyes. We were to breathe in and hold our breath for seven seconds, then expire strongly. After three rounds of breathing, we were to slowly raise our arms over our heads. "Imagine that you are bringing a bubble over you. Then tie the bubble on top of you with a golden bow. The golden bubble will protect you from other people's words, other people's animals." Another technique was "breaking the wooden chest." Paula led us outside to the back parking lot of the center. We stood in a circle and were to imagine "a big wooden chest in front of us. Inside the chest are all of our frustrations." "Imagine you have a big ax," Paula said. She instructed us to raise it above our heads and hit the imagined wooden chest over and over again until it broke into "pieces." During the techniques, some of the women and I tried to control our laughter, obviously feeling embarrassed or noting a kind of absurdity that pervaded the exercise. Others seemingly got into the fantasy, breaking the wooden box with palpable anger.

After the fourth session, Paula invited me to a dinner party with some of the other psychologists in the program who were working in clinics scattered through Santiago's *poblaciones*. The dinner was at the house of a psychologist who worked in the neighboring working-class municipality but lived in Alto Las Condes, a wealthy suburb. Laura, a psychologist in her midforties, lived with her husband, an orthopedic surgeon. Paula, Laura, two other women psychologists, and I sat in the living room drinking amaretto sours. Through the large French double doors, we looked out onto an outside patio, where the men stood around a barbecue pit. All of the couples lived in wealthy sectors of Santiago, from Las Condes to Vitacura to La Dehesa—the rich northeastern side of the city.

The psychologists reflected on their work, telling stories of particular patients and their frustrations with them, through jokes. I asked them, "Why continue if it is so frustrating?" One responded, "It's like . . . *charity*. We see them suffering, and we have to do something. Yes, most people burn out and start a private practice. But for two or three years, it's important to do this kind of work." She evoked Mother Theresa and Padre Hurtado—the Catholic priest who founded Hogar de Cristo, now the largest Catholic charity in Chile—as "examples of sacrifice and charity." Another responded in a half-joking manner: "We all have to pay our debts." Laura then told a story of a patient, "a drug addict," who continued to relapse. The story was disturbing. She laughed. Wiping tears from her eyes, she said, "In this work, *me entretengo*" (I entertain myself).

Such "entertainment" from humanitarian work recalls Didier Fassin's reflections on *pastoral altruism* among health care workers in which "an ambiguous ethical involvement among health professionals and social workers facing the sick or the needy whom they tried to assist and whose lack of will to extract themselves from their situations finally infuriates to the point that they [the health care workers] end up stigmatizing even more dramatically those they originally wanted to help" (Fassin 2007b, 209). The implicit religiosity of Fassin's "pastoral altruism" can be further explored.

Since the 1970s, conservative Catholic elites in Chile have drawn on theological justifications for wealth creation formulated by the Opus Dei and Legion of Christ movements. In response to the Church of Santiago's position on structural reform in the 1960s that made the dominant classes morally responsible for poverty, these movements advanced the idea that the free market was itself the "option for the poor."[9] Thus, rather than pay the debt of "temporal punishment" for present sin (the pleasure of wealth) through penitential works that would make them depart from their ordinary lives and social positions, the elites should positively strive to maximize their "ordinary life" in terms of work productivity and family commitment (Olave 2010; for "temporal punishment" see Vatican 2010, Article 4, Section X, "Indulgences").

As sociologist Thumala Olave argues, today conservative Catholic elites do not confront the parables of wealth and damnation through guilt and penance but rather have displaced its centrality through "a parable of talents," in which "business activity [is] a response to the religious imperative to develop individual talents." These elites see "professional excellence as a path to salvation, an alternative to the radical change in lifestyle which seemed to be the true Christian path of the 1960s" (Olave 2010, 21). Such a radical change would be exemplified in living in a *población*, for instance. The remarks of these psychologists lie somewhere between this radical change and the turn toward "ordinary life."[10] Their debts to God—a debt owed because they were born with talents and they sin in enjoying wealth—would be paid through charity work, producing both an attraction to the poor as a means to salvation and a visceral repugnance for them.

In the constant process of renewal that leads to individual salvation, this penance does not entail a dramatic altering of their social position, but does challenge them to uncomfortably acknowledge unequal life chances, even as they seek to maximize their inborn talents. Such attraction to and repugnance for the poor in the context of conservative Catholicism shows the specificity of the moral stakes of "pastoral altruism" and helps us understand the different affective shapes and tones in humanitarian works for the poor. With such debts paid, however, one could turn to the maximization of "ordinary life," the creation of a private practice and the generation of wealth.

My face betrayed me. The conversation became stifled. Paula's husband, hearing our conversation walked over and sat with us. "You know," he said, "We had a nanny at home when I was growing up, and I learned a lot from seeing how she dealt with things. She would tell me one terrible thing after another, about her son who was into drugs and about her husband. Nothing changed over the years. Paula knows her well, too. And then, I heard that phrase in psychology ... What was it? *Desamparo aprendido* [learned helplessness]. And, I thought, this is what she has, learned helplessness. So it's not like she was a bad person, but that she had learned to become helpless. She thought she could not change anything." Conversation then turned to how "our nannies can learn" from working in "our houses."

THE PARDON

The following week, I met Paula in her office before the session. I told her that I was disturbed by the dinner party conversation. She apologized for the others' words and said, "I want you to know, Clara, that this work is not entertainment for me." She lit a cigarette and continued. "Sometimes, I want to just break out and go crazy. I want to experience new things. I feel too protected, like I grew up protected." We heard a knock on her office door. The session had to start.

This time, Paula had decided to go on an "internal journey" with the women. With the sound of trickling water in the background, Paula began:

> Good, keep the eyes closed, very relaxed, very good. It is the hour in which your *vieja sabia* will leave your physical body. Imagine how it leaves your body, that it is equal to you but leaves you. You leave your seated physical

body and your *vieja sabia* leaves. Your *vieja sabia* does not feel hurt, does not feel pain. This *sabia* is perfect. It knows everything. It has all of the knowledge of the universe. It has all of the solutions. It is your part made of light. It can pass through the walls and does not have any limit; and since it does not have a limit, it can leave here and exit! And it starts to fly, starts to fly. I want you to focus, to put your attention on this flight, as you are feeling free, feeling the freedom in the air, feeling the breeze in your face. You want to jump out of everything that squeezes you; if you want to take off your clothes, take them off. There does not exist shame on this side. There does not exist evil, the bad. Shake down your hair, take off your clothes . . . do what you want to feel free . . . feel how you are, what you are feeling. Feel the pure air that enters into your nose and cleans your lungs and cleans your emotional body. You are free, and you continue flying like a bird. . . .

All of a sudden, from one cloud to the next you realize that there are stairs, and at the end of the stairs is a big door. It is a very big door, very wide, and gold in color. It is the door that opens to your spiritual world, to your internal world. We climb, climb one, two, three, four, and five. And you encounter this big, golden, precious, wide door. You touch the door, and someone opens it, and you realize that this is your guardian angel. How is your guardian angel? Focus on his rays, his movements, his hair, how he's dressed, the smell he has. Hug your angel. He missed you a lot. You receive his affection. And more, he was waiting especially for you. And receives you with a crown of flowers that he puts on your neck. You feel so much energy when you greet him, so much love. And he will lift you so you can know your internal world. I want you to paint your spiritual world as you like. Maybe there is a large, large pasture full of grass. Or maybe the grass is pink, or green. It is full of flowers, the ones you like the best, with distinct forms and colors, and it has an aroma so special, so special in your world, only you know this aroma. You continue to walk. He takes off your shoes and gives you a massage on your feet. It is very nice.

You continue to walk . . . you encounter a waterfall. It is not like any other waterfall. It has clear water, a transparent water. It is not just any water. It is a healing water that dissolves some pains, some angers, some rancor, traumas, negative influences that you have rooted very, very deep inside. And it leaves you happy. . . . Has dissolved a mountain of things that you had inside. Now you leave, and you realize that you are free now. How much more free you are now, not centered in your own fears, in your own anxieties, in your own complexes, in all of the negative things that have happened to you. You continue to walk, and you encounter a hill and start to climb. . . . You arrive at the top, and you encounter a big tree, a big fig tree. Under the tree there is a cushion only for you, and you sit there. At one side you have your guardian angel. On the other side you have Jesus, who is inside your internal world. And you will do an exercise before these three beings: your *vieja sabia*—or you—Jesus, and this angel. This exercise is not easy, because you have to do it only with the *vieja sabia*.

This exercise is the exercise of pardon. Pardon is the only thing that you will do to dissolve all of these hits, pains, angers, memories, and persons that have done harm to you in life. Your pardon is the only thing that will dissolve this so you will never see it again. And for you—in truth—to be an adult and a free woman. And, afterward, along with your *vieja sabia,* you will undo yourself of all the garbage that you have not wanted to undo because you have kept it like a valuable gem. And today you will make this change, and undo the habit, and decide to free yourself of all this.

First of all, you have to say to yourself: "I pardon myself for all of the times that I have felt guilty, for all of the negative energy that I have thrown at myself every day, for all of the times that I have said to myself: 'I am ugly, fat, wrinkled,' that 'I do not serve for anything.' I pardon myself for all of those times that I told myself that I was not intelligent, that I was useless, that I did not serve for anything, that I said to myself, 'Why was I born, why am I not dead?' I pardon myself for not valuing myself, for not seeing everything that I am, the beauty that I am. I pardon myself for all of those falls that I have had in life, for all of those errors and mistakes"—and above all, for that which only you know.

"I pardon myself. I pardon myself, and I am open to falling again and putting myself upright again. I pardon myself for this and much more. I undo all of this garbage that has served me all of these years. I root it out of me; I throw it away." Feel that with this pardon, all this garbage that you have in you starts to dissolve.

Magic the pardon.

"I pardon my mother because maybe I was a complicated baby. I pardon my mother because maybe she wanted a boy and I came out a girl. I pardon my mother for all the times that she treated me badly and made me feel bad and said ugly words to me. I pardon from my whole heart. . . .

"I pardon my father. Maybe he was not a good father, maybe I needed his warmth, his affection, his hug, his affection that only he could give to me and did not . . . because he was drunk and passed all day with his friends. . . . I pardon my father because he was perhaps a beater [domestic violence], because he touched my mother and made her cry, and did damage to her— for this and much more I pardon my father.

"I pardon whichever family member has done harm to me at some moment in life. . . . I pardon that family member who gossiped about me, who spoke badly of me. I pardon that family member to whom I lent money and who did not return it. . . . I pardon this friend who perhaps wanted to cheat on me with my husband, who humiliated me.

"And finally, I pardon once and for all this professional who humiliated me, who treated me badly . . . who made me feel like a little girl, who was unjust with me. To this person who attended to me, to this person who gave me anger, who made me feel so little—I pardon him and I pardon any other person who appears." Any person whom it really costs you to pardon. We will pardon without pride. Pride does not serve for anything. It only serves to make us continue to be sick. Clean yourself, heal yourself through pardon. Take out all of the garbage inside you.

Very good. Very good. You get up from the cushion with your guardian angel at one side and Jesus on the other. And I want you to feel what happens in this moment. How is your clean soul? How will things change from now on? How are you less of a slave to your past, to your garbage? You feel light, feel like a feather. You are happy, content; you want to live. You give one hand to Jesus and the other to your angel and you begin to come down the hill. You return like a feather. Observe your world well. You put in and take out what you want from your world. . . . You arrive at the door; you open it. You say to yourself that you already know how to go to this other world. You already know how to pardon. You already know. You have one tool more. Compare this flight with the flight when you came to the stairs, when you started. This flight is light, simple, more free, less slave. How do you feel?

As we opened our eyes, Paula asked the women how they felt. Macarena remarked, "I could not concentrate. I don't know, I was feeling my arms were too heavy, my legs." Paula responded, "It's your unconscious, which is still developing an ability to pardon. It means that, at bottom, your heart still does not want to pardon. And this means that you still continue to be sick." Honorina responded, "But, I don't know, I think. If someone does harm to you again, you have to pardon them again? I don't know. No." Paula responded, "The idea is that you do this exercise very often, because everyday we sustain harm. We pardon and pardon, I insist. It's not to put on another face. We have to respect ourselves. We have to speak, put up boundaries; we have to say to the other what we are not willing to accept, what we are not willing to live. But you pardon. What do you gain out of keeping angers, hates, humiliations, and so many things from the past? Do you take out something and construct? Nothing."

INTERVENTION AND THE "I"

Paula's exercise of pardon shows how the convention of pardon moves across therapeutic and political registers, changing in that migration. As we recall, Aylwin made an appeal for pardon as part of the accounting of the moral debt. This ethical work involved the reconciliation of victims, perpetrators, and witnesses who would come into agreement over the past. In this way, the past could be lived as past, and the reconciled nation could turn to the future. The pardon in the clinic took self-examination as a therapeutic for the self: through an internal journey, the self deciphers herself, identifying those inner impurities such as bad memories, anger, and hate in order to break free of them. Pardoning is the precondition for becoming, in Paula's words, "an adult and a free woman."

We might understand this breaking free of impurities as the kind of "purification of memory" advanced by the Vatican in the Great Jubilee 2000. The International Theological Commission's *Memory and Reconciliation: The Church and the Faults of the Past,* published in 1999, elaborated pardon as a "purification of memory" that entailed the Church's evaluation of the past and acknowledgment of "the sins committed in her name by its sons and daughters." Pardon for the Church, however, is an ethical task of the entire "community of the baptized": the Church is a "living society" in which "social sin" is the "accumulation and concentration of many personal sins" (see International Theological Commission 1999). Yet, in this "purification of memory," whereas sin is contained within the inner self, asking pardon and pardoning others always occurs in relation to a transcendent God, with whom and by whom the self is reconciled in Christ (International Theological Commission, 1999). The pardon in the clinic, on other hand, shifted this theological scene: the self was to perform pardon on oneself and others, purifying the self's memory, and then come back down to earth as a self-constituted "I." Jesus and a guardian angel would bear witness. It is a picture of moral autonomy, a self purified—through pardon—of relations.

Yet, when Honorina spoke of the difficulty of pardoning after being harmed again, she spoke from her actual relations; and when Macarena spoke of the heaviness of her body that did not permit this flight, she may have been indicating that her self was embodied differently, across her relations rather than apart from them. If this self is lived relationally, then the very understanding of how self and past relate would have to change, too. Indeed, the opening that Jung presents for memory is that of an *impersonal past,* archetypes autonomous from the willful self that nevertheless make up the transient crystalization of the self. For Paula, however, the inability to pardon was a symptom of the personal unconscious, an indication of a continued soul sickness.

What happened to the "historical debt" concerning the mental health of the population? By 2005, the program had been extended to every primary care center in Chile. Mental health officials, in conjunction with researchers from the University of Chile, published the results of their evaluation of the program—detailing its efficacy and cost-effectiveness—in the *Pan American Journal for Public Health* (Alvarado M. et al. 2005). In a sample of 229 patients, Alvarado and colleagues demonstrate that, after three months, 73.3 percent of the women had achieved "complete adherence" to their medication regime, while in contrast 37.8 percent of women adhered to group intervention. Overall, 77.2 percent of women showed a statistically significant improvement in depressive symptoms, according to the Beck Depression Index. The researchers state, "This data puts into relief the necessity to develop specific strategies to improve the adherence to treatment, in particular those of the psychosocial type [group intervention], which was unattended by close to 15 percent of the patients and had an irregular attendance of 40 percent of the patients" (p. 285).

In the midst of municipalization, psychosocial treatments are experiments geared toward creating community, through experiments with modes of relating. But these modes grow from existing relational modes. They also grow from an ethos of experiment constituted by a host of elements such as the qualities of physician care and local institutional arrangements. Together, these relations and elements compose the experiment as a singularity. How might the pharmacological aspect of the program differ in its local life? What might high rates of adherence both obscure and suggest?

CHAPTER 6

Life and Death, Care and Neglect

SELF-MEDICATION

In the streets of Santiago's center, a white-and-green billboard sits atop a high-rise building. In the image, a woman speaks to a pharmacist. The pharmacist in her white coat smiles at the well-coiffed woman, handing her a prescription. The text underneath the scene reads: "Self-medication is dangerous; talk to your pharmacist. Cruz Verde." Cruz Verde is one of the three pharmacy chains in Chile. The three chains, Cruz Verde, Farmacia Ahumada, and SalcoBrand, have a virtual oligopoly on the sales of pharmaceuticals in the Chilean market.[1] At the same time, they have developed partnerships with department stores to offer the sale of medications through department store credit. For instance, Farmacia Ahumada formed an alliance with Falabella, a major department store, allowing customers to buy pharmaceuticals as well as food and other household items using Falabella's credit card, the CMR card. SalcoBrand formed its own alliance with BCI bank, promoting the purchase of medications using BCI credit cards. With combined transactions of USD 900 million a year, these conglomerates are reshaping the relations between pharmaceutical and population, and between pharmacies (as the vendors of other brand-name and generic drugs) and the pharmaceutical industry.

In 2004, at the time that the billboards swathed the tops of buildings lining Alameda, the main street of Santiago's center, the three pharmacy chains were entering into a price war between themselves and were also in the midst of a confrontation with the international and national pharmaceutical industry. The price war began when Cruz Verde offered a 25 percent discount on all medications every Monday. SalcoBrand and Farmacias Ahumada responded immediately with their own discounts. SalcoBrand, drawing on its alliance with BCI bank, offered 30 to 35 percent reductions on all medications bought on the BCI credit card, while Farmacias Ahumada permanently discounted the prices of several hundred medications, particularly those on the state's National Drug Formulary List. With the price war came a media scandal. Even the right-wing newspaper *El Mercurio* admonished the pharmacy chains. For, with the price war, they had inadvertently shown how high their prices on medications had been all along. How was it possible to absorb price reductions of 35 percent? As *El Mercurio*'s editorial made clear, the consumer was "left with the sensation that he was being swindled, and not enjoying a vacation in San Juan under the courteous auspices of the pharmaceuticals" (*El Mercurio,* November 11, 2004, quoted in Fazio 2005, 218).

But even more important, the three chains worked together in a legislative, economic, and public relations struggle with the international and national pharmaceutical manufacturers. In an awkward but strategic alliance, the international pharmaceutical industry, represented by the Chamber of the Pharmaceutical Industry (Cámara de la Industria Farmacéutica), and the national pharmaceutical industry (the Asociación Industrial de Laboratorios Farmacéuticos) joined forces to lobby against the pharmacies' production of their own brand-name medications, medications that were off-patent and therefore could be produced by the pharmacies as so-called bio-equivalent medications. As the vice president of the Asociación Industrial de Laboratorios Farmacéuticos, Angélica Sánchez, commented to me in an interview in June 2004, "The pharmacies have the advantage of direct sales to consumers, and therefore they will preferentially sell their brand-name pharmaceuticals to clients. But, what we [her association and the Cámara] are working on is legislation for stricter guidelines in developing bio-equivalent medications. Because the pharmacies reap the profits of our research and development."

In this context, the advertisements of Cruz Verde instantiated themselves as sites of expert knowledge in relation to consumer-patients while also acknowledging the widespread practice of "self-medication" in a context in which pharmaceuticals for everyday ailments were

widely available.[2] In La Pincoya, the practice of self-medication implicated a "self." As I have discussed, the self is enmeshed in multiple
modes of relationality that are woven into economic difficulties and
unstable work patterns (see Das and Das 2006). Thus, discussing "self-
medication" in this neighborhood requires an understanding of these
relational modes, as well as of the local traffic in disease categories and
illness experiences.

LOCAL FORMULARY

Throughout my fieldwork, I was struck by the fact that people across
distinct social networks spoke of a "culture of self-medication," as if
this term were "common sense": from academics in the humanities and
social sciences to psychiatrists and mental health workers to neighbors
in La Pincoya. "We medicate everything," neighbors often ironically
remarked to me. Indeed, not only the advertising but also the buying,
selling, dispensing, and recycling of pharmaceuticals was apparent
throughout the city as one traversed Santiago's center to La Pincoya.
On buses to and from work, ambulatory sellers walked the aisles selling
anti-inflammatories, vitamins, and antibiotics for one hundred pesos a
pill (about twenty-five cents) to tired workers making their way back
home.

In La Pincoya, *almacén* owners kept shoeboxes full of antibiotics,
vitamins B and C, NSAIDS, anxiolytics, antidepressants, cough syrup,
and cold and flu medications. Examining the shoeboxes while asking
shopkeepers about common complaints, one can document a local formulary of everyday go-to medications and the everyday ailments experienced in this locality: headaches, backaches, lowered *ánimo, nervios,*
children's upper respiratory infections. Sra. Maria, a shopkeeper in La
Pincoya, went through her box with me. She stood across the counter
and conversed with me in her small storefront attached to her home. I
asked her how she managed to secure her supply of pharmaceuticals.
The pills came from a variety of sources, she explained.

For example, when specific pharmaceuticals were discounted in the
pharmacies, she would buy a supply on credit and charge slightly more
for them in La Pincoya to make a profit. Sometimes, however, she would
save her own pharmaceuticals from prescriptions given to her by the
local primary care center dispensary and sell those to neighbors as well.
Of course, she remarked to me, the pills as well as everything else in
the store could be sold "*al fiado*" (on trust), payable at the end of the

month, but only to those who were "trustworthy." Neighbors also sold their remaining prescription pharmaceuticals to Sra. Maria, which she then resold. In this way, pharmaceuticals not typically available without a medical prescription, such as antibiotics, anxiolytics, and antidepressants, were circulated in the neighborhood, establishing a formulary of necessary medications, defined locally.

But there were even more selling and buying locations. In the local market, there were vendors dedicated solely to selling pharmaceuticals for cash and on credit. *Muestras* (sample boxes) from clinics were brought back from doctor's appointments and saved, recirculated to friends, and also sold to the local corner store or the vendors in the *feria* (outdoor market). The availability of pharmaceuticals occurred through local circuits of exchange linking clinic to shop owner to neighbor and extending through families and neighborhood networks. And at the same time, it occurred through mechanisms of credit that linked the pharmacies with banks and department stores.

Antidepressants from the National Depression Treatment Program entered into these local circuits. Following how they were used, as one type among other medications, can help us explore how pharmaceuticals articulate with or mediate the bodily experiences of debt payments and unstable work.[3] Used sporadically to treat and thus mitigate bodily ailments emerging from confluences of the interpersonal and economic, antidepressants intimately tied to the affective configurations of the home and the temporality of economic scarcity. I think of "affective configurations" as tied into concrete living arrangements. They are shifting and partial, modest and dynamic, providing this tone of sadness and fear or that hue of joy or rage.

Antidepressant use occurs within modes of care, neglect, and violence that emerge from the interrelations and disjunctures of state programs, market demands, and intimate relations. I want to turn again to the questions of care within domestic relations that began this ethnography, specifically how the pharmaceutical is received in specific lives and affective configurations. While the state has displaced responsibilities for care onto individuals and families, this displacement does not necessarily mean that the pill is used as a disciplinary technology—that family members demand treatment compliance of kin with mental illness (see Biehl and Eskerod 2005). Rather, unique lives and configurations received pharmaceuticals differently and lent those pills—as actants—their force in relations.[4] Thus, exploring pharmaceuticals in affective configurations can open an inquiry into the quiet qualities of "making live" and "letting die" in the domestic, but it presupposes neither that life and death are opposed, nor that the antidepressant would have predictable effects, either because of its chemical composition or because of the disciplinary regimes of which it was initially an element (Foucault 1978). Attending to these qualities, however, can also show the limits of following a pharmaceutical in this lifeworld: that there are indeed matters of life and death for individuals that a focus on the pill would foreclose.

ÁNIMO AND SHARING

"We share them," Gladys told me. I sat with Gladys and her husband, Jorge, in their two-bedroom house that they shared with Gladys's daughter and granddaughter. Gladys and her husband were both in their fifties and had been married for the past thirty years. A petite woman with kind blue eyes, she spoke in a tremulous voice. Jorge was tall and wiry and had a warm disposition. We sat in a sparsely furnished living room with freshly painted white walls. Only the overstuffed blue couches and an old green sewing machine gave the room some color. When I entered their house, Gladys apologized. "It's not very welcoming," she said. They had just finished constructing a second bedroom, an extension of the main house. Before it was built, they had used the living room as a second bedroom, for her daughter.

Her daughter had had an off-and-on addiction to *pasta base* for several years. Attempting to break from the addiction, she smoked cigarette after cigarette in her room. "The walls were full of smoke," Gladys said. The smoke had sunk into the walls, staining them yellow and giving the entire house an acrid smell. Once the second bedroom was constructed, they worked on cleaning the walls, coating them with white paint. They removed the furniture, and bought new sofas on credit. The whiteness of the walls and the sparse clean furniture gave the house and its relations a chance at another family narrative. But Gladys and Jorge would have to contend with the demands of debt payments in the face of unemployment.

Seated next to Gladys, holding her hand, Jorge remarked, "All you see here, it was bought on credit. *Credit,*" he emphasized. "So it is not as if these sofas we are sitting on are really ours; they still belong to the department store. And we are paying the quotas, or we try to pay but are behind." Gladys explained, "You see, we paid for everything on credit, and that is why I got ill. Jorge lost his job in construction. They said he was too old, that he could not carry as much as the others. And we could not keep up with the payments." She pulled her hand out of Jorge's and began to rub her wrists. "I could not get out of bed," she went on. "The debts, they were tying me to the bed. I woke up in the morning, and the first thing I thought of were the debts. My body was tied to the bed. So Jorge took me to the primary care center, and they told me I had depression. And so I started taking the pills and going to the meetings with the psychologist."

A month had passed since the group sessions, and I asked her if the group meetings had helped her. "No, no, poor thing. The psychologist is such a good person, and pretty. I wanted to help her." She continued: "But the pills they gave me, they help my body get up. They told me to take one pill a day. But, I only take them when my body cannot get up from bed. The pills give you *ánimo*. So, last month Jorge started to look for work, but he wasn't finding anything. He rode his bicycle so far from here. He was riding his bicycle because we cannot pay bus fare. And I thought, my poor *viejo*, going around on bicycle all around the city. And he comes home for tea and a half of a round of bread. We had not even a *peso* for bread! I tried to start again in *la costura* (piece-meal sewing), but my body would not get up. I took the pills to get my body up from bed. I got a few *pololitos* [temporary jobs], and we had a little money to get through to the end of the month." But at that point, Gladys remarked, "Jorge also got sick, it [unemployment] was eating his nerves. So, we shared the pills. I told him, 'Take them, they help.'"

"I have worked my whole life in construction," Jorge told me. "And my wife, I never wanted to see her have to work again. For many years, she worked in sewing, but her wrists started to hurt. Sometimes she could not even pick up her cup of tea. It was too painful. When I got a contracted job in construction, I was earning well. And I told myself, I will never let that happen again. My wife, she can relax, she can be a grandmother to her grandchild. But then I lost my job. They told me I was too old to work. They fired me. It was like in one moment, we were doing well, moving up, renovating the house, and the next moment we did not even have a *peso* for bread. It was hard to look for work. At my age . . . They ask for young men thirty-five years old or younger. I am fifty-seven years old. Where will I find work? I rode all over the city, looking for work, and found one *pololito*, very hard labor. Yes, I took the pills that Gladys gave me. They helped me with the *ánimo*. I took them for a few days, but then I stopped when I found work. It was like, *whoosh* [he made a sweeping movement over his head, and smiled] . . .

It does not last for a long time, three months, but we can pay the debts in the meantime."

Gladys continued, "Yes, it was a relief. I felt like we could breathe again. We could buy bread. We could pay our debts. But I still worry. Workers die in construction. It's dangerous. He works in the most dangerous part. They tie a rope around him, and he has to work on the outside of the buildings. He could fall, the rope could fail." Jorge squeezed her hand. I asked Gladys if she was still taking the pills, with these ongoing worries. "No," she said, "now I save them for critical times, and it will be hard when Jorge has to look for work again. Why take them when we are better?" she asked.

In sharing pills, Gladys acknowledged Jorge's distress in the context of a mutually experienced economic precariousness. But further, in describing their mode of effectiveness and the temporality of those effects, Gladys and Jorge rendered the pill as a substance with a life-giving force that was immediately felt. As Gladys explained, "Te levanta el ánimo" (It raises the spirit/energy). Or, as Jorge described, "La pastilla me dio ánimo" (It gave me spirit/energy). The use of *ánimo* to describe the pill's effects in the context of the treatment for depression (*trastorno de ánimo*) could be seen as a reproduction of the language of the clinic within the home. Yet the word *ánimo* in colloquial usage intertwines multiple significations, as defined by the *Real Academia Española*: "the soul or the spirit that is the principle of human activity; value, force, energy; intention, will; attention and thought" (Real Academia 2010). For Gladys and Jorge, the pill was a dynamic vital force or energy felt immediately in the body, and it was to be saved for "critical moments." Thus, in their sharing, pills became agents in caring for others, lending vital force to relations themselves.

ENDURING

Carla too spoke of the antidepressant's vital force, but in relation to finding work. She cast this need to find work in the context of her relation with her husband, a relation that fluctuated between "enduring" and rupturing from betrayal and sexual coercion. Moments of economic scarcity and the need and desire to find employment worked into this fluctuation, like shifting tectonic plates. One month after the group sessions, I visited Carla in her home. Carla, who was in her midforties, lived with her husband and three children, her mother, Carla's brother, his wife, and their children. Carla's immediate family and her mother occupied the primary house, consisting of two rooms; her brother lived in a one-room shack attached to the back of the house with his wife and two children.

By the time I visited, Carla had a new job. She lost her job stringing racquets at the country club and now was a domestic worker two days a week. The change in work meant that she spent significantly more time at home, and that she earned less than half of what she earned before. Bills were now piling up, and this worked into the tension between Carla and her husband. We sat at the round dinner table covered with a lacy tablecloth while she fed her two-year-old son a cup of yogurt and intermittently checked on her five-year-old son as he played in the patio. As she explained to me, "The life of my husband is to work, pure work. There are bills to pay. . . . But what happens is that when I was working [in the country club], it was the same. But it was because he wanted it, because with what I earned I covered half of the costs of the house. That is to say, he did not concern himself with buying clothes, milk, medications, or anything for my children, because I bought everything. So, since I lost that job, he has had to pay for everything, and this has been hard for him to take on [*se la ha visto dura*]; and now the situation is more difficult."

Carla's sense that her husband had been only distantly involved in the economic and affective life of the home was marked by the way she spoke of her children: "*my* children," she emphasized, rather than "*the* children." Indeed, she had endured this distance since the birth of her first child, when she experienced the first of his betrayals. "He's never been here [for me], not even in the times when I needed him. When I was about to give birth, my mom took me to the hospital. He came to see me in the hospital after the baby had been born. Afterward, my mom and my brother came to get me [from the hospital]. He could not stop working. And with the little ones, it was the same thing. And that made me feel so bad. It's that I feel such a huge loneliness" (*soledad*). Three months earlier, she had discovered that he slept with another woman who worked in the same country club. The discovery precipitated her entrance into the depression treatment program. "I joined the group because the reproductive nurse [*matrona*] sent me. It was because, the day I went for contraceptives, she saw I was disturbed [*alterada*]. And I told her that I was not well. I was anxious [*ansiosa*]. I walked around very disturbed. And, earlier, I had been going to a group for alcoholics to accompany my brother, and I had heard of the psychologist. But you can't just go up and ask; you have to be sent."

Now, however, her husband's necessary involvement with the daili-ness of the house was producing forms of sexual coercion. "I've had to submit to him for the simple fact of my living together with him, for living here with my children, to maintain harmony." I asked her how much they earned. "He is earning 160 thousand pesos [USD 268], and it's not enough to cover the bills [*llevar las cuentas*]. Imagine it: for the house, just to be able to eat, I am given 60 [thousand (USD 100); this is her monthly income], 30 at midmonth, and 30 at the end of the month. But with this, I need to buy meat, bread, for all those days. And the light, telephone, water, buying [foodstuffs], and gas all need to be paid. These bills are costing 150 thousand [USD 252]." Carla was continuing to look for work: "I asked if I could add one more day [as domestic work staff], but no. So, although it's hard for me [*me cuesta*], I get up and search for work." On the days when she rode buses looking for work and going to interviews, she took the pills. "The pills lift the *ánimo,* so I take them before I leave the house."

One month later, I visited Carla again. She had found temporary work as an office cleaner for two more days a week. She looked and sounded noticeably more lively. I commented that she seemed better. She told me that she had confided to her mother about her husband's coercion. But her mother told her brother, and her brother beat up her husband. Her brother then moved into the main house, and her mother moved into the shack with her daughter-in-law and grandchildren. Since then her husband had not coerced her into having sex. But she viewed the future with apprehension: "It's been a month since we've had rela-tions. And I am happy. But I know that any day now he will oblige me [to have sex] again; in the meantime, I will continue with him. I will just have to endure it. What can I do? If he does not understand me, and I have told him everything that I feel? Since a man is more animal than the woman, he lets himself be guided by his instincts more than any-thing. But now it will be different, now he will search me and search me [*buscar*; literally, search out her sex or, more colloquially, pressure her to have sex]; and so that he leaves me in peace [*tranquila*], I will yield."

By sketching out the nature of this persistence, she intimated that there was a different kind of sexual violence occurring before. Now, the persistent fear of "searching" was what she had to live with. "And this gives me rage [*rabia*] because he's cheated on me twice, and when I work I pay for everything, and he doesn't pay one peso for the bills." When I asked her if she was still taking the pills, she replied, "What?"

"The antidepressants?" I asked. She said, "No, no. The pills, I stopped taking them for the moment."

For Carla, the antidepressant entered her life at critical moments, and her relations with her mother and brother helped her to "endure" (Biehl and Moran-Thomas 2009). Inconsistently taken, the antidepressant gave *ánimo* to look for work in a labor context where little was held constant, while the strength of her relation with her brother and mother produced an eventual shift in domestic living arrangements. This shift in arrangements produced a different affective configuration in the home, in which Carla moved from the actuality of sexual coercion to enduring fear of and rage at its possibility. For a different woman, Ana, antidepressants were, in contrast, intimately tied into her biography over time, and depression became a matrix through which extended family cared for her.

NEED FOR A WORKING BODY

"I was taking the pills [antidepressants] just to get up, so that my body could work," Ana told me. Ana, age forty-one, had just had an argument with her older son, Chino, when I came to visit her home, where she lived with her husband, Diego, and her two children—Chino, twenty-five years old, a son from an earlier relationship, and Kevin, eight years old. While we talked, she nervously smoked her Derby cigarettes, her trembling hand scattering ashes onto the couch where she sat. Thinking out loud, she said, "Maybe I should return to taking the pills."

Ana had been diagnosed with depression nine years earlier, after her husband left her for eight months to live with his new lover. At the time, Ana was pregnant with their son. She said the affair was "perverse." The lover had somehow gotten hold of the fax number of the clothing factory's head office where she worked ironing shirts. She sent a fax addressed to Ana detailing their trysts. Her boss, El Turco (the Turk), called her into the office and showed her the fax. Although her boss was sympathetic—"he gave me a hug"—the betrayal of her spouse and the feelings of humiliation "made me fall to the floor crying."

Ana was the youngest of six siblings. Her siblings, too, lived in La Pincoya, and they were known for being extremely gregarious and sociable. Ana, however, was so pained by the betrayal that she began withdrawing into her home. Her siblings made an appointment for her to see a private psychiatrist, who prescribed antidepressants for her. After Diego returned, she took antidepressants intermittently for the next several years. But then, about two years before she and I met, Ana had stopped taking them completely because she feared she was "becoming addicted." I asked her what "becoming addicted" meant to her. She replied that she had been taking the pills every day, and thought she would develop a "dependency": "I don't want to get to the point of needing pills every day, as if I cannot live without taking them."

A year and a half later, she developed vague pains in her neck and arms and trembling in her right hand. Ana went to the primary care clinic, where the physician told her she was experiencing psychosomatic symptoms. She was referred to the depression treatment program. As she explained to me, "They were giving out pills for free, and my older brother and sisters were going through difficult times [economically]." She began pharmacological treatment, but she stopped because of a lack of appetite and weight loss. Ana never attended group sessions. I met her through neighborhood relations. Her younger cousin was Antonio, who did auto body work in his patio, and whom I introduced in chapter 2.

When Ana continued to have symptoms, her siblings again pooled their money to pay for an appointment with a private psychiatrist based in Santiago's center. One of her older brothers bought on credit a different type of brand-name antidepressant that was prescribed for her, and the siblings agreed to collectively pay the monthly quotas. Taking the new antidepressant, Ana remarked, "I know these pills are a sacrifice for my siblings, so I save the pills for when I have crises. I determine when I need the pill myself, and stop when I feel better, usually after two or three days." She told me that she had never recuperated from the pain of her husband's betrayal, and that, given the problems of her older son as well, she continually "await[s] the next crisis."

It appeared that a new crisis had started as we spoke. Chino came home that morning after a night of drinking. In his drunken haze, he had lost his cell phone bought on credit, the fourth cell phone that he had lost in the past six months. Chino, like many young men in La Pincoya, depended on temporary work in construction. At the time, he was unemployed. He counted on the cell phone to secure this temporary work, receiving calls for immediate small jobs without warning. Without an income, however, he was unable to pay the quotas on all the lost cell phones.

Ana took over paying his debts out of her income, while they relied on Diego's income from construction work for all other household expenses. When I asked Ana why she took over Chino's debts, she remarked, "He is my first son. Diego is not his father. For many years, I raised Chino alone, and he spent more time alone than with his mother. I have worked my whole life. And he does not get along with Diego. Diego is much younger than me. He cannot control his rage. Once he found Chino in the street drunk, and he had so much rage. He beat up Chino, telling him, 'Your poor mother, how much you make her suffer.' I have so many conflicting feelings . . . So, if he cannot pay his debts, I must assume them."

Ana paid 160,000 pesos (about USD 270), half of the total household income, in monthly quotas. "The only way you can live is to be in debt," she said. "Look, I fought with Chino this morning, and told him, 'I kill myself working. Don't you see that the cell phones you lose mean all those hours when I kill myself at work? These cell phones are a sacrifice.'" Ana earned minimum wage in a clothing factory, where she had worked for the past twenty years without a significant raise. She stood twelve hours a day, ironing men's fine, collared shirts. The industrial iron heated the room to above ninety degrees Fahrenheit. Her wages depended on how many shirts she ironed per day, and because of this, Ana was worried that her "depressive crisis" could affect her pay. Running short on pills, she also worried that her siblings would have to pay for another prescription. "Look at my hand," she said to me, holding up her shaking right hand. "This always happens when I enter into crisis. And when my hand shakes, I can't iron, and I need to earn money to pay off these debts. This is why I tell you that my son is my sadness."

In 2007, Diego left Chile to work in Spain as an undocumented worker. He told me he was leaving because "there is no future in construction." He wanted to be able to earn money to make improvements to the house and send Kevin to good schools and to a university. In 2008, I visited Ana. When I arrived, she was pulling weeds from the sidewalk in front of her house in the evening light and invited me to have tea with her. Significant improvements had been made to the house, and there were new additions: a new room for Kevin, a second bathroom, a new leather couch, a microwave. Chino had a serious girlfriend and a job in construction. He spent most of his time in the home of his girlfriend's parents. Ana still had the same job, but now her home life was more "tranquil." "It's just my little one [Kevin] and me." Over tea and cigarettes, she told me that Diego was now living in Ibiza. Through his construction work there, he was able to pay off the debts they owed as well as make home improvements.

He called her every month, but in last month's phone call he had broken the news that he was not coming back. "He said that this place was nothing in comparison to there." "How painful," I said. "Yes, still, still, it is my sadness. I live with sadness. But now I try to move forward. I am finishing my high school degree at a night school here. I think that maybe when he [Diego] is an old man, he will come back to me. It hurts to think that, in the end, I will be alone. I try to keep it from Kevin, but he is slowly starting to realize that his father is not coming back. So, I have to take him to a psychologist, because he gets angry. Diego is a good worker. He sends money every month for Kevin's school. Because of him, Kevin is in a private school. But I live with the fear, *hasta cuándo* [until when]? Will he one day stop sending money? What will I do then? Ana put out her cigarette, taking an ashtray from the side table, where a postcard of the Virgin was propped up. A candle burned in front of the Virgin. Pointing to her, Ana said, "She listens to my tears and my pain. She is my solace in this house."

Ana's siblings' pooling of money, and the medications they purchased for her, show the force of kinship relations in constituting the experience of the self and the domestic. Through a remission in her symptoms, such relations enabled her to continue to work and to assume the debts of her son. As such, antidepressants, as indexical of these relations, were woven into her biography, and the interrelations between her trembling hand, her son, and debt constituted the tone of her sadness then. The sadness in Ana's biographical "moving forward" had a different tone. With debts paid and new trajectories for Diego and Chino, the loss of a future—of growing old with a partner—mixed with her present fear that his care for her and Kevin might someday end.

TAKE AWAY THE HUNGER

For Gladys, Carla, and Ana, antidepressants entered specific affective configurations of the home and domestic relations. They provided vital energy connected to work and tied to the life-giving qualities of relations. That the antidepressant is articulated so tightly with the energy needed to find work—temporary work to cover debts and household expenditures—speaks to life conditions in neoliberal Chile. These are conditions that I discussed before: the instability of the work contract; the massive expansion of credit for the poor, which serves as a way to tide one over in moments of scarcity; the selective nature of poverty programs.

But in situations of domestic neglect and abuse, antidepressants could also be taken up in ways that blurred boundaries between the life-giving and the potentially lethal qualities of relations. Neglect, violence, and pharmaceuticals worked in tandem to produce situations of damage and danger. As I learned in the case of another woman, Violeta, what constituted "domestic triaging" in families was more a question than a conclusion. Indeed, neglect occurred in relation to overlapping affective configurations that were very difficult to discern, and neglect occurred without a straightforward directionality (see Biehl 2004; Scheper-Hughes 1992). These affective configurations are enmeshed in economic pressures. Silence might exist at the edge of rage and fury. And subtle gestures introduced dark uncertainties, perhaps intimating a troubling domestic scene that I could not have access to.

"If I give money, I exist," said Violeta. It was October 2004. When I visited her in her shack situated behind her parents' house, Violeta had hardly eaten for a week and, for the most part, had remained in bed for the past week after a fight with her parents. Her cheekbones framed the hollows of her face. She wrapped herself in wool sweaters and heaped blankets on top of herself, although it was a pleasantly cool night. She spoke to me as a pair of intense brown-black eyes poking out from under the covers. Violeta told me that one week earlier she had taken twenty tablets of fluoxetine in a fit of rage and "pure nerves." She could not finish the rest of the tablets, she told me, because she fainted, and woke up the next day from her daughter's persistent calls.

Violeta was thirty-seven years old and single, and the mother of her dead younger brother's daughter, Marisol. That is, after her brother died, she became the child's mother through her care. She told me that the family's economic situation was getting worse. Her father, don Julio, seventy years old, had been out of work since April. He had worked as a parking lot attendant without a contract and received 120,000 pesos (USD 200) monthly. He quit after his boss denied him three days off from work to visit his wife in the hospital. She had metastatic breast cancer and was hospitalized for a host of complications arising as a result of chemotherapy and her uncontrolled diabetes. Since then, the household had depended on the contributions of two of his sons, who brought bread, tea, and vegetables. Violeta contributed income from temporary office cleaning. She earned 5,000 pesos (USD 9) a day without contract and benefits. This work was *por obra* (per work assignment), and Violeta often spent several weeks at a time out of work.

In February 2004, I met Violeta through Ruby. Ruby's sister's husband, Juan, was Violeta's younger brother. In the early 1990s, Juan had moved away from his parents' housing site to live with Ruby's sister in her mother's house. Because of this connection, I had heard many stories about Violeta's family and don Julio's hardness and violence toward his children and his wife. Violeta had shared the provisional wooden shack on the property with her younger sister, Andrea. During that time, the shack was full of cosmetics and bags of trendy clothes. Speakers from a boom box hung precariously from wires inserted in the wooden planks of the ceiling. They buzzed as Ricky Martin songs played at high volume. Pictures of Andrea with her boyfriend and friends were pegged like wallpaper on the far wall.

In July, Andrea left her parents' house to live with her boyfriend after her father slapped her during an argument. The walls were stripped bare, the wooden planks showing the residues of glue and scraps of photos. Violeta said, "Andrea couldn't stand it anymore, all the fighting, all the insults. But how could she just leave me thrown out? She didn't even tell me that she was leaving." With no one in the house as her ally, Violeta spent her time in bed, fasting, watching television, and getting up only to take care of her daughter, Marisol.

Several years earlier, Violeta had been diagnosed with chronic depression after attempting to commit suicide with an overdose of diazepam (Valium). Since that time, her family called her "*la loca*," which oscillated between endearing nickname and insult. Violeta told me that her depression started after her older sister died of lupus thirteen years earlier. Her older sister, with light skin, light brown hair, and an outgoing personality, was the favored child. She drew the love of her parents and the whole neighborhood. Violeta, on the other hand, had black hair and a brown complexion and had been quite timid as a child. "My mother never loved me," she remarked. As Violeta recounted, her mother told her during her sister's funeral that she "should have been the one that died."

In September, Violeta began receiving treatment for depression in the primary care center. However, she quit the group sessions while continuing to save her antidepressants. The group sessions, she told me, were "fantasy." "I liked being in the group; I never talked, but just listened to the psychologist talk and talk. I could even fall asleep for an hour there, in the group sessions. But, then, when the hour was up, it would be so *fome* [a downer] to return here [to the house], with the yelling and the insults. So I stopped going, because it was like being here [pointing to the sky] and then here [pointing around her], and *me bajoneó*" (it got me down). When I came to visit her, she recounted what happened right before her fit of rage. Her father had gone to look for her while she was visiting her friend Maria, who lived down the street in a one-bedroom house with her husband and two children.

I knew about Maria from other friends in the neighborhood. A few months earlier, Maria had been diagnosed with depression and was receiving a six-month's supply of fluoxetine as well as diazepam. As Maria explained to me, leading up to her diagnosis, Maria's husband had lost his job as manager of a sports store in La Dehesa, a wealthy municipality of Santiago. With only Maria's temporary office cleaning as a source of income, they could not keep up with their monthly debt payments. Maria had sold the DVD player and stereo that had taken "years to pay the quotas" for. The weight of debts and these losses had pressed down on Maria, and she could not sleep. She began taking the antidepressants "just to get out of bed so that my body could work."

But shortly after being diagnosed, she found stable work through a neighbor in an office-cleaning company, and her husband found temporary employment in construction. She stopped taking the medications because the contracted work was, in her words, "the remedy." She continued to receive the pills and passed them to Violeta, who, she said, had "a piece of my heart." Maria said, "She is such a good person, but her family, all are beaters, all are so crude. They have always been violent, so violent to their children. Look what Violeta does for Marisol; she cares for her and protects her from the others in her family. She lives for Marisol."

Violeta told me that she saved pills in a shoebox under her bed. I asked Violeta if I could see the shoebox. It was chock full of different pharmaceuticals: packs of fluoxetine, diazepam, and brand-name sample boxes of sertraline, bupropion, to name a few. There were also antibiotics, vitamins, and paracetamol. Other pills, I could not identify. Where did she get such pills? She responded somewhat cryptically, "They gave me prescriptions, and I save them."

> Clara: Who are they who gave you the prescriptions?
>
> Violeta: In the Psiquiátrico [Psychiatric Institute].
>
> Clara: But you're going to the consultorio [primary care center]?
>
> Violeta: For now. Before, I was going to the Psiquiátrico, but I got bored [aburrida] and annoyed [chorreada]. They made me sign some book of I don't know what, because they told me that if something more happened to me, they would intern me. And the only thing I think of is the daughter [la hija], la Marisol.

Violeta was extremely protective of Marisol. Outside of the everyday activities of picking her up from school, Violeta kept a close eye on her, even in the house. She watched her in the patio playing and preferred to have Marisol stay with her in her shack. For Marisol's sake, there was no way she would let herself be interned. She pointed out Maria's pills in this mass, saying, "She gives them to me as gifts. She gave me two boxes. She told me, 'Take them, I don't need them, they make you sleep and make you feel better.'" Violeta also turned to Maria for small cash loans or the use of her credit cards to buy Marisol clothes and school utilities. With her earnings from her sporadic work, Violeta paid the debts to Maria in small installments. "I am not one who takes advantage of another," said Violeta. But, when don Julio discovered that Violeta was giving money to her friend instead of paying the household bills, he was furious.

"He came to my friend's house," she told me, "*echando puro garabato* [saying/throwing out pure cuss words]. 'What are you doing, fucker, always walking around outside the house, you *tal por cual* [insults].' And I yelled back, '*Huevón*, why are you persecuting me? I am not your wife. I don't have a husband. I come and go, and I do not have to say to you where I go.' I was hysterical, I was shaking, I was capable of doing anything. He dragged me back home by my arm. He slapped me across the face. He told me that if I was not giving money, then I should work in the house. I was so ashamed. I took the bowl full of dog food and threw it against the wall, and it broke into pieces. I took my keys and threw them. My mother then started: 'You *tal por cual, desgraciada* [wretch]. You are *una loca*. You have always been *una loca*.' And I say to them, 'Am I *la loca*. Who is *la loca*? All of you, except me.' I tell you, pure nerves, and I starting taking the pills again. One, two, three, four . . . I didn't stop. I wanted to continue, but I got dizzy. Marisol was here, observing me, but she did not say anything. I think I scared her."

She continued: "Just now before you came, I was watching this program, this television series, about the emergency room, with Marisol. And there was this rich girl [*chica cuica*] that took a syrup [*jarabe*] to kill herself, and the doctors were taking everything from her stomach. And Marisol said, 'This girl is you [*soy tú*], mamá.' And I was cracking up with laughter [*cagando de la risa*; literally, 'shitting with laughter']. She notes everything, observes everything." For the next week, Violeta stayed in bed, taking seven to eight fluoxetine tablets a day to take away the hunger, watching television, and arising only to accompany Marisol to school and back. "And now they say I cannot have food. They told me, 'You have to earn to eat.'"

Violeta's story was so troubling not only because of the explicit violence but also because of its dark lining. The rage with which her father brought her back to the house, and Violeta's rejection of the role of his wife, intimated other possible underlying violences that I feared were happening but could not ask about. I was not immune to the rumors that had been circulating about don Julio for many years. In speaking of don Julio, neighbors said euphemistically with a knowing glance that he had "become twisted in his person" or that "he desires those he shouldn't." Accusations are not explicit; they stay in the register of suspicion. But subtle maneuvers within the domestic hint at such suspicions: a mother's efforts to afford protection by vigilantly watching her daughters and encouraging them to spend more time in the houses of extended kin living in the *población*. It is not simply a matter of just asking what is happening. I write with this uncertainty.

The following week, I visited Violeta in the evening. Violeta was waiting in the patio, huddled in a thick jacket. "It's better that we don't go through the house; there is pure idiocy happening in there." We walked to the side of the housing site and entered through a loose wooden plank in the fence, which led immediately to the door of her shack. But when we opened the door, don Julio was with Marisol in the room. Violeta became tense and silent. I was tense. He lingered as if he wanted to talk. As a courtesy, I asked him, "How are you?"

> Don Julio: *Más o menos, dentro de lo posible* [more or less, within what is possible].
>
> Clara: Oh . . .
>
> Don Julio (*speaking in a halting manner*): Because of so many things. Everything is bad. In the house.
>
> Clara: What is happening in the house?
>
> Don Julio: *De todo* [of everything]. *No hay para comer.* There is no money for food. My children are *malgeniado* [bad-charactered], *malgeniado* they are, *desgraciado* [wretched]. The other daughter [Andrea] comes and goes. None of them are committed to the house [*comprometido con la casa*]. None of them are concerned about the house. I have a problem with *la presión* [blood pressure] now.
>
> Clara: Because of what is happening in the house?
>
> Don Julio: Yes. It's because of my wife. Highs and lows. But mostly lows. She does not take care of herself, and does not know how to take care

of herself. [Sra. Maria, who had diabetes, did not take her insulin shots regularly. For the previous two months she had been in and out of the hospital for uncontrolled diabetes.]

Clara: Oh . . . and have you been able to find work?

Don Julio: No, no there is no work. Less for people of my age. I am old. I don't find work.

Clara: So, how are you enduring this?

Don Julio: Because of my two sons [*lolos*; he looks proud in this respect]. They are contributing.

Clara: Which sons? Marco and Juan? (Two sons whom I knew well.)

Don Julio: No, not them, no [with an ironic smile]. Well, Marco more than Juan. The two are Pedro, *el flaco* [the thin guy] who lives on the corner, and Nono, who lives in La Pintana [a different *población* in the southern zone].

By this point, don Julio had moved from standing in the doorway to sitting opposite me on Violeta's bed. Marisol was seated next to him. Violeta sat next to me on Marisol's bed, leaning against the wall and staring at the television. She looked censured, unable to speak in front of don Julio. I should never have continued asking him questions, I thought with frustration. I felt as if Violeta's space had been invaded. Don Julio hugged Marisol, "But this little spoiled [*regalonita*] daughter has everything." *Regalona,* deriving from *regalar,* or to give a gift, is usually spoken as a term of endearment, meaning that the child has been given a lot of love and attention. "She is the happiness of this house. *La regalona* of the house." As don Julio hugged her, Marisol scrunched her face up and tried to pull away from him. "Well, I came to visit Violeta. So . . . ," I said. Don Julio got the hint and said, "Good, so I will leave you all and let you converse." Violeta watched and observed carefully and cautiously as he entered the main house. She did not utter a word until the house door was shut, and then explained to me why she waited to speak: "*Capaz* [it would be possible] that he is listening to our conversation outside."

Violeta said she felt better when she was working. With work, she explained, her father could not "menace" her. But over a period of six months, Violeta had had only three jobs, the longest lasting two weeks, each approximately two months apart. Violeta had grown painfully thin, anorexic, her long black hair overwhelming the rest of her frail body. She told me that her parents denied her food, and that she took antidepressants to "take away the hunger," asserting her determination to not be hungry. She said she felt invisible in the house. She told me, "I am a ghost, I do not exist. I enter the house and speak to them, and it is as if I were speaking to the walls. They don't answer back. I move like a ghost; I feel like no one sees me."

NEW RELATIONS

In January 2005, Violeta began to attend Pentecostal meetings with her sister, Andrea. Her sister had been hospitalized for lupus-associated renal failure. After two critical weeks in the hospital, Andrea had returned to her parents' home. She had lost the function of both her kidneys and had to start dialysis three times a week. Andrea's body was wasted, and her once dramatically full curly brown hair had thinned so that her scalp was visible.

Although the two sisters had been estranged, Violeta cared for Andrea, accompanying her to dialysis and making her meals. Don Julio and Sra. Maria were also very attentive to Andrea, whom they said was "as beautiful as her older sister." I was struck by the care they gave her, even as they continued to belittle Violeta. Andrea's illness and the feeling of impending death enveloped the home. Violeta and Andrea began to attend Pentecostal meetings,[5] praying for a cure for Andrea. But the fights at home continued. In response to the fights with her parents, Violeta took pills in large quantities while increasingly seeking solace in the Pentecostal meetings, spending three nights a week with the group of approximately thirty members.

The meetings that Violeta attended took place in a former liquor store on the main street, Recoleta. Don Manuel was the brother who led the meetings. A thin man with leathery skin and gray hair, he explained to me that he had been an alcoholic years ago, but that the hand of God had touched him. Since then, he had been able to hold down a steady job laying ceramic tiles. Don Manuel's congregation was quickly expanding. Yet, as his popularity grew, so too did rumors of his thievery and dishonesty. Neighbors across religious and political affiliations had rancor toward him. Some said don Manuel often asked for food contributions for those "who were even poorer than us," collecting the food in cardboard boxes, but that in reality his family was storing and eating the food. Two neighbors claimed that his two sons had broken into their houses and had stolen electronic equipment and phones, and that when they had confronted don Manuel and his sons, the three had denied all wrongdoing. Violeta's parents took up these rumors to pressure her to stop going to the meetings.

I asked if I could accompany Violeta to the meetings. At the end of January, I attended a meeting with Violeta and Andrea. Violeta told me that she had taken more than twenty fluoxetine tablets over the weekend in response to a violent fight with her parents. She had not eaten, "not even a piece of bread." That morning, Violeta had had another argument with her mother, who had berated her for a plant that had gone missing from the patio. "And I took four pills after that," she remarked. In the span of a little more than forty-eight hours, Violeta had taken approximately twenty-five fluoxetine tablets.

Toward the close of the meeting, a tall man with gray curly hair, wearing a gray shirt and pants, entered the hall. He got down on his knees and prayed at the doorway. The worshippers sang and played guitars. The loudspeaker boomed out the pastor's voice. The man moved to the center of the hall. He hopped up and down, his eyes closed tightly. With his face pinched, he hugged himself, at times pointing around the room. He yelled, "I am a God," "I am not a God," "I am a confused God." The worshippers stopped singing. Men and women, speaking in tongues, grabbed the man's head, arms, trunk, skimmed their hands over his body, and then wiped their hands clean in the air. The sound of speaking in tongues belted through the loudspeakers, mixing with the crackles from the microphone as it lay on the podium.

Violeta was standing next to me. Turning to me, she said, "Does it give you fear?" And I whispered back, "No. But it makes me a little uncomfortable." She responded, "Ay, I don't like it when they *claman* [ask God to have mercy on a person and to use his power to effect a change in that person; exhortation of God]; it makes me nervous. I'm going outside." Violeta moved past me. She did not return until the pastor ended the session, shouting through the microphone, "We are closing, we are closing!" Those speaking in tongues stopped and returned to their places—all except the man with curly gray hair who continued to move his body. He gradually stopped as people began to leave.

Andrea, Violeta, and I took our leave, exiting through the side door. Suddenly, Violeta collapsed. Her thin body fell to the pavement, her head hitting the concrete with a dull thump. Her body seized on the sidewalk. "Carry her into the hall!" someone exclaimed. Don Manuel's son and I lifted her up and carried her into the hall. The son put a cushion under her head. Don Manuel knelt next to her head and began a laying on of hands (*ungiendo*). Others joined. At that moment, my thoughts were: "She's having a seizure. I wish they would stop. What should I do?"[6] Her body continued in a rhythmic spastic twitching. After what seemed like several minutes, the twitching stopped and she lay still. With her eyes still closed, she moved her mouth and then her head. I knelt down to hold her hand and turned her onto her side.

After a few minutes, Violeta opened her eyes. Dazed, she said nothing. She stayed that way for a minute, looking at my face. "Are you OK? Can you tell me where you are?" I asked. She did not answer, but instead sat up. She wiped her face with her hands and remained silent. Pushing herself up with her arms, she tried to stand but could not. I lifted her up, leading her to a chair. After several more minutes, she uttered, "It made me cold, when I went outside. It always happens when the man comes [the man with gray curly hair]. You saw me, Clara, I was trembling," referring to when she went outside. She did not seem to remember what had just occurred. I told her, "Violeta, you fainted, you were on the ground." She looked at me blankly.

Don Manuel's eldest son approached her, saying, "Sister, you have powers. You have the Spirit inside, and what happened is that the Spirit left when you were going [leaving the hall]. Why? Because we had a battle here because that man said that he is 'a confused God.' But God is not confused. God is transparent. And you have the power of the Spirit, a power of witchcraft" (*brujería*). Andrea mentioned that Violeta left when they were *clamando* (exhorting God), and that she should have stayed through it.

Don Manuel's eldest son said to Violeta: "What you need to do is *clamar* to God." Violeta did not answer. Another woman gave her a glass of water, saying, "Don't go now, stay here and rest." But Violeta stood up to leave. Don Manuel stopped her: "I will talk to you. You now have the demon. The Spirit left your body when you left [the hall]. You will heal here. You are sick." Violeta, again, did not speak, answering with a blank look. I walked her back to her house with Andrea, holding her arm firmly to steady her. While walking, Violeta spoke: "This has not happened in a long time. Something touched me." As we approached her house, she told me, "Do not mention this to my mother or father. This did not happen." In the following days, however, her parents heard gossip from the neighbors of the possession.

Over the next several months, as Violeta experienced more seizures both in the meetings and at home, the congregants alternated between saying that Violeta was possessed by demons and needed healing, and that she had the Spirit. At the same time, her parents began to more heavily oppose her attendance. She told me that they yelled at her. Don Julio hit her. They said she spent too much time there at the cost of completing her housework. Was she giving money to those thieves?

Violeta was anorexic. Neighbors saw her on the street with concern and dismay. "Poor girl," they remarked, at once condemning her family's relations and spreading more gossip. Members of the meetings greeted her on the street through a vocabulary of kinship. They chastised her with affection, remarking on how thin she had become. They invited her over for tea and would pass by her shack with a meal. Nevertheless, Violeta had no appetite. "It's this house, it takes away my hunger," she now said.

After witnessing two seizures, I confronted Violeta before another meeting: "Violeta, you take so many pills, and these are pills that affect your brain. Do you think that the pills could be giving you seizures? I say this only because I worry about you." "What? What are you talking about? Clara, now you put [construe] yourself as *doctora*," she said, laughing. "I tell you, you know me. You see how my family is with me. I am very alone in this house, but in the meetings, something touched me. And that cannot be explained by the pills." Whenever I visited her, I urged her to stop taking pills. I offered to take her to the psychiatric hospital for an evaluation of her seizures. I crossed the line. She became frustrated with me, snapping, "Ayyy, Clara, leave it be." At this point, psychiatric treatment had become obsolete, even as pharmaceuticals became possibly central to Violeta's bodily experiences.

Indeed, for Violeta, the pharmaceuticals, domestic violence, and the Pentecostal meetings spoke more to the complexity of the forces possessing her than did the idea of iatrogenesis that I advanced. Her bodily experiences were conditioned by economic insecurity but also lined by dark uncertainties. New relations with the Spirit and with the demon emerged as both promising and threatening forces. They connected her to new domestic relations, but in so doing they made her vulnerable to further beatings and insults at home. Pharmaceuticals became a damaging medium, even though received as a life-giving gesture. At the same time, the Pentecostal meetings emerged as a potent source of spiritual healing for Violeta, even as her body continued to sustain multiple damages from malnourishment and pharmaceuticals. In the difficulty of these relations, life and death are not opposed but are sketched into each other.

WRITING, SUFFERING, LIVING

Lalo also put into question any simple opposition between life and death. I met Lalo when I first arrived in La Pincoya in 1999. His fame preceded him: he was an infamous drug dealer of *pasta base* and widely known for his assaults and violence. As one of the main dealers in the *población*, he owned and operated out of three houses. But he proudly asserted that he sold only on the other side of the *población*, and did not sell to "*los de acá*" (those around here). Several local youths, however, had joined him dealing drugs, and it was commonly known that his dealings had resulted in several children becoming addicted to *pasta base* "here."

Moreover, he came from a family that was notorious in the neighborhood. Every son had been incarcerated for assault and drug running. The second oldest, still in prison, continued to direct drug trafficking and assaults from the prison. Lalo had been in prison twice, once for beating up his ex-wife and her lover when he caught them having sex in his home, and another time for "suspicion." (A common experience of many young men in La Pincoya, who are often taken into custody by the police on mere suspicion of wrongdoing.) It was rumored that the beating of his ex-wife and her lover had resulted in hospitalization for both of them. The ex-wife now lived with a long, disfiguring scar across her face.

I knew of Lalo through these stories and what some called his "big sin" of dealing drugs to children. For that reason, I had misgivings about speaking to him. Hearing more and more stories, and watching the way he held his pistols so casually in the street, I had begun to fear him. We greeted each other in the street, but I made my way cautiously around him, attempting to avoid further conversation.

Returning to La Pincoya in January 2004, however, I found that Lalo had radically changed. He was thirty-two years old, and his body was as thin as a wire. His face was drawn and chiseled from hunger. He had stopped dealing drugs after becoming addicted to *pasta base* himself. He had lost his fortune: money, cars, houses, and jewelry that he had stolen and bought with drug money. He lived in a shack at the back of his parents' property, a single wooden room divided in two by a sheet, separating the "bedroom" from the "living room." He was unemployed and sustaining himself with sporadic odd jobs. Eight months earlier, his girlfriend of eight years had left him without explanation, taking their two-month-old daughter. He had not seen them since and did not know where they were living. Neighbors considered Lalo dangerous and untrustworthy, referring to his history of dealing drugs in the *población* and the stories of his brutal beating of his ex-wife. Many warned me not to speak to him.

Lalo stood at a particular corner in the evenings when others were taking *once* (evening tea). Alone, he smoked his Belmont Lights. One night in March 2004 as I was passing by, he offered me a smoke. I decided to stop and talk, despite my fears that inclined me otherwise. The chat turned into regular conversations with him on that dusty corner in front of his family's home. He told me he was "suffering from abandonment." And because of this abandonment,

> everything has turned out badly, in my work, in my social relations, with my family. I have so many problems, so many problems. I am brought down, destroyed, alone. I feel a rejection [*rechazo*] toward my family, and my family rejects me too. My mom is always helping my brothers, and they take what they can from my mom. They never contribute, but she's always with them. And I have always contributed, always passing money to her. So when I am fine [economically] she draws near, but when I am fucked up, she criticizes me behind my back.

I asked him about his childhood. As the eldest in the family, he had dressed his younger brothers for school and prepared lunch for them. He had been held responsible if anything went wrong in the house. He continued to help his younger siblings, but felt a constant rejection from his mother.

> If I broke the handle of a cup, my mother beat the shit out of me. Even when nothing happened in the house, she beat me. And I realized that she was beating me because my dad was beating her. And one day, yeah, I asked her, "Why do you hit me so much, mom? Do you hit me because my dad hits you?" And she stood there thinking and said, "Yes, most likely, yes." And my brother Jesús—I gave him work, where I am working. I said to Jesús, "Look, they need more people there, come with me." And he was working with me. And then I discovered that he had robbed me of my birds, which are really expensive, and which I had in the cage out in front. So, you see how my family is with me.

Lalo's parents allowed him to stay on their property because he paid rent for the small shack that he inhabited. But because his work unloading trucks in Patronato (a commercial sector of the city occupied mainly by Koreans) was unstable, he was unable to regularly pay his rent. With his criminal record and lack of elementary school education, stable and contracted employment was difficult, if not almost impossible, for him to find. Lalo knew that he could go back to dealing drugs. Indeed, his contacts had called him, offering to set him up again. But, as Lalo told me, "It's something ethical. I want to do things correctly now." The desire to follow an ethical life came up against concrete obstacles.

> My work is so unstable. The other time that you came, Clarita, I had to leave to get my money, but they didn't pay me, and it's been delayed for a week, at times, two weeks. And I have costs, I have to pay rent; I can't wait two weeks. And at times, I say, "Ahhhh, I want to throw everything to shit." It's that, when I was doing bad things, I was doing well, and now that I am conscientious and want to do correct things, I'm doing badly. What conclusions do I take from this?

Intertwined with his feelings of abandonment and frustration was the loss of his girlfriend and his infant daughter. He told me that he did not know why Maria left, and he spent his time trying to figure out what he did wrong. "I always ask myself why she left, because she has never given me an explanation. And I stay with this uncertainty. I ask myself how I made a mistake, what I did. Is there something wrong with me? My pride is suffering." When he was not working or on the corner smoking, he spent his time in his shack watching a documentary he had about polar bears over and over again on a small television. He liked it very much and invited me to watch the "polar bear film" with him. "Polar bears are solitary animals," the documentary began.

Over the next year, Lalo's body disappeared as he lost weight. Without money to buy food, he went hungry. But he was not in the mood to eat. He preferred to spend the little money that he did have on cigarettes, which took the edge off his anxiety. He hurt himself because he was angry. "I have arrived at feeling pity for myself. It gives me so much anger, all these conflicted feelings. It gives me so much anger that I hit myself, I scraped the brick wall with my hands." He showed me his hands. His knuckles were scraped, darkened with dried blood. At times, he said, "I think that it would be better if I died. It would be better if I took a pistol and *pphhhfff*." He spoke to no one in his house; and outside the house, he said, "I wear a mask." But the mask was wearing thin, and after a few months Lalo stopped standing at the corner and retreated into his shack, where he passed entire days in front of the TV, speaking to no one.

In March 2005, Lalo began to tattoo his body. One tattoo a day for seven days. He only opened his door to the teenager who did the tattoos with a pin and the ink of broken pens, and to me. The first was on his neck: a large heart engulfed by a rose. The next were on his back: a sword wrapped by flowers; a woman in a black miniskirt with her legs crossed, slyly wielding a pistol in her hand. The next two were on his chest: a mermaid with big breasts, and a naked woman sitting forward seductively. The final two, one on each of his biceps, he did himself: one was the word *estoy* (I am), and the other was the word *muerto* (dead). The new tattoos tented up the skin with black ink, and the needle left a blood-marked border. I was cringing when my hand clasped his arm. I asked him, "But, didn't it hurt?" He answered, "Oh yes, it hurt me, but I liked the pain. For seven days I lived this pain, for seven days I was tattooing my body. It's because I *live* these experiences. It's not theory. I have lived, suffered. And I can live more, and suffer more."

His body was the page where he wrote his text and left his signature, his autobiography. Lalo's writing on his body performed his pain, in which dense relations murmured around him, but existentially, not through him. It was self-writing performed with the quality of conversion, and it was a provocation to himself as well as his family, neighbors, and me. How is a life force projected in and through this neglect, this rejection and abandonment? Through pain, he wrote his defiance.

From that conversion to a defiant life, Lalo turned again to his everyday life. Upon my urging, he began earning his high school diploma at a night school where I worked as a volunteer teacher. At the same time, he found temporary work laying down grass in a football field, a three-month work program for youth sponsored by a French nongovernmental organization. Once he found work and entered school, he resumed standing on the street at night. We stood in the cool evenings on the corner, but now talking through his mathematics problem sets, making calculations in the dust with sticks. He invited me to tea in his small shack. He carefully covered the coffee table made of unfinished wood with a red-and-white-checkered cloth and prepared a half round of bread for each of us, topping it with a slice of tomato and some dried oregano he had pilfered from his mother's kitchen. "Clarita, you can't tell me that I haven't conquered a little piece of your heart." Yes, you have.

But, his family's rejection endured. "I pay my rent now, and still they do not even acknowledge me." As Lalo again found, money was no guarantee of acknowledgment and care in the home. And yet he continued to attempt to reconcile with his family, passing any extra money that he earned to his mother. He struggled to understand why his mother continued to reject him. He was never invited to the main house for tea, nor did his parents invite him to their large Sunday meals or barbecues. The grill stood right before the door of his shack. The rejection seemed inexplicable. Having clearly aligned myself with Lalo, I found that the parents did not speak to me either.

SACRIFICE AND ACKNOWLEDGMENT

On October 20, 2006, Lalo was killed. I had returned to Cambridge, Massachusetts. I was in the midst of preparing my dissertation when I received a phone call from Ruby. She said, "I had to call you. I know you had much affection [*cariño*] for him, and how you worried about him." She related to me the details of his death. His younger sister had become involved with a drug trafficker in a neighborhood on the other side of the *población*. The drug trafficker had beaten her, and she had returned to the house with bruises on her face.

Lalo and his younger brother, Jesús, were furious. They went to the drug trafficker's house and roughed him up. The following night, a gang of teenagers with guns arrived at Lalo's house. They climbed over the brick walls surrounding the patio and entered the front door. In his shack, Lalo heard his mother screaming. The teenagers had her and her daughter at gunpoint in the living room. Lalo and Jesús entered through the back door. Jesús was fatally shot. They were about to shoot Lalo's mother, when Lalo threw himself over her body. He was shot in the abdomen and died almost immediately. The teenagers ran off. Hearing the gunshots, Leticia's children, Sebastián and Gonzalo, ran over. They drove Lalo in Sebastián's truck to the hospital, hoping that he could still be saved.

The news spread quickly of Lalo's and Jesús's deaths. Ruby's phone call two days later traveled the painful distance between Cambridge and La Pincoya. Such sadness. No service had been planned for the two brothers, but I later discovered that Leticia, who was Lalo's godmother, had stepped in to hold the brothers' *velorio* (wake) in her home. Leticia said that Lalo's mother was not capable of being a mother, and she felt it was her duty. Their bodies were buried in the Cementerio General.

In the weeks after Lalo's death, I spoke to many of his neighbors. Rumors circulated as to why Lalo died from "just one bullet to the stomach." Some said that Lalo had a cancer growing in his stomach, a cancer that grew from his family's rejection. As one neighbor recounted, "Lalo was rejected, abused by his parents since he was born. He was the eldest, and he was the one who got beat up. You have to understand, he grew up in a difficult time. His parents, like us, were in the Communist Party. They were both tortured. His father was an alcoholic. They were angry at Pinochet, but they took the anger out on Lalo. That was the mistake they made." Another neighbor recounted, "One night, after curfew—this was during the time of Pinocho—I heard the police coming. I looked across the street from the patio. There was a drunken man kicking a little boy in the street. The police arrested the man. The little boy was lying in the dust. That little boy was Lalo." And, as many told me, it was the fact that the bullet hit the cancer—an accumulation of his rejection and abuse—and "spread the pain in his body" that ultimately killed Lalo.

Returning to La Pincoya in July 2007, I asked Julieta to take me to Lalo's grave. As we rode the bus to the Cementerio General, Julieta told me that many neighbors showed up at the *velorio,* and that she was embittered by the emotional "show" of Lalo's mother. She said, "She was saying, 'My sons, my sons.' Crying and all that. What a hypocrite. She was always mistreating Lalo, beating the shit out of him. She couldn't care less when he was suffering." When we reached the cemetery, I bought flowers and put them on his grave. It was adorned by a basket of plastic flowers and a large flag of the Colo-Colo football team that Sebastián had put there. As I went from home to home, I heard new rumors: that Lalo had been infected with HIV. That he had resorted to male prostitution to make money to pay for *pasta base.* While remarking on how he had saved her life, his mother alluded to this rumor: "But, it was better that he died. He would have only lived more pain." Neighbors remarked to me: "At least this way, we can say that he finally had a moment of dignity. He died with dignity, instead of dying alone stigmatized with AIDS."

The circulation of these rumors, however, seemed to point back to the speakers. That is, in the tone in which they were spoken, with hesitation and retrospective justification, the rumors also voiced an unsettled feeling that the speaker had failed in being a neighbor to Lalo. Because Lalo was considered dangerous and untrustworthy among neighbors, the relations of the home were where he hoped he would be acknowledged. It is painfully striking that, in the last moment, Lalo sacrificed himself to save his mother's life. The ultimate attempt to be present to his family, through his death. Through the rituals for the dead, Lalo was brought back as neighbor, godson, brother, and son—a social world of vital connections, and an acknowledgment he had struggled to experience during his flesh-and-blood life.

Conclusion

Relations and Time

When I returned in August 2010 and visited neighbors, their memories of Lalo interspersed with their accounts of the changes in the neighborhood and in lives. Neighbors now spoke of him as an "ethical" drug dealer: he stood up for his *población* and only sold in the *barrio alto*. When I visited Julieta, she spoke of the changes in the *población* in the preceding few years, and Lalo wove into her memories. "He was something else, he was different," recounting how Lalo had himself been a militant in the Frente, along with her younger brother. "I miss that *loco* a lot," Julieta said. With regret in her voice, she said she had not appreciated his loyalty to "the people here." "We were blind to his suffering," Ruby said. "No one assumed the responsibility." "But, really," she added after hesitation, "he had done some terrible things." Their ambivalence and regret reveal the fragility and force of neighbor relations. Their narrative also shows how selves are not unitary subjects who are stable and fixed in time, but rather are enmeshed in multiple relations. Those relations themselves are revealed in time.

Julieta had moved from Leticia's house to the coast to take care of Tata, who was almost blind with cataracts. Julieta said that she took her children to live in San Antonio because "the street" was getting "too heavy" in La Pincoya. "The kids are selling drugs right here, on the corner!" Mama Ana had passed away three months earlier. Leticia was overcome with sorrow. Julieta told me bitterly that, in Mama Ana's final days, Leticia had pleaded with her not to die. Mama Ana had suffered a foot infection from uncontrolled diabetes that got into the bone and blood. "Yes, seeing Mama Ana so ill and delirious pained me, but I didn't plead with her to stay. I didn't want her to leave feeling that guilt. I wanted her to have peace. She lived a long life. She spent time with her grandchildren and saw Tata grow old. It was time to die."

I just happened to be walking to Leticia's house when I bumped into Julieta on the street corner. A few days earlier, she had returned from the coast for a visit. Emilio had stayed in La Pincoya, continuing to live in Leticia's house. His mother had died of cancer one year earlier, and his sisters and their children continued to live in the house across the street. Julieta now worked in San Antonio as a nanny for a young woman with a trust fund who fancied herself a melancholic artist. But the woman threw tantrums and was very spoiled. "Ufff, sounds painful," I said. She agreed, laughing. "Sometimes, I just think, 'Julieta, have patience, have patience.'" But the woman's family paid very well, she told me. Switching topics, she said she had finally "achieved it," meaning a kind of separation from Emilio that she could live with. "I told you Clarita, everything in its time." "But you come back to La Pincoya sometimes?" I asked. Julieta visited every other month. "It's my daughter. She has friends here. So I return for her. Yesterday, I woke up in a panic and felt like I was suffocating. I thought, that's strange. This house. I haven't felt it this strongly in a while."

FORCE OF RELATIONS

Julieta evoked a lived force of relations. She also shows that, although the identifiable form of the family—the family living together in the house—might change, the force of kinship can remain. Relations are lived in degrees of intensity; they are not an all-or-nothing presence or absence. Writing one year later, in 2011, it dawned on me that the very way I undertook this ethnography may have oriented me to the dynamic qualities of relations, to considering their different moments in their specificity. That is, moving with people in time reveals not only the work of time on relations but also the varying intensities they may take. But the writing of ethnography, too, entails a struggle: to allow oneself to be oriented in different ways in time and to time, so that one may be open to the field of relationality rather than foreclose it. Thus, attending to a slice of time—the contemporaneity of concealing-while-giving in everyday life—revealed the boundaries between neighbor and domestic relations, but also the possibilities of kindness and generosity.

And, rather than interpret Ruby's dream in terms of the deep psyche, for example, we might acknowledge her mourning with others. This mourning with others reveals the past continuous inhabiting actual conditions of economic precariousness.

Different ways of being oriented to and living in time allow one to attend to *how* the self is enmeshed in relations, and also help one appreciate everyday life as an achievement (Das 2007, 2010a). That is, relations might be lived in deep disconnection, but also might someday be lived as recovered. Or, confronted with multiple demands, an individual might be faced with, and have to suffer, her finiteness. Individuals are enmeshed in multiple relations that may be in play simultaneously, and these relations themselves may be composed of different elements, for example, blood and the everyday labors of caring. In this density of relations and elements, responsibility cannot be understood solely in terms of the willful autonomous subject. Rather, it might also be understood as responsiveness, and this responsiveness must be understood in concrete circumstances. Or, as Deleuze suggests, rather than apply judgment, ethnography might attend to the *"combats-between* that determine the composition of forces in the combatant"* (Deleuze 1997, 133, emphasis in original). The combat, for Deleuze, is not between self and other, but rather between forces that cross the self: "the process through which a force enriches itself by seizing hold of other forces and joining them into a new ensemble: a becoming" (p. 133). This scene of "combat" might also be understood as the scene where care takes shape, through patience, waiting, awakening, and enduring, but it might also be where cruelty manifests: the difficulty of being in another's present.

Attention to those forces helps destabilize parameters for ethnographic inquiry into the "social effects of neoliberalism" (Greenhouse 2010), in which the parameters are defined as the corrosive effects of or resistances to "consumer-based individualism so central to the social engineering inherent in neoliberal reform" (p. xiv). Such a formulation maintains an opposition between individuals (as autonomous and willful human beings) and forms of sociability. If we detach ourselves from this view and begin to think instead about the force of different relational modes, other avenues for inquiry into the circumstances of material scarcity may become available, and other possibilities for justice may be heard. Attending to time and relationality can bring about a critical understanding of the morbidities produced by unstable work and unpredictable wages, indebtedness, discontinuous and sometimes incompetent health care, and the pharmaceuticalization of public health.

Whereas public health and medicine have examined the differential distribution of health and disease in relation to socioeconomic inequality, ethnography can elucidate how specific institutional arrangements of state and market are lived through these relational modes, intensifying feelings of obligation and sometimes making these relations unbearable.

This reorientation can also introduce some hesitancy in the intense, and sometimes unwitting, moralization of "the family" in both policy and social analysis and, in so doing, introduce some hesitancy in assuming determinative effects of "neoliberalism." As we have seen in poverty programs, for example, the notion of an individual tied to legible family bonds is advanced as the basis for achieving dignity. One implication of this notion is that "the family," and particularly the mother, is assigned blame retrospectively for its inability to take responsibility for its members; at the same time, this family is also blamed for enduring certain kin, such as those with addiction and chronic mental illness, at the expense of family life. Such blame becomes intensely moralized precisely because the sociological family form is seen as the last bastion of social bonds and identity at the limit of neoliberalism. This picture, however, does not allow us to see the ways in which people are responding to many demands and desires, often under enormous economic pressures. A discourse of "the market" might be drawn on to retrospectively account for one's actions toward intimates in circumstances in which responsiveness becomes unbearable. But while such accounting for oneself in relation to others deflects this unbearability, it also voices the nature of relations themselves. The possibility of denial and disconnection are always already within relations themselves. Separateness as a condition of relations does not mean that ideas of relatedness themselves disintegrate, rather that acknowledgment of others must be repeatedly renewed (Das 2007, 217).

Setting aside a picture of all-or-nothing social bonds allows us to appreciate that concrete relations are constantly being achieved, and also failing. It opens ethnography to the multiple relational modes people are living and, in the play of these modes, offers a view into the possibilities for generosity and kindness that might not be apparent if we were to lock individuals within defined identities or take the "individualism" versus "social bonds" dyad at face value. Disconnection and connection are not all-or-nothing judgments about sociologically defined individuals. Rather, they occur within relational modes simultaneously lived, and they change over time. Thus, reorienting ourselves may make us give up our capacity to quickly judge others. However, we may instead become receptive to both the hurts *and* the possibilities in this world.

LOSS

It was August 2010, and I was able to return to La Pincoya after two years. On March 10 of that year, Sebastián Piñera of the Renovación Nacional party had been elected president. The multimillionaire owner of LAN Airlines and the Chilevision channel was the first democratically elected right-wing president in fifty years. Eleven days earlier, an earthquake measuring 8.8 on the Richter scale had hit the regions of Concepción and El Maule, followed by a tsunami in those same regions. The shocks were far-reaching, crumbling infrastructure in those regions as well as in Santiago. In the most affected regions, several hundred thousand people had been displaced and had lost their homes. After a delayed disaster response, in which the state attempted to assert its sovereignty in the face of the earthquake by waiting to accept international aid, scenes of looting took hold in the mainstream media. This prompted President Michelle Bachelet, in the final days of the Concertación's twenty-year governance, to declare a state of emergency in those regions and send in the military to create order before any humanitarian aid was accepted.[1]

I had been able to get in touch with Ruby after twenty-four hours. She and her family had not sustained injuries and were organizing to get water to the *población*. When I arrived in La Pincoya in August, my friends told me about their experiences during the earthquake, which they peppered with commentary about new uncertainties under Piñera. I saw Susana and Antonio. Antonio's auto body work was thriving, and Susana continued to work in food preparation for private schools. Their eldest son was now attending a private university and majoring in history. Antonio said, however, that he felt "*derrotado*" (defeated) both by Piñera's win and the sense that addiction to *pasta base* was becoming more and more common among the youth, who were, as he said, "*angustiados, borrados*" ("anguished," "erased," terms now used to describe addicts to *pasta base*). "Clarita, you should accompany me sometime to the hill at night. It's terrible. It's just that it is so much worse than before." He told me that many of his neighbors had voted for Piñera because he had promised a "*bono marzo*"—a monetary subsidy—of 40,000 pesos to those in the "humble sectors" of the Chilean population. But, Antonio said, "since Piñera got elected [*salió*], water has increased 36 percent, light 20 percent, bread 20 percent, Transantiago [the bus and metro system] 20 percent. Everything is increasing, and now I want to see the faces of those who voted for him. I would like to see them now."

I continued my visits with the neighbors. Walking up the street to Ruby's house, where I was staying for the month, I greeted a kindly elderly man, don Rodrigo, who sat on a stool on the sidewalk in front of the house he shared with his wife, Sra. Elva. "Hello!" Don Rodrigo did not seem to react. "Hello?" "Who is that?" He turned his head to the side. "It's Clara; do you remember me?" "Clarita! Ah, girl, it's that I don't see much." He stood up, and I held his hands. He said, "Let me call my wife." He made his way cautiously inside.

Sra. Elva came outside her house to greet me with don Rodrigo, giving me a kiss and a hug. "So nice to see you. You haven't changed one bit. It's like you've been pickled, well-conserved," she said. I asked her how they were doing. Her eyes filled with tears. "Not too well. . . . The little old man [*el viejito;* her husband] is almost blind [from cataracts]. He can't see anything. Today they announced that they will raise the price of bread to 1,000 pesos per kilo [from 780], because of the cost of wheat, they say. But for the poor, bread is mostly what we eat. Bread with a small salad."

She then told me that her daughter had passed away of uterine cancer, leaving the daughter's twin girls behind. The twins were now six years old. They had often stayed with Sra. Elva and don Rodrigo, and as toddlers had played in front of the house as their grandparents sat on their stools, greeting neighbors who walked up the street. Now, the twins rarely came to the house, because her daughter's husband's family most often took care of the children. Sra. Elva recounted how her daughter "endured and endured," without going to the doctor, because she always put the care of the children and her parents before herself.

"She had no time. She was always working, always working, trying to pay for things for the twins, pay for things for us." She had been diagnosed with metastatic uterine cancer when it was too late. "My daughter died the day of Christmas. She lasted three months, agonizing during *la pascua* [Christmas]. And then, you can imagine, remembering during the New Year. It has been seven months since she died. And for a mother to lose her child is the biggest grief of life. The children are everything. We have loves, but children are another thing. To lose one is . . . [Para la mamá perder su hijo es el duelo más grande de la vida.

Los hijos son todos. Tenemos amores, pero los hijos son otra, perder una es . . .] She cried, and so did don Rodrigo. "But with this pain, one has to continue. I am just waiting for God. It is the only thing I can say. But to see the little birds [the twins] without the mom . . . The earth hurts, for all the bad/evil that has been done."

KITE

Ruby saw me in the street and motioned to me from the gate of her house. I said good-bye to Sra. Elva and don Rodrigo with hugs. We would have another chance to visit in the coming weeks. Ruby wanted me to accompany her to a different *población* in the southern zone of the city, where she was now supervising an emergency work program. After being elected president of the Junta de Vecinos and winning a community development project, Ruby was now increasingly sought after by local nongovernmental organizations as well as by the municipality in advancing their political and social agendas. She was politically savvy, but she also had the courage to stand up to the authorities on more than one occasion.

One year earlier, she had been asked to work for a Chilean nongovernmental organization that ran emergency employment programs in *poblaciones* with official unemployment figures of greater than 10.8 percent. The program was highly reminiscent of the emergency work programs established under Pinochet to lower unemployment figures during the shock therapy of structural adjustment, but which offered salaries insufficient to survive on. This nongovernmental organization administered state funding for work programs and provided three-month work contracts. Thus, workers had a contract with the NGO, not the state. The women were paid less than minimum wage and were given jobs only in janitorial work and the maintenance of green areas.

Ruby, however, had her own aspirations. "We have to work here," she told me, sketching out an ethnographic project we could undertake together. She invited me to accompany her for the next month so she could introduce me to the women, the social organizers, and the parish priest in the other *población*. We took the hour-and-a-half bus ride from La Pincoya to the southern zone and back each day, raising questions and discussing them. "It's so different from La Pincoya. The sense of solidarity is different, the home is different. It's like another world. I'd like to know more about their history," she said. The *población* where she was working was notorious for drug trafficking and for an intense police presence that had led to the massive incarceration of men, but it was also known for its solidarity against the Pinochet regime and its network of social organizations.

On the afternoon when I left La Pincoya to go home again, Ruby had an unexpected meeting, so we could not say a proper good-bye. A proper good-bye would have meant spending the last hours talking, drinking tea, and waving good-bye as the taxi drove off. Unfortunately, that proper good-bye has never happened during the decade of our friendship, because of Ruby's work schedule. My last hours were spent instead with her eldest son, Davíd, and his little brother, Héctor, now seven years old. Héctor did not want to go to school, because I was leaving, and he threw a bit of a tantrum as Davíd tried to put on his school uniform. He wanted to stay and play games with me. One game we had devised was my keeping a "secret journal" of the foods he liked to eat, which, of course, I cannot share with you. Davíd was lenient this time. He said, however, we would have to do something other than stay inside the house. He wanted to teach Héctor how to fly a kite. We would fly it on the roof.

When we managed to climb on top of the corrugated iron roof, Johnny, Ruby's sister's partner, opened the gate. He had been addicted off and on to *pasta base* and was "involved" again, as Ruby said. He wanted a glass liter bottle to trade in for beer. The iron roof was littered with these bottles. Davíd said, "Sorry, we don't have any." "You sure?" Héctor got on his hands and knees to pick one up. He was about to hold it up, when Davíd kicked him gently on the butt (meaning, no!). "No, there's nothing up here." "Then you have 500 pesos?" "Sorry *tío*, I just spent the last 500 on buying candy and a kite for Héctor. I don't have money." "Oh, OK, OK."

After Johnny closed the gate, Davíd shook his head, and let out a little laugh. "Ahhh, Johnny." Héctor was scowling when Davíd turned his attention back to the kite. He threw it up in the air. There was a good breeze, and the kite caught the wind on the first try. The kite went higher and higher as the spool of thread ran out. "Look, Héctor, look!" "Wow!" Héctor said, a phrase I am pretty sure he learned from me. Héctor pointed up to the kite. The kite tugged at the spool. Davíd handed the spool to Héctor but kept his hand on the thread. With his other hand, he lit a cigarette. We spent the next hour on the roof, enjoying the sun and the breeze.

Notes

INTRODUCTION

1. The names given for all persons in La Pincoya are pseudonyms.

2. The use of *lifeworld* in this text draws from the idea of the lived world (*Lebenswelt*) in phenomenological and existential philosophy. See the extensive literature in anthropology, including Jackson 1996; Jackson 2009.

3. Michel Foucault's *The Birth of Biopolitics: Lectures at the Collège de France* outlines the conceptual underpinnings of American neoliberalism as compared to German ordoliberalism. American neoliberalism sought to extend market rationality to every aspect of life, from the rearrangement of the state, to intimacy, to our understanding of ourselves, to our human "nature" (Foucault 2008 [1978–1979]). See in particular lectures 9 through 12. Interestingly enough, Foucault does not mention Chile as the testing ground for these ideas, although the lectures occurred five years after the *golpe* and three years after Milton Friedman visited Chile and gave his famous lecture on Chile's "sick economy" at the behest of Pinochet. This lecture set the stage for the unveiling of the 1975 Economic Recovery Program in the midst of ongoing torture, disappearances, and executions.

4. There is an extensive critical literature on the "theory of marginality" and its relationship to theories of "advanced marginality" within contemporary sociological theory on poverty. See Janice Perlman, *The Myth of Marginality: Urban Politics and Poverty in Rio de Janeiro* (Berkeley: University of California Press, 1979), and *Favela: Four Decades of Living on the Edge in Rio de Janeiro* (Oxford: Oxford University Press, 2010); Peter Ward et al., "From Marginality of the 1960s to the 'New Poverty' of Today: A LARR Research Forum," *Latin American Research Review* 39, no. 1 (2004): 183–203. For the renewal of marginality in sociology, see Loïc Wacquant, *Urban Outcasts: A Comparative Sociology of Urban Poverty* (Cambridge: Polity Press, 2008). For a critical appraisal

of the use of marginality and the associated notion of "the ghetto," see Mario Luis Small, "Is There Such a Thing as 'the Ghetto'? The Perils of Assuming that the South Side of Chicago Represents Poor Black Neighborhoods," *City* 11, no. 3 (2007): 413–421.

5. Here, I follow Stanley Cavell's insightful reading of Wittgenstein and Heidegger in considering that the moral cannot be simply isolated from everyday life: "[A] moral claim upon us is leveled by the act of philosophizing itself, a claim that no *separate* subject of ethics would serve to study—as if what is wrong with us, what needs attention from philosophy, is our life as a whole (a claim that does not at once require us to articulate what that means, 'our life as a whole'") (Cavell 2005, 219, his emphasis).

1. SYMPTOMS OF ANOTHER LIFE

1. Pierre Bourdieu's formulation of time from the point of view of the agent is helpful. Bourdieu argues that time should not be understood as external to the subject, but rather that subjects themselves are temporalized (Bourdieu 2000). Yet his elaboration of the divide between subjective expectations and objective chances tends to assume a narrow mercantilistic and calculating subject. He writes, "This tendential law of human behaviors, whereby the subjective hope of profit tends to be adjusted to the objective probability of profit, governs the propensity to invest (money, work, time, emotion, etc.) in the various fields" (p. 216).

2. Given his account, the stroke could have been due to a patent foramen ovale.

3. What made this piece of pizza mean so much? Perhaps we could think of it indexing the uncertainty of Kevin's place in the home, and the possibility of separation.

4. *Light* here refers to electricity. In colloquial usage, *luz* (light) can refer to electricity as well as the electricity bill.

5. This is not to say that domestic triage—whose life should be cared for, whose could be neglected—is not happening every day in La Pincoya (cf. Biehl and Eskerod 2005). Domestic triage is not all or nothing, however. The expansion of this sense of responsibility among urban poor families shows how difficult and subtle the process of domestic triage is for family members, as well as elucidates its temporal dimensions.

6. Veena Das's essay on the relation between finite responsibility and the return to the everyday among urban poor neighborhoods in Delhi is helpful. New medical technologies can "expand the scope of kin obligations to such an extent that the immediate material conditions and limitations are lost from view" (Das 2010b, 44). Thus, "limiting the desire for infinite responsibility to the other is paradoxically what attaches one to life itself" (p. 32).

7. We might consider how anthropological method is involved in reaching very different conclusions regarding the nature of decision making in the home.

8. It is important to underline here how the tone and significance of this gift differ from Mauss's concept of gift. The bread was neither an object nor a service rendered within a system of "contractual morality" that holds together the

social order (Mauss and Halls 1990). Rather, this gift was the labor of the mother's hands for the sustenance of the daughter: an affirmation of life, an enactment of kinship. Jane Guyer's analysis of Mauss's *The Gift* in the context of where it was originally published—the 1923–24 issue of *L'Année sociologique*—provides a helpful reflection on how Mauss's narrow interest in the gift in relation to the history of contract did not prevent him from considering an ethics of generosity that analyses of the everyday could point to (Guyer 2010).

9. Villa Gremaldi was a notorious torture and disappearance camp established during the dictatorship. A large body of literature has been published on memory work in Chile and the politics of reconciliation and justice. See for example Gómez-Barris 2009; Loveman and Lira 2002; Richard and Moreiras 2001; Stern 2010.

2. SOCIAL DEBT, SILENT GIFT

1. The political stakes are evident in the regime's social policy documents as well as in Pinochet's public addresses admonishing Allende's democratic Socialist government. In 1978, Pinochet addressed the nation, saying, "The result of demagogic populism: 22% of Chileans living in extreme poverty," and calling for the eradication of extreme poverty through "the equality of opportunities before life" (Chile Oficina de Planificación Nacional, 1979). Ten years later, in 1988, the year of the plebiscite to vote for or against regime change, the Office of National Planning and the Ministry of the Secretary of State published a report outlining the achievements of the military regime, *Sabemos Hacia Donde Vamos: Algunos Logros del Gobierno del Presidente Augusto Pinochet Ugarte* (We Know Toward Where We Go: Some Achievements of the Government of President Augusto Pinochet Ugarte). An entire section is dedicated to "extreme poverty." Titled "Real Advance against Extreme Poverty," the regime's report cites statistics that show an apparent decrease of extreme poverty from 21 percent in 1970 to 14.2 percent in 1982 (Chile Secretaría General de Gobierno and Chile Oficina de Planificación Nacional, 1988). These numbers were a clear underrepresentation. Even independent pro-regime economists' calculations of extreme poverty, based on a basic-needs approach, showed that 25 percent of the population were extremely poor at that time (Petras et al. 1994, 35).

2. This principle of "growth with equity" would also increase national savings and produce a budget surplus from 1990 to 1994 (from 137 billion pesos to 368 in 1994; savings rose from 785 to 1.079), permitting a reduction of external debt through prepayments, even as one-third of the population remained below the poverty line and public infrastructures remained deteriorated after years of underfunding (Fazio 1999, 54).

3. MIDEPLAN (Ministerio de Planificación) follows the methodology for calculating the poverty line laid out by the United Nations Economic Commission for Latin America and the Caribbean. The poverty line and the indigence line are based on the basic nutritional requirements—calories and amount of protein—for the urban population. The cost of the basic family food basket (*canasta familiar*) per person is extrapolated from these nutritional requirements and takes into account internal availability, consumption habits of the

population, and relative price. The indigence line marks that income that would be necessary to satisfy alimentary needs. The poverty line is twice the indigence line. It doubles the cost of basic alimentary needs and, therefore, purportedly covers the cost of basic necessities such as clothes, transportation, housing, health, and education. MIDEPLAN recalculates these lines every two years for the Survey for National Socioeconomic Characterization, or CASEN. In 2003, the urban indigence line was calculated to be 21,856 pesos per person per month, while the urban poverty line was calculated to be 43,712 per person per month (MIDEPLAN 2004). These national indigence and poverty lines can be contrasted to the current World Bank's lines of USD 1 and USD 2 per day. The causalities for the decrease in poverty is a matter of debate. Several Chilean economists, sociologists, and World Bank economists have attributed this dramatic reduction to job creation stemming from economic growth, as well as to increased salaries for contracted labor, assigning a minimal role to the state's social spending (Arellano M. 2004; Larrañaga and Herrera 2008). Other scholars and government officials have attributed it to a combination of increased social spending and the way in which the government has harnessed economic growth for social programs (Hardy Raskovan and Amadeo 2004; Olavarria-Gambi 2003; Winn 2004).

4. See Peter Winn's important 2004 account of the history of the Chilean textile industry.

5. José Piñera is the older brother of the president of Chile, Sebastián Piñera (elected in 2010), who was one of the main forces behind the expansion of the credit card industry in Chile in the 1990s. The latter is the majority owner of LAN Airlines and the full owner of one of the major television networks, Chilevision.

6. Daniel Miller is helpful in challenging the moralism that frequently finds the consumption patterns of the poor as irrational. However, Miller would argue that the elimination of poverty "depends on industrialization and mass production" (Miller 2001b, 228). I am sympathetic to his defense of being open to consumption practices, but I am much more cautious about the assumptions about what poverty is and the idea that it is the same all the time, everywhere. Indeed, the shape of poverty in Santiago cannot be reduced to the absolute lack of goods. Rather, it must take into account the fluctuating nature of incomes that sustain the presence of goods in the context of the availability of institutional credit to low-income populations. Thus, the difficulty here is to explore poverty's highly dynamic shape, the layers of institutions that compose poverty, and the senses of responsibility woven into decision making by urban poor families. Microeconomists have shown the local contours of poverty by tracking cash flows in households over time, elucidating how events are absorbed back into everyday processes (see Collins et al. 2009).

7. See Polla Chilena, www.pollachilena.cl/index.php?option=com_content&task=view&id=40&Itemid=53.

8. The games related to sports, such as Polla Gol, Loto, Toto3, destine 15 percent of their earnings to the National Institute of Sports. Polla Chilena, www.pollachilena.cl/index.php?option=com_content&task=view&id=33&Itemid=46.

9. I draw from Deborah Poole's insightful study of juridical reform and the shadowy nature of legal documents in Ayacucho, Peru. Documents at once materialize "the law" and render "the law" illegible. The state here is thus experienced as both "just and coercive, [and as both] participatory and removed." In this context, Poole observes that while nongovernmental organizations and the state advance "the law" as universal and impartial, peasants "negotiate their daily lives in a series of calculations involving individuals and spaces that everyone knows exist 'outside the law'" (Poole 2004, 61).

10. Stefania Pandolfo's work on subjectivity and the political-theological imagination provides a helpful counterpoint here. In her article, she discusses how Moroccan youth experiencing despair and a "shrinking life" elaborate a work of creative imagination, between violation of the law and the eschatological elsewhere. In tracing the narratives, she observes that youth's conversations draw from a "theological referent" and Islamic vocabularies (Pandolfo 2007). In my ethnographic work, however, the "theological referent" and religious vocabulary was so obliquely drawn upon that it is difficult for me to interpret "the sacred" here as generating an "eschatological elsewhere" or theological imaginary. Indeed, the question of meaning—or the "referent"—may not define the parameters of this inquiry. Rather, we could explore *how* words are used, rather than relying on an a priori meaning. This approach opens an inquiry into the context that is emerging ethnographically (Das 1998; Wittgenstein 1953). Here, it is not a question of drawing on an alternative vocabulary to elaborate meaning and hope against the limits of one's cultural universe but a question of how the word is used that transfigures familiar forms.

11. Note here that the ordinary term used for money is *plata* (silver) and not *dinero* (coin).

12. I thank my colleague Aaron Goodfellow for this wonderful phrasing.

13. Arjun Appadurai discusses the "the illusion of permanence" of locality and the reproduction of social life (Appadurai 1996); similarly, we can think of the everyday itself as a scene of illusion—as Veena Das suggests—achieved again and again (Das 2007).

14. *Flaite* is a colloquial word that previously denoted a youth from the *poblaciones* who wore hip-hop clothes and listened to gangsta rap. The word gradually became associated with the criminal underworld of drugs and the *delinke*, or delinquent. But in common usage, it is often used to denote one who simulates being a "badass" but who really is more foolish than transgressive. It is thought to be derived from the English *fly*, which in Chilean colloquial Spanish relates to *vola'o*, which derives from *volar*, or *fly* in English (someone who is high, or "flying"; a drug addict).

15. I would like to emphasize that Cannell is specifically exploring Christian asceticism in terms of the dualism between matter and soul, and the inferiority posited between body and soul as a result of man's fallen nature. Clearly, such a discussion of asceticism would be different in other world religions and in pre-Augustinian experiments with Christianity (Brown 1988). Cannell is making the point that this specific version of Augustinian Christianity has been incorporated into European anthropological thought not only in the way this disci-

pline addresses Christianity but also in the ways in which this discipline itself contends with the body, genealogy, and modernity.

16. Jane Guyer has outlined a fascinating and very important contribution to thinking about *chesed,* the Hebrew word for loving kindness, that proves to be utterly pertinent here: "*Chesed* is both a divine and human attribute, one that is by definition unmotivated, uncalculated. It is a point at which newness can appear in a system of moral obligations: on an everyday basis and not just a prime mover or originator of whole systems. . . . Although dealing with death, *chesed shel emet* is a human, life-giving gesture" (Guyer 2010, 250).

17. I thank Veena Das for her suggestion to read "Pretending," a suggestion that led to a turning point in much of my thinking in this chapter.

18. The notion of the slice of time is akin to, but slightly different from, political theorist William Connolly's discussion of dwelling in a "crystal of time": "During such a moment, multiple layers of the past resonate with things unfolding in the current situation, sometimes issuing in something new as if from nowhere. The new is ushered into being through a process that exceeds rational calculation or the derivation of practical implications from universal principles" (Connolly 2011, 69). While dwelling in the crystal intermingles layers of past and anticipation, dwelling in the slice does not mingle past and anticipation but instead appreciates simultaneity or co-occurrence of acts. While dwelling in the crystal allows for the new to issue forth through this intermingling, dwelling in the slice allows for the "dawning of an aspect," or appreciating that which is right in front of us but which we are somehow blind to. The "new" in the slice is not necessarily new to the world, but it is new for the one dwelling, since it helps her appreciate what is already there. The "new" in the crystal seems to be new for the world—"You help to usher something new into the world" (p. 75)—and helps us appreciate the world as becoming. Yet if dwelling in the slice still yields "creative insight" into what is already there, and an appreciation of what is already there is our potential world, then would not this dwelling also lend itself to a "world of becoming"?

19. The urgency of concealing that protects a slide into an inhuman complicates Phillips and Taylor's remarks on "the kind life" by showing that how the human is experienced varies significantly according to history and place. As Phillips and Taylor remark, "The life lived in instinctive sympathetic identification with the vulnerabilities and attractions of others—is the life we are more inclined to live, and indeed is the one we are often living without letting ourselves know that this is what we are doing. People are leading secretly kind lives all the time but without a language in which to express this, or cultural support for it" (Phillips and Taylor 2009, 4). The issue may be more than simply "not letting ourselves know" what it is we are doing, premised on a psychological self; it may be that revealing kindness in this lifeworld is a real threat to a dignified life.

3. TORTURE, LOVE, AND THE EVERYDAY

1. The word *allegado* indicates a closeness or proximity. In Chile, the term is used in relation to persons inhabiting the house who may not be related by blood.

2. I am drawing inspiration here from Stanley Cavell's discussion of Shakespeare's *Antony and Cleopatra,* in which the "recession of the world is this play's interpretation of what I have called the truth of skepticism" (Cavell [1987] 2003, 25).

3. There is a large body of anthropological work exploring the legal, moral, and political implications of truth commissions in projects of national reconciliation. For work specific to Chile, please see Loveman and Lira 2002. Wilson and Borneman argue for retributive justice (Borneman 1997; Wilson 2001). Fiona Ross has argued that the shape of the truth commission narratives disallowed specific voices, particularly those of women (Ross 2003). On the other hand, Didier Fassin has explored how the violence of inequality must be taken into account in relation to global discourses of victimhood (see Fassin 2007b, 278). My inquiry overlaps and departs from this work by discussing how official attempts to acknowledge these violences are received in everyday life. We might appreciate that people not only make claims on the basis of their status as victims but also have a deep ambivalence about accepting the terms of acknowledgment through reparations.

4. The National Commission for Truth and Reconciliation, or the Rettig Commission, was named after its chair, Raúl Rettig, an elderly politician of the centrist Radical Party who had been elected to the Senate in 1949 and served as ambassador to Brazil during the Allende administration.

5. On June 30, 2008, Contreras was given a double life sentence for the assassination of General Carlos Prats and his wife, Sofía Cuthbert, in the Palermo District of Buenos Aires, Argentina, on September 30, 1974. Contreras was the former chief of the DINA (Dirección de Inteligencia Nacional), and had played a central role in Operación Condor, the coordinated effort between dictatorships in Chile, Argentina, Uruguay, and Bolivia to assassinate political opponents outside their sovereign territories. Judicial cases against Contreras for disappearances generated historic interpretations to the 1978 Amnesty Law, which opened the possibility of processing human rights violations considered closed by the Amnesty Law. The 1978 Amnesty Law provided amnesty to those convicted of criminal acts committed during the state of siege, between September 11, 1973, and March 10, 1978. In 2003, Judge Alejandro Solís used the figure of kidnapping as a crime that continued past the 1978 boundary in order to charge Contreras with the January 7, 1975, disappearance of Miguel Angél Sandoval Rodríguez, a militant of the Movimiento de la Izquierda Revolucionaria. While not annulling the Amnesty Law, this interpretation has allowed for the continued processing of cases, but not without significant difficulties (see www.memoriaviva.com/culpables/criminales_c/contreras.htm).

6. Stern provides an excellent account of the Supreme Court's invocation of the 1978 Amnesty Law in response to reactivated human rights cases and mounting evidence of mass killings discovered after the Rettig Report's release. He elaborates the context in terms of Pinochet and the army's scare and panic tactics when evidence tarnishing Pinochet's reputation as an austere leader emerged in the case of Pinochet's embezzling of money from the state ("Pinocheques"; see Stern 2010).

7. My interpretation of this moment differs from that of Paley, who ends her

account with President Aylwin citing Pope John Paul II's call for reconciliation. By ending the speech at that critical moment, without following his turning to the ethics of pardon, Paley can discuss how the Concertación relegated the violation of human rights to the past, "buried" them, in order to turn toward the future. While there is some merit to this analysis—in terms of a broader failure of institutional reforms and of the second Concertación administration under Frei Ruiz-Tagle, who effectively put human rights cases on the back burner in the interests of pursuing economic policy—I am interested in how the emphasis on the ethics of pardon kept the past open on specific moral grounds, officially speaking, thereby displacing responsibility for state violence onto "society" and the plane of transcendent values (Paley 2001, 127).

8. The names of the dogs illuminate their spiritual proximities. *Laico* means "independent from any religious organization or faith, in particular the Catholic faith." Indy was the daughter of Laico, a dog who Ruby said was aligned with the Mapuche people of Chile.

9. The Valech Commission was created in the wake of a series of high-profile political events: the embattled process of the Mesa de Diálogo (Dialogue Table) between 1999 and 2003 that brought human rights lawyers, high-level police and military officers, religious leaders, government officials, and academics together to bring new information to light about the detained-disappeared and to mutually revisit the past; the 1998 detention of Pinochet in London, his extradition to Chile and the stripping of his legal immunity in 2000, and the suspension of his trial in 2001, when he was declared to be mentally unfit; and finally, the 2003 proposal of the ultra-right-wing party, the Unión Democrática Independiente, to bring an end to the ongoing cases involving kidnapping with respect to the detained-disappeared.

10. For example, residents in La Pincoya recounted to me how the local football field, La Cancha Siete, was turned into a "concentration camp," in which men, from the young to the elderly, were held for several days. Youth were forced to watch their grandfathers run up and down the football field until they collapsed.

11. Individuals had to call a toll-free number staffed by outsourced CTC (Compañía de Telecomunicaciones de Chile) operators to set up an appointment for an interview (Ruy-Perez, personal communication).

12. A notice in the national newspaper *La Tercera* on December 13, 2003; a televised notice on Televisión Nacional for one week between March 29 and April 2, 2004.

13. Based on the CLP/USD November 2004 exchange rate: CLP 596.72/ USD 1. Source: Banco Central Base de Datos, http://si2.bcentral.cl/Basededato-seconomicos/951_417.asp?LlamadaPortada=SI. Last downloaded July 2, 2010.

14. There are several translations of *malestar,* including "unease, sickness, unrest, discontent," which do not seem to get to the existential sense of the word used here. So, I translate it literally as "ill-being."

15. It is important to emphasize here that Héctor's remark that all lives have equal value should be taken as an *expression of his aspirations*; he is not saying that all lives are valued equally in the *actual* political and economic system in

which he is living. Indeed, he makes this point clear in the way he frames his aspirations and his desire to continue criticizing society.

16. I draw here from Foucault's essay "Self Writing," in which he considers the differences between forms of the narrative of the self as these forms relate to moral philosophies. Foucault makes the distinction between Cicero's letters in which he "accounts for himself as a subject of action in connection with friends and enemies," and the correspondences of Seneca and Marcus Aurelius, which are accounts of the relation to the self—which "is a matter of bringing into congruence the gaze of the other and that gaze which one aims at oneself when one measures one's everyday actions according to the rules of a technique of living" (Foucault 1997, 221). Foucault's delineation of Cicero and Seneca presents very different ways of thinking about, writing, and living the moral, and therefore very different ways of accounting for oneself. I expand this discussion in relation to *testimonio* in the following chapter.

17. As Yúdice remarks, *testimonio* had been produced before the literary "boom" in Latin America, through Paulo Freire's consciousness-raising literacy movement, Christian Base Communities, and peasant and workers' mass organizations. But it was not brought into the literary sphere until Cuba's Casa de las Américas created a literary award for testimonial literature after a break with liberal Latin American intellectuals over Castro's defense of the Soviet invasion of Czechoslovakia (Yúdice 1991; see also Sommer 1991).

18. As an ethical practice of the self, *testimonio*—as a genre that grew from and in Latin American popular worlds—differs significantly from the "politics of testimony" of humanitarian psychiatry that Fassin and Rechtman examine. Fassin and Rechtman recall the dictatorships in Latin America, decolonization in Africa, and Palestine to delineate how a different politics of testimony has emerged, in which resilience of patients was emphasized over the resistance of fighters: "What we are seeing, in effect, is a phenomenon of ideological sedimentation, where one layer is deposited on the previous one, without completely obliterating it. . . . This is particularly the case given that many of those involved, particularly in the humanitarian movement, were left-wing militants in the 1960s and 1970s" (Fassin and Rechtman 2009, 160). I find it crucial to distinguish how *the self* differs across humanitarian testimony that Fassin and Rechtman posit—a testimony generated by physicians who "bear witness" to the symptoms and affects of those they define as "victims" and thus unify and homogenize unique experiences—and the genre of *testimonio* as self writing that does not substitute the unity of victims, collectively speaking, for the individual, but rather enacts a being-with that implicates very different moral selves. Consider Kay Warren's work on *testimonio* by Pan-Mayan activist Victor Montejo, in which "a collage of first-person accounts" is presented rather than a single narrator, and in which a "subjectivity shaped by Maya hermeneutics . . . stress[es] Maya cultural struggles and their distinctive moral discourse" (Warren 1998, 130). In writing on violence in San Andrés, Warren herself as anthropologist is worked on by this "moral discourse": "the challenge of representing violence compelled me to shift to a more polyphonic text. . . . I quoted a long, magical-realist narrative . . . and discussed Maya hermeneutics to show

that realist fragments were only one of a variety of ways Mayas used to represent the effect of violence on their lives" (p. 129). To discuss *testimonio* and not only humanitarian testimony, I think it is necessary to attend to this relational making of the self, a self that is not necessarily that self posited in global psychiatry.

19. Please see Cavell's discussion of Coriolanus, in which Cavell elaborates how the infiniteness of desire is not from the endless reserves of desire, but that desire has a "structure of endlessness" that might be imposed upon the finiteness of the human body (Cavell [1987] 2003, 66).

20. While I could write a detailed account of his detentions, I choose to leave this as a silent presence in the text. I believe that this silent presence speaks more to what Héctor desires and also conveys how this silence pervades the family's everyday life.

21. On July 1, 1996, the Association of Progressive Lawyers filed a criminal suit against Pinochet and his top military officers for the crimes of genocide, terrorism, and torture. Five days later, the Foundation Presidente Allende, represented by Joan Garcés, further clarified the international scope of terrorism involving Operación Condor. Initially, Judge Manuel García-Castellón had taken the Chile case, while Garzón had taken the Argentinean case. However, with the arrest order of Pinochet by Garzón, the two cases were consolidated under Garzón. (See also Davis 2003; Roht-Arriaza 2005; Wilson 2003).

22. This suit was also based on the December 10, 1998, Writ of Indictment of Pinochet, in which Garcés made a dollar estimate of the damages and losses sustained by those he represented. He proposed a sum of 300,506 euros for each person assassinated, detained, or missing, and 30,000 euros for each person tortured. The total estimated amount for damages was more than 3 billion euros. See Sumario 19/1997 Pieza Separada, Al Juzgado Central de Instrucción No. 5, July 19, 2004 (Garcés 2004).

23. This executive commission was headed by Helmut Frenz, a Lutheran pastor and cofounder of the Fundación de Ayuda Social de Iglesias Cristianas and Comité Pro Paz, the network of priests, ministers, and human rights lawyers founded in 1973 that provided legal assistance to those arrested and detained during the dictatorship.

24. Based on the June 2005 exchange rate: CLP 595.48/USD 1.

25. *Limosnear* is derived from *limosna*, alms given to the poor or indigent. In the act of almsgiving, the giver is in the presence of God incarnate. It is not coincidental that Ruby alludes to a Catholic moral economy in relation to state reparations, given how charity has come to characterize a host of resources and state services in the *población*, but also how the state's discourse of reconciliation is based on Catholic values of pardon and forgiveness.

26. Most of the costs of production are absorbed by the women themselves: electricity to run sewing machines and ambient lighting are part of household bills. The lockstitch sewing machines and overlock machines (which both cut and finish a seam) are usually bought on credit by the women, with subsidies from the state.

27. In a way, we can think of the dream as a dilation of time itself.

4. NEOLIBERAL DEPRESSION

1. See Julieta Kirkwood's foundational work for Chilean feminism, *Ser política en Chile: Las feministas y los partidos* (Kirkwood [1986] 2010) and Nelly Richard's acute analysis of Kirkwood, in her discussion of "the feminine" as minoritarian (Richard 1993). See also Sonia Montecino Aguirre 1996 and 2008. For historian Alejandra Brito, motherhood must be understood within the transformations of nineteenth-century urbanization and modernization. As semirural women were moved from the city's periphery to the interior, medicine and public health transformed motherhood from an "intimate and private practice" to a "responsibility with social character" (Brito Peña 2008, 122). And as anthropologist María Elena Acuña Moenne has noted, contemporary motherhood was reconfigured through the Pinochet regime's pro-natalist policy in order to refound La Patria (Acuña Moenne 2005).

2. See Nara Milanich's historical account of the liberal Chilean Civil Code of 1857, which abolished paternity investigations, which had previously been conducted in pre-Code courts according to Iberian law. Under this liberal code, paternity was established through contract, in which the man freely acknowledged his relationship as father to a child. In 1998, the New Filiation Act, reinstated paternity investigation and abolished the distinction between legitimate and illegitimate children (Milanich 2009).

3. I reproduce only excerpts of this testimony, since it is composed of addresses, dates, and names, and thus might make Leticia and, by extension, her family, easily identifiable.

4. We might contrast this testimonial writing with Diamela Eltit's *El Padre Mío*, the fragmented testimony of a homeless schizophrenic man who, to Eltit, embodies the "marginal" of Santiago (Eltit 1989). The figure of the madman is posed against the linear history of official Chile. It is interesting to note how this figure of homelessness as madness may hinge upon and reinstate the security of home as order and domesticity: home, order, officialdom are the foil for the madness of a homeless man and his fragments of testimony. Yet, in Leticia's writing, home is clearly what is at stake: a problem and an existential margin. Through reworking conventions of *testimonio*, Leticia attempts to make herself present to others, even if that making present might also be incongruent to others, indeed may present insanity to others. Writing of *El Padre Mío*, literary scholar Michael Lazzara elaborates the "limits of testimony": the unspeakableness of "traumatic memory" and the impossibility of language in the face of state violence (Lazzara 2006). Yet framing state violence as an all-or-nothing matter (the impossibility of language) may block us from considering the experimentation with literary genres that people are engaged in, experiments that also put one's sanity at risk (see Yúdice 1991).

5. I thank Veena Das for this suggestion.

6. See Código Penal, Libro 2, Titulo 7, "Crímenes y simples delitos contra el orden de las familias y contra la moralidad pública" Art. 342–345, www.leychile.cl/Navegar/?idNorma=1984&idParte=0. Last accessed July 15, 2010.

7. Since abortions are undertaken clandestinely, the estimated number of abortions is generally based on the assumption that for every woman hospital-

ized for abortion, five abortions go unobserved (see Blofield 2001, 16). Since women are unlikely to volunteer that they have induced an abortion, official statistics based on hospital stay likely significantly underreport abortion rates.

8. *Tata* derives from Quechua and in colloquial usage means "grandpa." *Mama* also derives from Quechua and is colloquially used as a term of endearment for a woman.

5. COMMUNITY EXPERIMENTS

1. Simultaneously, health care financing was massively transformed. Until the late 1970s, the National Health Service for the working class was funded by tax revenue and payroll contributions, while the white-collar workers' National Medical Service for Employees was funded by payroll contributions and out-of-pocket payments. After 1979, these systems were consolidated into one National Health Service System financed by a new financial body, the National Fund for Health (FONASA). Decree Law No. 3 (1981) legalized private insurance companies, called Instituciones de Salud Previsionales (ISAPRES), opening the door to enormous health and economic disparities between the two systems. Workers are required to contribute 7 percent of their income to either the FONASA or the ISAPRES. Inequalities between the systems arose as the ISAPRES matched contributions to estimated health risks, and adjusted premiums according to changes in health status, while the FONASA accepted any citizen irrespective of risk. Thus, the ISAPRES created a pool of healthier and wealthier clients who could contribute more to their collective insurance pool, while the FONASA shouldered poorer and more ill clients. At the same time, since the ISAPRES would often break its contracts with clients upon a diagnosis of catastrophic illness, the FONASA had to bear the brunt of costs for catastrophic illnesses, even for those clients who had not been paying into the pool.

2. This reimbursement was called the Facturación por Atención Prestada por Municipalidades.

3. Indeed, upon his death Marconi was eulogized by the Ministry of Health's Mental Health Unit: "Through these images of Marconi as genius, Marconi as master, and Marconi as social fighter, we would have liked to have been with him in this moment of our recognition and gratitude by his disciples. Dedicate to him as well the recent honor that Chile, along with Brazil, has received from the Pan American Health Organization and World Health Organization, as the two National Plans in Mental Health with the most development in Latin America and the Caribbean" (Unidad de Salud Mental 2005).

4. Intracommunity psychiatry was informed by Latin American Social Medicine, advancing a break from cultural colonialism and a critique of capitalist relations. In his 1973 article "The Chilean Cultural Revolution in Mental Health Programs," published in *Acta Psiquiátrica y Psicológica de America Latina,* Marconi elaborates on the intracommunity psychiatry approach, premising his conceptual elaborations on a critique of capitalist society: "If the prevalence of the most frequent mental disorders in Chile, neurosis, alcoholism, epilepsy, is intimately tied to the structure of the capitalist society, of social

classes, then whatever honest and scientifically founded program in Mental Health [that exists] must postulate the abolition of a class society" (Marconi T. 1973, 19). He posits an evolution along three axes of the field of mental health: services (*asistencia*); teaching, or formation of personnel (*docencia*); and research (*investigación*). Along these axes, Marconi charts an historical movement from (1) *asilo*, feudal society's attempt to isolate the mentally ill (1952), to (2) the psychiatric hospital, an institutionalization of mental health care in the psychiatric hospital and an increasing "cultural colonialism" of European psychiatric categories (1953–1970), and finally to (3) the mental health of the community—a "psychiatry of the masses" forged through "national creativity" and an involvement of the community in "the creation, implementation, and evaluation of popular Mental Health programs [that would] definitively break the cultural colonialism" (1971 to "the present"; Marconi T. 1973, 18). As he outlines these stages, he asks rhetorically, "Can we pass from a feudal structure in Mental Health, represented by isolation, modernized in the Psychiatric Hospital, to a psychiatry of the masses? Is an intermediate stage of Psychiatric Services in General Hospitals or Mental Health Units throughout the whole country essential before planning a national solution that is massive and intra-communitarian? We live a revolution in mental health, but . . . Technocratic revolution or cultural revolution?" (p. 18).

5. It is important to point out that, while the existing community mental health movement does draw inspiration from intracommunity psychiatry, the narrative is not simply linear. When the possibility of community mental health emerged after the dictatorship ended, the state itself had changed.

6. Thus, we might consider the "virtuous social cycle" that Behforouz and colleagues discuss in their work on community-based treatment of HIV in this light. See Behforouz et al. 2004.

7. I am not arguing for or against the program's effectiveness in general. Rather, I am interested in what we take to be criteria for a program's effectiveness, given the differences in local worlds.

8. Critically assessing sociologist Pedro Morandé's opposition between neoliberal technocrats and their inability to understand the "'Latin American ethos' founded in a Catholic substrate and indigenous traditions," literary critic Luis Cárcamo-Huechante examines how the texts of neoconservative elites propose participation in the market as a consumer as achieving moral transcendence and perfection.

9. Throughout the 1960s, Catholicism in Chile, as well as regionally, turned significantly to the political left. Supported by Vatican II reforms and the call for radical transformation from a meeting of 150 bishops in Medellín, the Chilean Catholic Church supported social activism and structural reform while examining the relationship between Marxism and Catholicism. After the *golpe,* under the leadership of Cardinal Raúl Silva Henríquez, the Church allied itself with the victims of human rights violations.

10. As Olave points out, the opening chapter of a book of homilies by Escrivá de Balaguer, founder of Opus Dei, is called "The Richness of Ordinary Life."

6. LIFE AND DEATH, CARE AND NEGLECT

1. The presence of the Chilean pharmacy market is felt throughout Latin America. Farmacia Ahumada S.A., for instance, has emerged as the largest and most lucrative chain of pharmacies in Latin America. Earning 70 percent of its revenue outside of Chile, and with more than 1,000 establishments across Chile, Peru, Brazil, and Mexico, the company serves 167 million clients annually (Fazio 2005, 215). In Chile, its shops are known as Farmacia Ahumada; in Peru, Boticas Fasa; in Mexico, Farmacias Benavides; and in Brazil, Drogamed. SalcoBrand, the smallest chain of the three, has 234 stores in the Metropolitan Region of Santiago, with 130 in other regions. Cruz Verde, on the other hand, has extended its 365 stores throughout Chile, establishing pharmacies in the most remote of locations, where access even to proper medical care is scarce.

2. Anthropologists have shown how pharmaceutical markets diverge and leak into black markets. For example, Anne Lovell addresses these aspects in her work on pharmaceutical leakage and diversion in addiction markets (Lovell 2006). While there are local markets for everyday pharmaceuticals, such as the generic antibiotic amoxicillin, anti-inflammatories, and supplements that do not require a controlled prescription, controlled pharmaceuticals such as antidepressants, anxiolytics, and Viagra leak into the local markets through their sale or through gift giving. On the other hand, medications for rare diseases, and treatments that cause fewer side effects and are marketed as more effective for common complaints, such as birth control, acne medication, and other antibiotics, exceed the household budget, sometimes being secured through Phase IV "seeding." For a discussion of the clinical trial industry in relation to the treatment of rare disease in low-income populations, please see Petryna 2009.

3. Here, we can see how what João Biehl calls the "pharmaceuticalization of public health" and "pharmaceutical governance"—public health's shift from a concern with continuous clinical care and substantive welfare systems to a concern with securing the right to medications—is received and transformed within local markets and localities that have generated knowledges about common conditions (Biehl 2008; Biehl 2007).

4. Medications have been understood as vehicles for meanings; or, in their circulation and exchange, medications—like other material objects—can mark specific social relations (Geest et al. 1996; Whyte et al. 2002). Following this, Sjaak van der Geest and colleagues elaborate the "biography of pharmaceuticals," which examines the different phases in the production of the pharmaceutical and the relations implicated therein. Here, I am particularly interested in how pharmaceuticals gain force in dynamic and singular affective configurations, a perspective informed by Aaron Goodfellow's elaboration of the pharmaceutical as nonhuman actant (Goodfellow 2008).

5. These meetings are explicitly called "*reuniones*" (meetings) and not church services. When I described the meeting place as a "church," I was quickly corrected by members, who said, "It is not church like the Catholic Church; it is a meeting, closer to the people."

6. The fact that I was in medical training at the time did not lend moral clarity to the situation, as if by virtue of being a Harvard medical student I could

magically dissolve the concrete circumstances and relations in which this was occurring and simply "successfully manage" the person as patient. Such a view assumes that medicine or a medical student is authorized to define what the context is and can impose that vision at will. This is not to say that intervention is unwarranted or impossible, but rather that, for physicians and anthropologists, intervention takes place in social worlds. Faced with the uncertainty of the moment, I responded by remaining on the scene.

CONCLUSION

1. I have written elsewhere about the earthquake; see Han 2010.

References

Acuña Moenne, María Elena. 2005. "Embodying Memory: Women and the Legacy of the Military Government in Chile." *Feminist Review* 79:150–161.

Addo, Ping-Ann, and Niko Besnier. 2008. When Gifts Become Commodities: Pawnshops, Valuables, and Shame in Tonga and the Tongan Diaspora." *Journal of the Royal Anthropological Institute* 14:39–59.

Agamben, Giorgio. 1998. *Homo Sacer: Sovereign Power and Bare Life*. Stanford, CA: Stanford University Press.

Agencias. 2005. "Presidente Lagos estima que la transición chilena ha concluido." *Emol* (July 14).

Alvarado M., Rubén. 1993. "Estado actual y proyecciones para la epidemiología en salud mental." In *Psicología Comunitaria y Salud Mental en Chile*, edited by R.M. Olave and L. Zambrano, 128–147. Santiago: Editorial Universidad Diego Portales.

Alvarado M., Rubén, Jorge Vega, Gabriel Sanhueza, and María Graciela Muñoz. 2005. "Evaluación del programa para la detección, diagnóstico y tratamiento integral de la depresión en atención primaria, en Chile." *Pan American Journal of Public Health* 18 (4–5): 278–286.

Appadurai, Arjun. 1996. *Modernity at Large: Cultural Dimensions of Globalization*. Minneapolis: University of Minnesota Press.

Araya, Ricardo. 1995. *Trastornos Mentales en la Atención Primaria, Santiago, Chile*. Santiago: Universidad de Chile, Departamento de Psiquiatría.

Araya, Ricardo, Graciela Rojas, Rosemarie Fritsch, Julia Acuña, and Glyn Lewis. 2001. "Common Mental Disorders in Santiago, Chile." *British Journal of Psychiatry* (176): 228–233.

Araya, Ricardo, Graciela Rojas, Rosemarie Fritsch, Jorge Gaete, Maritza Rojas, Greg Simon, and Tim Peters. 2003. "Treating Depression in Primary Care in

Low-Income Women in Santiago, Chile: A Randomised Controlled Trial." *The Lancet* (361): 995–1000.

Arellano M., José Pablo. 2004. "Políticas sociales para el crecimiento con equidad Chile 1990–2002." *Estudios Cieplan* 26:1–19.

Arriagada, Irma. 2010. "La crisis del cuidado en Chile." In *Construyendo redes: Mujeres latinoamericanas en las cadenas globales de cuidado.* Santiago: Centro de Estudios de la Mujer/INSTRAW.

Ashforth, Adam. 2005. *Witchcraft, Violence, and Democracy in South Africa.* Chicago: University of Chicago Press.

Austin, J.L. 1958. "Pretending." *Proceedings of the Aristotelian Society*(32): 261–278.

Aylwin Azócar, Patricio. 1990. *Discurso del Presidente de la República Patricio Aylwin Azócar: El inicio de la Legislatura Ordinaria del Congreso National, 21 de Mayo, 1990,* www.bcn.cl/susparlamentarios/mensajes_presidenciales/21m1990.pdf.

———. 1992. *La transición chilena: Discursos escogidos, marzo 1990–1992.* Santiago: Editorial Andrés Bello.

Banco Central de Chile. 2005. *Informe de estabilidad financiera, segundo semestre 2005.* Santiago: Banco Central.

Barcia, Roque. 1889. *Diccionario General Etimológico de la Lengua Española.* Madrid: Álvarre Hermanos.

Behforouz, H.L., P.E. Farmer, and J.S. Muhkerjee. 2004. "From Directly Observed Therapy to *Accompagnateurs:* Enhancing AIDS Treatment Outcomes in Haiti and in Boston." *Clinical Infectious Diseases* 38:S429–436.

Bersani, Leo and Adam Phillips. 2008. *intimacies.* Chicago: University of Chicago Press.

Beverley, John. 2004. *Testimonio: On the Politics of Truth.* Minneapolis: University of Minnesota Press.

Biehl, João. 2004. "Life of the Mind: The Interface of Psychopharmaceuticals, Domestic Economies, and Social Abandonment." *American Ethnologist* 31 (4): 475–496.

———. 2007. *Will to Live: AIDS Therapies and the Politics of Survival.* Princeton, NJ: Princeton University Press.

———. 2008. "Pharmaceuticalization: AIDS Treatment and Global Health Politics." *Anthropology Quarterly* 80 (4): 1083–1126.

Biehl, João, and Torben Eskerod. 2005. *Vita: Life in a Zone of Social Abandonment.* Berkeley: University of California Press.

Biehl, João, and Amy Moran-Thomas. 2009. "Symptom: Subjectivities, Social Ills, Technologies." *Annual Review of Anthropology* 38:267–288.

Blofield, Merike Helena. 2001. *The Politics of "Moral Sin": A Study of Abortion and Divorce in Catholic Chile since 1990. In Nueva Serie,* edited by FLACSO. Santiago: FLACSO.

Borneman, John. 1997. *Settling Accounts: Violence, Justice, and Accountability in Postsocialist Europe.* Princeton, NJ: Princeton University Press.

Bourdieu, Pierre. [1980] 1990. *The Logic of Practice.* Stanford, CA: Stanford University Press.

———. 2000. *Pascalian Meditations.* Cambridge, U.K.: Polity Press.

Brito Peña, Alejandra. 2008. "Mujeres del mundo popular urbano: La búsqueda de un espacio." In *Mujeres chilenas: Fragmentos de una historia,* edited by S. Montecino Aguirre, 119–128. Santiago: Editorial Catalonia.

Brown, Cynthia G., Human Rights Watch (Organization), and Americas Watch Committee (U.S.). 1991. *Human Rights and the "Politics of Agreements": Chile during President Aylwin's First Year.* New York: Human Rights Watch.

Brown, Peter. 1981. *The Cult of Saints: Its Rise and Function in Latin Christianity.* Chicago: University of Chicago Press.

———. 1988. *The Body and Society: Men, Women, and Sexual Renunciation in Early Christianity.* New York: Columbia University Press.

Burchell, Graham. 1991. "Peculiar Interests: Civil Society and Governing 'The System of Natural Liberty.'" In *The Foucault Effect: Studies in Governmentality, with Two Lectures by and an Interview with Michel Foucault,* edited by G. Burchell, C. Gordon, and P. Miller, 119–150. Chicago: University of Chicago Press.

Butler, Judith. 2005. *Giving an Account of Oneself.* New York: Fordham University Press.

Canguilhem, Georges. 2008. "The Normal and the Pathological." In *Knowledge of Life,* edited by P. Marrati and T. Meyers, 121–133. New York: Fordham University Press.

Cannell, Fenella. 2004. "The Christianity of Anthropology." *Journal of the Royal Anthropological Institute* 11:335–356.

Cárcamo-Huechante, Luis E. 2001. "El discurso de Friedman: Mercado, universidad y ajuste cultural en Chile." *Revista Crítica Cultural* 23:46–51.

———. 2007. *Tramas del Mercado: Imaginación económica, cultura pública y literatura en el Chile de fines del siglo veinte.* Santiago: Editorial Cuarto Propio.

Carrithers, Michael. 2005. "Anthropology as a Moral Science of Possibilities." *Current Anthropology* 46 (3): 433–456.

Carsten, Janet. 2003. *After Kinship.* Cambridge: Cambridge University Press.

Castel, Robert. 1991. "From Dangerousness to Risk." In *The Foucault Effect: Studies in Governmentality,* edited by G. Burchell, C. Gordon, and P. Miller, 281–297. Chicago: University of Chicago Press.

Castells, Manuel. 1983. *The City and the Grassroots: A Cross-Cultural Theory of Urban Social Movements.* London: Edward Arnold.

Cauas, Jorge. 1975. "The Government Economic Recovery Program: Report on the State of Public Finance, 1975." In *Chilean Economic Policy,* edited by J.C. Méndez G., 155–190. Santiago: Budget Directorate.

Cavell, Stanley. [1969] 2002. *Must We Mean What We Say?* Cambridge: Cambridge University Press.

———. 1979. *The Claim of Reason: Wittgenstein, Skepticism, Morality, and Tragedy.* Oxford: Oxford University Press.

———. [1987] 2003. *Disowning Knowledge in Seven Plays of Shakespeare.* Cambridge: Cambridge University Press.

———. 1988. *In Quest of the Ordinary: Lines of Skepticism and Romanticism.* Chicago: University of Chicago Press.

———. 2003. *Emerson's Transcendental Etudes.* Stanford, CA: Stanford University Press.

————. 2005. *Philosophy the Day after Tomorrow.* Cambridge, MA: Harvard University Press, Belknap Press.

Chile Oficina de Planificación Nacional. 1979. *Plan nacional indicativo de desarrollo, 1979–1984.* [Santiago]: Odeplan.

Chile Secretaría General de Gobierno, and Chile Oficina de Planificación Nacional. 1988. *Sabemos hacia donde vamos: Algunos logros del gobierno del presidente Augusto Pinochet Ugarte.* [Santiago]: Ministerio Secretaría General de Gobierno: Oficina de Planificación Nacional.

CINTRAS. N.d. "The Reparation for Survivors of Torture: An Inconclusive Task." Unpublished manuscript.

CNPPT. 2004. *Informe de la Comisión Nacional sobre Prisión Política y Tortura.* Santiago: La Nación-Ministerio del Interior.

Coleman, Norm, and Carl Levin. 2004. *Money Laundering and Foreign Corruption: Enforcement and Effectiveness of the Patriot Act Case Study Involving Riggs Bank.* Edited by United States Senate Permanent Subcommittee on Investigations, Committee on Governmental Affairs.

Collins, Daryl, Jonathan Morduch, Stuart Rutherford, and Orlanda Ruthven. 2009. *Portfolios of the Poor: How the World's Poor Live on $2 a Day.* Princeton, NJ: Princeton University Press.

CONACE. 2006. *Informe anual de la situación de las drogas en Chile.* Edited by Ministerio de Interior. Santiago: Gobierno de Chile.

CONADECUS. 2007. "Endeudamiento: ¿Chilenos endeudados o sobreendeudados?" *Observatorio del Consumidor.* Santiago: CONADECUS. Digital video.

Connolly, William E. 2011. *A World of Becoming.* Durham, NC: Duke University Press.

Constable, Marianne. 2005. *Just Silences: The Limits and Possibilities of Modern Law.* Princeton, NJ: Princeton University Press.

Cowan, Kevin, and José De Gregorio. 2003. "Credit Information and Market Performance: The Case of Chile." In *Credit Reporting Systems and the International Economy*, edited by M.J. Miller, 163–202. Cambridge: MIT Press.

Cruz Feliciano, Héctor M., and Fernando Véliz Montero. 2007. "Endeudamiento, control social y mercado en Chile." Paper presented at the *Latin American Studies Association Meetings*, Montreal, Canada.

Das, Veena. 1995. *Critical Events: An Anthropological Perspective on Contemporary India.* Delhi: Oxford University Press.

————. 1998. "Wittgenstein and Anthropology." *Annual Review of Anthropology* 27:171–195.

————. 2006. "Secularism and the Argument from Nature." In *Powers of the Secular Modern: Talal Asad and His Interlocutors,* edited by C. Hirschkind and D. Scott, 93–112. Stanford, CA: Stanford University Press.

————. 2007. *Life and Words: Violence and the Descent into the Ordinary.* Berkeley: University of California Press.

————. 2008. "Violence, Gender, and Subjectivity." *Annual Review of Anthropology* 37:283–299.

————. 2010a. "Engaging the Life of the Other: Love and Everyday Life." In *Ordinary Ethics: Anthropology, Language, and Action,* edited by M. Lambek, 376–399. New York: Fordham University Press.

———. 2010b. "The Life of Humans and the Life of Roaming Spirits." In *Rethinking the Human,* edited by J.M. Molina and D.K. Swearer, 31–45. Cambridge, MA: Harvard University Press.

Das, Veena, and Renu Addlakha. 2001. "Disability and Domestic Citizenship: Voice, Gender, and the Making of the Subject." *Public Culture* 13 (3): 511–531.

Das, Veena, and Ranendra Das. 2006. "Pharmaceuticals in Urban Ecologies: The Register of the Local." In *Global Pharmaceuticals: Ethics, Markets, Practices,* edited by A. Petryna, A. Lakoff, and A. Kleinman, 66–97. Durham, NC: Duke University Press.

Das, Veena, Arthur Kleinman, Mamphela Ramphele, and Pamela Reynolds, eds. 2000. *Violence and Subjectivity.* Berkeley: University of California Press.

Davis, Madeleine. 2003. *The Pinochet Case: Origins, Progress, and Implications.* London: Institute of Latin American Studies.

Deleuze, Gilles. 1997. *Essays Critical and Clinical.* Minneapolis: University of Minnesota Press.

Deleuze, Gilles, and Félix Guattari. 1986. *Kafka: Toward a Minor Literature.* Minneapolis: University of Minnesota Press.

———. 1987. *A Thousand Plateaus: Capitalism and Schizophrenia.* Minneapolis: University of Minnesota Press.

Desjarlais, Robert R. 2003. *Sensory Biographies: Lives and Deaths among Nepal's Yolmo Buddhists.* Berkeley: University of California Press.

Dockendorff, Eduardo. 1990. Santiago, dos ciudades: Análisis de la estructura socio-económica espacial del Gran Santiago. Santiago: Centro de Estudios del Desarrollo.

Eltit, Diamela. 1989. *El padre mío.* Santiago: Francisco Zegers Editor.

Espinoza, Vicente. 1989. *Para una historia de los pobres de la ciudad.* Santiago: Ediciones SUR.

Esposito, Roberto. 2010. *Communitas: The Origin and Destiny of Community.* Stanford, CA: Stanford University Press.

Evans-Pritchard, E.E. 1976. *Witchcraft, Oracles, and Magic among the Azande.* Oxford: Clarendon Press.

Farmer, Paul. 2003. *Pathologies of Power: Health, Human Rights, and the New War on the Poor.* Berkeley: University of California Press.

Fassin, Didier. 2007a. "Humanitarianism as a Politics of Life." *Public Culture* 19 (3): 499–520.

———. 2007b. *When Bodies Remember: Experiences and Politics of AIDS in South Africa.* Berkeley: University of California Press.

———. 2010. "Ethics of Survival: A Democratic Approach to the Politics of Life." *Humanity: An International Journal of Human Rights, Humanitarianism, and Development* (Fall): 81–95.

———. 2012. *Humanitarian Reason: A Moral History of the Present.* Berkeley: University of California Press.

Fassin, Didier, and Richard Rechtman. 2009. *The Empire of Trauma: An Inquiry into the Condition of Victimhood.* Princeton, NJ: Princeton University Press.

Fazio, Hugo. 1996. *El programa abandonado: Balance económico social del gobierno de Aylwin.* Santiago: Arcis Universidad / LOM Ediciones / CENDA.

———. 1997. *Mapa actual de la extrema riqueza en Chile.* Santiago: ARCIS Universidad / LOM Ediciones / CENDA.

———. 1999. *El sur en el nuevo sistema mundial.* Santafé de Bogotá: Siglo del Hombre Editores / IEPRI Universidad Nacional.

———. 2005. *Mapa de la extrema riqueza al año 2005.* Santiago: LOM Ediciones.

Ffrench-Davis, Ricardo. 2004. *Entre el neoliberalismo y el crecimiento con equidad: Tres décadas de política económica en Chile.* Buenos Aires: Fundación OSDE / Siglo Veintiuno Editores Argentina.

Foerster, Rolf. 1995. *Introducción a la religiosidad mapuche.* Santiago: Editorial Universitaria.

Foucault, Michel. 1978. *The History of Sexuality.* New York: Pantheon Books.

———. [1978–1979] 2008. *The Birth of Biopolitics: Lectures at the Collège de France, 1978–1979.* Translated by Graham Burchell. New York: Palgrave Macmillan.

———. 1980. "The Politics of Health in the Eighteenth Century." In *Power/Knowledge: Selected Interviews and Writings, 1972–1977,* edited by C. Gordon, 166–182. New York: Pantheon Books.

———. 1991. "Governmentality." In *The Foucault Effect: Studies in Governmentality: With Two Lectures by and an Interview with Michel Foucault,* edited by G. Burchell, C. Gordon, and P. Miller, 87–104. Chicago: University of Chicago Press.

———. 1997. "Self Writing." In *Ethics: Subjectivity and Truth,* edited by P. Rabinow. New York: New Press.

Frank, Volker. 2004. "Politics without Policy: The Failure of Social Concertation in Democratic Chile, 1990–2000." In *Victims of the Chilean Miracle: Workers and Neoliberalism in the Pinochet Era, 1972–2002,* edited by P. Winn, 71–124. Durham, NC: Duke University Press.

Freud, Sigmund. 1966. *Introductory Lectures on Psycho-Analysis.* New York: W. W. Norton and Company.

———. 1995. "The 'Uncanny.'" In *Sigmund Freud: Psychological Letters and Writings,* edited by S. L. Gilman, 120–153. New York: Continuum.

Fullwiley, Duana. 2011. *The Enculturated Gene: Sickle Cell Health Politics and Biological Difference in West Africa.* Princeton: Princeton University Press.

Garcés, Juan. 2004. "Sumario 19/1997 Pieza Separada. Al Juzgado Central de Instrucción No. 5," July 19, www.elclarin.cl/fpa/pdf/p_190704.pdf.

Garcés, Mario. 1997. *Historia de la comuna de Huechuraba: Memoria y oralidad popular urbana.* Santiago: ECO Educación y Comunicaciones.

Garcia, Angela. 2010. *The Pastoral Clinic: Addiction and Dispossession along the Rio Grande.* Berkeley: University of California Press.

Geest, Sjaak van der, Susan Reynolds Whyte, and Anita Hardon. 1996. "The Anthropology of Pharmaceuticals: A Biographical Approach." *Annual Review of Anthropology* 25:153–178.

Gideon, Jasmine. 2001. "The Decentralization of Primary Health Care Delivery in Chile." *Public Administration and Development* 21:223–231.

Gómez-Barris, Macarena. 2009. *Where Memory Dwells: Culture and State Violence in Chile.* Berkeley: University of California Press.

Good, Byron. 1994. *Medicine, Rationality, and Experience*. Cambridge: Cambridge University Press.

Goodfellow, Aaron. 2008. "Pharmaceutical Intimacy: Sex, Death, and Methamphetamine." *Home Cultures* 5 (3): 271–300.

Grandin, Greg. 2005. "The Instruction of Great Catastrophe: Truth Commissions, National History, and State Formation in Argentina, Chile, and Guatemala." *American Historical Review* 110 (1): 46–67.

Greaves, Edward. 2005. "Panoptic Municipalities, the Spatial Dimensions of the Political, and Passive Revolution in Post-Dictatorship Chile." *City and Community* 4 (2): 189–215.

Greenhouse, Carol. 2010. *Ethnographies of Neoliberalism*. Philadelphia: University of Pennsylvania Press.

Guyer, Jane. 2004. *Marginal Gains: Monetary Transactions in Atlantic Africa*. Chicago: University of Chicago Press.

———. 2010. "The True Gift: Thoughts on *L'Année sociologique*." *Review du M.A.U.S.S.* 36:283–253.

Han, Clara. 2010. "Earthquake in Chile: Poverty and Social Diagnoses." *LASA Forum* 41 (3): 9–12.

Hardy, Clarisa. 1987. *Organizarse para vivir: Pobreza urbana y organización popular*. Santiago: Programa del Economía del Trabajo.

Hardy Raskovan, Clarisa, and Eduardo Amadeo. 2004. *Equidad y protección social: Desafíos de políticas sociales en América Latina*. Santiago: LOM Ediciones / Chile 21.

Henríquez, Helia, and Verónica Riquelme. 2006. *Lejos del Trabajo Decente: El empleo desprotegido en Chile*. Santiago: Departamento de Estudios / Dirección del Trabajo.

Herrera Rodríguez, Susana. 2004. *El aborto inducido: ¿Víctimas o victimarias?* Santiago: Editorial Catalonia.

———. 2008. "Aborto inducido: ¿Un secreto de mujeres o una problemática de género?" *In Mujeres chilenas: Fragmentos de una historia*, edited by S. Montecino Aguirre, 599–610. Santiago: Editorial Catalonia.

Illanes, María Angélica. 2007. *Cuerpo y sangre de la política: La construcción histórica de las Visitadores Sociales (1887–1940)*. Santiago: LOM Ediciones.

International Theological Commission. 1999. *Memory and Reconciliation: The Church and the Faults of the Past*. Rome: Vatican, www.vatican.va/roman_curia/congregations/cfaith/cti_documents/rc_con_cfaith_doc_20000307_memory-reconc-itc_en.html.

Jackson, Michael, ed. 1996. *Things As They Are: New Directions in Phenomenological Anthropology*. Bloomington: Indiana University Press.

———. 2009. "Where Thought Belongs: An Anthropological Critique of the Project of Philosophy." *Anthropological Theory* 9 (3): 235–251.

John Paul II. 1987. *Seis Discursos del Papa Juan Pablo II en Chile*. Santiago: Centro de Estudios Públicos.

Jung, Carl G. 1958. *Psychology and Religion*. New Haven, CT: Yale University Press.

Junta Militar. 1974. "Declaration of Principles of the Chilean Government." In

Chilean Economic Policy, edited by J.C. Méndez G., 23–44. Santiago: Budget Directorate.

Kast Rist, Miguel, and Sergio Molina Silva. 1975. *Mapa extrema pobreza.* Santiago: ODEPLAN.

Keane, Webb. 2005. "Signs Are Not the Garb of Meaning: On the Social Analysis of Material Things." In *Materiality,* edited by D. Miller, 182–205. Durham, NC: Duke University Press.

———. 2007. *Christian Moderns: Freedoms and Fetish in the Mission Encounter.* Berkeley: University of California Press.

———. 2008. "Market, Materiality, and Moral Metalanguage." *Anthropological Theory* 8 (1): 27–42.

———. 2010. "Minds, Surfaces, and Reasons in the Anthropology of Ethics." In *Ordinary Ethics: Anthropology, Language, and Action,* edited by M. Lambek, 64–83. New York: Fordham University Press.

Kirkwood, Julieta. [1986] 2010. *Ser política en Chile: Las feministas y los partidos.* Santiago: LOM Ediciones.

Kleinman, Arthur. 2000. "The Violences of Everyday Life: The Multiple Forms and Dynamics of Social Violence." In *Violence and Subjectivity,* edited by V. Das, A. Kleinman, M. Ramphele, and P. Reynolds, 226–241. Berkeley: University of California Press.

———. 2006. *What Really Matters: Living a Moral Life Amidst Uncertainty and Danger.* Oxford: Oxford University Press.

———. 2010. "Caregiving: The Divided Meaning of Being Human and the Divided Self of the Caregiver." In *Rethinking the Human,* edited by J.M. Molina and D.K. Swearer. Cambridge, MA: Harvard University Press.

Kleinman, Arthur, Veena Das, and Margaret Lock. 1997. *Social Suffering.* Berkeley: University of California Press.

Kubal, Mary Rose. 2006. "Contradictions and Constraints in Chile's Health Care and Education Decentralization." *Latin American Politics and Society* 48 (4): 105–135.

La Cuarta. 2002. "Ley Dicom: Un millón 800 mil familias salen de la pantalla," June 7.

Lagos, Ricardo. 2004. "El Presidente de la República da a conocer el Informe de la Comisión sobre Prisión Política y Tortura," www.archivochile.com/ Derechos_humanos/com_valech/gob_otros_estado/hhddgobotros0017.pdf.

Lambek, Michael. 2010. "Towards an Ethics of the Act." In *Ordinary Ethics: Anthropology, Language, and Action,* edited by M. Lambek, 39–63. New York: Fordham University Press.

———. 2011. "Kinship as Gift and Theft: Acts of Succession in Mayotte and Ancient Israel." *American Ethnologist* 38 (1): 2–16.

Larrañaga, Osvaldo. 2005. "Focalización de Programas en Chile: El Sistema CAS." In *Serie de informes sobre redes de protección social,* edited by W. B. Institute. Washington, DC: World Bank.

Larrañaga, Osvaldo, and Rodrigo Herrera. 2008. "Los recientes cambios en la desigualdad y la pobreza en Chile." *Estudios Públicos* 109:149–186.

Lazzara, Michael J. 2006. "The Poetics of Impossibility: Diamela Eltit's *El Padre Mío.*" *Chasqui: Revista de literatura latinoamericano* 35 (1): 106–118.

Lemke, Thomas. 2001. "The Birth of Bio-politics": Michel Foucault's Lecture at the Collège de France on Neo-liberal Governmentality. *Economy and Society* 30 (2): 190–207.

Lewis, Oscar. 1966. *La Vida: A Puerto Rican Family in the Culture of Poverty— San Juan and New York.* New York: Random House.

Lovell, Anne. 2006. "Addiction Markets: The Case of High-Dose Buprenorphine in France." In *Global Pharmaceuticals: Ethics, Markets, Practices,* ed. A. Petryna, A. Lakoff, and A. Kleinman, 136–170. Durham, NC: Duke University Press.

Loveman, Brian. 1988. *Chile: The Legacy of Hispanic Capitalism.* New York: Oxford University Press.

Loveman, Brian, and Elizabeth Lira. 2002. *El espejismo de la reconciliación política: Chile 1990–2002.* Santiago: LOM Ediciones / DIBAM.

Madariaga, Carlos. 2005. "Visión desde los equipos de salud mental y psiquiatría." In *Enfermedad Mental, Derechos Humanos, y Exclusión Social,* edited by Ministerio de Salud, 38–66. Santiago: Ministerio de Salud, Gobierno de Chile.

Marconi T., Juan. 1973. "La revolución cultural chilena en programas de salud mental." *Acta Psiquiátrica y Psicológica de America Latina* 19 (1): 17–33.

Márquez, Francisca. 2006. "Políticas sociales de vivienda en Chile: De la autoconstrucción tutelada a la privatización segregada 1967–1997." *Cadernos Gestão Pública e Cidadania* 11 (49): 79–108.

Marrati, Paola, and Todd Meyers. 2008. "Forward: Life, as Such." In *Knowledge of Life,* edited by P. Marrati and T. Meyers, vii–xii. New York: Fordham University Press.

McFarland, Ian A. 2001. "Who Is My Neighbor?: The Good Samaritan as a Source for Theological Anthropology." *Modern Theology* 17 (1): 57–66.

Meller, Patricio. 1996. *Un siglo de economía política chilena (1890–1990).* Santiago: Editorial Andrés Bello.

MEMCH. 2010. *Movimiento Pro-Emancipación de la Mujer.* Santiago: MEMCH, www.memch.cl/.

Mendive, Susana. 2004. "Entrevista al Dr. Juan Marconi, Creador de la Psiquiatría Intracomunitaria: Reflexiones Acerca de su Legado Para la Psicología Comunitaria Chilena." *Psykhe* 13 (2): 187–199.

El Mercurio de Valparaíso. 2000. "El riesgo de vivir en cuotas," July 29.

MIDEPLAN. 2004. *Conceptos Fundamentales Sistema de Protección Social: Chile Solidario,* edited by MIDEPLAN. Santiago: Gobierno de Chile.

———. 2006. *Encuesta de Caracterización Socioeconómica Nacional (CASEN).* Santiago: Gobierno de Chile.

Milanich, Nara. 2009. *Children of Fate: Childhood, Class, and the State in Chile, 1850–1930.* Durham, NC: Duke University Press.

Miller, Daniel. 1995. "Consumption Studies and the Transformation of Anthropology." In *Acknowledging Consumption: A Review of the New Studies,* edited by D. Miller. New York: Routledge.

———. 2001a. *Home Possessions: Material Culture Behind Closed Doors.* Oxford: Berg.

————. 2001b. "The Poverty of Morality." *Journal of Consumer Culture* 1:225–243.

Ministerio de Salud. 1993. *Políticas y Plan Nacional de Salud Mental*. Santiago: Unidad de Salud Mental, Gobierno de Chile.

————. 2000. *Plan Nacional de Salud Mental y Psiquiatría*. Santiago: Gobierno de Chile.

Ministerio Secretaria General de la Presidencia. 1999. *Protección de Datos de Carácter Personal*. Ley 19.628.

Montecino Aguirre, Sonia. 1996. *Madres y Huachos: Alegorías del mestizaje chileno*. Santiago: Editorial Sudamerica.

————. 2008. "Hacia una antropología del género en Chile." In *Mujeres Chilenas: Fragmentos de una historia*, edited by S. Montecino Aguirre, 395–404. Santiago: Editorial Catalonia.

Moulian, Tomás. 1997. *Chile actual: Anatomía de un mito*. [Santiago]: ARCIS Universidad / LOM Ediciones.

————. 2000. "La liturgia de la reconciliación." In *Políticas y estéticas de la memoria*, edited by N. Richard, 15–22. Serie Ensayo. Providencia, Santiago: Editorial Cuarto Propio.

Nelson, Diane. 2009. *Reckoning: The Ends of War in Guatemala*. Durham, NC: Duke University Press.

Olavarria-Gambi, Mauricio. 2003. "Poverty Reduction in Chile: Has Economic Growth Been Enough?" *Journal of Human Development* 4 (1): 103–123.

Olave, Thumala A. 2010. "The Richness of Ordinary Life: Religious Justification among Chile's Business Elite." *Religion* 40:14–26.

PAHO. 1990. *Declaración de Caracas: Reestructuración de la Atención Psiquiátrica en América Latina*. Caracas, Venezuela: Pan American Health Organization.

Paley, Julia. 2001. *Marketing Democracy: Power and Social Movements in Post-dictatorship Chile*. Berkeley: University of California Press.

Palma, Julieta, and Raúl Urzúa. 2005. "Políticas contra la pobreza y ciudadanía social: El caso de Chile Solidario." *Políticas Sociales* 12:1–37.

Pandolfo, Stefania. 1997. *Impasse of Angels: Scenes from a Moroccan Space of Memory*. Chicago: University of Chicago Press.

————. 2007. "'The Burning': Finitude and the Politico-Theological Imagination of Illegal Migration." *Anthropological Theory* 7 (3): 329–363.

Parker Gumucio, Cristián. 1991. "Christianity and Popular Movements in the Twentieth Century." In *Popular Culture in Chile: Resistance and Survival*, edited by K. Aman and C. Parker Gumucio, 41–68. Boulder, CO: Westview Press.

Parry, Jonathan. 1985. "*The Gift*, the Indian Gift, and the 'Indian Gift.'" *Man* 21:453–473.

Pateman, Carol. 1988. *The Sexual Contract*. Stanford, CA: Stanford University Press.

Perlman, Janice. 1979. *The Myth of Marginality: Urban Politics and Poverty in Rio de Janeiro*. Berkeley: University of California Press.

————. 2010. *Favela: Four Decades of Living on the Edge in Rio de Janeiro*. Oxford: Oxford University Press.

Petras, James F., Fernando Ignacio Leiva, and Henry Veltmeyer. 1994. *Democracy and Poverty in Chile: The Limits to Electoral Politics*. Boulder, CO.: Westview Press.

Petryna, Adriana. 2002. *Life Exposed: Biological Citizens after Chernobyl*. Princeton, NJ: Princeton University Press.

———. 2009. *When Experiments Travel: Clinical Trials and the Global Search for Human Subjects*. Princeton, NJ: Princeton University Press.

Phillips, Adam, and Barbara Taylor. 2009. *On Kindness*. New York: Picador.

PNUD. 2002. *Desarrollo humano en Chile: Nosotros los chilenos: Un desafío social*. Santiago: Naciones Unidas.

Poole, Deborah. 2004. "Between Threat and Guarantee: Justice and Community in the Margins of the Peruvian State." In *Anthropology in the margins of the state*, edited by V. Das and D. Poole, 35–66. Santa Fe, NM: School of American Research.

Povinelli, Elizabeth A. 2006. *The Empire of Love: Toward a Theory of Intimacy, Genealogy, and Carnality*. Durham, NC: Duke University Press.

Price, Joshua. 2002. "The Apotheosis of Home and the Maintenance of Spaces of Violence." *Hypatia* 17 (4): 39–70.

Rabinow, Paul, George Marcus, James D. Faubion, and Tobias Rees. 2008. *Designs for an Anthropology of the Contemporary*. Durham, NC: Duke University Press.

Raczynski, Dagmar. 2008. "Sistema Chile Solidario y la Política de Protección Social de Chile: Lecciones del pasado y agenda para el futuro." In *Una nueva agenda económica y social para América Latina*, edited by Instituto Fernando Henrique Cardoso y Corporación de Estudios para Latinoamérica. Santiago: iFHC/CIEPLAN.

Raczynski, Dagmar, Claudia Serrano, and Manuela Valle. 2002. *Eventos de Quiebre de Ingreso y Mecanismos de Protección Social: Estudios de Hogares de Ingreso Medio y Bajo*. Santiago: Banco Mundial.

Razeto M., Luis. 1986. *Economía Popular de Solidaridad: Identidad y proyecto en una visión integradora*. Santiago: Area Pastoral Social de la Conferencia Episcopal de Chile.

———. 1990. *Las Organizaciones económicas populares, 1973–1990*. Santiago: Programa de Economía del Trabajo.

Real Academia. 2010. *Diccionario de la Lengua Española*, http://buscon.rae.es/drael/.

Richard, Nelly. 1993. *Masculino/feminino: Prácticas de la diferencia y la cultura democrática*. Santiago: Francisco Zegers Editor.

———. 2000. *Políticas y estéticas de la memoria*. Providencia, Santiago: Editorial Cuarto Propio.

Richard, Nelly, and Alberto Moreiras. 2001. *Pensar en-la postdictadura*. Santiago: Editorial Cuarto Propio.

Riesco, Manuel. 2005. "Trabajo y previsión social en el Gobierno de Lagos." In *Gobierno de Lagos: Balance crítico*, edited by G. Salazar Vergara, 43–70. Santiago: LOM Ediciones.

Rivas, Jéssica. 2006. "Endeudamiento de chilenos se disparó en los últimos 5 años." *El Mercurio*, May 8, 2006.

Roht-Arriaza, Naomi. 2005. *The Pinochet Effect: Transnational Justice in the Age of Human Rights*. Philadelphia: University of Pennsylvania Press.

Ross, Fiona C. 2003. *Bearing Witness: Women and the Truth and Reconciliation Commission in South Africa*. London: Pluto Press.

Ruiz, Carlos. 2000. Democracia, consenso, y memoria: Una reflexión sobre la experiencia chilena. In *Políticas y estéticas de la memoria*, edited by N. Richard, 15–22. Serie Ensayo. Providencia, Santiago: Editorial Cuarto Propio.

Ruiz, Mauricio. 2002. "Dicom invita a los deudores a revisar gratis su situación commercial." *Las Últimas Noticias* (June 14).

Salazar Vergara, Gabriel. 2005. "Ricardo Lagos, 2000–2005: Perfíl histórico, trasfondo popular." In *Gobierno de Lagos: Balance crítico*, edited by G. Salazar Vergara, 71–100. Santiago: LOM Ediciones.

Salazar Vergara, Gabriel, and Julio Pinto. 1999. *Historia contemporánea de Chile*. Santiago: LOM Ediciones.

Scheper-Hughes, Nancy. 1992. *Death without Weeping: The Violence of Everyday Life in Brazil*. Berkeley: University of California Press.

Schild, Verónica. 2007. "Empowering 'Consumer-Citizens' or Governing Poor Female Subjects." *Journal of Consumer Culture* 7 (2): 179–203.

Scully, Timothy. 1992. *Rethinking the Center: Party Politics in Nineteenth- and Twentieth-Century Chile*. Stanford, CA: Stanford University Press.

Silva, Consuelo. 2007. "La subcontratación en Chile: Aproximación sectorial." In *Trabajo y equidad*. Santiago: Consejo Asesor Presidencial.

Silva, Eduardo. 1996. *The State and Capital in Chile: Business Elites, Technocrats, and Market Economics*. Boulder, CO: Westview Press.

Silverstein, Michael. 1976. "Shifters, Linguistic Categories, and Cultural Description." In *Meaning in Anthropology*, edited by K. Basso and H. A. Selby, 11–56. Albuquerque: School of American Research, University of New Mexico Press.

Small, Mario Luis. 2007. "Is There Such a Thing as 'the Ghetto'? The Perils of Assuming that the South Side of Chicago Represents Poor Black Neighborhoods" *City* 11 (3): 413–421.

Smith, Brian H. 1982. *The Church and Politics in Chile: Challenges to Modern Catholicism*. Princeton, N.J.: Princeton University Press.

Sommer, Doris. 1991. "Rigoberta's Secrets." *Latin American Perspectives* 18 (3): 32–50.

Stack, Carol. 1974. *All Our Kin*. New York: Basic Books.

Stern, Steve J. 2004. *Remembering Pinochet's Chile: On the Eve of London, 1998*. Durham, NC: Duke University Press.

———. 2010. *Reckoning with Pinochet: The Memory Question in Democratic Chile, 1989–2006*. Durham, NC: Duke University Press.

Strathern, Marilyn. 1981. *Kinship at the Core: An Anthropology of Elmdon, a Village in North-West Essex in the Nineteen Sixties*. Cambridge: Cambridge University Press.

———. 1995. "Nostalgia and the New Genetics." In *The Rhetorics of Self-Making*, edited by D. Battaglia, 97–120. Berkeley: University of California Press.

———. 1996. "Cutting the Network." *Journal of the Royal Anthropological Institute*, n.s., 2: 517–535.

———. 2005. *Kinship, Law and the Unexpected: Relatives Are Always a Surprise*. Cambridge: Cambridge University Press.

Szot M., Jorge, and Cristina Moreno W. 2003. "Mortalidad por aborto en Chile: Análisis Epidemiológico 1985–2000." *Revista chilena de obstetricia y ginecología* 68 (4): 309–314.

Teitelboim G, Berta. 2001. "Estadísticas Sociales al Nivel Local." In *Fourth Meeting of the Expert Group on Poverty Statistics*. Rio de Janeiro: CEPAL.

Ticktin, Miriam. 2011. *Casualties of Care: Immigration and the Politics of Humanitarianism in France*. Berkeley: University of California Press.

Tinsman, Heidi. 2002. *Partners in Conflict: The Politics of Gender, Sexuality, and Labor in the Chilean Agrarian Reform, 1950–1973*. Durham, NC: Duke University Press.

Tironi Barrios, Eugenio. 1990. *Autoritarismo, modernización y marginalidad: El caso de Chile, 1973–1989*. Santiago: Ediciones SUR.

Traverso, Ana. 2007. "Modernización y regionalismo en la poesía de Jorge Tellier." *Anales de Literatura Chilena* 8 (8): 133–154.

Unidad de Salud Mental. 2005. "Juan Marconi Tassara." Obituary. MINSAL, www.minsal.cl, accessed June 19, 2006.

Valdés, Juan Gabriel. 1995. *Pinochet's Economists: The Chicago School in Chile*. Cambridge: Cambridge University Press.

Valdés, Teresa, Ximena Valdés, FLACSO (Organization) Programa Chile, and Centro de Estudios para el Desarrollo de la Mujer. 2005. *Familia y vida privada: Transformaciones, tensiones, resistencias y nuevos sentidos?* Vitacura: FLACSO-Chile / CEDEM.

Valdés, Ximena. 2007. "Notas sobre la metamorfosis de la familia en Chile." In *Futuro de las familias y desafíos para las políticas públicas*, 1–13. Naciones Unidas CEPAL, UNFPA. Santiago: CEPAL.

Varas C., Sofia. 2008. "Tarjetas de crédito están cambiando el endeudamiento de los chilenos (Cooperativa)." In *CONADECUS: Consumidores Chile*. Vol. 2008. Santiago: CONADECUS.

Vatican. 2010. *Catechism of the Catholic Church*. Vol. 2010. Rome: Vatican.

Vergara, Pilar. 1984. "Auge y caída del neoliberalismo en Chile: Un estudio sobre la evolución ideológica del régimen militar." In *Documento de Trabajo*, vol. 216, edited by FLACSO, 369: Santiago: FLACSO.

———. 1990. *Políticas hacia la extrema pobreza en Chile, 1973–1988*. [Santiago]: Facultad Latinoamericana de Ciencias Sociales.

Wacquant, Loïc. 2008. *Urban Outcasts: A Comparative Sociology of Urban Poverty*. Cambridge: Polity Press.

Ward, Peter, et al. 2004. "From Marginality of the 1960s to the 'New Poverty' of Today: A LARR Research Forum." *Latin American Research Review* 39 (1): 183–203.

Warren, Kay B. 1998. *Indigenous Movements and Their Critics: Pan-Maya Activism in Guatemala*. Princeton, NJ: Princeton University Press.

WHO. 2001. *The World Health Report—Mental Health: New Understanding, New Hope*. Geneva: World Health Organization.

Whyte, Susan Reynolds, Sjaak van der Geest, and Anita Hardon. 2002. *Social Lives of Medicines*. Cambridge: Cambridge University Press.

Wilson, Richard. 2001. *The Politics of Truth and Reconciliation in South Africa: Legitimizing the Post-apartheid State*. Cambridge: Cambridge University Press.

———. 2003. "The Anthropological Study of Truth Commissions." *Anthropological Theory* 3 (3): 367–387.

Winn, Peter. 2004. *Victims of the Chilean Miracle: Workers and Neoliberalism in the Pinochet Era, 1972–2002*. Durham, NC: Duke University Press.

Wittgenstein, Ludwig. 1953. *Philosophical Investigations*. Malden, MA: Blackwell Publishers.

Yúdice, George. 1991. "Testimonio and Postmodernism." *Latin American Perspectives* 18 (3): 15–31.

Index

Page numbers in italics indicate illustrations.

abandonment: overview of, 22; limits around, 24–25; mother militant and, 134, 143–44, 146, 151; pharmaceuticals and, 209, 213–14, 221, 224, 226–30

abortion, 155–56, 158, 159–61, 249n7. *See also* maternity

absorbing mechanism *(amortiguador/a)*, 99, 118–19

acknowledgement, 24, 86–87, 119, 229–30. *See also* kindness; limit/s; separateness

actants, pharmaceuticals as, 205, 252n4

active awaiting or waiting or, as modality of care, 31, 56, 240n1

active solidarities, 70–75

adaptations, and reconciliation, 127–28

addiction to *pasta base*: children's, 36, 111, 185–86, 235; domestic violence and, 48; men's, 27, 30, 35–36, 38–39, 43, 48, 50, 53, 151, 190, 225, 238; Pinochet as responsible for, 111; statistics for, 36; treatments for, 30, 53; women's, 35, 50, 53, 54, 150, 206. *See also* domestic struggles to care for kin; *pasta base* (cocaine base paste)

addiction to pharmaceuticals, 212

Administradores de Fondos de Cesantía, 77

affection *(cariño)*, 118, 153, 229. *See also* love

affective configurations, and domestic relations, 22, 147, 205–6, 214–15

agency, 132, 208

aguantar (endure), 76, 81. *See also* enduring

Alessandri, Arturo, 71

Alianza parties, 173–74

Allende, Salvador, 1–3, 7, 15, 17–18, 132–33, 135, 142

Almacenes París, 32, 37, 40, 63, 159

Alvarado, Rubén, 170, 171, 200

amitriptyline, 173, 180

Amnesty Law of 1978, 96, 245nn5–6

amortiguador/a (absorbing mechanism), 99, 118–19

ánimo (spirit/energy), 6, 206, 207–8, 210–11

anthropology: of care, 22–28, 240n5; method and, 49, 83–84, 240n7, 243n10, 243n15; research methodology and, 5–6, 16–17. *See also* ethnography

antidepressants, 173, 180, 216, 217. *See also specific antidepressants*

Appadurai, Arjun, 243n13

Araya, Ricardo, 172, 179–81

asking and begging, 77–78, 87. *See also limosnear* (to beg for)

aspiration/s: overview of, 4, 6, 11; democracy and, 19, 21, 97, 108, 128; economic precariousness and, 17; intimate relations

aspiration/s *(continued)*
  and, 93, 100–101, 127; mourning of, 127;
  for political community, 97, 108, 127;
  reconciliation and, 93–94, 100–101, 108,
  112–14, 246n15; state institutions and, 17
Augustinian asceticism, 84, 243n15
Austin, J. L., 85–87
autobiography, and writing on the body, 140,
  227–28. *See also* biography over time
autoconstruction *(auto-construcción)*, 15–
  16, 29
Aylwin (Azócar), Patricio: community mental health program and, 199; Concertación government and, 58, 168; economic growth policies and, 59; Labor
  Code reform and, 61; reconciliation
  and, 94–96; Rettig Report and, 93–95,
  116, 127, 245n4; on social debt and
  poverty, 56–57, 245n7; on temporality
  of moral healing, 94–95

Bachelet, Michelle, 2, 235
Baraona, Pablo, 7
Bardón, Alvaro, 7
barrio alto (wealthy urban neighborhoods),
  18, 76, 99, 123, 156, 194, 217, 231
Beck Depression Index, 201
becoming aware of connections/
  disconnections, 5
becoming minor, 75–76
to beg for *(limosnear)*, 117, 248n25. *See
  also* begging and asking
begging and asking, 77–78, 87. See also
  limosnear (to beg for)
Biehl, João, 25, 252n3
biography over time, 211–14. *See also* autobiography, and writing on the body
biopolitics, 25–26
birth, as force in everyday lives, 100–103
black market for pharmaceuticals, 203–5,
  252n2
the body: bodying forth of relations and,
  160; need for a working, 35, 207–8,
  211, 213, 217; writing on in relation to
  autobiography and, 140, 227–28. *See
  also* embodiment
boundary/ies: begging and asking, 77–78,
  87; dignity in domestic relations and,
  69, 75–79; kindness in relation to, 88–
  89; kinship and, 4; the moral subject as
  refracted through relations and, 4; the
  political subject as refracted through
  relations and, 4; reciprocity in domestic

relations and, 77–80, 87; of speech and
  silence, 56, 89–90; state violence and
  care, 4–5, 47–50, 53, 240nn7–8. *See
  also* neighbors and neighborhoods
Bourdieu, Pierre, 86, 240n1
Butler, Judith, 26

cachar (to catch in relation to critical
  moment), 81, 86, 88, 90, 118
Cámara de la Industria Farmacéutica
  (Chamber of the Pharmaceutical
  Industry), 203
Canguilhem, Georges, 26–27
Cannell, Fennela, 83–84, 243n15
Cárcamo-Huechante, Luis, 9, 189, 251n8
care: abandonment by kin and, 209, 213–
  14, 221, 224, 226–30; anthropology
  of, 22–28, 240n5; becoming aware
  of connections/disconnections and, 5;
  democratic transition and, 4; doctors
  in community mental health program
  and, 182–83; in everyday life, 5; finite
  responsibility and, 43–47, 240n4,
  240n6; hope and, 31, 33, 47, 53; infinite responsibility and, 21, 31, 46–47,
  240n6, 248n19; kinship and, 20, 26,
  209, 212, 213–14, 221, 224; life in time
  and, 20; lifeworld and, 5, 239n2; the
  moral and, 38; neoliberal social reforms
  and, 5; pharmaceuticals and, 209, 212,
  213–14, 221, 224; self-, 5, 28, 65–66,
  188; state institutions for, 4; state violence boundary with, 4–5, 47–50, 53,
  240nn7–8; as waiting or active awaiting, 31, 56, 240n1. *See also* domestic
  struggles to care for kin
cariño (affection), 118, 153, 229. *See also*
  love
Carsten, Janet, 15, 17
casa de sangre (house of blood), 16, 20, 33
to catch in relation to critical moment
  (cachar), 81, 86, 88, 90, 118
Catholicism: charity and, 78, 116–17, 194–
  95, 248n25; Christian Base Communities and, 73, 247n17; community mental
  health program and, 176, 186, 191, 195,
  197–200, 251n9; debt to God owed by
  doctors and, 195–96; First Communion
  and, 138–39; free market option for
  the poor and, 195; human rights and,
  251n9; Legion of Christ and, 195; liberation theology and, 73, 247n17; marginality and, 13–14; marianism and,

65, 143; the market and, 155, 195–96; moral debt and, 96, 116–17, 248n25; Opus Dei and, 62, 195, 251n10; pardon and, 200; poverty and, 13; spiritual dimensions and, 246n8; *testimonio* and, 138–39. *See also* Christianity

Cavell, Stanley, 30–31, 49, 88, 137, 240n5, 245n2, 248n19

Center for Information of Commercial Documentation (DICOM), 40–43

Central Unitaria de Trabajadores (CUT), 62–63

Centro Comunitario de Salud Mental (COSAM), 167–68, 175, 185

Centro Integral de Derechos Humanos y Salud Mental (CINTRAS), 104, 105

Centro National de Informaciones; National Center of Information (CNI), 136

Centro para el Desarrollo Económica y Social de América Latina (DESAL), 13–14

Chamber of the Pharmaceutical Industry (Cámara de la Industria Farmacéutica), 203

charity: Catholicism and, 78, 116–17, 194–95, 248n25; community mental health program and, 194–96, 251nn9–10; shame and, 78

Chicago Boys, 6–7, 40

children, and addiction to *pasta base,* 36, 111, 185–86, 235

ChileSolidario, 64

Christian Base Communities, 73, 247n17

Christian Democrats, 13–14, 131–32, 182

Christianity, 83–85, 88, 243n15. *See also* Catholicism

citizenship, 131–34, 153, 249n1. *See also* state

coalition of democratic parties (Concertación). *See* Concertación (coalition of democratic parties)

cocaine base paste *(pasta base).* See *pasta base* (cocaine base paste)

CODEPU (Corporación para la Defensa del Pueblo), 105, 116, 122, 127

Comités de Asistencia Social (Ficha-CAS) and Ficha-CAS II, 57–58

commitment to the house *(compromiso con la casa),* 16. *See also* kinship

communal cooking *(ollas comunes),* 73, 74

Communist Party, 99, 106, 108–10, 114–16, 134–35, 161, 230

community: actual and eventual, 108, 134, 143; democracy and, 10; political, 133–

34, 161–62; social mobilization for resolution of local needs and, 10, 116–17. *See also* neighbors and neighborhoods; poor urban neighborhoods *(poblaciones)*

community mental health program: overview of, 22, 169, 200–201; caring doctors and, 182–83; Catholicism and, 176, 186, 191, 195, 197–200, 251n9; charity work and, 194–96, 251nn9–10; debts to God and, 195–96; decentralization affects on, 183–84, 251nn5–6; democratic transition and, 169; economic precariousness/debts and, 178–79; epidemiological studies and, 169–72; experiment and, 179–84; historical debt and, 170–73, 251nn3–5; intracommunity psychiatry and, 170, 250n4, 251n5; Jung and, 186–87, 200; local lifeworld and, 183, 251n6; memory and, 199–200; Mental Health Unit manual and, 187–88; municipality and state friction and, 173–78, 185, 188; municipalization and, 167–69; National Depression Treatment Program and, 22, 25, 169, 180, 205; the pardon in group session and, 196–99; pastoral altruism and, 193–96, 251nn9–10; pharmacotherapy and, 5, 181, 191, 201; the self and self-help and, 183, 187–93, 199–200; self-help groups and, 180, 182–83; spiritual dimensions of state and, 188–89, 251n8; statistics for, 200–201; surgery of the soul and, 185–89; *vieja sabia* and, 186–87, 192–94, 196–98. *See also* depression; pharmaceuticals

compromiso con la casa (commitment to the house), 16. *See also* kinship

concealment, and dignity, 27, 87

Concertación (coalition of democratic parties): Bachelet and, 235; center-left parties and, 173; Christian Democrat membership and, 185; economic growth policies and, 59, 96; human rights and, 96, 105, 245n7; La Bandera membership and, 185; Labor Code reform and, 61; Lagos administration and, 173, 182; municipalization and, 168; Pinochet's administration on economics and, 59; poverty programs and, 58, 94; reconciliation rhetoric and, 96, 105–6

Conchalí municipality, 18, 135

Connolly, William, 244n18

Constable, Marianne, 90

Consultorio La Pincoya, 167, 175, 178, 185
consumer credit. *See* credit
consumerism *(consumismo):* consumer culture and, 5; consumer goods and, 63–64; credit expansion and, 31; economic analyses and, 31; poverty dynamics and, 64, 242n6; poverty line calculations and, 241n3; sexuality and, 131, 148, 149; social debt and, 63–64; spiritual dimensions of, 188–89, 251n8
contemporaneity, and time, 85, 90, 232
contracts: community development programs through state, 19; Family Contract document and, 65, 67, 68, 88–89; subcontractors and, 61–62, 77; work, 62, 214, 237
contratistas (subcontractors), 61–62, 77
Contreras Sepúlveda, Manuel, 94, 245n5
Corporación Nacional de Consumidores y Usuarios (National Corporation of Consumers and Users), 32
Corporación para la Defensa del Pueblo (CODEPU), 105, 116, 122, 127
COSAM (Centro Comunitario de Salud Mental), 167–68, 175, 185
countergifts and gifts. *See* gifts and countergifts
coup d'état of 9/11/73 *(golpe del estado),* 1–3, 17–18, 135
crack cocaine, 36. See also *pasta base* (cocaine base paste)
credit: democratic transition and, 32; DICOM Law and, 41; dignity and, 39–42; disciplinary technologies and, 40; expansion of, 39–40; future possibilities and, 11, 52–53; institutions of, 21, 31–32, 36–37, 39–42, 40, 63, 159; as resource, 20–21, 38–43, 52–53; social debt and, 63; subjects of, 31–33, 105–6. *See also* debt payments; debt/s; household indebtedness
criminal prosecutions, and reconciliation, 96, 245nn5–6
critical event/s, 1–3, 17–18, 135
critical moment/s: overview of, 55–56, 63; catching the, 81, 86, 88, 90, 118; economic precariousness and, 56, 63–64, 87–88; enduring hardships in relation to, 76, 78–79, 81, 85–88; obligation and, 78; pharmaceuticals and, 208, 210–11; social debt and, 55–56, 63, 81, 86–88, 90
"crone" *(vieja sabia),* 186–87, 192–94, 196–98. *See also* community mental health program

Cruz Verde, 202, 203, 252n1
culture of poverty, 13
CUT (Central Unitaria de Trabajadores), 62–63

Das, Veena, 24, 47, 89, 93, 133, 234, 240n6, 243n13
death: citizenship and, 133, 153; health issues and, 55; life as sketched into, 25, 28, 133–34, 206, 214–15, 222, 224; lived life alongside, 25, 28, 128, 227–28; the market and, 25; mother militant and, 25, 133–34, 143–44; mourning of, 128; political community and, 133–34, 161–62; reparations and, 95; state violence and, 51–52, 105, 121, 136. *See also* mortality and morbidity
debt payments: pharmaceuticals and, 205, 206, 212–13, 252n2; repayment of *la polla* loans and, 70, 72, 74, 80; temporality of, 38, 42–43, 56. *See also* debt/s; household indebtedness
debt/s: overview of, 5–6; for abortion, 159–61; community mental health program and, 178–79, 195–96; to God owed by doctors, 195–96; moral debt and, 4, 94–97, 116–17, 245nn4–5, 248n25; performative break between past and present, 4; public, 8, 11; reconciliation without disclaiming past, 4; state violence and care boundary and, 4–5, 48–49, 240n7. *See also* debt payments; household indebtedness; social debt in context of domestic relations
decentralization policies, 17–18, 22, 168, 169–70, 183–84, 251nn5–6
Declaration of Principles in 1974, 9–10
Decree Law, 61, 250n1
Deleuze, Gilles, 42, 74–75, 86–87, 233
democracia entre comillas (democracy in quotation marks), 93
democracy: aspiration and, 19, 21, 97, 108, 112, 128; community and, 10; individual mobilization and, 116–17; neoliberal economic model and, 11; in quotation marks, 93; sacrifice for, 97–100; *tomando conciencia* and, 111–12. *See also* Concertación (coalition of democratic parties)
democracy in quotation marks *(democracia entre comillas),* 93
democratic transition, 2, 4, 10, 32, 56–57, 59, 169
depresión a ratos (depression from time to time), 26

depresión neoliberal (neoliberal depression), 129, 131

depression: embodiment of, 206–7; enduring in relation to, 60, 208–11; exiled mother militant and, 146, 162; group sessions and, 60, 180, 182–83, 196–200, 207, 216; neoliberal, 129, 131; pharmaceuticals and, 207; pharmaceuticals for, 207, 208, 209, 212; sexuality and, 146, 162; statistics for, 25; symptoms of, 173, 178–81, 187–88, 192, 201; from time to time, 26; treatment programs for, 22, 25, 60, 169, 180, 205, 207–9, 212; treatments for, 60, 173, 207, 208, 209, 212. *See also* community mental health program; mental health; pharmaceuticals

depression from time to time *(depresión a ratos)*, 26

DESAL (Centro para el Desarrollo Económica y Social de América Latina), 13–14

desire: to endure, 81; limiting, 21, 24, 44, 46–49, 113, 248nn19–20

DICOM (Center for Information of Commercial Documentation), 40–43

DICOM Law (Protection of Data of Personal Character), 41

dictatorship/s, 1, 245n5, 247n18. *See also* state; state violence; *specific dictators*

dignity: boundaries in domestic relations and, 69, 75–79; concealment and, 27, 87; credit and, 39–42; dignified life and, 39–42, 90, 244n19; living with, 56, 69, 86, 88–90; state visions of the poor frictions with living with, 56, 69, 86, 88–90

disappearances, 3, 94–96, 111, 121–22, 245n5

disciplinary technologies, 40, 64–69

disorientation or losing self, 146–47

doctors, in community mental health program, 182–83, 193–96, 251nn9–10. *See also* community mental health program

domestic relations: overview and description of, 33, 44–46, 75; affective configurations and, 22, 147, 205–6, 214–15; dignity and boundaries in, 69, 75–79; economic scarcity as mitigated through, 70–72; ethnographic engagement in, 19–20, 234; exiled mother militant and, 17, 20–21, 131, 151–53; illusions in, 80–81, 243n13; intimate relations and, 93, 100–101, 127, 134, 160, 208–11; as lived through the market, 20, 234; neoliberalism effects on, 144; obligations

and, 56, 234; Pentacostal meetings with new, 221–24, 252n5; reciprocity and boundaries in, 77–80, 87; relatedness and, 11, 15, 16, 33; sacrifice and, 229–30; sexuality and, 153–54, 162–66; time and, 20, 231–32; torture compared with embodiment of, 51–52, 241n9. *See also* domestic struggles to care for kin; neighbors and neighborhoods; social debt in context of domestic relations

domestic struggles to care for kin: overview of, 20–21, 29–31, 52–53; credit as resource and, 20–21, 38–43, 52–53; DICOM and, 40–43; domestic relations described and, 33, 44–46; domestic violence and, 43–47, 240nn3–6; embodiment of, 30, 39, 46, 48–49, 50–51; everyday life with different future and, 52–53; finite responsibility and, 43–47, 240n4, 240n6; household indebtedness and, 31, 36; infinite responsibility and, 21, 31, 46–47, 240n6, 248n19; institutions of credit and, 31–32, 36, 39–42; limiting desire and, 21, 24, 44, 46–49; made or making time for change in loved ones and, 34–38; maintaining the image and, 42, 46, 59; state violence and care boundary and, 47–50, 53, 240nn7–8; subjects of credit and, 31–33; temporality of debt payments and, 38, 42–43, 56; unstable work for men and, 29–30, 31–32, 34, 44, 51; waiting or active awaiting as modality of care and, 31, 240n1. *See also* addiction to *pasta base*

domestic triaging, 22, 25, 215

domestic violence: addiction to *pasta base* and, 48; domestic struggles to care for kin and, 43–47, 240nn3–6; pharmaceuticals and, 214–21, 222, 224, 226; state violence as cause for, 229–30

double celebration of mother militant, 132–33, 143

double sense of everyday life, 81

dreams, as opening time, 126–27, 248n27

drop of time, 87, 90–91, 238

drug trafficking, 225, 229, 231, 237–38. See also *pasta base* (cocaine base paste)

economic precariousness: overview of, 235–36; aspiration and, 17; community mental health program and, 178–79; critical moment and, 56, 63–64, 87–88; for men, 123, 124–25, 144; pharmaceuticals and,

economic precariousness *(continued)*
208; social debt and, 56, 63–65, 69, 87–
90; for women, 122–25, 123, 144, 147–
48, 155–56, 248n26; work contracts
and, 62, 214, 237
Economic Recovery Program of 1975, 8,
239n3
economics: democratic transition and, 10;
economic analyses and, 31; economic
growth policies and, 58–59, 241nn2–3;
economic scarcity and, 70–72, 205;
homo economicus and, 6–7; neoliberal
experiment and, 6–11; private financial
system and, 8–9. *See also* the market
embodiment: of depression, 206–7; depression and, 26; of domestic relations compared with torture, 51–52, 241n9; of
domestic struggles to care for kin, 30,
39, 46, 48–49, 50–51; economic precariousness and, 30; of pain, 23, 26–27, 46,
52, 79, 228; waiting or active awaiting
as modality of care and, 31, 56, 240n1.
See also the body
employment: DICOM Law and, 41; Labor
Code and, 61–62, 168; Labor Plan and,
61, 242n5; labor unions and, 8, 9, 62–
63; unemployment and, 39, 77, 108, 124,
172, 183, 206–7, 237. *See also* unstable
work for men; unstable work for women
endure *(aguantar)*, 76, 81. *See also* enduring
enduring: critical moment in relation to, 76,
78–79, 81, 85–88; depression in relation
to, 60, 208–11
epidemiological studies, 169–72. *See also*
economic precariousness
Espinoza, Vicente, 105–6
Esposito, Roberto, 143
ethical and political awakening *(tomando
conciencia)*, 111–12
ethics: acknowledgement and, 86–87; of
experiment, 181, 183–84, 201; *pasta
base* and, 226–27, 231; reparations and,
108–10; self-making and, 24; *tomando
conciencia* and, 111–12
ethnography: generality in, 169; kindness
and, 232, 234; kinship and, 232; relational modes and, 4–5, 20, 27, 232–34,
252n6; as scene, 24; of self enmeshed in
relations, 19–20, 234; silence and, 89–
90, 252n6; specificity in, 232; time and,
232. *See also* anthropology
everyday language, 106–7
everyday life: birth as force in, 100–103;
care in, 5; with different future, 11, 52–

53; gifts as concealed through illusion
of, 81–89; limiting desire to inhabit,
113, 248nn19–20; norms and normative
relation to, 27–28; reinhabiting, 4, 93,
131, 134; state as layered in, 17, 24
exiled mother militant: depression and, 146,
162; domestic relations and, 17, 20–21,
131, 151–53; health care and, 96; in
home country exile, 129, 131, 146–47;
indemnifications and, 116; maternity
and, 131, 134, 143, 160; self-making
and, 26. *See also* mother militant;
sexuality
experiment: community-based, 170, 180,
251n6; economic precariousness and,
179–84; ethical ethos and, 181, 183–84,
201; neoliberal, 6–11; *testimonio* and,
27, 140–41, 249n4

family: ethnographic engagement in relations and, 234; moralization of, 234;
as parapolity, 10, 25, 66; in relation
to state, 131–34, 152–53, 249n1,
249nn1–2, 249n2. *See also* father;
mother; sexuality; women
Family Contract document, 65, 67, 68,
88–89
Fassin, Didier, 23, 89, 108, 195, 245n3,
247n18
father, 133–34, 141, 143, 145, 151–53, 156,
160. *See also* family; mother; paternity
Ficha-CAS (Comités de Asistencia Social)
and Ficha-CAS II, 57–58
finite responsibility, and care, 43–47, 240n4,
240n6. *See also* infinite responsibility,
and care
First Communion, 138–39. *See also*
Catholicism
fluoxetine, 60, 146, 162, 173, 180, 215,
217–18, 222
FONASA (National Fund for Health), 250n1
Fondo Solidario e Inversion Social (Solidary
Fund and Social Investment), 64–65
Foucault, Michel, 26, 65–66, 112, 140,
205–6, 239n3, 247n16
Foundation for Documentation and Archive
of the Vicariate of Solidarity, 121–22
Frei Montalva, Eduardo, 13–15, 120, 131–
32, 151
Frente Patriótico Manuel Rodríguez (FPMR),
135–36, 151
Freud, Sigmund, 126
Friedman, Milton, 6, 8, 239n2
friendship, 4, 26, 77, 79, 87–89. *See also*

domestic relations; neighbors and
neighborhoods
Fullwiley, Duana, x, 27
Fundación Presidente Allende, 116, 127
future: for national identity, 96, 245n7;
possibilities for, 11, 52–53, 74. See
also present

games of honor, 86
Garcia, Angela, x, 27
Garzón, Baltazar, 115
Gauttari, Félix, 74–75, 86–87
Geest, Sjaak van der, 252n4
generality, in ethnographic engagement, 169
Gideon, Jasmine, 168
gifts and countergifts: as concealed through
illusion of everyday life, 81–89, 243n15,
244n16, 244nn18–19; contemporaneity
of, 85–86, 232, 244n18; as games of
honor, 86; giving and, 81, 85–90; moral
contracts and, 240n8; pharmaceuticals
as shared, 207–8; silent, 87, 244n19;
state violence and care boundary and,
49, 240n8
giving, 81, 85–90. See also gifts and
countergifts
golpe del estado (9/11/73 coup d'état), 1–3,
17–18, 135
Good, Byron, ix, x
Goodfellow, Aaron, 252n4
gossip of neighbors, 55, 70, 79, 80–81
governmentality, 65–66
Government Economic Recovery Program
of 1975, 8
government of the poor, 66–69
government poverty programs, 64–69, 88–89
government services funding, 71, 242n8
Greenhouse, Carol, 5, 233
group sessions, 60, 180, 182–83, 196–200,
207, 216
growth with equity, 58–59, 241n2
Grupos Acción Popular, 2
Guyer, Jane, 73, 240n8, 244n16

Hamilton Rating Scale for Depression,
180–81
health and illnesses: alcoholism, 53, 97–98,
156–57, 212; anxiety, 34, 53, 162, 168,
172, 227; biopolitics and, 25–26; cancer,
51, 55, 75, 167, 215, 229–30, 232, 236;
death and, 55; diabetes, 215, 220, 231–
32; headache in the eye, 125–26; lupus,
216, 221; medicalization and, 25–26;
mental illness, 50; osteoporosis, 125;

schizophrenia, 97–98, 249n4; stroke,
34–35, 51, 98, 125–26, 240n2; temporality of pharmaceutical effects and,
208. See also addiction to pasta base;
health care
health care, 8, 96, 105, 168, 250nn1–2;
pharmaceuticalization of public, 204,
252n3. See also community mental
health program; doctors; health and
illnesses
Health Service of the Northern Metropolitan Region (SSMN), 174–75, 177–79,
185, 188
Herrer Rodríguez, Susana, 155, 159–60
historical debt, and community mental
health program, 170–73, 251nn3–5
home/house. See house/home
homo economicus, 6–7
household indebtedness, 31, 36, 147–50,
148, 159, 241n1
house/home: autoconstruction within neighborhoods and, 15–16; housing crisis
and, 14–15; kinship and, 15–16; pieza/
pieza atras in, 16; subsidies for, 105
house of blood (casa de sangre), 16, 20, 33
Huechuraba municipality, 18. See also La
Pincoya
humanitarianism, 23, 103–4, 235, 246n11–
12, 248n18
human rights: Catholicism and, 251n9;
Concertación and, 96, 105, 245n7;
neoliberalism and, 105; pardon and,
95–96; reconciliation and, 96, 103–6,
246nn9–13; testimonies and, 103–6,
246nn9–13
hunger/malnourishment, and pharmaceuticals, 215, 216, 218–19, 220–22, 224

Illanes, María Angélica, 65, 78
illnesses and health issues. See health and
illnesses
illusion/s, in domestic relations, 81–89,
243n13, 243n15, 244n16, 244nn18–19
imipramine, 173, 180
indemnifications, and state violence, 115–18,
119–22, 127–28, 248nn23–25
Independent Democratic Union (Unión
Democrática Independiente), 62, 173–74
individualism, 10, 27, 131, 233, 234
individuality, 27, 134
individual mobilization, 116–17
infinite responsibility, and care, 21, 31,
46–47, 240n6, 248n19. See also finite
responsibility, and care

Instituciones de Salud Previsionales (ISA-PRES), 250n1
institutions of credit, 31–32, 36–37, 39–42, 40, 63, 159
Inter-American Convention to Prevent and Sanction Torture, 104
Inter-American Development Bank, 9
interdependence and la polla, 74–75
International Monetary Fund, 8–9
International Theological Commission, 200
intimate relations, 93, 100–101, 127, 134, 160, 208–11
intracommunity psychiatry, 170, 250n4, 251n5
ISAPRES (Instituciones de Salud Previsionales), 250n1

Jung, Carl G., 186–87, 200
Junta de Vecinos (Neighborhood Council), 18, 128, 237
justice, and social debt, 9, 21, 56–57, 59, 90–91, 161

Keane, Webb, 68–69, 72, 74, 87
kindness: acts of, 70, 79, 81, 83–88, 90, 244n16; concealment of, 85; ethnography and, 232, 234; in everyday life, 20, 21, 79, 81, 83–88, 90, 244n16; games of honor and, 86; silent, 70, 79, 86–87, 89–90, 244n19. See also acknowledgement
kinship: autoconstruction within neighborhoods and, 15–16; birth as force in everyday life and, 101; boundaries and, 4; care and, 20, 26, 209, 212, 213–14, 221, 224; ethnography and, 232; ethnography of self is enmeshed in multiple relations, 19–20, 234; gifts as moral contracts and, 240n8; house/home and, 15–16; house of blood and, 16, 20, 33; obligations and, 16, 33, 53, 234, 240n6; sexuality and, 131; social debt and, 77, 92. See also domestic struggles to care for kin
Kleinman, Arthur, ix, 24, 146
Kubal, Mary Rose, 168

La Bandera, 180–82, 184
Labor Code, 61–62, 168
Labor Plan, 61, 242n5
labor unions, 8, 9, 62–63. See also employment
La Dehesa, 76, 99, 123, 194, 217
La Florída, 99, 119–20

Lagos, Ricardo, 59, 64, 103–5, 109, 173, 182
La Pincoya, 11–19, 98, 120, 189
Lazzara, Michael, 249n4
Legion of Christ, 195. See also Catholicism
Lewis, Oscar, 13
liberal imagination, of political community, 21–22, 133–34, 153
liberal political community. See political community
liberation theology, 73, 247n17. See also Catholicism
life as sketched into death, 25, 28, 133–34, 206, 214–15, 222, 224
life-giving, pharmaceuticals as, 214–15, 224
life in time, 20
lifeworld: care and, 5, 239n2; local, 183, 251n6; of poor urban neighborhoods, 4–5, 16–17, 39, 113, 206, 244n19
limit/s: around abandonment, 24–25; finite responsibility in relation to, 43–47, 240n4, 240n6; limiting desire and, 21, 24, 44, 46–49, 113, 248nn19–20; waiting or active awaiting and, 31, 56, 240n1. See also acknowledgement
limosnear (to beg for), 117, 248n25. See also begging and asking
lived life alongside death, 25, 28, 128, 227–28
to live with dignity (vivir con dignida), 56, 69, 86, 88–90. See also dignity
local formulary, of pharmaceuticals, 204–6, 217, 252n3–4
losing self or disorientation, 146–47
love: affection and, 118, 153, 229; changing tone of, 117–19; limit of, 119; love affects and, 28, 99, 117–19; loving kindness and, 84–85, 88, 244n16; misericordia and, 84; as patiency, 119; as quiet absorbing, 99, 118–19. See also kindness

Madariaga, Carlos, 171
madness, 178, 249n4
Madre-huacho, 143. See also mother
madre soltera (single mother), 129, 137, 143–44. See also mother
maintaining the image (manteniendo la imagen), 42, 46, 59
malnourishment/hunger, and pharmaceuticals, 215, 216, 218–19, 220–22, 224
manteniendo la imagen (maintaining the image), 42, 46, 59
Mapuche, 139, 246n8
Marconi, Juan, 170, 250nn3–4

marginality, 13–14, 23, 172
marianism, 65, 143. *See also* Catholicism
Marín, Gladys, 106, 144, 161, 163
the market: autoregulation of, 6; Catholic
   conservatives and, 155, 195–96; Chicago
   Boys and, 7; death and, 25; domestic relations as lived through, 20, 234; extreme
   poverty produced by, 9, 42, 57; faith in,
   188–89; household indebtedness and,
   31; moral transcendence and, 251n8;
   as option for the poor, 195; subsidiary
   state and, 10; as value neutral, 176. *See
   also* economics
Marks, Harry, 169
marriage/s, 44–46, 133, 141, 208, 210, 211
Massacre of Corpus Christi (Operación
   Albania), 136
maternity: abortion and, 155–56, 158, 159–
   61, 249n7; citizenship and, 132; exiled
   mother militant and, 131, 134, 143,
   160; mortality rates and, 155; mother
   militant and, 131–34, 143, 146, 152,
   153, 160; pregnancies and, 154–56,
   158, 160; reproduction and, 10, 131–
   33, 153; *testimonio* and, 141–42. *See
   also* mother; women
McFarland, Ian, 84
medicalization, 25–26
MEMCH (Movimiento Pro-Emancipación
   de La Mujer Chilena), 129–30
memory/ies, 19, 96–97, 108–9, 199–200
men: addiction to *pasta base* by, 27, 30, 35–
   36, 38–39, 43, 48, 50, 53, 151, 190,
   225, 238; as breadwinners, 131–32;
   economic precariousness for, 123, 124–
   25, 144; family in relation to state and,
   132–33, 249n2; marriage and, 44–46,
   133, 141, 208, 210, 211; militancy and,
   131–32, 152; patriarchy and, 131–32.
   See also sexuality; unstable work for
   men; women
mental health, 34, 50, 53, 97–98, 162, 168,
   172, 227, 249n4. *See also* community
   mental health program; depression;
   health and illnesses
Mental Health Unit of the Ministry of
   Health, 170, 172–73, 174, 187–88,
   251nn3
MIDEPLAN (Ministerio de Planificación),
   32, 241n3
militancy: democratic movements and, 113,
   120, 136; men and, 131–32, 152; *testimonio* and, 113; women and, 129–34,
   152, 160. *See also* mother militant

Miller, Daniel, 242n6
Ministerio de Planificación (MIDEPLAN),
   32, 241n3
Ministry of Health, 168, 170, 172, 185
Ministry of Health's Mental Health Unit,
   170, 172–73, 174, 187–88, 250n3,
   251nn3
Ministry of Housing, 15
MIR (Movimiento de la Izquierda Revolucionaria), 99, 120
misericordia, 84
Montecino, Sonia, 143
the moral: care and, 38; in everyday life, 15–
   16; gifts as moral contracts and, 240n8;
   moral debt and, 4, 94–97, 116–17,
   245nn4–5, 248n25; moral healing and,
   94–95; moralization of family and, 234;
   moral obligations and, 86, 244n16; moral
   striving and, 86–87; the moral subject
   and, 4; moral transcendence and, 251n8
mortality and morbidity: abortions and,
   155; Declaration of Principles in 1974
   and, 10; ethnographic engagement in
   relations and, 233; infant, 24–25. *See
   also* death
mother: citizenship and, 131, 132, 249n1;
   household indebtedness and, 148; loss
   of, 231–32, 236–37; Madre-huacho
   and, 143; marianism and, 65; mother
   militant and, 164–65; political community and, 131, 249n1; single, 129, 137,
   143–44. *See also* family; father; maternity; mother militant; women
mother militant: abandonment and, 134,
   143–44, 146, 151; death and, 25, 133–
   34, 143–44; disorientation of, 146–47;
   double celebration of, 132–33, 143;
   household indebtedness and, 147–
   50; internal conflict of, 144–46; life as
   sketched into death and, 25, 133–34;
   maternity and, 131–34, 143, 146, 152,
   153, 160; memory and, 147; sacrifice
   and, 134, 143–44; the social for, 146,
   149, 163; *testimonio* and, 113, 134,
   136–44. *See also* exiled mother militant;
   maternity; militancy; women
mourning, 5, 127, 128, 233
movement in time, 30–31
Movimiento de la Izquierda Revolucionaria
   (MIR), 99, 120
Movimiento Pro-Emancipación de La Mujer
   Chilena (MEMCH), 129–30
Municipal Government Law, 18
municipalities, 18, 173–78, 185, 188

Municipality of Conchalí, 18, 135
Municipality of Huechuraba, 18. See also
    La Pincoya
municipalization, 167–69

National Commission for Truth and Recon-
    ciliation (Rettig Commission), 93–95,
    116, 127, 245n4
National Commission on Political Impris-
    onment and Torture (Valech Commis-
    sion and Report), 103–7, 110, 116,
    246nn9–13
National Corporation of Consumers and
    Users (Corporación Nacional de Consu-
    midores y Usuarios), 32
National Depression Treatment Program,
    22, 25, 169, 180, 205
National Drug Formulary List, 203
National Fund for Health (FONASA), 250n1
National Health Service, 250n1
national identity, 96, 245n7
National Medical Service for Employees,
    250n1
National Plan for Mental Health (now
    National Plan for Mental Health and
    Psychiatry), 170, 172–73
nature, as understood by Chicago Boys, 6–7
Neighborhood Council (Junta de Vecinos),
    18, 128, 237
neighbors and neighborhoods: auto-
    contrucción within, 15–16; economic
    scarcity mitigated through relations
    among, 70–72; ethnography of self
    enmeshed in multiple relations among,
    19–20, 234; gossip of, 55, 70, 79, 80–
    81; relations among, 16; wealthy urban,
    18, 76, 99, 123, 156, 194, 217, 231.
    See also community; domestic relations;
    poor urban neighborhoods (poblaciones);
    specific neighborhoods
neoliberal depression (depresión neoliberal),
    129, 131
neoliberal experiment, 6–11
neoliberalism, 6–11, 105, 144, 188–89,
    234, 251n8
neoliberal social reforms: care and, 5; con-
    sumer culture and, 5; corporate sector
    and, 8–9; Declaration of Principles in
    1974 and, 9–10; unstable work and, 8,
    29–30, 31–32, 34, 44, 51. See also neo-
    liberal experiment; neoliberalism
9/11/73 coup d'état (golpe del estado), 1–3,
    17–18, 135
norms and normative relation to life, 27–28

obligation/s: critical moments and, 78;
    domestic relations and, 56, 234; kin-
    ship, 16, 33, 53, 234, 240n6; moral, 86,
    244n16; to la polla system, 72; reciproc-
    ity and, 78, 79; to state, 68
La Obra, 188–89
Oficina Muncipal de Información Laboral
    (OMIL), 124
Olave, Thumala, 195, 251n10
ollas comunes (communal cooking), 73, 74
Operación Albania (Massacre of Corpus
    Christi), 136
Operación Condor, 245n5, 248n21
Operación Sitio, 14–15, 120
Opus Dei, 62, 195, 251n10. See also
    Catholicism

Paley, Julia, 10–11, 96, 183, 245n7
Pan American Health Organization's Cara-
    cas Declaration, 170, 250n3
Pandolfo, Stefania, 127, 243n10
parable of the Good Samaritan, 84–85, 88.
    See also Catholicism; Christianity
parapolity, family as, 10, 25, 66
pardon, 93, 95–96, 200, 245n7, 248n5
the pardon, and group sessions, 196–200
Parry, Jonathan, 83
past, and relation to present, 4, 24, 47,
    125–26
pasta base (cocaine base paste): drug traf-
    ficking and, 225, 229, 231, 237–38;
    ethics and, 226–27, 231; household
    indebtedness and, 36; sex sold for, 50,
    51, 54; statistics for, 36, 53; writing
    on the body and, 140, 227–28. See also
    addiction to pasta base; pharmaceuticals
pastoral altruism, 193–96, 251nn9–10. See
    also community mental health program
Pateman, Carol, 131
paternity, 133, 134, 151–53, 160, 249n2.
    See also father
patiency, 119
patriarchy, 131–32
Perlman, Janice, 13–14
Petryna, Adriana, 184
pharmaceuticals: abandonment and, 209,
    213–14, 221, 224, 226–30; as actants,
    205, 252n4; addiction to, 212; agency
    and, 208; ánimo and, 206, 207–8, 210–
    11; antidepressants and, 173, 180, 216,
    217; biography over time and, 211–14;
    black market, 203–5, 252n2; care and,
    209, 212, 213–14, 221, 224; critical
    moments and, 208, 210–11; debt pay-

ments and, 205, 206, 212–13, 252n2; depression and, 207, 212, 216–17; depression treatment programs and, 22, 25, 60, 169, 180, 205, 207–9, 212; domestic triaging and, 22, 25, 215; domestic violence and, 214–21, 222, 224, 226; economic precariousness and, 208; embodiment of depression and, 206–7; enduring intimate relations and, 208–11; fluoxetine and, 60, 146, 162, 173, 180, 215, 217–18, 222; group sessions and, 207, 216; hunger/malnutrition and, 215, 216, 218–19, 220–22, 224; life as sketched into death and, 28, 206, 214–15, 222, 224; as life-giving, 214–15, 224; local formulary of, 204–6, 217, 252n3–4; need for a working body and, 35, 207–8, 211, 217; pharmaceuticalization of public health and, 204, 252n3; pharmacy market and, 202–4, 252nn1–2; seizures and, 222–24; self-medication and, 202–5, 222–24, 252n2; sharing and gift of, 207–8; state involvement in pharmaceutical industries and, 9; suicide attempts and, 216, 218; temporality of effects of, 208; unstable work and, 205, 206–7, 209, 210. *See also* community mental health program; depression; *pasta base* (cocaine base paste)

pharmacotherapy, 5, 181, 191, 201

pharmacy market, 202–4, 252nn1–2

Phillips, Adam, 84–85, 244n19

pieza/pieza atras (room/separate room), 16

Piñera, Sebastián, 61, 235–36, 242n5

Pinochet, Augusto: credit for the poor and, 39; decentralization policy and, 17–18; Decree Law and, 61, 250n1; disappearances and, 3, 94–95, 245n5; Economic Recovery Program of 1975 and, 8, 239n3; extreme poverty assessments and, 56–57, 241n1; Labor Plan and, 61, 242n5; Municipal Government Law and, 18; municipalization and, 168, 250n1; neoliberal experiment and, 6–11; 9/11/73 coup d'état by, 1–3, 17–18, 135; *pasts base* addiction responsibilities and, 111; Riggs Case and, 114–16, 114–18, 248nn21–23; social debt to the poor and, 56

poblaciones (poor urban neighborhoods). *See* poor urban neighborhoods *(poblaciones)*

pobladores (poor urban peoples), 14–15, 130, 183. *See also* poor urban neighborhoods

political community: death and, 133–34, 161–62; eventual or aspiration for, 97, 108, 127; liberal imagination of, 21–22, 133–34, 153; mother and, 131, 249n1; sacrifice for, 108, 134, 143–44. *See also* sexuality

political mobilization, in poor urban neighborhoods, 10, 14–15, 116–17

the political subject, 4

political violence. *See* state violence

politics. *See* Concertación (coalition of democratic parties); political community; *specific political party*

la polla (rotating credit association): overview of, 70–72; active solidarities and, 74; becoming minor and, 75–76; future possibilities and, 74; illegal-legal systems and, 71–72, 243nn9–10; interdependence and, 74–75; Polla Chilena de Beneficencia and, 71–72, 242n8; popular economic forms relations with, 72–73; repayment of loans and, 70, 72, 74, 80; as sacred money, 72, 243n11. *See also* social debt in context of domestic relations

Polla Chilena de Beneficencia, 71–72, 242n8

La Polla de Beneficiencia, 71–72, 242n8

Poole, Deborah, 72, 243n9

the poor: government of, 66–69; living with dignity frictions with state visions of, 56, 69, 86, 88–90. *See also* credit; poverty; social debt in context of domestic relations

poor urban neighborhoods *(poblaciones)*: housing crisis and, 14–15; housing subsidies and, 105; La Pincoya and, 11–19, 98, 120, 189; lifeworld of, 4–5, 16–17, 39, 113, 183, 206, 244n19, 251n6; 9/11/73 commemorations in, 1–3, 17; *pobladores* and, 14–15, 130, 183; political mobilization in, 10, 14–15, 116–17. *See also* community; neighbors and neighborhoods; poverty

poor urban peoples *(pobladores)*, 14–15, 130, 183. *See also* poor urban neighborhoods

popular economic forms, 72–73. See also *la polla* (rotating credit association)

popular movement for housing *(tomas de terreno)*, 13–15, 29, 98, 120, 135, 189

Popular Unity, 132–33, 142. *See also* Allende, Salvador Ricardo

possession, 222–24

poverty: assessments of, 55–60, 63, 241n1;
Aylwin on social debt and, 56–57;
Catholicism and, 13; consumerism and,
64, 242n6; culture of, 13; democratic
transition and, 56–57; dynamics of, 64,
242n6; economic growth policies and,
58–59, 241nn2–3; extreme, 9, 42, 57;
free market as option and, 195; government programs and, 64–69, 88–89; the
moral dimensions of, 56, 64, 66–69,
91–92, 242n6; neoliberal experiment
and, 8–9; poverty line calculations and,
241n3; statistics for, 32, 241n3. *See also*
the poor; poor urban neighborhoods
(poblaciones)
Povinelli, Beth, 5, 87
PRAIS (Programa de Reparación y Atención
Integral de Salud), 96, 105
pregnancies, 154–56, 158, 160. *See also*
maternity
present: acknowledgement of, 24; being in
another's, 20, 85–86, 141–42, 164, 169,
214, 233; indeterminacy in, 47; making,
249n4; past and, 4, 24, 47, 125–26; self
as, 27–28. *See also* future
pretending, 79, 85–88, 99, 111–12, 114
private financial system, 8–9
Programa de Reparación y Atención Integral
de Salud (PRAIS), 96, 105
Programa Puentes, 64–66
property ownership, 10, 14–15, 120, 143
prostitution, for *pasta base*, 50, 51, 54
Protection of Data of Personal Character
(DICOM Law), 41
Psychiatric Institute, 50, 217
public debt, 8, 11

Razeto, M. Luis, 73
Rechtman, Richard, 108, 247n18
reciprocity, 77–80, 87
reconciliation: overview of, 92–94, 128;
adaptations and, 127–28; Amnesty Law
of 1978 and, 96, 245nn5–6; aspiration
and, 93–94, 100–101, 108, 112–14,
246n15; birth as force in everyday life
and, 100–103; criminal prosecutions
and, 96, 245nn5–6; democracy as aspiration and, 108, 112; disappearances
and, 3, 94–96, 111, 121–22, 245n5;
dreams as opening time and, 126–27,
248n27; economic precariousness for
men and, 123, 124–25; economic precariousness for women and, 122–25,
123, 248n26; free health care and, 96;

hope and, 93–94; human rights and,
96, 103–6, 246nn9–13; indemnifications and, 115–18, 119–22, 127–28,
248nn23–25; individual mobilization
and, 116–17; limiting desire to inhabit
everyday life and, 113, 248nn19–20;
love affects and, 28, 99, 117–19; memory and, 96–97; moral debt and, 4, 94–
97, 245nn4–5; the past actualized in the
present and, 125–26; past violence and
future national identity and, 96, 245n7;
reparations and, 96, 105–10, 246nn13–
14; Rettig Report and, 93–95, 116, 127,
245n4; Riggs Case concerning Pinochet's
money and, 114–18, 248nn21–23; sacrifice for democracy and, 97–100; silence
lived and, 92–94, 110–11, 113, 117,
248n20; subjects of credit and, 105–6;
truth commission testimonies and, 103–
6, 246nn9–13; unstable work and, 92,
98, 99, 101, 102, 119, 122–28, 123;
Valech Commission and Report and,
103–7, 110, 116, 246nn9–13; withdrawal from/by the world and, 92–93,
245n2. *See also* torture
regret, 231
relatedness, 11, 15, 16, 33
relations, domestic. *See* domestic relations
Renovación Nacional party, 59, 173, 235
reparations, 96, 105–10, 246nn13–14
reproduction, 10, 131–33, 153. *See also*
maternity
research methodology, 5–6, 16–17
research sites for community intervention
study, 180–82, 184
responsibility: finite, 43–47, 240n4, 240n6;
infinite, 21, 31, 46–47, 240n6, 248n19
responsiveness, 20, 52, 88, 90–91, 233–34
Rettig Comission (National Commission for
Truth and Reconciliation), 93–95, 116,
127, 245n4
Rettig Report, 93–95, 116, 127, 245n4
Riggs Case, 114–16, 114–18, 248nn21–23
Rojas, Graciela, 172, 179–80, 182–83
room/separate room *(pieza/pieza atras)*, 16,
128
rotating credit association *(la polla)*. *See la
polla* (rotating credit association)
la rueda, 122–24
Ruy-Perez, Simona, 105, 246n11

sacred money, and *la polla*, 72, 243n11
sacrifice: acknowledgement of, 229–30; for
democracy, 97–100; domestic relations

and, 229–30; mother militant and, 134, 143–44; pharmaceuticals and, 229–30; for political community, 108, 134, 143–44; sexuality and, 108, 134, 143–44

SalcoBrand, 202, 203, 252n1

Sánchez, Angelica, 203

sanity and insanity, 249n4

scarcity, economic, 70–72, 205

Scheper-Hughes, Nancy, 24–25, 215

Schild, Verónica, 33

seductresses, 133, 152. *See also* women

seizures, 222–24

the self: disorientation or losing, 146–47; ethical work on, 95–96; self-care/self-responsibility and, 5, 28, 65–66, 188; self-help and, 183, 187–93, 199–200; self-help groups and, 180, 182–83; self-making and, 24, 26, 113, 248n18; self-medication and, 202–5, 252n2; self writing and, 112–13, 140, 228, 247n16. *See also* care; community mental health program

separateness, 36, 45, 129, 141–43. *See also* acknowledgement

sexual coersion/violence, 44–46, 208, 210, 211

sexuality: overview and description of, 148–50, 218; overview of, 134, 153; abortion and, 155–56, 158, 159–61, 160; agency and women and, 132; alcoholism and, 156–57; citizenship and, 131–34, 249n1; consumerism and, 131, 148, 149; depression and, 146, 162; domestic relations and, 153–54, 162–66; economic precariousness for men and, 144; economic precariousness for women and, 144, 147–48, 155–56; father and, 133–34, 141, 143, 145, 151–53, 156, 160; household indebtedness and, 147–50, 159; paternity and, 133, 134, 151–53, 160, 249n2; pregnancies and, 154–56, 158, 160; reproduction and, 10, 131–33, 153; sacrifice and, 108, 134, 143–44; seductresses and, 133, 152; separateness for women and, 129, 141–43; shame and, 148–50, 218; silent debt for abortion and, 159–61; single mother and, 129, 137, 143–44; social debt and, 54–56, 76–79; subjectivity/subject of action and, 113, 140, 143, 153, 247n16; *testimonio* and, 113, 136–44. *See also* exiled mother militant; father; maternity; men; mother; mother militant; political community; women

shame, 54–56, 76–79, 148–50, 218

sharing and gift of pharmaceuticals, 207–8

silence: acknowledgement/moral striving and, 86–87; keeping world intact through, 161; lived, 92–94, 110–11, 113, 117, 248n20; silent debt for abortion and, 159–61; silent kindness and, 70, 79, 86–87, 89–90, 244n19

single mother *(madre soltera)*, 129, 137, 143–44. *See also* mother

slice of time, 232, 234n18

the social, 6, 7, 146, 149, 163

social bonds, 234

social debt in context of domestic relations: overview of, 4, 20–21, 54–56; active solidarities and, 70–75; begging and asking boundary and, 77–78, 87; consumer goods and, 63–64; credit and, 63; critical moment and, 55–56, 63, 81, 86–88, 90; dignity in domestic relations informed by boundaries and, 69, 75–79; disciplinary technologies and, 64–69; economic growth policies and, 58–59, 241nn2–3; economic precariousness and, 56, 63–65, 69, 87–90; economic scarcity mitigated through domestic relations and, 70–72; enduring hardships and, 76, 78–79, 81, 85–88; Family Contract document and, 65, 67, 68, 88–89; gifts as concealed through illusion of everyday life and, 81–89, 243n15, 244n16, 244nn18–19; gossip of neighbors and, 55, 70, 79, 80–81; government of the poor and, 66–69; illusions in domestic relations and, 80–81, 243n13; justice and, 9, 21, 56–57, 59, 90–91, 161; kindness in everyday life and, 70, 79, 81, 83–88, 90, 244n16; kindness in relation to boundaries and, 88–89; Labor Code and, 61–62; living with dignity frictions with state visions of the poor and, 56, 69, 86, 89–90; moral dimensions of poverty and, 64, 66–69, 91–92, 242n6; popular economic forms and la polla relations and, 72–73; poverty assessments and, 55–60, 63, 241n1; poverty dynamics and, 64, 242n6; reciprocity and boundaries in domestic relations and, 77–80, 87; repayment of *la polla* loans and, 70, 72, 74, 80; self-responsible women and, 65–66; shame and, 54–56, 76–79; silent kindness and, 70, 79, 86–87, 89–90, 244n19; speech and silence boundaries

social debt in context of domestic relations
(*continued*)
and, 56, 89–90; state poverty programs
and, 64–69, 88–89; subcontractors and,
61–62, 77; unstable work and, 54, 60–
62, 63, 71, 76–77; work contracts and,
62, 214, 237. *See also* debt; *la polla*
(rotating credit association); social debt
solidarities, active, 70–75
Solidary Fund and Social Investment (Fondo
Solidario e Inversion Social), 64–65
Sommer, Doris, 113
southern zone, 99, 119–20, 237–38
specificity, in ethnography, 232
spirit/energy (*ánimo*), 6, 206, 207–8, 210–11
spiritual dimensions, 188–89, 246n8, 251n8
SSMN (Health Service of the Northern Metropolitan Region), 174–75, 177–79,
185, 188
Stack, Carol, 33
state: citizenship and, 131–34, 132, 133,
153, 249n1; democratic transition of, 2,
4, 10, 32, 56–57, 59, 169; disciplinary
technologies and, 40; disciplinary technologies of, 64–69; family as parapolity
and, 10, 25, 66; family in relation to,
131–34, 152–53, 249n1, 249nn1–2,
249n2; governmentality and, 65–66; as
layered in everyday life, 17, 24; municipalities' friction with, 173–78, 185, 188;
national identity and, 96, 245n7; patriarchy and, 131–32; pharmaceutical industries and, 9; poverty programs and,
64–69, 88–89; spiritual dimensions of,
188–89, 251n8; subsidiary state and, 10
state institutions, 4, 17, 31–32, 36, 39–42.
See also specific institutions
state violence: care boundary with, 4–5, 47–
50, 53, 240nn7–8; death and, 51–52,
105, 121, 136; disappearances and, 3,
94–96, 111, 121–22, 245n5; domestic
violence as a result of, 229–30; indemnifications and, 115–18, 119–22, 127–28,
248nn23–25; against labor unions and
democratic movement, 8. *See also* torture; *specific operations*
Stern, Steve, 96–97, 245n6
Strathern, Marilyn, 5, 78
structural adjustment loan plan, 8–9, 40,
73, 74, 237
subcontractors (*contratistas*), 61–62, 77
subjectivity/subject of action: sexuality and,
113, 140, 143, 153, 247n16; subjects

of credit and, 31–33, 105–6; *testimonio*
and, 113, 140, 247n16
suffering, representation of, 23–24
suicides and suicide attempts, 32, 190, 216,
218
Superintendent of Banks and Financial Institutions, 32, 40–41
surgery of the soul, 185–89. *See also* community mental health program
symbolic reparations, 105
symptoms, 126, 173, 178–81, 187–88, 192,
201

Taylor, Barbara, 84–85, 244n19
temporality: of debt payments, 38, 42–43,
56; of economic scarcity, 205; of moral
healing, 94–95; of pardons, 199–200;
of pharmaceutical effects, 208; of state
violence, 94
testimonies: humanitarian, 103–4, 246n11–
12, 248n18; human rights and, 103–6,
246nn9–13; self-making and, 248n18;
testimonio in relation to, 113, 137–38,
247nn17–18; torture and, 104–5,
246nn11–12
testimonio: overview of, 113, 247n17;
Catholicism and, 138–39; experiment
and, 27, 140–41, 249n4; marriage and,
141; maternity and, 141–42; militancy
and, 113; mother militant and, 113,
134, 136–44; personal and impersonal
aspects of and, 112–13, 200; self-making
and, 113, 248n18; self writing and, 137,
140–41; sexuality and, 113, 136–44;
subjectivity/subject of action and, 113,
140, 247n16; testimonies in relation to,
113, 137–38, 247nn17–18; time and,
140–43; women and, 137–41, 164
Ticktin, Miriam, 23
time: biography over, 211–14; contemporaneity and, 85, 90, 232; domestic relations
and, 20, 231–32; dreams as opening,
126–27, 248n27; drop of, 87, 90–91,
238; ethnography and, 232; life in, 20;
made or making, 34–38; movement in,
30–31; slice of, 232, 234n18; *testimonio*
and, 140–43
Tinsman, Heidi, 131–32
tomando conciencia (ethical and political
awakening), 111–12
tomas de terreno (popular movement for
housing), 13–15, 29, 98, 120, 135, 189
torture: overview and definition of, 104,

246n10; embodiment of domestic relations compared with, 51–52, 241n9; in everyday language, 106–7; indexing of actual life conditions and, 107–8; reparations for, 96, 105–10, 246n13, 246nn13–14; testimonies and, 104–5, 246nn11–12; trauma and, 23, 108; Villa Gremaldi camp and, 51, 241n9. *See also* reconciliation; state violence

transition, democratic, 2, 4, 10, 32, 56–57, 59, 169

trauma, 23, 108

truth commissions, 103–6, 245n3, 246nn9–13. *See also specific truth commissions*

unemployment, 39, 77, 108, 124, 172, 183, 206–7, 237. *See also* employment; unstable work for men; unstable work for women

Unión Democrática Independiente (Independent Democratic Union), 62, 173–74

United Nations Convention against Torture and Other Cruel, Inhuman or Degrading Treatment or Punishment, 104

United Nations Development Program, 11

United Nations Economic Commission for Latin America and the Caribbean, 241n3

University of Chicago, Deptartment of Economics, 6–7, 40

unstable work for men: overview of, 8, 205, 206–7, 209, 210; neoliberal social reforms and, 29–30, 31–32, 34, 44, 51; pharmaceuticals and, 206–7; reconciliation and, 102, 119, 123, 128; social debt and, 60–62, 71, 76; torture in everyday language and, 106–7. *See also* employment; men; unstable work for women

unstable work for women: overview of, 8, 205, 206–7, 209, 210; pharmaceuticals and, 209, 210; reconciliation and, 92, 98, 99, 101, 102, 122–27, 123; social debt and, 54, 63, 76–77. *See also* employment; unstable work for men; women

Valdés, Juan, 6–7

Valech, Sergio, 103

Valech Commission and Report (National Commission on Political Imprisonment and Torture), 103–7, 110, 116, 246nn9–13

Vekemans, Roger, 13–14

vieja sabia ("crone"), 186–87, 192–94, 196–98. *See also* community mental health program

Villa Gremaldi camp, 51, 241n9. *See also* torture

violence, sexual, 44–46, 208, 210, 211. *See also* domestic violence; state violence

vivir con dignida (to live with dignity), 56, 69, 86, 88–90. *See also* dignity

vivir con dignida (to live with dignity), 56, 69, 86, 88–90

Wacquant, Loïc, 23

waiting or active awaiting, as modality of care, 31, 56, 240n1

Warren, Kay B., 247n18

wealthy urban neighborhoods *(barrio alto)*, 18, 76, 99, 123, 156, 194, 217, 231

WHO (World Health Organization), 25, 250n3

Whyte, Susan Reynolds, 252n4

Winn, Peter, 61

withdrawal from/by the world, 92–93, 245n2

women: addiction to *pasta base* by, 35, 50, 53, 54, 150, 206; agency for, 132; Declaration of Principles in 1974, 10; dignity in domestic relations informed by boundaries and, 75–79; economic precariousness for, 122–25, 123, 144, 147–48, 155–56, 248n26; endure hardships and, 76; family in relation to state and, 131–33, 249n1; Madre-huacho and, 143; marriage and, 44–46, 133, 141, 208, 210, 211; militancy and, 129–34, 152, 160; political involvement chronology and, 134–36, 135; prostitution for *pasta base* and, 50, 51, 54; as seductresses, 133, 152; self-responsible role of, 65–66; separateness for, 36, 45, 129, 141–43; shame and, 78; *testimonio* and, 137–41, 164. *See also* community mental health program; maternity; men; mother; mother militant; sexuality; unstable work for women

World Bank, 8–9, 241n3

writing on the body, 140, 227–28

Yúdice, George, 247n17

TEXT:	10/13 Sabon
DISPLAY:	Sabon
COMPOSITOR:	BookMatters, Berkeley
PRINTER AND BINDER:	IBT Global